Abortion Bibliography

for 1982

Abortion Bibliography

for 1982

Compiled by

Polly T. Goode

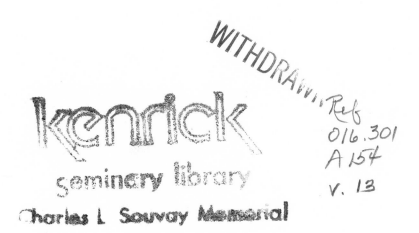
The Whitston Publishing Company
Troy, New York
1985

TABLE OF CONTENTS

PREFACE

ABORTION BIBLIOGRAPHY for 1982 is the thirteenth annual list of books and articles surrounding the subject of abortion in the preceding year. It appears serially each fall as a contribution toward documenting in one place as comprehensively as possible the literature of one of our central social issues. It is an attempt at a comprehensive world bibliography. Searches in compiling this material have covered the following sources: ABSTRACTS ON CRIMINOLOGY AND PENOLOGY; ABSTRACTS ON POLICE SCIENCE; ACCESS; AIR UNIVERSITY LIBRARY INDEX TO MILITARY PERIODICALS; AMERICA: HISTORY AND LIFE; AMERICAN HUMANITIES INDEX; AMERICAN REFERENCE BOOKS ANNUAL; APPLIED SCIENCE AND TECHNOLOGY INDEX; ART INDEX; BIBLIOGRAPHIC INDEX; BIOLOGICAL ABSTRACTS; BIOLOGICAL AND AGRICULTURAL INDEX; BRITISH HUMANITIES INDEX; BUSINESS PERIODICALS INDEX; CANADIAN EDUCATION INDEX; CANADIAN PERIODICALS INDEX; CATHOLIC PERIODICAL AND LITERATURE INDEX; COMMUNICATION ABSTRACTS; COLLEGE STUDENT PERSONNEL ABSTRACTS; COMPLETED RESEARCH IN HEALTH, PHYSICAL EDUCATION AND RECREATION; CRIMINAL JUSTICE ABSTRACTS; CRIMINAL JUSTICE PERIODICAL INDEX; CUMULATIVE BOOK INDEX; CUMULATIVE INDEX TO NURSING AND ALLIED HEALTH LITERATURE; CURRENT INDEX TO JOURNALS IN EDUCATION; DISSERTATION ABSTRACTS INTERNATIONAL: SCIENCES AND ENGINEERING: DISSERTATION ABSTRACTS INTERNATIONAL: SOCIAL SCIENCES AND HUMANITIES; EDUCATION INDEX; ENVIRONMENT ABSTRACTS; ESSAY AND GENERAL LITERATURE INDEX; HOSPITAL LITERATURE INDEX; HUMAN RESOURCES ABSTRACTS; HUMANITIES INDEX: INDEX MEDICUS; INDEX TO JEWISH PERIODICALS; INDEX TO LEGAL PERIODICALS; INTERNATIONAL NURSING INDEX; MASTERS ABSTRACTS; MEDIA REVIEW DIGEST; MONTHLY PERIODICAL INDEX; MUSIC INDEX; PAIS; PAIS FOREIGN LANGUAGE INDEX; PHILOSOPHER'S INDEX; PSYCHOLOGICAL ABSTRACTS; PSYCHOPHARMACOLOGY ABSTRACTS; READERS GUIDE TO PERIODICAL LITERATURE; RELIGION INDEX ONE: PERIODICALS; RELIGIOUS AND THEOLOGICAL ABSTRACTS; SAGE URBAN STUDIES ABSTRACTS; SOCIAL SCIENCES INDEX; SOCIAL WORK RESEARCH AND ABSTRACTS; SOCIOLOGICAL ABSTRACTS; WOMEN'S STUDIES ABSTRACTS.

The Bibliography is divided into two sections: a title section in alphabetical order; and a subject section. Thus, if the researcher does not wish to observe the subject heads of the compiler, he can use the title section exclusively. The subject heads have been allowed to issue from the nature of the material indexed rather than being imposed from Library of Congress subject heads or other standard lists.

The Book section includes Government Publications and Monographs.

The Subject Head Index includes page numbers.

Polly T. Goode
Troy, New York

LIST OF SUBJECT HEADINGS

AMB: REVISTA DA ASSOCIACAO MEDICA BRASILEIRA
AORN JOURNAL: ASSOCIATION OF OPERATING ROOM NURSES
ACQUISITIONS MEDICALES RECENTES
ACROSS THE BOARD
ACTA CLINICA BELGICA
ACTA ENDOCRINOLOGICA
ACTA EUROPAEA FERTILITATIS
ACTA GENETICAE MEDICAE ET GEMELLOLOGIAE
ACTA MEDICA IUGOSLAVICA
ACTA OBSTETRICIA ET GYNECOLOGICA SCANDINAVICA
ACTA OBSTETRICIA ET GYNECOLOGICA SCANDINAVICA. SUPPLEMENT
ACTA OTO-LARYNGOLOGICA
ACTA PSYCHIATRICA SANDINAVICA
ACTA REPRODUCTION TURCICA
ACTA UNIVERSITATIS PALACKIANAE OLOMUCENSIS FACULTATIS MEDICAE
ACTA VETERINARIA SCANDINAVICA. SUPPLEMENT
ADOLESCENCE
ADVANCE DATA
ADVANCES IN EXPERIMENTAL MEDICINE AND BIOLOGY
ADVERTISING AGE
AFRICAN JOURNAL OF MEDICINE AND MEDICAL SCIENCES
AGRESSOLOGIE
AKUSHERSTVO I GINEKOLOGIIA
ALBERTA REPORT
AMERICA
AMERICAN BAR ASSOCIATION JOURNAL
AMERICAN COLLEGE OF PHYSICIANS
AMERICAN DRUGGIST
AMERICAN FAMILY PHYSICIAN
AMERICAN JOURNAL OF CLINICAL NUTRITION
AMERICAN JOURNAL OF EPIDEMIOLOGY
AMERICAN JOURNAL OF GASTROENTEROLOGY
AMERICAN JOURNAL OF HUMAN GENETICS
AMERICAN JOURNAL OF INDUSTRIAL MEDICINE
AMERICAN JOURNAL OF JURISPRUDENCE
AMERICAN JOURNAL OF LAW AND MEDICINE
AMERICAN JOURNAL OF MEDICAL GENETICS
AMERICAN JOURNAL OF MENTAL DEFICIENCY
AMERICAN JOURNAL OF NURSING
AMERICAN JOURNAL OF OBSTETRICS AND GYNECOLOGY
AMERICAN JOURNAL OF OPTOMETRY AND PHYSIOLOGICAL OPTICS
AMERICAN JOURNAL OF POLITICAL SCIENCE
AMERICAN JOURNAL OF PUBLIC HEALTH
AMERICAN JOURNAL OF REPRODUCTIVE IMMUNOLOGY
AMERICAN JOURNAL OF TRIAL ADVOCACY
AMERICAN JOURNAL OF VETERINARY RESEARCH
AMERICAN PHARMACY
AMERICAN POLITICAL QUARTERLY
AMERICAN SPECTATOR

AMERICAN UNIVERSITY LAW REVIEW
ANAESTHESIA
ANALES DE LA ACADEMIA NACIONAL DE MEDICINA
ANDROLOGIA
ANESTHESIOLOGY
ANNALES CHIRURGIAE ET GYNAECOLOGIAE
ANNALES MEDICO-PSYCHOLOGIQUES
ANNALI DELL OSPEDALE MARIA VITTORIA DI TORINO
ANNALI DI OSTETRICIA GINECOLOGIA, MEDICINA PERINATALE
ANNALS OF CLINICAL BIOCHEMISTRY
ANNALS OF EMERGENCY MEDICINE
ANNALS OF HUMAN GENETICS
ANNALS OF THE NEW YORK ACADEMY OF SCIENCES
ANTHROPOLOGICAL QUARTERLY
ARCHIV FUR EXPERIMENTELLE VETERINARMEDIZIN
ARCHIVES OF ANDROLOGY
ARCHIVES OF ENVIRONMENTAL HEALTH
ARCHIVES OF GYNECOLOGY
ARCHIVES OF INTERNAL MEDICINE
ARCHIVES OF OBSTETRICS AND GYNECOLOGY
ARCHIVES OF PATHOLOGY AND LABORATORY MEDICINE
ARCHIVES OF SEXUAL BEHAVIOR
ARCHIVES ROUMAINES DE PATHOLOGIE EXPERIMENTALE ET DE MICROBIOLOGIE
ARCHIVIO DE VECCHI PER L ANATOMIA PATOLOGICA E LA MEDICINA CLINICA
ARCHIVIO PER LA SCIENZE MEDICHE
ARTERIOSCLEROSIS
ARTERY
ARTHRITIS AND RHEUMATISM
ARZNEIMITTEL-FORSCHUNG
ARZTLICHE JUGENDKUNDE
ASIAN SURVEY
AUDUBON
AUSTRALASIAN NURSES JOURNAL
AUSTRALIAN AND NEW ZEALAND JOURNAL OF OBSTETRICS AND GYNAECOLOGY
AUSTRALIAN JOURNAL OF SOCIAL ISSUES
AUSTRALIAN NURSES' JOURNAL
AUSTRALIAN VETERINARY JOURNAL

BAPTIST HISTORY AND HERITAGE
BEIJING REVIEW
BEITRAEGE ZUR GERICHTLICHEN MEDIZIN
BIOCHEMICAL MEDICINE
BIOLOGICAL REPRODUCTION
BIOORGANICHESKAYA KHIMIYA
BIOSCIENCE
BIRTH
BIRTH DEFECTS
BLOOD
BLOOD VESSELS
BOLLETINO DI PSICOLOGIA APPLICATA
BOLLETTINO DELLA SOCIETA ITALIANA DE BIOLOGIA SPERIMENTALE
BRIGHAM YOUNG UNIVERSITY LAW REVIEW
BRITISH JOURNAL OF ANAESTHESIA
BRITISH JOURNAL OF CANCER
BRITISH JOURNAL OF CLINICAL PHARMACOLOGY
BRITISH JOURNAL OF CLINICAL PRACTICE
BRITISH JOURNAL OF CLINICAL PSYCHOLOGY
BRITISH JOURNAL OF HAEMATOLOGY
BRITISH JOURNAL OF HOSPITAL MEDICINE

BRITISH JOURNAL OF MEDICAL PSYCHOLOGY
BRITISH JOURNAL OF OBSTETRICS AND GYNAECOLOGY
BRITISH JOURNAL OF PSYCHIATRY
BRITISH JOURNAL OF UROLOGY
BRITISH JOURNAL OF VENEREAL DISEASES
BRITISH MEDICAL JOURNAL
BULLETIN DE L'ACADEMIE NATIONALE DE MEDICINE
BULLETIN DU CANCER
BULLETIN OF THE PAN AMERICAN HEALTH ORGANIZATION
BUSINESS INSURANCE

CAHIERS DE DROIT
CAHIERS QUEBECOIS DE DEMOGRAPHIE
CALIFORNIA LAW REVIEW
CALIFORNIA WESTERN LAW REVIEW
CALVIN THEOLOGICAL JOURNAL
CANADIAN CONSUMER
CANADIAN JOURNAL OF PHYSIOLOGY AND PHARMACOLOGY
CANADIAN JOURNAL OF PUBLIC HEALTH
CANADIAN MEDICAL ASSOCIATION JOURNAL
CANADIAN NURSE
CANADIAN VETERINARY JOURNAL
CANCER
CAPITAL UNIVERSITY LAW REVIEW
CARCINOGENESIS
CASE WESTERN RESERVE LAW REVIEW
CATHOLIC LAWYER
CATHOLIC MEDICAL COLLEGE JOURNAL
CENTER MAGAZINE
CESKOSLOVENSKA GYNEKOLOGIE
CHANGING TIMES
CHANNELS
CHATELAINE
CHEMICAL AND ENGINEERING NEWS
CHEMOTHERAPY
CHRISTIAN CENTURY
CHRISTIANITY AND CRISIS
CHRISTIANITY TODAY
CHUNG HUA FU CHAN KO TSA CHIH
CHUNG-KUO YAO LI HSUEH PAO
CLINICA CHIMICA ACTA
CLINICAL AND EXPERIMENTAL OBSTETRICS AND GYNECOLOGY
CLINICAL AND INVESTIGATIVE MEDICINE
CLINICAL CHEMISTRY
CLINICAL ENDOCRINOLOGY
CLINICAL GENETICS
CLINICAL NEPHROLOGY
CLINICAL OBSTETRICS AND GYNECOLOGY
CLINICAL ONCOLOGY
CLINICAL PEDIATRICS
CLINICAL PHARMACOLOGY AND THERAPEUTICS
CLINICAL SCIENCE
CLINICAL THERAPEUTICS
CLINICAL TRIALS JOURNAL
CLINICS IN HAEMOTOLOGY
COLUMBIA HUMAN RIGHTS LAW REVIEW
COLUMBIA LAW REVIEW
COMMONWEAL
COMMUNIO

FBI LAW ENFORCEMENT BULLETIN
FAMILY CIRCLE
FAMILY COMMUNITY HEALTH
FAMILY LAW REPORTER
FAMILY LAW REPORTER: COURT OPINIONS
FAMILY PLANNING PERSPECTIVES
FAMILY RELATIONS
FAR EASTERN ECONOMIC REVIEW
FARMAKOLOGYA I TOKSIKOLOGYA
FEDERAL REGISTER
FEL'DSHER I AKUSHERKA
FEMINISM AND PROCESS THOUGHT
FERTILITY AND STERILITY
FINANCIAL POST
FLORIDA STATE UNIVERSITY LAW REVIEW
FOLIA MEDICA
FOLIA MEDICA CRACOVIENSIA
FORBES
FORTSCHRITTE DER MEDIZIN

GACETA MEDICA DE MEXICO
GASTROENTEROLOGIE CLINIQUE ET BIOLOGIQUE
GASTROENTEROLOGY
GEBURTSHILFE UND FRAUENHEILKUNDE
GENERAL PHARMACOLOGY
GIGIENA TRUDA I PROFESSIONALNYE ZABOLEVANIA
GINECOLOGIA Y OBSTETRICIA DE MEXICO
GINEKOLOGIA POLSKA
GLAMOUR
GOLDEN GATE UNIVERSITY LAW REVIEW
GOOD HOUSEKEEPING
GUARDIAN
GYNAEKOLOGISCHE RUNDSCHAU
GYNECOLOGIC AND OBSTETRIC INVESTIGATION
GYNECOLOGIC ONCOLOGY

HAEMATOLOGICA
HAREFUAH
HASTINGS CENTER REPORT
THE HASTINGS LAW JOURNAL
HEALTH
HEALTH BULLETIN
HEALTH EDUCATION
HEALTH EDUCATION JOURNAL
HEALTH POLICY AND EDUCATION
HEALTH VISITOR
HEPATOLOGY
HEREDITY
HIGH SCHOOL JOURNAL
HIROSHIMA JOURNAL OF MEDICAL SCIENCES
HOFSTRA LAW REVIEW
HOME ECONOMICS RESEARCH JOURNAL
HOME MAGAZINE
HOMILETIC AND PASTORAL REVIEW
HORMONE AND METABOLIC RESEARCH

HOSPITAL AND COMMUNITY PSYCHIATRY
HOSPITAL/HEALTH CARE TRAINING
HOSPITAL PRACTICE
HOSPITAL PROGRESS
HOSPITALS
HOWARD LAW REVIEW
HU LI TSA CHIH
HUMAN BIOLOGY
HUMAN EVENTS
HUMAN GENETICS
HUMAN HEREDITY
HUMAN RIGHTS
HUMANIST

IPPF: INTERNATIONAL PLANNED PARENTHOOD FEDERATION MEDICAL BULLETIN
ILLINOIS BAR JOURNAL
INDIAN JOURNAL OF CLINICAL PSYCHOLOGY
INDIAN JOURNAL OF EXPERIMENTAL BIOLOGY
INDIAN JOURNAL OF MEDICAL RESEARCH
INDIAN JOURNAL OF MEDICAL SCIENCES
INDIAN JOURNAL OF PATHOLOGY AND MICROBIOLOGY
INDIAN JOURNAL OF PEDIATRICS
INDIAN JOURNAL OF PHYSIOLOGY AND PHARMACOLOGY
INDUSTRY OF FREE CHINA
INFECTION CONTROL AND UROLOGICAL CARE
INFIRMIERE CANADIENNE
INFIRMIERE FRANCAISE
INFORMATION
INQUIRY
INTERCOM
INTERFACES
INTERNATIONAL ANESTHESIOLOGY CLINICS
INTERNATIONAL ECONOMIC REVIEW
INTERNATIONAL FAMILY PLANNING PERSPECTIVES
INTERNATIONAL JOURNAL FOR VITAMIN AND NUTRITION RESEARCH
INTERNATIONAL JOURNAL OF ANDROLOGY
INTERNATIONAL JOURNAL OF BIOLOGICAL RESEARCH IN PREGNANCY
INTERNATIONAL JOURNAL OF CANCER
INTERNATIONAL JOURNAL OF EPIDEMIOLOGY
INTERNATIONAL JOURNAL OF FERTILITY
INTERNATIONAL JOURNAL OF GYNAECOLOGY AND OBSTETRICS
INTERNATIONAL JOURNAL OF HEALTH EDUCATION
INTERNATIONAL JOURNAL OF HEALTH SERVICES
INTERNATIONAL JOURNAL OF IMMUNOPHARMACOLOGY
INTERNATIONAL JOURNAL OF NURSING STUDIES
INTERNATIONAL JOURNAL ON TISSUE REACTIONS
INTERNATIONAL MIGRATION REVIEW
INTERNATIONAL SURGERY
IRISH JURIST
IRISH MEDICAL JOURNAL
ISRAEL JOURNAL OF MEDICAL SCIENCES
ISSUES IN HEALTH CARE OF WOMEN

JAMA: JOURNAL OF THE AMERICAN MEDICAL ASSOCIATION
JAOA: JOURNAL OF THE AMERICAN OPTOMETRIC ASSOCIATION
JNCI: JOURNAL OF THE NATIONAL CANCER INSTITUTE
JOGN NURSING: JOURNAL OF OBSTETRIC GYNECOLOGIC AND NEONATAL NURSING
JAMES JOYCE QUARTERLY

JAPANESE JOURNAL OF FERTILITY AND STERILITY
JEWISH FRONTIER
JOHNS HOPKINS MEDICAL JOURNAL
JORDEMODERN
JOSANPU ZASSHI
JOURNAL DE GENETIQUE HUMAINE
JOURNAL DE GYNECOLOGIE, OBSTETRIQUE ET BIOLOGIE DE LA REPRODUCTION
JOURNAL DES MALADIES VASCULAIRES
JOURNAL FOR THE SCIENTIFIC STUDY OF RELIGION
JOURNAL OF ADOLESCENT HEALTH CARE
JOURNAL OF THE AMERICAN ACADEMY OF CHILD PSYCHIATRY
JOURNAL OF THE AMERICAN ACADEMY OF DERMATOLOGY
JOURNAL OF THE AMERICAN COLLEGE HEALTH ASSOCIATION
JOURNAL OF THE AMERICAN MEDICAL WOMEN'S ASSOCIATION
JOURNAL OF THE AMERICAN SCIENTIFIC AFFILIATION
JOURNAL OF THE AMERICAN VETERINARY MEDICAL ASSOCIATION
JOURNAL OF APPLIED DEVELOPMENTAL PSYCHOLOGY
JOURNAL OF APPLIED SOCIAL PSYCHOLOGY
JOURNAL OF BIOLOGICAL SCIENCE
JOURNAL OF BIOMEDICAL MATERIALS RESEARCH
JOURNAL OF BIOSOCIAL SCIENCE
JOURNAL OF CHRONIC DISEASES
JOURNAL OF CLINICAL ENDOCRINOLOGY AND METABOLISM
JOURNAL OF CLINICAL GASTROENTEROLOGY
JOURNAL OF CLINICAL PATHOLOGY
JOURNAL OF CLINICAL PSYCHOPHARMACOLOGY
JOURNAL OF CONTEMPORARY HISTORY
JOURNAL OF COUNSELING PSYCHOLOGY
JOURNAL OF CRIMINAL LAW AND CRIMINOLOGY
JOURNAL OF ENDOCRINOLOGY
JOURNAL OF ETHNOPHARMACOLOGY
JOURNAL OF FAMILY HISTORY
JOURNAL OF FAMILY LAW
JOURNAL OF FAMILY PRACTICE
JOURNAL OF FAMILY WELFARE
JOURNAL OF HEALTH AND SOCIAL BEHAVIOR
JOURNAL OF HEREDITY
JOURNAL OF THE INDIAN MEDICAL ASSOCIATION
JOURNAL OF INTERNATIONAL MEDICAL RESEARCH
JOURNAL OF THE IOWA MEDICAL SOCIETY
JOURNAL OF LABORATORY AND CLINICAL MEDICINE
JOURNAL OF LEGAL MEDICINE
JOURNAL OF MARRIAGE AND THE FAMILY
JOURNAL OF THE MEDICAL ASSOCIATION OF GEORGIA
JOURNAL OF THE MEDICAL ASSOCIATION OF THAILAND
JOURNAL OF MEDICAL PRIMATOLOGY
JOURNAL OF THE MEDICAL SOCIETY OF TOKO UNIVERSITY
JOURNAL OF MEDICINAL CHEMISTRY
JOURNAL OF MODERN AFRICAN STUDIES
JOURNAL OF THE NATIONAL MEDICAL ASSOCIATION
JOURNAL OF NEAR EASTERN STUDIES
JOURNAL OF PERIODONTOLOGY
JOURNAL OF PERSONALITY AND SOCIAL PSYCHOLOGY
JOURNAL OF PHARMACEUTICAL SCIENCES
JOURNAL OF PHARMACOBIO-DYNAMICS
JOURNAL OF PRACTICAL NURSING
JOURNAL OF PSYCHOSOMATIC RESEARCH
JOURNAL OF REPRODUCTIVE FERTILITY
JOURNAL OF REPRODUCTIVE MEDICINE

JOURNAL OF THE ROYAL COLLEGE OF GENERAL PRACTITIONERS.
JOURNAL OF THE ROYAL COLLEGE OF SURGEONS OF EDINBURGH.
JOURNAL OF THE ROYAL SOCIETY OF MEDICINE.
JOURNAL OF SCHOOL HEALTH
JOURNAL OF THE SCIENTIFIC STUDY OF RELIGION.
JOURNAL OF SEX RESEARCH
JOURNAL OF SOCIAL PSYCHOLOGY
JOURNAL OF THE SOUTH CAROLINA MEDICAL ASSOCIATION.
JOURNAL OF STEROID BIOCHEMISTRY
JOURNAL OF SUBMICROSCOPIC CYTOLOGY
JOURNAL OF SURGICAL ONCOLOGY
JOURNAL OF THE TENNESSEE MEDICAL ASSOCIATION
JOURNAL OF THEORETICAL BIOLOGY
JOURNAL OF TROPICAL PEDIATRICS
JOURNAL OF UROLOGY
JOURNAL OF VALUE INQUIRY
JUGOSLAVENSKA GINEKOLOGIJA I OPSTETRICIJA
JURIST

KATILOLEHTI
KINESIS: GRADUATE JOURNAL OF PHILOSOPHY
KLINISCHE MONATSBLAETTER FUR AUGENHEILKUNDE
KLINISCHE WOCHENSCHRFIT

LABORATORNOE DELO
LABORATORY ANIMALS
LABORATORY INVESTIGATION
LABOUR WORLD
L'ACTUALITE
LADIES HOME JOURNAL
LAKARTIDNINGEN
LANCET
LAW, MEDICINE AND HEALTH CARE
LEBENSVERSICHERUNGSMEDIZIN
LEBER, MAGEN, DARM
LIGUORIAN
LIJECNICKI VJESNIK
LINACRE QUARTERLY
LIPIDS
LISTENER
LOYOLA LAW REVIEW
LUTHERAN THEOLOGICAL JOURNAL

MCN: AMERICAN JOURNAL OF MATERNAL CHILD NURSING
MMW: MUENCHENER MEDIZINISCHE WOCHENSCHRIFT
MMWR: MORBIDITY AND MORALITY WEEKLY REPORT
MACLEAN'S
MADEMOISELLE
MAJOR PROBLEMS IN OBSTETRICS AND GYNECOLOGY
MARKETING AND MEDIA DECISIONS
MARRIAGE
MARYLAND STATE MEDICAL JOURNAL
McGILL LAW JOURNAL
MEDICAL BIOLOGY
MEDICAL CARE
MEDICAL HYPOTHESES
MEDICAL JOURNAL OF AUSTRALIA

MEDICAL JOURNAL OF MALAYSIA
MEDICAL WORLD NEWS
MEDICINE AND SCIENCE IN SPORTS AND EXERCISE
MEDICINSKI PREGLED
MEDICINSKI RAZGLEDI
MEDITSINSKAIA SESTRA
MEDIZINISCHE WELT
METAMEDICINE
MIDWIFE, HEALTH VISITOR AND COMMUNITY NURSE
MIND
MINERVA ANESTESIOLOGICA
MINERVA GINECOLOGIA
MINERVA PEDIATRICA
MISSOURI MEDICINE
MODERN MINISTRIES
THE MONIST.
MONOGRAPHS IN PATHOLOGY
MONTH
MOTHER JONES
MS
MUTATION RESEARCH

NAHRUNG
NATIONAL CATHOLIC REPORTER
NATIONAL JOURNAL
NATIONAL REVIEW
NATURE
NEDERLANDS TIJDSCHRIFT VOOR GENEESKUNDE
NERVENARZT
NEUROBIOLOGIA
NEUROTOXICOLOGY
NEW DIRECTIONS FOR WOMEN
NEW ENGLAND JOURNAL OF MEDICINE
NEW ENGLAND LAW REVIEW
NEW REPUBLIC
NEW SCIENTIST
NEW SOCIETY
NEW STATESMAN
NEW YORK STATE JOURNAL OF MEDICINE
NEW YORK STATE LAW SCHOOL LAW REVIEW
NEW YORK TIMES MAGAZINE
NEW ZEALAND JOURNAL OF HISTORY
NEW ZEALAND MEDICAL JOURNAL
NEW ZEALAND NURSING FORUM
NEWSETTE
NEWSWEEK
NIPPON SANKA FUJINKA GAKKAI ZASSHI
NIPPON YAKURIGAKU ZASSHI
NORDISK MEDICIN
NORTH CAROLINA LAW REVIEW
NORTHWESTERN UNIVERSITY LAW REVIEW
NOUVELLE PRESSE MEDICALE
NOUVELLE REVUE THEOLOGIQUE
NOVA LAW JOURNAL
NUESTRO
NUEVA ENFERMERIA
NURSE PRACTITIONER
NURSES DRUG ALERT
NURSING

NURSING AND HEALTH CARE
NURSING JOURNAL OF INDIA
NURSING MANAGEMENT
NURSING MIRROR AND MIDWIVE'S JOURNAL
NURSING MONTREAL
NURSING OUTLOOK
NURSING QUEBEC
NURSING TIMES
NURSINGLIFE

OBSERVER
OBSTETRICAL AND GYNECOLOGICAL SURVEY
OBSTETRICS AND GYNECOLOGY
OBSTETRICS AND GYNECOLOGY ANNUAL
OEFFENTLICHE GESUNDHEITSWESEN
OFF OUR BACKS
OHIO NORTHERN UNIVERSITY LAW REVIEW
ORIGINS
ORVOSI HETILAP
OTHER SIDE
OUR SUNDAY VISITOR

PAEDIATRIE UND PAEDOLOGIE
PANMINERVA MEDICA
PAPAU NEW GUINEA MEDICAL JOURNAL
PARENTS
PAST AND PRESENT
PATHOLOGE
PATOLOGIA POLSKA
PEACE AND CHANGE
PEDIATRIC ANNALS
PEDIATRICS
PEOPLE WEEKLY
PERCEPTUAL AND MOTOR SKILLS
PERSONAL COMPUTING
PERSONNEL AND GUIDANCE JOURNAL
PHILOSOPHICAL INVESTIGATIONS
PHILOSOPHICAL STUDIES
PHILOSOPHY AND PUBLIC AFFAIRS
PHLEBOLOGIE
PHYSIOLOGIA BOHEMOSLOVACA
PHYSIOLOGY AND BEHAVIOR
PIELEGNIARKA I POLOZNA
PLANTA MEDICA
PLAYBOY
POLITICAL THEORY
POLSKI TYGODNIK LEKARSKI
POPULATION
POPULATION AND DEVELOPMENT REVIEW
POPULATION AND ENVIRONMENT
POPULATION AND ENVIRONMENT: BEHAVIORAL AND SOCIAL ISSUES
POPULATION BULLETIN
POPULATION REPORTS
POPULATION STUDIES
POPULI
POSTGRADUATE MEDICAL JOURNAL
PRACTITIONER
PRAXIS

PREVENTIVE MEDICINE
PRIEST
PROCEEDINGS OF THE ANNUAL SYMPOSIUM OF EUGENICS SOCIETY
PROFESSIONAL GEOGRAPHER
PROFESSIONI INFERMIERISTICHE
PROGRESIVE
PROGRESS IN CLINICAL AND BIOLOGICAL RESEARCH
PROGRESS IN DRUG RESEARCH
PROGRESS IN LIPID RESEARCH
PROGRESSIVE GROCER
PROSTAGLANDINS
PROSTAGLANDINS LEUKOTRIENES AND MEDICINE
PSICHIATRIA GENERALE E DELL ETA EVOLUTIVA
PSICO
PSYCHOLOGICAL REPORTS
PSYCHOLOGY OF WOMEN QUARTERLY
PSYCHONEUROENDOCRINOLOGY
PUBLIC HEALTH
PUBLIC HEALTH REPORTS
PUBLIC OPINION QUARTERLY

RN
RADICAL AMERICAN
READERS DIGEST
REASON
RECENTI PROGRESSI IN MEDICINA
RECONSTRUCTIONIST
REFRACTORY GIRL
REGAN REPORT ON NURSING LAW
RELATIONS
REPRODUCCION
RESEARCH COMMUNICATIONS IN CHEMICAL PATHOLOGY AND PHARMACOLOGY
RESPIRATION
REVIEW OF RADICAL POLITICAL ECONOMY
REVISTA CHILENA DE OBSTETRICIA Y GINECOLOGIA
REVISTA DE ENFERMAGEN
REVISTA DE INFORMACAO LEGISLATIVA
REVISTA DE MEDICINA DE LA UNIVERSIDAD DE NAVARRA
REVISTA DE SANIDAD E HIGIENE PUBLICA
REVISTA DOCTOR COMNIS
REVISTA ESPANOLA DE INVESTIGACIONES SOCIOLOGICAS
REVISTA ESPANOLA DE LAS ENFERMEDADES DEL APARATO DIGESTIVO
REVISTA MEDICA DE CHILE
REVISTRA DI SERVIZIO SOCIALE
LA REVUE JURIDIQUE THEMES
REVUE MEDICALE DE BRUXELLES
REVUE MEDICALE DE LIEGE
REVUE MEDICALE DE LA SUISSE ROMANDE
RIVISTA DI NEUROBIOLOGIA
RIVISTA ITALIANA DI GINECOLOGIA
ROLLING STONE
RUTGERS LAW REVIEW

SPM: SALUD PUBLICA DE MEXICO
ST. LOUIS UNIVERSITY LAW JOURNAL
SAN FRANCISCO
SATURDAY EVENING POST
SATURDAY NIGHT

SBORNIK LEKARSKY
SCANDINAVIAN JOURNAL OF CLINICAL AND LABORATORY INVESTIGATION
SCANDINAVIAN JOURNAL OF INFECTIOUS DISEASES
SCANDINAVIAN JOURNAL OF SOCIAL MEDICINE
SCHWEIZERISCHE MEDIZINISCHE WOCHENSCHRIFT
SCIENCE
SCIENCE DIGEST
SCIENCE NEWS
SCOTTISH MEDICAL JOURNAL
SEMAINES DES HOPITAUX DE PARIS
SEMINARS IN LIVER DISEASE
SEOUL JOURNAL OF MEDICINE
SIGN
SINGAPORE MEDICAL JOURNAL
SISTERS TODAY
SOCIAL BIOLOGY
SOCIAL CASEWORK
SOCIAL JUSTICE REVIEW
SOCIAL PSYCHOLOGY QUARTERLY
SOCIAL SCIENCE AND MEDICINE
SOCIAL SCIENCE RESEARCH
SOCIAL THEORY AND PRACTICE
SOCIETY
SOCIOLOGIA DEL DIRITTO
SOCIOLOGICAL ANALYSIS
SOCIOLOGICAL SPECTRUM
SOCIOLOGY AND SOCIAL RESEARCH
THE SOLICITORS' JOURNAL
SOUTH
SOUTH AFRICAN JOURNAL OF CRIMINAL LAW AND CRIMINOLOGY
SOUTH AFRICAN MEDICAL JOURNAL
SOUTHERN JOURNAL OF PHILOSOPHY
SOUTHERN MEDICAL JOURNAL
SOUTHWEST PHILOSOPHICAL STUDIES
SOVETSKAIA MEDITSINA
STEROIDS
STUDIES IN FAMILY PLANNING
SUBSTANCE AND ALCOHOL ACTIONS/MISUSE
SUNDAY TIMES
SYKEPLEIEN
SYRACUSE LAW REVIEW

TV GUIDE
TABLET
TEEN
TEMPLE LAW QUARTERLY
TENNESSEE LAW REVIEW
TERATOLOGY
TEXAS TECH LAW REVIEW
THERAPEUTISCHE UMSCHAU
THERAPIE DER GEGENWART
THERAPIE HUNAGIRCA
THOUGHT
THROMBOSIS RESEARCH
TIJDSCHRIFT VOOR DIERGENEESKUNDE
TIJDSCHRIFT VOR ZIEKENVERPLEGING
TIMES (London)
TIMES HIGHER EDUCATIONAL SUPPLEMENT
TIMES LITERARY SUPPLEMENT

TISSUE ANTIGENS
TODAY
TOXICOLOGY
TRIAL
TROPICAL DOCTOR
TSITOL I GENETIKA
TULANE LAW REVIEW
TUMORI

UMKC LAW REVIEW.
USA TODAY
US CATHOLIC
US NEWS AND WORLD REPORT
UGESKRIFT FOR LAEGER
UNION MEDICALE DU CANADA
UNION W.A.G.E.
UNIVERSITY OF CINCINNATI LAW REVIEW
UNIVERSITY OF RICHMOND LAW REVIEW
THE UNIVERSITY OF TOLEDO LAW REVIEW
UROLOGIA INTERNATIONALIS
UROLOGY
VARDFACKET
VETERINARNI MEDICINA
VETERINARY CLINICS OF NORTH AMERICA. SMALL ANIMAL PRACTICE
VETERINARY RECORD
VIITORUL SOCIAL
VILLAGE VETERINARY RECORD
THE VOICE
VIRGINIA LAW REVIEW
VITA MEDICALA
VITAL HEALTH SERVICES
VITAL HEALTH STATISTICS
VOGUE
VOPROSY OKHRANY MATERINSTVA I DETSTVA

WHO OFFSET PUBLICATIONS
WALL STREET JOURNAL
WASHINGTON AND LEE LAW REVIEW
WASHINGTON LAW REVIEW
WASHINGTON UNIVERSITY LAW QUARTERLY
WESTERN JOURNAL OF MEDICINE
WHITTIER LAW REVIEW
WIADOMOSCI LEKARSKIE
WIENER KLINISCHE WOCHENSCHRIFT
WIENER MEDIZINISCHE WOCHENSCHRIFT
WISCONSIN LAW REVIEW
WISCONSIN MEDICAL JOURNAL
WISSENSCHAFTLICHE SCHRIFTENREIHE DER HUMBOLDT-UNIVERSITAT
WOMEN AND HEALTH
WOMEN'S RIGHTS LAW REPORTER
WOMEN'S STUDIES INTERNATIONAL FORUM
WOMEN'S STUDIES INTERNATIONAL QUARTERLY
WORLD HEALTH
WORLD POLITICS

XENOBIOTICA

YALE JOURNAL OF BIOLOGY AND MEDICINE
YAO HSUEH HSUEH PAO: ACTA PHARMACEUTICA SINICA

ZFA: ZEITSCHRIFT FUR ALLGEMEINMEDIZIN
ZAHN-, MUND-, UND KIEFERHEILKUNDE MIT ZENTRALBLATT
ZDRAVOOKHRANENIYE BELORUSSII
ZEITSCHRIFT FUR ARZTLICHE FORTBILDUNG
ZEITSCHRIFT FUR DIE BEVOLKERUNGSWISSENSCHAFT
ZEITSCHRIFT FUR DIE GESAMTE HYGIENE
ZEITSCHRIFT FUR DIE GESAMTE INNERE MEDIZIN
ZEITSCHRIFT FUR GEBURTSCHILFE UND PERINATOLOGIE
ZEITSCHRIFT FUR NATURFORSCHUNG TEIL B
ZENTRALBLATT FUR CHIRURGIE
ZENTRALBLATT FUR GYNAEKOLOGIE
ZHURNAL NEVROPATOLOGII I PSIKHIATRII

BOOKS, GOVERNMENT PUBLICATIONS,
AND MONOGRAPHS

ABORTION BIBLIOGRAPHY FOR 1979. Troy, New York: Whitston Publishing,
    1982.

Beale, Calvin L. RURAL AND SMALL TOWN POPULATION CHANGE, 1970-1980.
    Washington: G.P.O., United States Department of Agriculture, 1981.

Brody, Eugene B. SEX, CONTRACEPTION, AND MOTHERHOOD IN JAMAICA.
    Cambridge: Harvard University Press, 1981.

Burtchaell, James T. RACHEL WEEPING, AND OTHER ESSAYS ON ABORTION.
    Fairway, Kansas: Andrews and McMeel, 1982.

David, Henry P., et al. TEEN PROBLEM PREGNANCIES: PEER COUNSELORS'
    PERCEPTIONS ABOUT COMMUNITY CONCERNS AND SOLUTIONS. New York:
    Planned Parenthood/Transnational Family Research Institute Report,
    1981.

Dow, Thomas E., Jr., et al. CONTINUITY AND CHANGE IN METROPOLITAN
    AND RURAL ATTITUDES TOWARDS FAMILY SIZE AND FAMILY PLANNING IN
    KENYA BETWEEN 1966-1977/1978. Nairobi, Kenya: Population Studies
    and Research Institute, University of Nairobi, 1981.

--. NOTE ON MODERN, TRANSITIONAL AND TRADITIONAL DEMOGRAPHIC AND
    CONTRACEPTIVE PATTERNS AMONG KENYAN WOMEN, 1977-1978. Nairobi,
    Kenya: Population Studies and Research Institute, University of
    Nairobi, 1981.

Eckard, Eugenia. United States. National Center for Health Statis-
    tics. Division of Health Care Statistics. TEENAGERS WHO USE OR-
    GANIZED FAMILY PLANNING SERVICES: UNITED STATES, 1978. Rockville,
    Maryland: Department of Health and Human Services, 1981.

FAMILY PLANNING IN THE 1980's: CHALLENGES AND OPPORTUNITIES; report
    of the ..., Jakarta, Indonesia. New York: The Population Council,
    International Conference on Family Planning in the 1980's, 1981.

Gallagher, Charles F. POPULATION AND DEVELOPMENT IN EGYPT: I. Birth
    and death on the Nile. Washington, D.C.: American University,
    1981.

Gish, D. T. MANIPULATING LIFE, WHERE DOES IT STOP? San Diego,
    California: Creation-Life, 1981.

Hatch, Maureen, et al. SPONTANEOUS ABORTION AND EXPOSURE DURING
    PREGNANCY TO THE HERBICIDE 2,4,5-T. Washington: American Public
    Health Association, NTIS Report, 1981.

Hendershot, Gerry E., et al. United States. National Center for

1

Health Statistics. USE OF SERVICES FOR FAMILY PLANNING AND IN-
FERTILITY: UNITED STATES. Rockville, Maryland: Department of
Health and Human Services, 1981.

INVESTIGACIONES COOPERATIVAS. Bogota, Colombia: Corporacion Centro
Regional de Poblacion (CRRP). Area Biomedica. Programa Regional de
Investigaciones en Fecundidad (PRIF), 1981.

Isaacs, Stephen L. POPULATION LAW AND POLICY: SOURCE MATERIALS AND
ISSUES. New York: Human Sciences Press, 1981.

Jain, Sagar C., et al. MANAGEMENT DEVELOPMENT IN POPULATION PROGRAMS
[Developing Countries]. Chapel Hill: University of North Carolina,
Department of Health Policy and Administration, School of Public
Health, 1981.

Kolbe, Helen K. ORAL CONTRACEPTIVES ABSTRACTS: A GUIDE TO LITERA-
TURE, 1977-1979. New York: Plenum Publishing Corporation, 1980.

Maine, Deborah. FAMILY PLANNING [Developing Countries]: ITS IMPACT
ON THE HEALTH OF WOMEN AND CHILDREN. New York: Columbia University
Press, Center for Population and Family Health, College of Physi-
cians and Surgeons, 1981.

Mamlouk, Maria. KNOWLEDGE AND USE OF CONTRACEPTION IN TWENTY DE-
VELOPING COUNTRIES. Washington: Populationa Reference Bureau,
1982.

Merton, Andrew H. ENEMIES OF CHOICE: THE RIGHT-TO-LIFE MOVEMENT AND
ITS THREAT TO ABORTION. Boston: Beacon Press, 1981.

Mishell, Daniel. ADVANCES IN FERTILITY REEARCH. New York: Raven
Press, 1982.

Montgomery, J. W. SLAUGHTER OF THE INNOCENTS. Westchester, Illinois: Good News Publishers, 1981.

Morgan, Susanne. COPING WITH A HYSTERECTOMY; YOUR OWN CHOICE, YOUR
OWN SOLUTIONS. New York: Dial Press, 1982.

Muldoon, Maureen. ABORTION; An Annotated Indexed Bibliography.
Lewiston, New York: Edwin Mellen Press, 1980.

NATIONAL CONFERENCE ON ABORTION, 1979. ABORTION PARLEY. Fairway,
Kansas: Andrews and McMeel, 1980.

New York State. Department of Health. State Center for Health Statistics. INDUCED ABORTIONS RECORDED IN NEW YORK STATE 1980, With five
year summary, 1976-1980. Albany, New York, 1981.

Ooms, Theodora. TEENAGE PREGNANCY IN A FAMILY CONTEXT: IMPLICATIONS
FOR POLICY [United States]. Philadelphia: Temple University Press,
1981.

PLAN FOR ACTION. Old Tappan, New Jersey: Fleming H. Revell Company,
1980.

POPULATION COUNCIL: 1980 ANNUAL REPORT. New York: The Population
Council, 1980.

Rubin, Eva R. ABORTION, POLITICS, AND THE COURTS: Roe v. Wade and its aftermath. Westport, Connecticut: Greenwood Press, 1982.

Saw, Swee-Hock. POPULATION CONTROL FOR ZERO GROWTH IN SINGAPORE. New York: Oxford University Press, 1980.

Shapiro, Constance H. ADOLESCENT PREGNANCY PREVENTION: SCHOOL-COMMUNITY COOPERATION. Springfield, Illinois: Charles C. Thomas, Publisher, 1981.

Smith, E. D. ABORTION. New York: Appleton-Century-Crofts, 1982.

Stettner, Allison G., et al. HEALTH ASPECTS OF FAMILY PLANNING: A GUIDE TO RESOURCES IN THE UNITED STATES. New York: Human Sciences Press, 1982.

Tatalovich, Raymond, et al. POLITICS OF ABORTION: A STUDY OF COMMUNITY CONFLICT IN PUBLIC POLICY MAKING [United States]. New York: Praeger Publishers, 1981.

United States. Bureau of Community Health Services. DESIGNING YOUR FAMILY PLANNING EDUCATION PROGRAM. Rockville, Maryland: Department of Health and Human Services, 1980.

United States. National Center for Health Statistics. Division of Health Care Statistics. THE NATIONAL INVENTORY OF FAMILY PLANNING SERVICES: 1978 survey results. Rockville, Maryland: Department of Health and Human Services, 1982.

United States. National Center for Health Statistics. Division of Vital Statistics. TRENDS IN CONTRACEPTIVE P]RACTICE: UNITED STATES, 1965-1976. Rockville, Maryland: Department of Health and Human Services, 1982.

United States. Senate. Committee on the Judiciary. Subcommittee on Separation of Powers. HUMAN LIFE BILL: hearings: v. 1-2, April 23-June 18, [1981], on S. 158, a bill to provide that human life shall be deemed to exist from conception. Washington: G.P.O., 1982.

United States. Senate. Committee on the Judiciary. Subcommittee on Separation of Powers. HUMAN LIFE BILL--S. 158: report, together with additional and minority views. Washington: G.P.O., 1981.

United States. Senate. Committee on Labor and Human Resources. OVERSIGHT OF FAMILY PLANNING PROGRAMS, 1981: hearing, March 31, 1981, on examination on the role of the federal government in birth control, abortion referral, and sex education programs. Washington: G.P.O., 1981.

United States. Senate. Committee on Labor and Human Resources. Subcommittee on Aging, Family and Human Services. OVERSIGHT ON FAMILY PLANNING PROGRAMS UNDER TITLE X OF THE PUBLIC HEALTH SERVICE ACT, 1981: hearing, June 23 and September 28, 1981, on oversight on the role of the federal government in family planning administered under Title X of the Public Health Service Act. Washington: G.P.O., 1981.

Wardle, L. D. LAWYER LOOKS AT ABORTION. Provo, Utah: Brigham Young University Press, 1982.

Abdominal approach in cerclage for treatment of repeated abortion due
to segmental cervical insufficiency, by R. Grio, et al. MINERVA
GINECOLOGIA. 33(12):1131-1136, December 1981

Abnormalities of sperm morphology in cases of persistent infertility
after vasectomy reversal, by R. J. Pelfrey, et al. FERTILITY AND
STERILITY. 38(1):112-114, July 1982

Abortifacient action of endotoxin on pregnant rats and its inhibitory
action on placental mitochondrial Mg++-ATPase, by M. Ema, et al.
EISEI SHIKENJO HOKOKU. 99:68-73, 1981

The abortifacient effect of 16,16-dimethyl-trans-delta 2-PGE1 methyl
ester, a new prostaglandin analogue, on mid-trimester pregnancies
and long-term follow-up observations, by S. Takagi, et al. PROSTA-
GLANDINS. 23(4):591-601, April 1982

Abortion. NEW ZEALAND MEDICAL JOURNAL. 94(698):472-473, December
23, 1981

--OUR SUNDAY VISITOR. 70:3, January 17, 1982

--, by R. H. Bube. JOURNAL OF THE AMERICAN SCIENTIFIC AFFILIATION.
33(3):158-165, 1981

--[letter], by V. J. Hartfield. NEW ZEALAND MEDICAL JOURNAL.
95(700):57-58, January 27, 1982

--[letter], by A. Simpson, et al. NEW ZEALAND MEDICAL JOURNAL.
94(697):433-434, December 9, 1981

The abortion activists, by D. Granberg. FAMILY PLANNING PERSPEC-
TIVES. 13(4):157-163, July-August 1981

Abortion affects men too, by P. Black. NEW YORK TIMES MAGAZINE.
pp. 76-78+, March 28, 1982

Abortion alarums [editorial], by C. Tietze. AMERICAN JOURNAL OF
PUBLIC HEALTH. 72(6):534-535, June 1982

An abortion alternative, by J. Gilhooley. AMERICA. 147:289-290,
November 13, 1982

Abortion and accident proneness: a Danish validation study, by R. L.
Somers. JOURNAL OF BIOLOGICAL SCIENCE. 13(4):425-429, October
1981

Abortion and American pluralism, by M. Bunson. SOCIAL JUSTICE RE-
VIEW. 72:198-204, November-December 1981

Abortion and birth control in Canton, China, by M. Vink. WALL STREET
JOURNAL. 198:26, November 30, 1981

Abortion and the consideration of fundamental, irreconcilable interests, by C. J. Jones. SYRACUSE LAW REVIEW. 33:565-613, Spring
1982

Abortion and contraception in the Korean fertility transition, by P.
J. Donaldson, et al. POPULATION STUDIES. 36:227-235, July 1982

Abortion and the death of the fetus, by S. L. Ross. PHILOSOPHY AND
PUBLIC AFFAIRS. 11:232-245, Summer 1982

Abortion and the Hatch Amendment, by E. Bryce. AMERICA. 146(9):166-
168, March 6, 1982

Abortion & healing, by M. T. Mannion. MODERN MINISTRIES. 3:22-25+,
April 1982

Abortion and infant mortality before and after the 1973 US Supreme
Court decision on abortion, by L. S. Robertson. JOURNAL OF BIO-
LOGICAL SCIENCE. 13(3):275-280, July 1981

Abortion and informed consent requirements, by M. B. Kapp. AMERICAN
JOURNAL OF OBSTETRICS AND GYNECOLOGY. 144(1):1-4, September 1,
1982

Abortion and international law: the status and possible extension
of women's right to privacy, by A. E. Michel. JOURNAL OF FAMILY
LAW. 20(2):241, 1982

Abortion and the public opinion polls. Morality and legality. Part I,
by S. K. Henshaw, et al. FAMILY PLANNING PERSPECTIVES. 14(2):53-
55+, March-April 1982

Abortion and the public opinion polls (United States), by S. K. Henshaw, et al. FAMILY PLANNING PERSPECTIVES. 14:53-55+, March-April
1982

Abortion and reverence for human life, by H. Kraatz, et al. DEUT-
SCHES GESUNDHEITSWESEN. 36(21):ix-xiii, 1981

Abortion and the rhetoric of individual rights: why the abortion debate isterile, by L. R. Churchill, et al. HASTINGS CENTER REPORT.
12:9-12, February 1982

Abortion and women's health: a meeting of the National Abortion Federation, by J. H. Johnson. FAMILY PLANNING PERSPECTIVES. 14:327-
328, November-December 1982

Abortion at midpregnancy by catheter or catheter-balloon supplemented
by intravenous oxytocin and prostaglandin F_2alpha, by Y. Manabe,
et al. INTERNATIONAL JOURNAL OF BIOLOGICAL RESEARCH IN PREGNANCY.
2(2):85-89, 1981

Abortion attitudes. by C. Doyle. OBSERVER. p. 27, July 13, 1982

5

Abortion battles, by J. McLaughlin. NATIONAL REVIEW. 34:1599, December 24, 1982

Abortion: British conference [National Abortion Campaign (NAC) national conference, May 22-23, 1981], by A. Henry. OFF OUR BACKS. 12:5, July 1982

Abortion, capital punishment and the Judco-Christian ethic, by P. Cameron. LINACRE QUARTERLY. 48:316-332, November 1981

Abortion cases pending in Supreme Court, by N. Hunter. OFF OUR BACKS. 12:12, October 1982

Abortion clinics and the organization of work: a case study of Charles Circle, by N. R. Aries. REVIEW OF RADICAL POLITICAL ECONOMY. 12(2):53-62, 1980

The abortion controversy and the claim that this body is mine, by M. R. Wicclair. SOCIAL THEORY AND PRACTICE. 7(3):337-346, 1981

Abortion death toll rises, but rate tapers off in 1980. OUR SUNDAY VISITOR. 70:7, March 14, 1982

Abortion: the debate begins. NEWSWEEK. 100:29, August 30, 1982

Abortion debate [editorial], by M. Istona. CHATELAINE. 55:6, March 1982

Abortion debate in Senate. NEW DIRECTIONS FOR WOMEN. 11:1+, September-October 1982

Abortion during mid-pregnancy by rivanol-catheter supplemented with PGF2 alpha drip-infusion or quinine hydrocholoride, by Y. Manabe, et al. CONTRACEPTION. 23(6):621-628, June 1981

Abortion ethics, by M. J. Fromer. NURSING OUTLOOK. 30(4):234-240, April 1982

Abortion: exercise in biomedical ethics, by D. G. Jones. JOURNAL OF THE AMERICAN SCIENTIFIC AFFILIATION. 34(1):6-17, 1982

Abortion: first round in a long fight (Senate debate). US NEWS AND WORLD REPORT. 93:7, August 30, 1982

Abortion for fetal abnormalities [letter], by J. E. McArthur. NEW ZEALAND MEDICAL JOURNAL. 94(698):473, December 23, 1981

Abortion in the Philippines: a study of clients and practitioners, by M. Gallen. STUDIES IN FAMILY PLANNING. 13(2):35-44, February 1982

Abortion in single girls in Hong Kong, by G. W. Tang. JOURNAL OF ADOLESCENT HEALTH CARE. 2(3):213-216, March 1982

Abortion in the U.S., 1977-1978, by J. D. Forrest, et al. FAMILY PLANNING PERSPECTIVES. 11(6):329-341, November-December 1979

Abortion induced for eugenic reasons [editorial], by K. Betke. MMW: MUENCHENER MEDIZINISCHE WOCHENSCHRIFT. 123(39):1441-1442, September 25, 1981

Abortion--an industrial issue (ACTU Congress, 1981 [Australian trade union]), by D. Hague, et al. REFRACTORY GIRL. (23):15-16, March 1982

Abortion--insurance. FAMILY LAW REPORTER: COURT OPINIONS. 7(50): 2789, October 27, 1981

Abortion is not a banner-waving issue [letter], by J. P. James. JOGN NURSING: JOURNAL OF OBSTETRIC GYNECOLOGIC AND NEONATAL NURSING. 10(6):458-459, November-December 1981

Abortion--judicial consent--children's rights--parental consultation. FAMILY LAW REPORTER: COURT OPINIONS. 7(41):2652, August 25, 1981

Abortion legislation. Implications for medicine, by A. Milunsky, et al. JAMA: JOURNAL OF THE AMERICAN MEDICAL ASSOCIATION. 248(7): 833-834, August 20, 1982

Abortion--legislation restricting access to abortion services during first trimester must meet strict scrutiny test and may not un- reasonably confine or burden aborting physician's practice. Re- strictions must be based on medical necessity and will be voided if not narrowly tailored to meet needs asserted or supported by medi- cal necessity. JOURNAL OF FAMILY LAW. 19:745-750, August 1981

Abortion may sensitize the mother to HLA antigens, by A. Gelabert, et al. TISSUE ANTIGENS. 17(4):353-356, 1981

The abortion mess in Los Angeles (controversy over disposition of dead fetuses found at defunct private pathology lab), by D. W. Pawley. CHRISTIANITY TODAY. 26:46+, September 17, 1982

Abortion myths and realities: who is misleading whom?, by W. Cates, Jr. AMERICAN JOURNAL OF OBSTETRICS AND GYNECOLOGY. 142(8):954- 956, April 15, 1982

Abortion: a national security issue, by S. D. Mumford. AMERICAN JOURNAL OF OBSTETRICS AND GYNECOLOGY. 142(8):951-953, April 15, 1982

--(alleged threats posed to the United States by continued world population growth; abortion as a possible solution), by S. D. Mum- ford. HUMANIST. 42:12-13+, September-October 1982

Abortion of a 5-month pregnancy caused by fistula cervicolaqueatica, by K. Pekhlivanov. AKUSHERSTVO I GINEKOLOGIIA. 20(5):418-419, 1981

Abortion: one man's view, by H. Bray. ESSENCE. 12:146, April 1982

Abortion or birth? Discriminators in problem pregnancy decisions, by D. Williams, et al. SOCIOLOGICAL SPECTRUM. 1(2):115-133, April- June 1981

Abortion, personhood, and moral rights, by D. Algeo. THE MONIST. 64:543-549, October 1981

Abortion: Planned Parenthood Association of Kansas City, Missouri, Inc. v. Ashcroft (655 F 2d 848): Missouri loses latest round in battle over permissible abortion regulations. UMKC LAW REVIEW.

50:320-339, Spring 1982

Abortion: a plea for moral sensitivity, by J. M. Orenduff. SOUTHWEST
PHILOSOPHICAL STUDIES. 6:69-74, April 1981

Abortion--a police response, by G. H. Kleinknecht, et al. FBI LAW
ENFORCEMENT BULLETIN. 51:20-23, March 1982

Abortion practices and attitudes in cross-cultural perspective, by R.
N. Shain. AMERICAN JOURNAL OF OBSTETRICS AND GYNECOLOGY. 142(3):
245-251, February 1, 1982

Abortion: readers respond. COMMONWEAL. 109:75-84, February 12, 1982

Abortion--referrals--family planning services. FAMILY LAW REPORTER:
COURT OPINIONS. 8(1):2009, November 3, 1981

Abortion--restrictions. FAMILY LAW REPORTER: COURT OPINIONS. 7(35):
2567, July 14, 1981

Abortion--restrictions--county hospitals. FAMILY LAW REPORTER: COURT
OPINIONS. 8(4):2049, November 24, 1981

Abortion rights group opposes bill, by M. Meehan. NATIONAL CATHOLIC
REPORTER. 18:28, July 2, 1982

Abortion rights in danger, by E. Doerr. HUMANIST. 45:52-66, May-
June 1982

Abortion services in the United States, 1979 and 1980, by S. K. Henshaw, et al. FAMILY PLANNING PERSPECTIVES. 14(1):5-8+, January-
February 1982

Abortion: stalled in Congress, trouble in the states, by T. Dejanikus. OFF OUR BACKS. 12:21, March 1982

Abortion--State Budget Act restricting circumstances under which
public funds would be authorized to pay for abortions for Medi-Cal
recipients held unconstitutional. JOURNAL OF FAMILY LAW. 20:345-
351, January 1982

Abortion statistics 1980. HEALTH BULLETIN. 39(6):382-383, November
1981

Abortion strategies for 1983, by T. Dejanikus. OFF OUR BACKS. 13:
10, January 1983

Abortion surveillance, 1979--provisional statistics. MMWR: MORBIDITY
AND MORALITY WEEKLY REPORT. 31(4):47-50, February 5, 1982

Abortion: a technique for working through grief, by N. B. Buckles.
JOURNAL OF THE AMERICAN COLLEGE HEALTH ASSOCIATION. 30(4):181-182,
February 1982

Abortion test cases, by J. G. Deedy. TABLET. 236:1007-1008, October
9, 1982

Abortion, tuition tax credits fall short of mark, by J. Castelli.
OUR SUNDAY VISITOR. 71:3, October 3, 1982

Abortion: what kind of moral issue?, by L. Nicholson. JOURNAL OF
VALUE INQUIRY. 15:235-242, 1981

Abortion: winning at the state level (Pennsylvania), by T. Sgrignoll.
MS. 10:26, April 1982

Abortion: a woman's decision, by J. B. Conlin. HOSPITAL/HEALTH CARE
TRAINING. 8(2):38, 1981

Abortions and hydatidiform mole: the genetic link [editorial], by R.
Toaff. HAREFUAH. 101(5-6):120-122, September 1981

Abortions and moles, by K. Benirschke. MONOGRAPHS IN PATHOLOGY.
(22):23-48, 1981

Abortions because of unavailability of prenatal diagnosis [letter],
by E. B. Hook, et al. LANCET. 2(8252):936, October 24, 1981

Abortions--hospitals. FAMILY LAW REPORTER: COURT OPINIONS. 7(33):
2535, June 23, 1981

Abortions preventable by contraceptive practice, by C. F. Westoff, et
al. FAMILY PLANNING PERSPECTIVES. 13(5):218-223, September-October 1981

Abortions--regulation by state and local municipalities--a municipal
ordinance which requires that all abortion facilities be equipped
with expensive and unnecessary equipment similar to that of a hos-
pi'al operating room is an unconstitutional burden on a woman's
right to choose to abort a pregnancy. CAPITAL UNIVERSITY LAW RE-
VIEW. 10:925-930, Summer 1981

About the clinical value of estimations of plasma progesterone levels
and urinary pregnandiol output in cases of imminent abortion during
the first half of pregnancy, by I. Misinger, et al. CESKOSLOVENSKA
GYNEKOLOGIE. 46(9):668-672, November 1981

Acceptability of the contraceptive vaginal ring by rural and urban
population in two Latin American countries, by A. Faundes, et al.
CONTRACEPTION. 24(4):393-414, October 1981

The acceptability of day stay for termination of pregnancy, by J. M.
Cundy, et al. BRITISH JOURNAL OF CLINICAL PRACTICE. 35(6):215-
218, June 1981

Acceptability of medroxyprogesterone acetate in rural areas of
Mexico, by V. Velasco Murillo, et al. GINECOLOGIA Y OBSTETRICIA
DE MEXICO. 49(293):153-161, March 1981

Access to data and the information explosion: oral contraceptives and
risk of cancer, by J. M. Weiner, et al. CONTRACEPTION. 24(3):301-
313, September 1981

Access to postpartum sterilization in southeast Brazil, by B. Janowitz, et al. MEDICAL CARE. 20(5):526-534, May 1982

Access to sterilization in two hospitals in Honduras, by B. Janowitz,
et al. BULLETIN OF THE PAN AMERICAN HEALTH ORGANIZATION. 15(3):
226-230, 1981

Accommodation of conscientious objection to abortion: a case study of
the nursing profession, by W. C. Durham, Jr., et al. BRIGHAM YOUNG
UNIVERSITY LAW REVIEW. 1982:253-370, 1982

Actinomyces-like organisms and IUD use linked but clinical importance
of the finding is unclear. FAMILY PLANNING PERSPECTIVES. 14:34-
35, January-February 1982

Action of oral contraceptives on circulating immune complexes, by B.
Petermann, et al. ZENTRALBLATT FUR GYNAEKOLOGIE. 104(6):349-353,
1982

Action of prostaglandin F2 alpha on 1st-trimester pregnancy, by M.
Talas, et al. AKUSHERSTVO I GINEKOLOGIIA. (11):52, November 1981

Activities of a commission on the termination pregnancy for medical
reasons, by E. Khristzova, et al. AKUSHERSTVO I GINEKOLOGIIA.
21(1):16-20, 1982

Activities of various 6-chloro-6-deoxysugars and (S) alpha-chlorohy-
drin in producing spermatocoeles in rats and paralysis in mice and
in inhibiting glucose metabolism in bull spermatozoa in vitro, by
W. C. Ford, et al. JOURNAL OF REPRODUCTIVE FERTILITY. 65(1):177-
183, May 1982

Acute renal failure. Experience over a 22-year period, by M. Alvo, et
al. REVISTA MEDICA DE CHILE. 109(5):420-427, May 1981

Administrative, counseling and medical practices in National Abortion
Federation facilities, by U. Landy, et al. FAMILY PLANNING PER-
SPECTIVES. 14:257-280, September-October 1982

Adolescent aborters. Factors associated with gestational age, by J.
Poliak, et al. NEW YORK STATE JOURNAL OF MEDICINE. 82(2):176-179,
February 1982

Adolescent abortions in the United States, by W. Cates, Jr. JOURNAL
OF ADOLESCENT HEALTH CARE. 1(1):18-25, September 1980

Adolescent contraception, by G. C. Bolton. CLINICAL OBSTETRICS AND
GYNECOLOGY. 24(3):977-986, September 1981

Adolescent induced abortion in Benin City, Nigeria, by A. E. Omu, et
al. INTERNATIONAL JOURNAL OF GYNAECOLOGY AND OBSTETRICS. 19(6):
495-499, December 1981

Adolescent sex, by W. Girstenbrey. MEDIZINISCHE WELT. 32(44):3,
October 30, 1981

Adolescent suicide attempts following elective abortion: a special
case of anniversary reaction, by C. Tishler. PEDIATRICS. 68(5):
670-671, 1981

Adolescents, parents, and birth control, by N. Brozan. NEW YORK
TIMES MAGAZINE. p. B6, March 8, 1982

Adolescents' use of a hospital-based contraceptive program (based on
a study of the Adolescent Reproductive Health Care Program Columbia-Presbyterian Medical Center, New York City, 1977-80), by J. B.
Jones, et al. FAMILY PLANNING PERSPECTIVES. 14:224-225+, July-

August 1982

Adoption wins tax break, by M. Meehan. NATIONAL CATHOLIC REPORTER. 18:2, February 19, 1982

Adrenal function in hirsutism. II. Effect of an oral contraceptive, by R. A. Wild, et al. JOURNAL OF CLINICAL ENDOCRINOLOGY AND ME-TABOLISM. 54(4):676-681, April 1982

Advances in contraception (glossypol), by S. Katz. CHATELAINE. 55:36, February 1982

Advantages and risks of hormonal contraception, by M. Mall-Haefeli. FORTSCHRITTE DER MEDIZIN. 100(16):723-728, April 29, 1982

Aetiology of delivery during the second trimester and performance in subsequent pregnancies, by G. J. Ratten. MEDICAL JOURNAL OF AUS-TRALIA. 2(12-13):654-656, December 12-26, 1981

The after-care of abortion patients, by J. R. Ashton. JOURNAL OF THE ROYAL COLLEGE OF GENERAL PRACTITIONERS. 31(225):217-222, April 1981

Age and birth control, by N. Mallovy. HOME MAGAZINE. 17:80X, May 1982

Age of consent to abortion [letter], by M. Colvin, et al. LANCET. 1(8286):1418, June 19, 1982

Age-specific secular changes in oral contraceptive use [letter], by S. Shapiro, et al. AMERICAN JOURNAL OF EPIDEMIOLOGY. 114(4):604, October 1981

Airing contraceptive commercials, by P. Donovan. FAMILY PLANNING PERSPECTIVES. 14:321-323, November-December 1982

Alaska courts have jurisdiction to order sterilization. FAMILY LAW REPORTER: COURT OPINIONS. 7(28):2452-2453, May 19, 1981

Alpha-difluoromethylornithine as a postcoitally effective antifer-tility agent in female rats, by P. R. Reddy, et al. CONTRACEPTION. 24(2):215-221, August 1981

Alteration in blood pressures associated with combined alcohol and oral contraceptive use--the Lipid Research Clinics Prevalence study, by R. B. Wallace, et al. JOURNAL OF CHRONIC DISEASES. 35(4):251-257, 1982

Alterations in clinical chemistry measures associated with oral con-traceptive and estrogen use: the Lipid Research Clinics Program Prevalence Study, by L. D. Cowan, et al. JOURNAL OF REPRODUCTIVE MEDICINE. 27(5):275-282, May 1982

Am I getting paid for this? (TV news story about a woman's decision to have an abortion: excerpt), by B. Rollin. VOGUE. 172:308-310, August 1982

Amniocentesis and the apotheosis of human quality control, by J. M. Nolan-Haley. JOURNAL OF LEGAL MEDICINE. 2(3):347-363, September 1981

11

Amniocentesis and selective abortion, by T. J. Silber. PEDIATRIC
ANNALS. 10(10):31-34, October 1981

Amount of tissue evacuated by vacuum aspiration in therapeutic
abortions, by P. Rasmussen. ACTA OBSTETRICIA ET GYNECOLOGICA
SCANDINAVICA. 60(5):475-479, 1981

Anaerobic sepsis and septic shock in criminal abortion, by A. Angelov, et al. AKUSHERSTVO I GINEKOLOGIIA. 20(3):262-264, 1981

Anaesthesia for outpatient termination of pregnancy. A comparison
of two anaesthetic techniques, by G. H. Hackett, et al. BRITISH
JOURNAL OF ANAESTHESIA. 54(8):865-870, August 1982

An analysis of continuity-descontinuity in natural family planning:
an Australian factor analysis, by J. A. Johnston. INTERNATIONAL
JOURNAL OF FERTILITY. 26(3):231-238, 1981

An analysis of electrocardiographic changes during artificial abortion in 51 cases. CHUNG HUA FU CHAN KO TSA CHIH. 14(2):116-117,
April 1979

Analysis of pathological process in fallopian tubes after injection
with mucilago phenol in relation to its sterilization effectiveness, by M. Y. Chen. CHUNG HUA FU CHAN KO TSA CHIH. 14(2):84-86,
April 1979

Analysis of the results and considerations on the organizatinal
aspects of the implementation of the Law 194/78 in a provincial
hospital, by L. Pacilli, et al. MINERVA GINECOLOGIA. 33(9):811-
816, September 1981

The analysis of spontaneous abortion using a new half-sib model for
qualitative traits, by W. L. Golden, et al. PROGRESS IN CLINICAL
AND BIOLOGICAL RESEARCH. 69A:197-202, 1981

Ancient Greek ethical perspectives on abortion and euthanasia, by P.
J. Carrick. DISSERTATION ABSTRACTS INTERNATIONAL. A. p. 5146,
1982

Ancora in materia di pianificazione familiare e di interruzione
volontaria della gravidanzam, by V. Segre. SOCIOLOGIA DEL DIRITTO.
7(3):159-176, 1980

And now? OR: How not to get into trouble. Practical advice on contraception, by E. Revelli. ANNALI DELL OSPEDALE MARIA VITTORIA DI
TORINO. 22(7-12):339-359, July-December 1979

Anesthesia in the pregnant myasthenic patient (considerations on 2
cases of voluntary interruption of pregnancy), by M. Chiefari, et
al. ARCHIVES OF OBSTETRICS AND GYNECOLOGY. 85(4):259-270, July-
August 1980

Antecedents to contraceptive innovation: evidence from rural Northern
Thailand, by D. P. Hogan, et al. DEMOGRAPHY. 18(4):597-614,
November 1981

Anti-abortion bid fails in Congress, by T. Dejanikus. OFF OUR BACKS.
12:13, October 1982

The anti-abortion campaign (Soviet Union), by M. Ryan. BRITISH
MEDICAL JOURNAL. 283(6303):1378-1379, November 21, 1981

Anti-abortion doctors: why a former foetus killer heads a pro-
life campaign, by S. McCarthy. ALBERTA REPORT. 9:34, May 17,
1982

Anti-abortion march marks court ruling, by M. Holahan. NATIONAL
CATHOLIC REPORTER. 18:4, January 29, 1982

Antiabortion measures loom before congress, by M. J. England. JOUR-
NAL OF THE AMERICAN MEDICAL WOMEN'S ASSOCIATION. 37(2):34-35,
February 1982

Antiabortion movement broadens (statement signed by 200 American
religious leaders). CHRISTIANITY TODAY. 26:64+, January 18,
1982

Anti-abortion protestors had no right to necessity charge at trespass
trial. CRIMINAL LAW REPORTER: COURT DECISIONS AND PROCEEDINGS.
29(22):2475-2476, Septemer 2, 1981

Antiandrogenic effects of cyproterone acetate and chloromadinone
acetate on the rat hypothalamus as revealed by electroencephalo-
graphic responses, by C. Kaur, et al. PHYSIOLOGIA BOHEMOSLOVACA.
30(4):365-373, 1981

Antiestrogenic and antifertility actions of anordrin (2 alpha 17
alpha-diethynyl-A-nor-5 alpha-androstane-2 beta, 17 beta-diol
2,17-dipropionate), by R. R. Mehta, et al. STEROIDS. 38(6):679-
691, December 1981

Anti-factor XI, direct positive Coombs's test and recurrent abortion
in a system lupus erythematosus [letter], by J. R. Duran-Suarez, et
al. HAEMATOLOGICA. 66(3):383-384, June 1981

Anti-fertility activity of a benzene extract of hibiscus rosa-
sinensis flowers on female albino rats, by M. P. Singh, et al.
PLANTA MEDICA. 44(3):171-174, March 1982

Antifertility effect of azastene mediated by prostaglandin, by A.
Helvacioglu, et al. AMERICAN JOURNAL OF OBSTETRICS AND GYNECOLOGY.
141(2):138-144, September 15, 1981

Antifertility effects of GnRH, by H. M. Fraser. JOURNAL OF REPRO-
DUCTIVE FERTILITY. 64(2):503-515, March 1982

Antifertility effects of gossypol and its impurities on male hamsters, by D. P. Waller, et al. CONTRACEPTION. 23(6):653-660, June
1981

Antifertility effects of luteinizing hormone-releasing hormone (LHRH)
agonists, by F. Labrie, et al. PROGRESS IN CLINICAL AND BIOLOGICAL
RESEARCH. 74:273-291, 1981

Antimicrobial prophylaxis for termination of pregnancy?. DRUG AND
THERAPEUTICS BULLETIN. 20(7):28, April 2, 1982

Antipyrine elimination in saliva after low-dose combined or progestogen-only oral contraceptive steroids, by D. M. Chambers, et al. BRITISH JOURNAL OF CLINICAL PHARMACOLOGY. 13(2):229-232, February 1982

Antisperm antibodies in infertility: the role of condom therapy [letter], by L. B. Greentree. FERTILITY AND STERILITY. 37(3):451-452, March 1982

Apostle of abortion, by G. Epps. SCIENCE. 3(2):70, March 1982

Un appel en faveur de la vie: pourquoi si mal recu?, by J. Harvey. RELATIONS. 42:32-37+, January-February 1982

Application of laparoscope for female sterilization (analysis of 74 cases), by C. H. He, et al. CHUNG HUA FU CHAN KO TSA CHIH. 3(2): 106-109, June 1981

Applying humanae vitae solution, by C. W. Thomson. NATIONAL CATHOLIC REPORTER. 18:18, June 4, 1982

Are hormonal contraceptives relevant for family planning?, by J. M. Wenderlein. MMW: MUENCHENER MEDIZINISCHE WOCHENSCHRIFT. 124(2): 487-488, May 21, 1982

Are spermicides dangerous?. READERS DIGEST. 120:44, June 1982

Are we ignoring the needs of the woman with a spontaneous abortion?, by S. K. Wetzel. MCN: AMERICAN JOURNAL OF MATERNAL CHILD NURSING. 7(4):258-259, July-August 1982

Arias-Stella reaction with prominent nuclear pseudoinclusins simulating herpetic endometritis, by L. E. Dardi, et al. DIAGNOSTIC GYNECOLOGY AND OBSTETRICS. 4(2):127-132, Summer 1982

Aspects of reproduction related to human rights. II. Contraception, by J. Martinez-Manautou. GACETA MEDICA DE MEXICO. 117(7):266-268, July 1981

--III. Artificial termination of pregnancy, by L. Castelazo-Ayala. GACETA MEDICA DE MEXICO. 117(7):268-272, July 1981

--IV. Sterilization by surgical means, by C. MacGregor. GACETA MEDICA DE MEXICO. 117(7):272-274, July 1981

Assisting at abortions: can you really say no?, by W. A. Regan. RN. 45:71, June 1982

Association between endometriosis and spontaneous abortion: a retrospective clinical study, by D. L. Olive, et al. JOURNAL OF REPRODUCTIVE MEDICINE. 27(6):333-338, 1982

At what age is contraception no longer necessary?, by J. H. Meuwissen. NEDERLANDS TIJDSCHRIFT VOOR GENEESKUNDE. 100(16):743-745, April 29, 1982

Atherosclerosis and oral contraceptive use. Serum from oral contraceptive users stimulates growth of arterial smooth muscle cells, by J. D. Bagdade, et al. ARTERIOSCLEROSIS. 2(2):170-176, March-April 1982

The attitude toward abortion in Middle English writings: a note on the history of ideas, by R. R. Barkley. COMMUNIO. 9:176-183, Summer 1982

Attitude toward and use of induced abortion among Taiwanese women [research], by J. F. Wang. ISSUES IN HEALTH CARE OF WOMEN. 3:179-202, May-June 1981

Attitudes of Chinese women towards sexuality and birth control, by D. Ellis, et al. CANADIAN NURSE. 78(3):28-31, March 1982

Attitudes of rural Bangladesh physicans toward abortion, by M. J. Rosenberg, et al. STUDIES IN FAMILY PLANNING. 12(8-9):318, August-September 1981

Attitudes of selected secondary students toward family planning education, by J. Mercier, et al. HOME ECONOMICS RESEARCH JOURNAL. 10(2):127-136, December 1981

Attitudes to pregnancy [editorial]. JOURNAL OF THE ROYAL COLLEGE OF GENERAL PRACTITIONERS. 31(229):452-453, August 1981

Attitudes toward male oral contraceptives: implications for models of the relationship between beliefs and attitudes, by J. Jaccard, et al. JOURNAL OF APPLIED SOCIAL PSYCHOLOGY. 11(3):181-191, May-June 1981

Atypical reserve cell hyperplasia of cervical glands, simulating adenocarcinoma. An undescribed reversible lesion in a woman taking oral contraceptives, by M. Filotico, et al. TUMORI. 67(5):491-496, October 31, 1981

Avoiding shame: the ethical context of abortion in Ghana, by W. Bleek. ANTHROPOLOGICAL QUARTERLY. 54:203-209, October 1981

Avortement et securite sociale; vers l'avortement gratuit?, by P. Verspieren. ETUDES. 356:321-327, March 1982

Babies and bishops, by M. Holland. NEW STATESMAN. pp. 8-9, July 30, 1982

The baby our doctors told us we'd never have (ed. by M. Fuerst), by J. Koblas. GOOD HOUSEKEEPING. 195:122+, October 1982

Back to basics ... a CAC report. CANADIAN CONSUMER. 12:10-14, July 1982

Bacteriologic studies in second-trimester pregnancy termination: a comparison of intra- and extra-amniotic methods, by J. Reichman, et al. INTERNATIONAL JOURNAL OF GYNAECOLOGY AND OBSTETRICS. 19(5): 409-412, 1981

Balanced translocation karyotypes in patients with repetitive abortion. Case study and literature review, by J. R. Davis, et al. AMERICAN JOURNAL OF OBSTETRICS AND GYNECOLOGY. 144(2):229-233, September 15, 1982

The band-aid operation (tubal ligation and vasectomy). HEALTH. 14: 52, March 1982

Barrier contraception: a trend toward older methods, by R. L. Young.
CONSULTANT. 22:297-301, June 1982

Barrier-method contraceptives and pelvic inflammatory disease, by J.
Kelaghan, et al. JAMA: JOURNAL OF THE AMERICAN MEDICAL ASSOCIA-
TION. 248(2):184-187, July 9, 1982

Basal body temperature [letter], by B. Kambic. FERTILITY AND STERIL-
ITY. 38(1):120-121, July 1982

Battle over abortion moves back to high court, by R. B. Shaw. OUR
SUNDAY VISITOR. 71:4, October 24, 1982

The beginnings of hormonal contraception and the Munchener Medizinische Wochenschrift, by H. H. Summer. MMW: MUENCHENER MEDIZINISCHE
WOCHENSCHRIFT. 124(2):499-503, May 21, 1982

Behavioral factors contributing to abortion deaths: a new approach to
mortality studies, by R. M. Selik, et al. OBSTETRICS AND GYNECOLO-
GY. 58(5):631-635, November 1981

Behaviour of ujoviridin exposures test (ICG) in conjunction with application of hormonal contraceptives, by E. Brugmann, et al. ZEN-
TRALBLATT FUR GYNAEKOLOGIE. 103(14):823-826, 1981

Behind the anti-abortion lines, by L. Bush. THE VILLAGE VOICE.
26(4):18+, November 25, 1981

Benefit of the 'pill' may outweigh the risks [news]. AMERICAN FAMILY
PHYSICIAN. 26(3):258-259, September 1982

Benign hepatic tumour and oral contraception, by A. Lavy, et al.
HAREFUAH. 102(3):107-108, February 1, 1982

Better birth control pill seen. NEW YORK TIMES MAGAZINE. p. 33,
January 1, 1982

Bevolkerungspolitische zielsetzungen in der volksrepublik China und
ihre sozio-okonomische begrundung, by H. Schubnell. ZEITSCHRIFT
FUR DIE BEVOLKERUNGSWISSENSCHAFT. 7(1):3-57, 1981

Beyond abortion: the potential reach of a human life amendment, by D.
Westfall. AMERICAN JOURNAL OF LAW AND MEDICINE. 8:97-135, Summer
1982

Beyond the limits of reproductive choice: the contribution of the
abortion-funding cases to fundamental-rights analysis and to the
welfare-rights thesis, by S. F. Appleton. COLUMBIA LAW REVIEW.
81(4):721-758, May 1981

Beyond the pill: contraceptives of the future, by E. P. Frank.
MADEMOISELLE. 88:130-132+, October 1982

Biliary lipids, bile acids, and gallbladder function in the human
female: effects of contraceptive steroids, by F. Kern, Jr., et al.
JOURNAL OF LABORATORY AND CLINICAL MEDICINE. 99(6):798-805, June
1982

Biochemical and steroidal indicators in the use of monogest, a progesterone contraceptive, by J. Kobiikova, et al. CESKOSLOVENSKA

GYNEKOLOGIE. 46(7):540-541, August 1981

Biologic and physical means of assessing the threat of miscarriage, by J. P. Schaaps. REVUE MEDICALE DE LIEGE. 37(4):114-117, February 15, 1982

Biology--contraception--adolescence (part 2), by P. Lonchambon, et al. INFIRMIERE FRANCAISE. (237):7-16, July 1982

--. From the physiology of puberty to the possible physiopathology of contraception in the formative years, by P. Lonchambon, et al. INFIRMIERE FRANCAISE. (236):21-30+, June 1982

Biophysical studies on molecular mechanism of abortificient action of prostaglandins. I. The study of molecular electrostatic potential distribution of PGF2 alpha, PGF1 beta and PGA1, by V. Kothekar, et al. JOURNAL OF THEORETICAL BIOLOGY. 93(1):7-23, November 7, 1981

--II. The study of the long and short range inter action between different fragments of PGF2 alpha, PGF1 beta and PGA1, by V. Kothekar, et al. JOURNAL OF THEORETICAL BIOLOGY. 93(1):25-40, November 7, 1981

--IV. Conformation energy calculation of PGA1, PGB1 and PGE1, by V. Kothekar. JOURNAL OF THEORETICAL BIOLOGY. 94(4):943-949, February 21, 1982

The biotechnological revolution: the hidden pro-life issue, by R. McMunn. OUR SUNDAY VISITOR. 70:6-7+, January 17, 1982

The birth control blues, by S. Levy. ROLLING STONE. pp. 25-26+, March 4, 1982

Birth control: contraception, by A. Bicego, et al. PROFESSIONI INFERMIERISTICHE. 34(3):149-159, July-September 1981

Birth control: 4-day pill is promising in early test, by R. Eder. NEW YORK TIMES MAGAZINE. p. C1, April 20, 1982

Birth-control in the West in the thirteenth and early fourteenth centuries, by P. P. A. Biller. PAST AND PRESENT. (94):3-26, February 1982

Birth control: lay challenge to medical authority over childbirth, by M. J. Steckevicz. DISSERTATION ABSTRACTS INTERNATIONAL. A. p. 4168, 1982

Birth control pills and pancreatitis, by J. W. Liu. MARYLAND STATE MEDICAL JOURNAL. 31(2):66-67, February 1982

Birth control plugs (silicon plug for Fallopian tubes). SCIENCE NEWS. 122:41, July 17, 1982

Birth control-sex preference and sex ratio, by M. A. Toro. HEREDITY. 47:417-423, December 1981

Birth control today: his kicks, your risks?, by C. L. Mithers. MADEMOISELLE. 88:34, November 1982

Birth control: a view from a Chinese village, by S. W. Mosher. ASIAN

SURVEY. 22:356-368, April 1982

Birth defects and vaginal spermicides, by S. Shapiro, et al. JAMA: JOURNAL OF THE AMERICAN MEDICAL ASSOCIATION. 247(17):2381, May 7, 1982

Birth planning in Cuba: a basic human right, by J. M. Swanson. INTERNATIONAL JOURNAL OF NURSING STUDIES. 18(2):81-88, 1981

The bishops and the Hatch Amendment, by W. F. Buckley. NATIONAL REVIEW. 34:132-133, February 5, 1982

Bitter pill: the birth control pill is losing popularity as evidence mounts about its harmful side effects, by G. B. Sinclair. SATURDAY NIGHT. 96:13, December 16, 1981

Bladder perforation owing to a unipolar coagulating device, by J. Pakter, et al. AMERICAN JOURNAL OF OBSTETRICS AND GYNECOLOGY. 141(2):227, September 15, 1981

Blood cloting defects in second-trimester D and E easy to treat, say MDs. FAMILY PLANNING PERSPECTIVES. 13:279-280, November-December 1981

Blood levels of ethynylestradiol, caffeine, aldosterone and desoxy-corticosterone in hypertensive oral contraceptive users, by L. Kaul, et al. CONTRACEPTION. 23(6):643-651, June 1981

Blood loss and side effects in day case abortion, by G. W. Cochrane, et al. BRITISH JOURNAL OF OBSTETRICS AND GYNAECOLOGY. 88(11): 1120-1123, November 1981

Blood pressure and contraceptive use, by C. R. Kay. BRITISH MEDICAL JOURNAL. 285(6343):737-738, September 11, 1982

--, by K. T. Khaw, et al. BRITISH MEDICAL JOURNAL. 285(6339):403-407, August 7, 1982

Body image of and contraceptive use by college females, by M. Young. PERCEPTUAL AND MOTOR SKILLS. 53(2):456-458, October 1981

Breast cancer and the condom [editorial], by G. Tibblin. CLINICAL AND INVESTIGATIVE MEDICINE. 4(3-4):153-154, 1981

Breast cancer and oral contraception: findings in Oxford-Family Planning Association contraceptive study, by M. P. Vessey, et al. BRITISH MEDICAL JOURNAL. 282(6282):2093-2094, 1981

Breast cancer and the pill [editorial], by I. S. Fraser. MEDICAL JOURNAL OF AUSTRALIA. 1(1):6, January 9, 1982

Breast cancer and use of antihypertensive drugs and oral contraceptives: results of a case-control study, by F. Clavel, et al. BULLETIN DU CANCER. 68(5):449-455, 1981

Breast cancer, pregnancy, and the pill, by J. O. Drife. BRITISH MEDICAL JOURNAL. 283(6294):778-779, September 19, 1981

Breast-feeding and family planning: a review of the relationships between breast-feeding and family planning, by R. E. Brown.

AMERICAN JOURNAL OF CLINICAL NUTRITION. 35(1):162-171, January 1982

Breast-feeding, fertility and family planning, by M. F. McCann, et al. POPULATION REPORTS (24):J525-575, November-December 1981

British embrace a gentler postcoital contraceptive. MEDICAL WORLD NEWS. 23:28-29, October 11, 1982

The Brook Advisory Centres. HELATH VISITOR. 55:177-178, April 1982

Buck v. Bell: 'felt necessities' v. fundamental values?, by R. J. Cynkar. COLUMBIA LAW REVIEW. 81(7):1418-1461, November 1981

Budd-Chiari syndrome and hepatic adenomas associated with oral contraceptives [a case report], by H. K. Tong, et al. SINGAPORE MEDICAL JOURNAL. 22(3):168-172, June 1981

Budd-Chiari syndrome and OCs ... oral contraceptives. NURSES DRUG ALERT. 5:86, September 1981

C.S.C. justifying abortion, by J. Burtchaell. SIGN. 61:18-22+, February 1982

Cu-7 IUD can be used up to 4 years with low pregnancy rates. FAMILY PLANNING PERSPECTIVES. 14:35-36, January-February 1982

A calm look at abortion arguments: legislation relating to abortion must hinge on the question: when does the right to life begin?, by R. Bissell. REASON. 13:27-31, September 1981

Can Congress settle the abortion issue?, by M. C. Segers. HASTINGS CENTER REPORT. 12(3):20-28, June 1982

Can contraception kill romance?, by J. Labreche. CHATELAINE. 55:47+, August 1982

Can 'doctor's orders' include involuntary sterilization?. RN. 45(1):34-35, January 1982

Carbohydrate metabolism during treatment with estrogen, progestogen, and low-dose oral contraceptives, by W. N. Spellacy. AMERICAN JOURNAL OF OBSTETRICS AND GYNECOLOGY. 142(6 Pt 2):732-734, March 15, 1982

Carbohydrate metabolism studies in women using Brevicon, a low-estrogen type of oral contraceptive, for one year, by W. N. Spellacy, et al. AMERICAN JOURNAL OF OBSTETRICS AND GYNECOLOGY. 142(1):105-108, January 1, 1982

Cardiovascular effects and progestins in oral contraceptives, by V. Wynn. AMERICAN JOURNAL OF OBSTETRICS AND GYNECOLOGY. 142(6 Pt 2):718, March 15, 1982

Care of a pre-eclampsia multipara with repeated pregnancy loss, by C. H. Chou. HU LI TSA CHIH. 28:11-16, July 1981

Careers: family planning, fundamental to care. by A. Cowper. NURSING MIRROR AND MIDWIVE'S JOURNAL. 154(25):58, June 23, 1982

A case-control study of cancer of the endometrium, by J. L. Kelsey, et al. AMERICAN JOURNAL OF EPIDEMIOLOGY. 116(2):333-342, August 1982

A case of female pseudohermaphroditism of difficult interpretation, by T. De Toni, et al. MINERVA PEDIATRICA. 34(8):361-365, April 30, 1982

A case of hepatoma in pregnancy associated with earlier oral contraception, by S. E. Christensen, et al. ACTA OBSTETRICIA ET GYNECOLOGICA SCANDINAVICA. 60(5):519, 1981

A case of porcine abortion caused by nocardia asteroides [letter], by R. W. Mason. AUSTRALIAN VETERINARY JOURNAL. 57(8):398-399, August 1981

Case records of the Massachusetts General Hospital. Weekly clinico-pathological exercises. Case 40-1982. Tender hepatomegaly in a 29-year-old woman. NEW ENGLAND JOURNAL OF MEDICINE. 307(15):934-942, October 7, 1982

A case report: ureterouterine fistula as a complication of elective abortion, by G. T. Keegan, et al. JOURNAL OF UROLOGY. 128(1):137-138, July 1982

Case studies of indigenous abortion practitioners in rural Bangladesh, by S. Islam. STUDIES IN FAMILY PLANNING. 13(3):86-93, March 1982

Cases of abortion, premature labor and fetal anoxia after treatment of anovulation, by J. Krzysiek, et al. GINEKOLOGIA POLSKA. 52(1):45-50, January 1981

Castracao, esterilizacao, "mudanca" artificial de sexo (conference paper, some emphasis on Brazil), by A. Chaves. REVISTA DE INFORMACAO LEGISLATIVA. 18:261-272, January-March 1981

Catholic, non-Catholic clinic patients endorse abortion legality, oppose Church stand. FAMILY PLANNING PERSPECTIVES. 14:98-99, March-April 1982

Catholics and sex, by J. Garvey. COMMONWEAL. 109:134-136, March 12, 1982

--[discussion]. COMMONWEAL. 109:412-414, July 16, 1982

Causes of chromosome anomalies suggested by cytogenetic epidemiology of induced abortions, by M. Yamamoto, et al. HUMAN GENETICS. 60(4):360-364, 1982

Cellular and humoral factors of immunity in threatened abortion, by V. S. Rakut, et al. ZDRAVOOKHRANENIYE BELORUSSII. (1):24-25, 1981

Cellular and humoral immunity in habitual abortion, by K. A. Khashimova, et al. VOPROSY OKHRANY MATERINSTVA I DETSTVA. 26(5):66-68, 1981

Cellular immunity in normal pregnancy and abortion: subpopulations of T lymphocytes bearing Fc receptors for IgG and IgM, by Y. Sumiyoshi, et al. AMERICAN JOURNAL OF REPRODUCTIVE IMMUNOLOGY. 1(3):

20

145-149, 1981

Cenni sulla valutazione dell'aborto hella religione islamica, by M.
Vallaro. SOCIOLOGIA DEL DIRITTO. 7(3):87-106, 1980

Centric fission of chromosome no. 7 in three generations, by D.
Janke. HUMAN GENETICS. 60(2):200-201, 1982

Cerebral circulation disturbances due to the use of contraceptives,
by D. Khadzhiev, et al. ZHURNAL NEVROPATOLOGII I PSIKHIATRII.
81(1):64-67, 1981

Cervical adenocarcinoma in users of oral contraceptives [clinical
case], by E. Roa, et al. REVISTA CHILENA DE OBSTETRICIA Y GINE-
COLOGIA. 45(4):225-228, 1980

The cervical cap. An alternate barier contraceptive method, by W. M.
Gilbirds, 2n, et al. MISSOURI MEDICINE. 79(4):216-218+, April
1982

Cervical dilatation in late first trimester termination by prostaglandin, hylase and isogel, by A. V. Mandlekar, et al. PROSTA-
GLANDINS LEUKOTRIENES AND MEDICINE. 6(4):381-387, April 1981

Cervical mucus penetration test for in vitro assay of vaginal contraceptive agents, by N. J. Alexander, et al. FERTILITY AND STERIL-
ITY. 36(4):516-520, October 1981

Cervical suture in Scotland; strengths and weaknesses in the use of
routine clinical summaries, by S. K. Cole. BRITISH JOURNAL OF OB-
STETRICS AND GYNAECOLOGY. 89(7):528-535, July 1982

Chances of abortion prophylaxis in early pregnancy, by S. Koller.
GEBURTSHILFE UND FRAUENHEILKUNDE. 42(3):204-212, March 1982

Changes in intraocular pressure during prostaglandin-induced abortion, by M. Ober, et al. KLINISCHE MONATSBLAETTER FUR AUGEN-
HEILKUNDE. 180(3):230-231, March 1981

Changes in the legislation regulating the legal status of artificial
abortion in the world in the past 10 years, by D. Vasilev. AKUS-
HERSTVO I GINEKOLOGIIA. 20(4):269-275, 1981

Changes in physiological, EEG, and psychological paremeters in women
during the spontaneous menstrual cycle and following oral contraceptives, by D. Becker, et al. PSYCHONEUROENDOCRINOLOGY. 7(1):
75-90, March 1982

Changes in the reproductive behavior in East Germany (1970-1979) in
connection with measures of family policy. I., by U. Fritsche.
ZEITSCHRIFT FUR ARZTLICHE FORTBILDUNG. 75(10):489-492, May 15,
1981

Changes in sexual desire after voluntary sterilization, by F. D.
Bean, et al. SOCIAL BIOLOGY. 27(3):186-193, Fall 1980

Changes of gap junctions in myometrium of guinea pig at parturition
and abortion, by R. E. Garfield, et al. CANADIAN JOURNAL OF
PHYSIOLOGY AND PHARMACOLOGY. 60(3):335-341, 1982

Changing contraceptive usage intentions: a test of the Fishbein model of intention, by D. McCarty. JOURNAL OF APPLIED SOCIAL PSYCHOLOGY. 11(3):192-211, May-June 1981

Changing patterns of contraception, by J. Peel. PROCEEDINGS OF THE ANNUAL SYMPOSIUM OF EUGENICS SOCIETY. 16:41-48, 1981

Changing profile of IUD users in family planning clinics in rural Bangladesh, by S. Bhatia, et al. JOURNAL OF BIOSOCIAL SCIENCE. 13(2):169-177, April 1981

Characteristics and attitudes of family planners in Khartoum, Sudan, by M. A. Khalifa. JOURNAL OF BIOSOCIAL SCIENCE. 14(1):7-16, January 1982

Characteristics of contraceptive acceptors in rural Zaire, by J. E. Brown, et al. STUDIES IN FAMILY PLANNING. 11(12):378-384, December 1980

Characteristics of medical termination of pregnancy acceptors in Pondicherry State, 1972-1976, by N. S. Rao. INDIAN JOURNAL OF MEDICAL SCIENCES. 35(3):43-46, March 1981

Characteristics of successful distributors in the community-based distribution of contraceptives in Guatemala, by J. T. Bertrand, et al. STUDIES IN FAMILIY PLANNING. 11(9-10):274-285, September-October 1980

Characteristics of women recruited to a long-term study of the seque-lae of induced abortion. Report from a joint RCGP/RCOG Study co--ordinated by the Royal College of General Practitioners' Manchester Research Unit, by C. R. Kay, et al. JOURNAL OF THE ROYAL COL-LEGE OF GENERAL PRACTITIONERS. 31(229):473-477, August 1981

The child in the silent walk, by D. De Marco. LINACRE QUARTERLY. 48:333-339, November 1981

Child mortality and fertility in Colombia: individual and community effects, by M. R. Rosenzweig, et al. HEALTH POLICY AND EDUCATION. 2(3-4):305-348, March 1982

Child psychiatry and the law; developmental rights to privacy and in-dependent decision-making, by M. J. Guyer, et al. JOURNAL OF THE AMERICAN ACADEMY OF CHILD PSYCHIATRY. 21:298-302, May 1982

Childlessness in a transitional population: the U.S. at the turn of the century, by S. E. Tolnay, et al. JOURNAL OF FAMILY HISTORY. 7:200-219, Summer 1982

China and the one-child family, by J. Mirsky. NEW SOCIETY. pp. 264-265, February 18, 1982

China: planning or persecution? China is using a mix of incentives and deterrents to meet its population reduction target; but the campaign has led to excesses, by D. Lee. SOUTH. pp. 35-37, November 1981

China's one-child drive: another long march, by L. C. Landman. IN-TER NATIONAL FAMILY PLANNING PERSPECTIVES. 7:102-107, September 1981

China's one-child family: policy and public response, by L. F. Goodstadt. POPULATION AND DEVELOPMENT REVIEW. 8:37-58, March 1982

China's 'one-child' population future. INTERCOM. 9(8):1, August
1981

China's population policy, by K.-I. Chen. CURRENT HISTORY. 81:251-
254+, September 1982

Choice of ecbolic and the morbidity of day-case terminations of pregnancy, by D. B. Garrioch, et al. BRITISH JOURNAL OF OBSTETRICS AND
GYNAECOLOGY. 88(10):1029-1032, October 1981

The choice of sterilization procedure among married couples, by L. M.
Markman, et al. JOURNAL OF FAMILY PRACTICE. 14(1):27-30, January
1982

Choices that make us whate we are; abortion and the bomb--U.S. bishops' meeting, by J. R. Roach. ORIGINS. 12:377+, November 25,
1982

Choisis done in vie, by G. Huyghe. DOCUMENTATION CATHOLIQUE. (1a).
79:457-458, May 2, 1982

Cholesterol ester metabolism in plasma during estrogen and anti-
androgen treatment in men with carcinoma of the prostate, by L.
Wallentin. et al. JOURNAL OF LABORATORY AND CLINICAL MEDICINE.
98(6):906-916, December 1981

Chorea associated with the use of oral contraceptives: report of a
case and review of the literature, by W. B. Wadlington, et al.
CLINICAL PEDIATRICS. 20(12):804-806, December 1981

Christian freedom and ethical inquiry, by P. H. Van Ness. CALVIN
THEOLOGICAL JOURNAL. 17:26-52, April 1982

Les Christiens et le probleme social de l'avortement: table-ronde, by
P. Cote, et al. RELATIONS. 42:28-31, January-February 1982

Chromosomal analysis of baboons and their mothers, following application to mothers of potentially post-ovulation fertility-inhabiting
steroids, by Z. A. Jemilev, et al. ZENTRALBLATT FUR GYNAEKOLOGIE.
103(20):1215-1219, 1981

The chromosomal effects of the oral contraceptive, by N. P. Bishun.
JOURNAL OF SURGICAL ONCOLOGY. 20(2):115-118, June 1982

Chromosome abnormalities in 150 couples with multiple spontaneous
abortions, by P. Husslein, et al. FERTILITY AND STERILITY. 37(3):
379-383, March 1982

Chromosome analyses in couples with repeated pregnancy loss, by T.
Andrews, et al. JOURNAL OF BIOLOGICAL SCIENCE. 14(1):33-52,
January 1982

Chromosome translocations in couples with multiple spontaneous
abortions, by V. V. Michels, et al. AMERICAN JOURNAL OF HUMAN
GENETICS. 34(3):507-513, May 1982

Chromosomes, crime and the courts: the XXY and XYY quandary, by H. J.

Grace. SOUTH AFRICAN JOURNAL OF CRIMINAL LAW AND CRIMINOLOGY. 5(3):223-227, 1981

Chronic intestinal ischemia associated with oral contraceptive use, by G. L. Arnold, et al. AMERICAN JOURNAL OF GASTROENTEROLOGY. 77(1):32-34, 1982

Chronic treatment with a LH-RH-agonist: a new contraceptive method?, by M. Schmidt-Gollwitzer, et al. ACTA EUROPAEA FERTILITATIS. 12(3):275-276, September 1981

Church teaching and the immorality of contraception, by W. E. May. HOMILETIC AND PASTORAL REVIEW. 18:23, January 15, 1982

City appeals overturn of abortion consent rule. NATIONAL CATHOLIC REPORTER. 18:23, September 17, 1982

Civil liability of physicians following unsuccessful sterilization, by H. Franzki. FORTSCHRITTE DER MEDIZIN. 99(4):79-80, January 29, 1981

Clarity can be confusing, by W. S. Coffin, Jr. CHRISTIANITY AND CRISIS. 41:274+, October 19, 1981

Cliff-hanger Hatch plan vote likely, by M. Meehan. NATIONAL CATHOLIC REPORTER. 18:3, February 19, 1982

Clinical and biochemical results during the treatment with marvelon, a new oral contraceptive, by M. Mall-Haefeli, et al. GEBURTSHILFE UND FRAUENHEILKUNDE. 42(3):215-222, March 1982

Clinical and epidemiological aspects of voluntary interruption of pregnancy 2 years after law No. 194 on abortion, by M. G. Ricci, et al. RIVISTA ITALIANA DI GINECOLOGIA. 59(4/5):405-420, ?

Clinical and immunological responses with Pr-beta-hCG-TT vaccine, by S. M. Shahani, et al. CONTRACEPTION. 25(4):421-434, April 1982

Clinical, epidemiological, morphological and etiopathogenetic aspects of benign tumors of hepatocytic derivation, with description of a case of focal nodular hyperplasia, by L. Bontempini, et al. ARCHIVIO DE VECCHI PER L ANATOMIA PATOLOGICA E LA MEDICINA CLINICA. 64(3):547-568, December 1981

Clinical experience with sulprostone, by W. Brabec, et al. WIENER KLINISCHE WOCHENSCHRIFT. 93(6):193-197, March 20, 1981

Clinical experience with use of a jet injector for paracervical blocks in office practice, by A. D. Kovacs. OBSTETRICS AND GYNE-COLOGY. 59(3):373-374, March 1982

Clinical experience with vasovasostomy utilizing absorbable intra-vasal stent, by J. F. Redman. UROLOGY. 20(1):59-61, July 1982

Clinical forum 4. Gynecological nursing: sense of sensitivity, by G. Bichard, et al. NURSING MIRROR AND MIDWIVE'S JOURNAL. 154(15): xiii-xvi, April 14, 1982

Clinical forum 9. Obstetrics II: Postpartum family planning, by S. Walker. NURSING MIRROR AND MIDWIVE'S JOURNAL. 153(11 Suppl):xxii-

The clinical nurse specialist's role in the management of gestational trophoblastic neoplasms, by A. R. Marean. MAJOR PROBLEMS IN OBSTETRICS AND GYNECOLOGY. 14:229-241, 1982

Clinical observations on long-acting oral contraceptives--a report of 43,373. CHUNG HUA FU CHAN KO TSA CHIH. 14(2):65-67, April 1979

Clinical performance of a new levonorgestrel-releasing intrauterine device: a randomized comparison with a nova-T-copper device, by C. G. Nilsson, et al. CONTRACEPTION. 25(4):345-356, 1982

Clinical pharmacology and common minor side effects of oral contraceptives, by J. E. DeLia, et al. CLINICAL OBSTETRICS AND GYNECOLOGY. 24(3):879-892, September 1981

Clinical reprography of women seeking medical termination of pregnancy at AIIMS Hospital, New Delhi, by R. Singh, et al. JOURNAL OF FAMILY WELFARE. 28:3-17, June 1982

Clinical study of gossypol as a male contraceptive, by G. Z. Liu. REPRODUCCION. 5(3):189-193, July-September 1981

A clinical trial of norethisterone oenanthate (Norigest) injected every two months, by G. Howard, et al. CONTRACEPTION. 25(4):333-340, April 1982

Clinical trial of an oral contraceptive containing desogestrel and ethynyl estradiol, by M. J. Weijers. CLINICAL THERAPEUTICS. 4(5):359-366, 1982

The clinical use of me-quingestanol contraceptive pill. CHUNG HUA FU CHAN KO TSA CHIH. 14(2):68-72, April 1979

Clostridium perfringens sepsis following criminal abortion, by A. Meijernik, et al. NEDERLANDS TIJDSCHRIFT VOOR GENEESKUNDE. 126(14):613-616, April 3, 1982

Coagulation factors in women using oral contraceptives or intrauterine contraceptive devices immediately after abortion, by P. Lahteenmaki, et al. AMERICAN JOURNAL OF OBSTETRICS AND GYNECOLOGY. 141(2):175-179, September 15, 1981

Cognitive-behavioral prevention of adolescent pregnancy, by S. P. Schinke, et al. JOURNAL OF COUNSELING PSYCHOLOGY. 28(5):451-454, September 1981

Colposcopic study of the effect of steroid contraceptives on the uterine cervix, by J. Y. Zhou. CHUNG HUA FU CHAN KO TSA CHIH. 16(1):55-58, January 1981

A combined device of negative pressure bottle with injector for artificial abortion, by J. K. Zhou. CHUNG HUA FU CHAN KO TSA CHIH. 61(9):551, September 1981

Comments to the United States Senate Judiciary Subcommittee on Separation of Powers. A bill to provide that human life shall be deemed to exist from conception [editorial]. TERATOLOGY. 24(1): 107-109, August 1981

Committee to Defend Reproductive Rights v. Myers: abortion funding as
an unconstitutional condition, by C. W. Sherman. CALIFORNIA LAW
REVIEW. 70:978-1013, July 1982

--[625 P 2d 119 (Cal)]: the constitutionality of conditions on public
benefits in California. THE HASTINGS LAW JOURNAL. 33:1475-1500,
July 1982

--[625 P 2d 779 (Cal)]: procreative choice guaranteed for all women.
GOLDEN GATE UNIVERSITY LAW REVIEW. 12:691-716, Summer 1982

Communist party of the Soviet Union and the women's question: the
case of the 1936 decree in defence of mother and child, by J.
Evans. JOURNAL OF CONTEMPORARY HISTORY. 16:757-775, October 1981

Community availability of contraceptives and family limitation, by A.
O. Tsui, et al. DEMOGRAPHY. 18(4):615-625, November 1981

Community forum. 2. Contraception, by Z. Pauncefort. NURSING MIRROR
AND MIDWIVE'S JOURNAL. 154(6 Suppl):i-xii, February 10, 1982

Comparative risk of death from induced abortion at less than equal to
12 weeks gestation performed with local vs. general anesthesia, by
H. Peterson, et al. AMERICAN JOURNAL OF OBSTETRICS AND GYNECOLOGY.
141(7):763-768, December 1, 1981

Comparative study of the action of phytohemagglutinin on DNA fluorescence in the lymphocytes of women with physiological pregnancy and
in threatened abortion, by V. S. Tolmachev, et al. TSITOL I
GENETIKA. 15(4):16-18, July-August 1981

Comparison of the Lippes Loop D and tapered Lippes Loop D intrauterine devices, by B. Behlilovic, et al. CONTRACEPTION. 25(3):
293-298, 1982

Comparison of the metabolic effects of two hormonal contraceptive
methods: an oral formulation and a vaginal ring. I. Carbohydrate
metabolism and liver function, by T. Ahren, et al. CONTRACEPTION.
24(4):415-427, October 1981

--II. Serum lipoproteins and apolipoproteins, by T. Ahren, et al.
CONTRACEPTION. 24(4):451-468, October 1981

A comparison of moral and ego development in women: a quantative and
qualitative study of the reconstruction of the abortion decision,
by L. M. Connor. DISSERTATION ABSTRACTS INTERNATIONAL. A. p.
1085, 1982

Comparison of 2 therapeutic schemes in threatened premature labor, by
G. C. Di Renzo, et al. MINERVA GINECOLOGIA. 33(9):841-850, September 1981

Compelling state interest justifies spousal notice burden on abortion. FAMILY LAW REPORTER: COURT OPINIONS. 8(2):2018-2020,
November 10, 1981

Compensation for incorrect sterilization--remarks on the judgment of
the German Supreme Court of 18 March 1980, by K. Handel. BEITRAEGE
ZUR GERICHTLICHEN MEDIZIN. 39:233-237, 1981

Complications and contraindications of oral contraception, by W. W. Beck, Jr. CLINICAL OBSTETRICS AND GYNECOLOGY. 24(3):893-901, September 1981

Complications following the vaginal use of potassium permanganate for an abortion, by A. Atanasov, et al. AKUSHERSTVO I GINEKOLOGIIA. 20(4):355-357, 1981

Complications in women after operative sterilization, by B. Gavric, et al. JUGOSLAVENSKA GINEKOLOGIJA I OPSTETRICIJA. 21(3-4):81-82, May-August 1981

Complications of pregnancy and labor in former oral contraceptive users, by S. Harlap, et al. CONTRACEPTION. 24(1):1-13, July 1981

Computerized patient-flow analysis of local family planning clinics, by J. L. Graves, et al. FAMILY PLANNING PERSPECTIVES. 13(4):164-170, July-August 1981

Concentration of hormones in early pregnancy in response to prosta-glandin-induced abortion, by B. Seifert, et al. ZENTRALBLATT FUR GYNAEKOLOGIE. 104(1):45-51, 1982

Concepts of abortion and their relevance to the abortion debate, by M. B. Mahowald. SOUTHERN JOURNAL OF PHILOSOPHY. 20:195-208, Summer 1982

The condom as contraceptive and prophylactic [a reappraisal], by P. D. Shenefelt. WISCONSIN MEDICAL JOURNAL. 80(9):19-20, September 1981

Condom sales surge, as venereal diseases rise, by R. Raldt. AMERICAN DRUGGIST. 185:60+, January 1982

Confidentiality and the pill [letter], by R. Taines. AMERICAN FAMILY PHYSICIAN. 25(5):53, May 1982

Conflict of choice: California considers statutory authority for in-voluntary sterilization of the severely mentally retarded. WHIT-TIER LAW REVIEW. 4:495-516, 1982

Congenital defects and miscarriages among New Zealand 2, 4, 5-T sprayers, by A. H. Smith, et al. ARCHIVES OF ENVIRONMENTAL HEALTH. 37(4):197-200, July-August 1982

Congressional power and constitutional rights: reflections on pro-posed "human life" legislation (whether recent U.S. Supreme Court decisions on abortion can be undone by ordinary legislation), by S. Estreicher. VIRGINIA LAW REVIEW. 68:333-358, February 1982

Congressional withdrawal of jurisdiction from federal courts: a reply to Professor Uddo, by M. Vitiello. LOYOLA LAW REVIEW. 28:61-76, Winter 1982

Conoscenza dell'aborto e organizzazione del lavoro consultoriale, by A. Capodilupo. REVISTRA DI SERVIZIO SOCIALE. 21(2):74-81, 1981

Le conseil familial et conjugal en France, by J. Rigaux. SOCIOLOGIA DEL DIRITTO. 7(2):111-124, 1980

Consent and privacy in the National Survey of Family Growth: a report on the pilot study for cycle III, by K. Tanfer, et al. VITAL HEALTH STATISTICS. 2(91):1-47, March 1982

Conservatism, attitude to abortion and Macoby's biophilia, by J. J. Ray, et al. JOURNAL OF SOCIAL PSYCHOLOGY. 118(1):143, October 1982

Constitution law--right to privacy--parental notice requirements in abortion statutes. TENNESSEE LAW REVIEW. 48:974-999, Summer 1981

Constitutional law/abortion. ILLINOIS BAR JOURNAL. 70:515-519, April 1982

Constitutional law--abortion--Utah's parental notification statute held constitutional. H.L. v. Matheson (101 S Ct 1164). CUMBERLAND LAW REVIEW. 12:711-725, 1981-1982

Constitutional law--fourteenth amendment--right to privacy--contraceptives--minors--the United States Court of Appeals for the Sixth Circuit has held that a state-funded family planning center's distribution of contraceptives to minors without parental notice does not violate the parents' constitutional rights. DUSQUESNE LAW REVIEW. 20:111-121, Fall 1981

Constitutional law--Medicaid funding restriction does not unconstitutionally burden the right to terminate a pregnancy. TULANE LAW REVIEW. 56:435-446, December 1981

Constitutional law--the minor, parent, state triangle and the requirement of parental notification: H.L. v. Matheson (101 S Ct 1164). HOWARD LAW REVIEW. 25:299-322, 1982

Constitutional law--privacy rights--consent requirements and abortions for minors. NEW YORK STATE LAW SCHOOL LAW REVIEW. 26:837-854, 1981

Constitutional law--right of privacy--abortion--family law--parent and child--standing--as applied to immature, unemancipated and dependent minors, a state statute requiring a physician to notify a pregnant minor's parents prior to the performing of an abortion is constitutional--H.L. v. Matheson. UNIVERSITY OF CINCINNATI LAW REVIEW. 50:867-881, 1981

Constitutional law--a state statute, which requires physicians to notify the parents of immature and unemancipated minors before performing an abortion, does not violate the minors' fundamental right to have an abortion. DRAKE LAW REVIEW. 31:476-485, 1981-1982

Constitutional law--United States Supreme Court upholds the unconstitutionality of the Hyde Amendment, withholding Medicaid funds for therapeutic abortions unless the life of the mother is endangered. TEMPLE LAW QUARTERLY. 54:109-144, 1981

Consultori per la pianificazione familiare in Brasile, by C. Souto, et al. SOCIOLOGIA DEL DIRITTO. 7(2):125-137, 1980

Consultorio familiare e politica sociale. Un approccio sociologico-giuridico, by M. Corsale. SOCIOLOGIA DEL DIRITTO. 7(2):35-62,

1980

Contact dermatitis from a copper-containing intrauterine contraceptive device, by C. Romaguera, et al. CONTACT DERMATITIS. 7(3):
163-164, May 1981

Context effects on survey responses to questions about abortion, by
H. Schuman, et al. PUBLIC OPINION QUARTERLY. 45(2):216-223, Summer 1981

A contextual approach to decisions about pregnancy and abortion, by
J. Lambert. FEMINISM AND PROCESS THOUGHT. pp. 106-137, 1981

Continuation of injectable contraceptions in Thailand, by T. Narkavonnakit, et al. STUDIES IN FAMILY PLANNING. 13(4):99-105, April
1982

Continued follow-up study of 120 persons born after refusal of application for therapeutic abortion, by H. Forssman, et al. ACTA PSY-
CHIATRICA SANDINAVICA. 64(2):142-149, 1981

The continuing need for contraceptive research [editorial], by J. J.
Sciarra. FERTILITY AND STERILITY. 53(3):439-452, September 1981

Contraception and multiple sclerosis, by S. Poser. NERVENARZT.
53(6):323-326, June 1982

Contraception and toxic-shock syndrome: a reanalysis, by J. D. Shelton, et al. CONTRACEPTION. 24(6):631-634, December 1981

La contraception artificielle: conflit de devoirs ou acte a double
effet, by N. Hendricks. NOUVELLE REVUE THEOLOGIQUE. 204:396-413,
May-July 1982

Contraception by diet probed, by P. S. Lefevere. NATIONAL CATHOLIC
REPORTER. 18(1):5, February 12, 1982

Contraception choices of female university students [research], by A.
Ayvazian. JOGN NURSING: JOURNAL OF OBSTETRIC GYNECOLOGIC AND NEO-
NATAL NURSING. 10(6):426-429, November-December 1981

Contraception: condoms, rhythm, spermicidal agents, diaphragms, intrauterine devices, by J. A. Gans. AMERICAN DRUGGIST. 185:35-38+,
March 1982

Contraception during lactation, by I. Aref, et al. CONTRACEPTIVE
DELIVERY SYSTEMS. 3(1):47-52, 1982

Contraception for adolescent girls, by J. E. DeLia. CONSULTANT.
21:63-64+, March 1981

Contraception for adolescents, by J. Huber. THERAPEUTISCHE UMSCHAU.
39(6):469-471, June 1982

Contraception for adolescents ... test yourself. AMERICAN JOURNAL OF
NURSING. 81:2191+, December 1981

Contraception for the under 16s: better safe than sorry [research],
by A. Cook. NURSING MIRROR AND MIDWIVE'S JOURNAL. 153(12):24-26,
September 16, 1981

Contraception: how many will heed the Pope?, by C. Longley. TIMES (London). p. 10, May 7, 1982

Contraception in adolescence, by S. Vandal. NURSING QUEBEC. 2(2): 18-23, January-February 1982

Contraception in adolescents according to recent scientific understanding, by M. Mall-Haefeli. THERAPEUTISCHE UMSCHAU. 39(6):448-457, June 1982

Contraception in ethnic minority groups in Bedford [research], by P. Beard. HEALTH VISITOR. 55:417+, August 1982

Contraception in the future, by H. S. Jacobs. PROCEEDINGS OF THE ANNUAL SYMPOSIUM OF EUGENICS SOCIETY. 16:49-57, 1981

Contraception is less risky for teenagers than is pregnancy, worldwide study finds. FAMILY PLANNING PERSPECTIVES. 14:274-275, September-October 1982

Contraception: the pill, by V. A. Serrano. AMERICAN DRUGGIST. 185: 45+, March 1982

Contraception, pregnancy management and the clinic: opinions of 1271 puerperas in a large hospital on the northern border of Milan, by P. Dall'Aglio. ANNALI DI OSTETRICIA GINECOLOGIA, MEDICINA PERINATALE. 103(1):48-59, January-February 1982

Contraception, pregnancy management and the family-planning clinic (findings on 410 puerperas in a Lombard hospital), by M. Semeria. ANNALI DI OSTETRICIA GINECOLOGIA, MEDICINA PERINATALE. 103(1):93-101, January-February 1982

Contraception: which method will you prescribe, and why?, by G. Weiss. CONSULTANT. 21:285-286+, November 1981

Contraception with LHRH agonists, a new physiological approach, by F. Labrie, et al. REPRODUCCION. 5(4):229-241, October-December 1981

Contraception--a woman's delimma, by S. Wigington. NURSING TIMES. 77:1765-1768, October 1981

Contraception: yesterday & today (1979), by B. Morrison. FAMILY RELATIONS. 30(1):141, January 1981

Contraceptive activity and mechanism of action of 6-methylsubstituted D'$_6$-pentaranes combined with nestranol, by V. V. Korkhov, et al. FARMAKOLOGYA I TOKSIKOLOGYA. 44(1):95-98, 1981

Contraceptive availability differentials in use and fertility, by A. O. Tsui, et al. STUDIES IN FAMILY PLANNING. 12(11):381-393, November 1981

Contraceptive choice and maternal image, by M. Viglione. DISSERTAtion ABSTRACTS INTERNATIONAL. B. p. 2010, 1982

Contraceptive cover for rubella vaccination, by S. Rowlands, et al. PRACTITIONER. 226(1368):1155-1156, June 1982

Contraceptive effect of breast feeding, by P. W. Howie, et al. JOUR-

NAL OF TROPICAL PEDIATRICS. 28(1):ii-v, February 1982

Contraceptive efficacy of 200 microgram R2323 and 10 microgram R2858, by H. Rall. CLINICAL TRIALS JOURNAL. 18(6):395-400, 1981

Contraceptive failure in the United States: the impact of social, economic and demographic factors [research], by A. L. Schirm, et al. FAMILY PLANNING PERSPECTIVES. 14(2):68-75, March-April 1982

Contraceptive intentions and subsequent behavior in rural Bangladesh, by S. Bhatia. STUDIES IN FAMILY PLANNING. 13:24, January 1982

Contraceptive method switching among American female adolescents, 1979, by M. B. Hirsch. DISSERTATION ABSTRACTS INTERNATIONAL. A. p. 1303, 1982

Contraceptive methods. NUEVA ENFERMERIA. (11):12-16, May 1980

--, by M. E. Creus. REVISTA DE ENFERMAGEN. 4(34):36-40, May 1981

Contraceptive methods and abortion: one question, by L. Balestriere. ANNALES MEDICO-PSYCHOLOGIQUES. 139(5):513-528, May 1981

Contraceptive patterns of college students who experienced early coitus [research], by M. L. Vincent, et al. JOURNAL OF SCHOOL HEALTH. 51(10):667-672, December 1981

Contraceptive practice in Bangladesh: a study of mediators and differentials, by S. M. Shahidullah. DISSERTATION ABSTRACTS INTERNA-TIONAL. A. p. 5261, 1982

Contraceptive preferences of adolescents and the role of counseling, by M. Endler, et al. THERAPEUTISCHE UMSCHAU. 39(6):458-461, June 1982

Contraceptive research on the value and cost of children, by K. Sadashivaiah. JOURNAL OF FAMILY WELFARE. 28:25-32, June 1982

Contraceptive sterilization in four Latin American countries, by J. McCarthy. JOURNAL OF BIOLOGICAL SCIENCE. 14(2):189-201, April 1982

Contraceptive steroids, age, and the cardiovascular system, by E. R. Plunkett. AMERICAN JOURNAL OF OBSTETRICS AND GYNECOLOGY. 142(6 Pt 2):747-751, March 15, 1982

Contraceptive use and family planning services along the U.S.-Mexico border, by C. W. Warren, et al. INTERNATIONAL FAMILY PLANNING PER-SPECTIVES. 7:52-59, June 1981

Contraceptive use and fertility in the Republic of Panama, by R. S. Monteith, et al. STUDIES IN FAMILY PLANNING. 12(10):331-340, October 1981

Contraceptive use patterns, prior source, and pregnancy history of female family planning patients: United States, 1980, by E. Eckard. ADVANCE DATA. (82):1-12, June 16, 1982

Contraceptive use, pregnancy intentions and pregnancy outcomes among U.S. women [research], by J. G. Dryfoos. FAMILY PLANNING PERSPEC-

TIVES. 14(2):81-94, March-April 1982

Contraceptives, by I. R. McFadyen. INFORMATION. (5):95, 1981

--, by B. P. Quinby. MADEMOISELLE. 88:66-67, January 1982

Contraceptives and the conceptus. II. Sex of the fetus and neonate
    after oral contraceptive use, by H. P. Klinger, et al. CONTRA-
    CEPTION. 23(4):367-374, April 1981

Contraceptives and the female undergraduates in Ibadan, Nigeria, by
    J. A. Adeleye. EAST AFRICAN MEDICAL JOURNAL. 58(8):616-621,
    August 1981

Contraceptives and the liver, by M. Schmid. LEBER, MAGEN, DARM.
    11(5):216-226, September 1981

Contraceptives: back to the barriers, by R. Serlin. NEW SCIENTIST.
    91(1264):281-284, July 30, 1981

Contraceptives go on trial for diabetics. NEW SCIENTIST. 91;463,
    August 20, 1981

Contradiction isn't unreasonableness, by C. Sureau. ACQUISITIONS
    MEDICALES RECENTES. 198:173-178, 1981

Contribution of auxiliary sanitary personnel to the care of patients
    with toxico-septic abortion, by A. Koros. VITA MEDICALA. 29(6):
    129-133, June 1981

Contribution of HCG radioimmunoassay in the diagnosis of pathological
    states in early pregnancy, by H. Fingerova, et al. CESKOSLOVENSKA
    GYNEKOLOGIE. 46(9):673-680, November 1981

Contributo all'analisi del ruolo dell'operatore in un consultorio
    pubblico di fronte alla richiesta di interruzione di gravidanza, by
    M. Ghezzi. REVISTRA DI SERVIZIO SOCIALE. 21(1):82-90, 1981

Control of the effect of treatment in late threatened abortions using
    the DU-1 Dynamo-uterograph, by D. Tsenov, et al. AKUSHERSTVO I
    GINEKOLOGIIA. 21(1):11-15, 1982

Control of uterine contraction with tocolytic agents (ritodrine).
    2. Use in cases of threatened abortion, cervical incontinence and
    gynecologic surgery in pregnancy, by P. A. Colombo, et al. ANNALI
    DI OSTETRICIA GINECOLOGIA, MEDICINA PERINATALE. 102(6):431-440,
    November-December 1981

Controlling population growth. BEIJING REVIEW. 25:6-7, May 17, 1982

Copper as a male contraceptive, by S. S. Riar, et al. INDIAN JOURNAL
    OF EXPERIMENTAL BIOLOGY. 19(12):1121-1123, December 1981

Correlates of contraceptive use among urban poor in Colombia, by J.
    T. Bertrand, et al. JOURNAL OF BIOSOCIAL SCIENCE. 13(4):431-441,
    October 1981

Cottonseed oil as a vaginal contraceptive. ARCHIVES OF ANDROLOGY.
    8(1):11-14, 1982

Counseling for sterilization, by B. L. Gonzales. JOURNAL OF REPRO-
   DUCTIVE MEDICINE. 26(10):538-540, October 1981

Counseling on contraception following interruption of pregnancy.
   Responsibility of the hospital gynecologist. Model of contraceptive
   counseling at the Gynecological Clinic Berlin-Neukolln, by S. Ufer,
   et al. FORTSCHRITTE DER MEDIZIN. 100(16):746-748, April 29, 1982

Counselling needs of women seeking abortions, by M. J. Hare, et al.
   JOURNAL OF BIOLOGICAL SCIENCE. 13(3):269-273, July 1981

Couple-directed contraceptive counseling, by M. A. Redmond. CANADIAN
   NURSE. 78:38-39, September 1982

Couple to Couple League an idea whose time has come, by C. A.
   Savitskas, Jr. OUR SUNDAY VISITOR. 70:6, March 28, 1982

The course of intrauterine pregnancy with a coil in situ, by J. J.
   Kjer, et al. UGESKRIFT FOR LAEGER. 143(7):416-417, February 9,
   1981

Court finds pill defectively designed. TRIAL. 17(6):13, June 1981

Court: public college paper can't reject abortion ads (Portland
   Community College), by F. King. EDITOR AND PUBLISHER--THE FOURTH
   ESTATE. 114:20, October 10, 1981

Court upholds parental notice requirement before allowing abortions
   on minors, by P. A. Ewer. JOURNAL OF CRIMINAL LAW AND CRIMINOLOGY.
   72(4):1461-1481

Court won't intervene to compel girl to have abortion urged by
   mother. FAMILY LAW REPORTER: COURT OPINIONS. 8(10):2140-2141,
   January 11, 1982

Criminal liability for complicity in abortions committed outside
   Ireland, by M. J. Findlay. IRISH JURIST. 15:88-98, Summer 1980

Critical abortion litigation, by D. J. Horan. CATHOLIC LAWYER. 26:
   198-208, Summer 1981

Crushing freedom in the name of life, by N. Dorsen. HUMAN RIGHTS.
   10:19-21+, Spring 1982

Cultural influenes in birth practices in Papua New Guinea, by E. E.
   Drakum. AUSTRALASIAN NURSES JOURNAL. 11:14-15+, June 1982

Curbing sexual appetite (Depo Provera lowers testosterone levels:
   work of Fred S. Berlin and John Money), by W. Herbert. SCIENCE
   NEWS. 122:270, October 23, 1982

Current birth control methods: know your choices, by C. West.
   ESSENCE. 1:60+ March 1982

Currently used methods in induced abortion, by A. A. Haspels.
   TIJDSCHRIFT VOR ZIEKENVERPLEGING. 34(17):745-749, August 25, 1981

Cyclic hepatitis' in a young woman [case presentation], by H. J.
   Dworken, et al. HOSPITAL PRACTICE. 16(11):48G-H, November 1981

Cyematopathology. Principles and recommendations for practical handling of pathologico-anatomic and histologic examinations in abortions, diseases and death of premature and full-term infants, by K.
Kloos. PATHOLOGE. 3(3):121-126,

Cyproterone acetate in the treatment of acne vulgaris in adult females, by B. Hansted, et al. DERMATOLOGICA. 164(2):117-126, February 1982

Cytogenetic examinations of married couples with obstetrical failures, by H. Kedzia, et al. GINEKOLOGIA POLSKA. 52(9):80-1804,
September 1981

Cytogenetic studies in recurrent fetal loss, by M. T. Mulcahy. AUS-
TRALIAN AND NEW ZEALAND JOURNAL OF OBSTETRICS AND GYNAECOLOGY.
22(1):29-30, February 1982

A cytogenetic study of 1000 spontaneous abortions, by T. Hassold, et
al. ANNALS OF HUMAN GENETICS. 44(Pt 2):151-178, October 1980

Cytogenetics of spontaneous abortions, by L. Zergollern, et al. ACTA
MEDICA IUGOSLAVICA. 36(2):107-113, 1982

Dalkon shield controversy continues. TRIAL. 17(6):13, June 1981

Damage awards for wrongful birth and wrongful life, by A. H. Bernstein. HOSPITALS. 56(5):65-67, March 1, 1982

Damaged placenta in mid-trimenon abortion, by A. Jakobovits. JUGO-
SLAVENSKA GINEKOLOGIJA I OPSTETRICIJA. 21(3-40:72-74, May-August
1981

Death following puncture of the aorta during laparoscopic sterilization, by H. B. Peterson, et al. OBSTETRICS AND GYNECOLOGY. 59(1):
133-134, January 1982

Death from amniotic fluid embolism and disseminated intravascular
coagulation after a curettage abortion, by W. Cates, Jr., et al.
AMERICAN JOURNAL OF OBSTETRICS AND GYNECOLOGY. 141(3):346-348,
October 1, 1981

A death in a hospital (liberals silent as unwanted child is starved
to death in Indiana hospital; they are busy protesting the danger
of nuclear weapons to human life), by R. E. Tyrrell, Jr. AMERICAN
SPECTATOR. 15:6+, June 1981

Deaths following female sterilization with unipolar electrocoagulat-
ing devices. CONNECTICUT MEDICINE. 46(1):31-32, January 1982

Deaths from second trimester abortion by dilatation and evacuation:
causes, prevention, facilities, by W. Cates, Jr., et al. OBSTE-
TRICS AND GYNECOLOGY. 58(4):401-408, October 1981

The debate over life, by C. M. Odell. OUR SUNDAY VISITOR. 70:10-
11+, January 17, 1982

Decidual vasculopathy and extensive placental infarction in a patient
with repeated thromboembolic accidents, recurrent fetal loss, and a
lupus anticoagulant, by F. De Wolf, et al. AMERICAN JOURNAL OF OB-
STETRICS AND GYNECOLOGY. 142(7):829-834, April 1, 1982

Decision analysis for assessing the impact of female sterilization in Bangladesh, by M. J. Rosenberg, et al. STUDIES IN FAMILY PLANNING. 13(2):59, February 1982

The decline of fertility in Costa Rica: literacy, modernization and family planning, by J. M. Stycos. POPULATION STUDIES. 36(1):15-30, March 1982

Decreased adenosine 3'-5'-cyclic monophosphate concentration in amniotic fluid during rivanol-induced abortion, by P. Bistoletti, et al. GYNECOLOGIC AND OBSTETRIC INVESTIGATION. 13(3):184-188, 1982

Decreased cyclic A M P concentration in amniotic fluid during rivanol-induced abortion, by P. Bistoletti, et al. GYNECOLOGIC AND OBSTETRIC INVESTIGATION. 13(3):184-188, 1982

A defence of abortion: a question for Judith Jarvis Thomson. PHILOSOPHICAL INVESTIGATIONS. 5:142-145, April 1982

Delay in conception for former 'pill' users, by S. Linn, et al. JAMA: JOURNAL OF THE AMERICAN MEDICAL ASSOCIATION. 247(5):629-632, February 5, 1982

The demographic impact of the contraceptive distribution project in Matlab, Bangladesh, by W. S. Stinson, et al. STUDIES IN FAMILY PLANNING. 13(5):141-148, May 1982

The demographic impact of the family planning--health services project in Matlab, Bangladesh, by J. F. Phillips, et al. STUDIES IN FAMILY PLANNING. 13(5):131-140, May 1982

Demographic trends in tubal sterilization: United States, 1970-1978, by F. DeStefano, et al. AMERICAN JOURNAL OF PUBLIC HEALTH. 72(5): 480-484, May 1982

Demonstration of an early abortifacient effect of norethisterone (NET) in the primate (baboon), by L. R. Beck, et al. CONTRACEPTION. 25(1):97-105, January 1982

Demonstration of a spirocheticidal effect by chemical contraceptives on treponema pallidum, by B. Singh, et al. BULLETIN OF THE PAN AMERICAN HEALTH ORGANIZATION. 16(1):59-64, 1982

Depo-provera debate revs up at FDA, by M. Sun. SCIENCE. 217:424-428, July 30, 1982

Depo-provera for better or worse?, by P. MacMillan. NURSING TIMES. 78(11):467, March 17-23, 1982

Depo provera in perspective, by I. A. McGoldrick. PAPAU NEW GUINEA MEDICAL JOURNAL. 24(4):274-279, December 1981

Depo-provera: an injectable contraceptive, by S. Wigington. NURSING TIMES. 77:1794-1798, October 1981

Deregulation and the right to life, by A. Yankauer. AMERICAN JOURNAL OF PUBLIC HEALTH. 71:797-801, August 1981

Dermal changes in response to hormonal contraceptives, by C. Scholz, et al. ZENTRALBLATT FUR GYNAEKOLOGIE. 103(19):1158-1164, 1981

Dermatoglyphic characteristics in abortion, by N. A. Bel'tseva, et al. AKUSHERSTVO I GINEKOLOGIIA. (3):44-47, March 1982

Detection of subclinical abortion in infertile women by beta-hCG radioimmunoassay, by T. Onoue, et al. NIPPON SANKA FUJINKA GAKKAI ZASSHI. 33(8):1255-1258, August 1981

The development and role of the Marriage and Family Section in the establishment of socialist family policies in East Germany. ZEIT-SCHRIFT FUR DIE GESAMTE HYGIENE. 27(7):514-516, July 7, 1981

The development and role of the Marriage and Family Section in the Social Hygiene Society of East Germany, by B. Wegner. ZEITSCHRIFT FUR DIE GESAMTE HYGIENE. 27(7):516-518, July 7, 1981

Development of a male contraceptive--a beginning [editorial], by W. J. Crowley, Jr. NEW ENGLAND JOURNAL OF MEDICINE. 305:695-696, September 17, 1981

Development of pregnancy following sterilization of the woman, by L. C. van Otterlo, et al. NEDERLANDS TIJDSCHRIFT VOOR GENEESKUNDE. 126(6):241-244, February 6, 1982

Diagnostic and prognostic value of colpocytosmears in threatened abortion in the first half of pregnancy, by S. Hristamian. FOLIA MEDICA. 23(3-4):24-29, 1981

Diaphragm failure [letter], by W. R. Atkinson. MEDICAL JOURNAL OF AUSTRALIA. 2(4):206-207, August 22, 1981

Diaphragms rediscovered, by S. O'Malley. COSMOPOLITAN. 192(3):171+, March 1982

Dietary deprivation induces fetal loss and abortion in rabbits, by T. Matsuzawa, et al. TOXICOLOGY. 22(3):255-259, 1981

Dilatation and evacuation procedures and second-trimester abortions. The role of physician skill and hospital setting, by W. Cates, Jr., et al. JAMA: JOURNAL OF THE AMERICAN MEDICAL ASSOCIATION. 248(5): 559-563, August 6, 1982

Dilatation of hepatic sinusoids after use of oral contraceptives, by M. Balazs, et al. DEUTSCHE MEDIZINISCHE WOCHENSCHRIFT. 106(41): 1345-1349, October 9, 1981

Dilatation of hepatic sinusoids caused by oral contraceptives, by M. Balazs, et al. ORVOSI HETILAP. 122(34):2071-2074, August 23, 1981

Dinamica demografica, planificacion familiar y politica de poblacion en Costa Rica, by L. Rosero Bixby. DEMOGRAFIA Y ECONOMIA. 15(1): 59-84, 1981

Diphyllobothriasis in Americans and Asians [letter]. JAMA: JOURNAL OF THE AMERICAN MEDICAL ASSOCIATION. 247(16):2230, April 23, 1982

Discontinuance of oral contraceptives [letter], by P. T. Hohe. ARCHIVES OF INTERNAL MEDICINE. 142(8):1585, August 1982

Disposition of intravenous diazepam in young men and women, by H. G. Giles, et al. EUROPEAN JOURNAL OF CLINICAL PHARMACOLOGY. 20(3):

207-213, 1981

Divergent perspectives in abortion counseling, by G. D. Gibb, et al.
 PSYCHOLOGICAL REPORTS. 50(3 Pt 1):819-822, June 1982

The do it yourself abortion, by G. Sherry. OUR SUNDAY VISITOR. 70:
 12+, March 28, 1982

Do zygotes become people?, by W. R. Carter. MIND. 91:77-95, January
 1982

Does oral contraception cause deep venous thromboses?, by R. Lambrecht, et al. ZENTRALBLATT FUR CHIRURGIE. 106(16):1074-1080,
 1981

Does progestogen reduction in oral contraception parallel reduced
 lipid metabolic effects?, by N. Crona, et al. ACTA OBSTETRICIA ET
 GYNECOLOGICA SCANDINAVICA. SUPPLEMENT. 105:41-44, 1982

Doing as the ancient Egyptians did--the sponge, by V. Morgan. TIMES
 (London). p. 9, March 16, 1982

The doubtful value of transitory contraception after laparoscopic
 electrocoagulation of the fallopian tubes, by J. J. Kjer, et al.
 ACTA OBSTETRICIA ET GYNECOLOGICA SCANDINAVICA. 60(4):403-405, 1981

Down go the abortion and school prayer bills, by B. Spring. CHRIS-
 TIANITY TODAY. 26:56-58, October 22, 1982

The dream of love and the reality of contraception. Current adolescent sexual behaviour and contraceptive methods, by K. Thormann, et
 al. THERAPEUTISCHE UMSCHAU. 39(6):462-468, June 1982

Drug blocks pregnancy after fertilization, by J. Fox. CHEMICAL AND
 ENGINEERING NEWS. 60:26, May 17, 1982

Duration of brest-feeding and development of children after insertion
 of a levo-norgestrel-releasing intrauterine contraceptive device,
 by M. Heikkila, et al. CONTRACEPTION. 25(3):279-292, 1982

Duration of lactation and return of menstruation in lactating women
 using hormonal contraception and intrauterine devices, by K. Prema.
 CONTRACEPTIVE DELIVERY SYSTEMS. 3(1):39-46, 1982

The dynamics of the abortion debate, by J. G. Johnson. AMERICA.
 146:106-109, February 13, 1982

Dynamics of policy politics: the cases of abortion funding and family
 planning in the state of Oregon, by G. L. Keiser. DISSERTATION
 ABSTRACTS INTERNATIONAL. A. p. 4919, 1982

Early adolescent childbearing: a changing morbidity?, by R. E.
 Kreipe, et al. JOURNAL OF ADOLESCENT HEALTH CARE. 2(2):127-131,
 December 1981

Early complications and sequence of pregnancy interruption with
 hypertonic saline, by R. Borenstein, et al. INTERNATIONAL JOURNAL
 OF FERTILITY. 25(2):88-93, 1980

Early complications of induced abortion in primigravidae, by K.

Dalaker, et al. ANNALES CHIRURGIAE ET GYNAECOLOGIAE. 70(6):331-336, 1981

Early fetal loss by Z. Stein. BIRTH DEFECTS. 17(1):95-111, 1981

Early pregnancy factor as a monitor for fertilization in women wearing intrauterine devices, by Y. C. Smart, et al. FERTILITY AND STERILITY. 37(2):201-204, 1982

Early therapy for the incompetent cervix in patients with habitual abortion, by J. W. Ayers, et al. FERTILITY AND STERILITY. 38(2):177-181, August 1982

Early total occlusion of os uteri to prevent habitual abortion and premature deliveries, by E. Saling. ZEITSCHRIFT FUR GEBURTSCHILFE UND PERINATOLOGIE. 185(5):259-261, 1981

Eastern Europe: pronatalist policies and private behavior, by H. P. David. POPULATION BULLETIN. 36(6):48, February 1982

Echographic examinations in 246 cases of voluntary interruption of pregnancy, by P. Rattazzi, et al. MINERVA GINECOLOGIA. 33(12):1173-1178, December 1981

An economic interpretation of the distribution and organization of abortion services (Georgia; based on conference paper), by B. J. Kay, et al. INQUIRY. 18(4):322-331, Winter 1981

Ectopic pregnancies: rising incidence rates in northern California, by P. H. Shiono, et al. AMERICAN JOURNAL OF PUBLIC HEALTH. 72:173-175, February 1982

Ectopic pregnancy after tubal sterilization. Mechanism of recanalization [case report], by P. Rimdusit. JOURNAL OF THE MEDICAL ASSOCIATION OF THAILAND. 65(2):101-105, February 1982

Ectopic pregnancy and prior induced abortion [research], by A. A. Levin, et al. AMERICAN JOURNAL OF PUBLIC HEALTH. 72(3):253-256, March 1982

Education and contraceptive choice: a conditional demand framework, by M. R. Rosenzweig, et al. INTERNATIONAL ECONOMIC REVIEW. 23:171-198, February 1982

Effect of aflatoxin B1 on hepatic drug-metabolizing enzymes in female rats. Interaction with a contraceptive agent, by L. Kamdem, et al. XENOBIOTICA. 11(4):275-279, April 1981

Effect of blood pressure or changing from high to low dose steroid preparations in women with oral contraceptive induced hypertension, by R. J. Weir. SCOTTISH MEDICAL JOURNAL. 27(3):212-215, July 1982

Effect of the blood serum from pregnant women with early and late toxicoses and threatened abortions on spontaneous contractile activity of smooth muscle, by S. Sharankov, et al. AKUSHERSTVO I GINEKOLOGIIA. 20(3):190-197, 1981

Effect of castration and oral contraceptives on hepatic ethanol and acetaldehyde metabolizing enzymes in the male rat, by F. S. Messiha, et al. SUBSTANCE AND ALCOHOL ACTIONS/MISUSE. 1(2):197-

202, 1980

Effect of combined oral contraceptives on glycosylated haemoglobin, by N. Oakley, et al. JOURNAL OF THE ROYAL SOCIETY OF MEDICINE. 75(4):234-236, April 1982

Effect of contraceptive steroids on creatine kinase activity in serum [letter], by U. Gupta, et al. CLINICAL CHEMISTRY. 28(6):1402-1403, June 1982

The effect of contraceptive steroids on the incorporation of uniformly carbon-14-labeled glucose into porcine aortic lipids, by W. C. Kent, et al. ARTERY. 9(6):425-436, 1981

The effect of a contraceptive vaginal ring and oral contraceptives on the vaginal flora, by S. Roy, et al. CONTRACEPTION. 24(4):481-491, October 1981

Effect of contraceptives on the digestibility of dietary protein and nitrogen balance, by K. Gruhn, et al. NAHRUNG. 25(8):779-788, 1981

The effect of cyproterone acetate on pituitary-ovarian function and clinical symptoms in hirsute women, by N. O. Lunell, et al. ACTA ENDOCRINOLOGICA. 100(1):91-97, May 1982

Effect of duration of low-dose oral contraceptive administration on carbohydrate metabolism, by V. Wynn. AMERICAN JOURNAL OF OBSTETRICS AND GYNECOLOGY. 142(6 Pt 2):739-746, March 15, 1982

Effect of exogenous human chorionic gonadotropin on the endogenous hormoral milieu of serum estradiol-17 beta and progesterone in the patient with threatened abortion, by B. H. Park, et al. CATHOLIC MEDICAL COLLEGE JOURNAL. 34(2):349-358, 1981

Effect of 15-methyl-prostaglandin F2 alpha used for dilating the cervix uteri before abortion on endogenous prostaglandin F2 alpha systhesis, by V. N. Goncharova, et al. AKUSHERSTVO I GINEKOLOGIIA. (12):37-38, December 1981

The effect of high doses of 6-chloro-6-deoxyglucose on the rat, by W. C. Ford, et al. CONTRACEPTION. 24(5):577-588, November 1981

Effect of hormonal contraceptives containing 0.05 mg ethinyl estradiol and 0.125 mg desogestrel in normophasic regimen (Oviol), by M. J. Weijers. FORTSCHRITTE DER MEDIZIN. 100(16):764-767, April 29, 1982

Effect of injectable norethisterone oenanthate (Norigest) on blood lipid levels, by K. Fotherby, et al. CONTRACEPTION. 25(4):435-446, April 1982

Effect of intra amniotic saline and prostaglandin on fibrinolytic activity, prothrombin time and serum electrolytes [a comparative study], by V. D. Joshi, et al. INDIAN JOURNAL OF PHYSIOLOGY AND PHARMACOLOGY. 25(2):167-170, April-June 1981

Effect of intrauterine drug contraceptives on the endometrium, by T. A. Shirokova, et al. LABORATORNOE DELO. (11):665-667, 1981

Effect of low gestagen doses on the kidneys and urodynamics of the upper urinary tract, by A. G. Khomauridze, et al. AKUSHERSTVO I GINEKOLOGIIA. (4):56-57, April 1982

Effect of a low-protein diet on contraceptive steroid-induced chole-stasis in rats, by U. A. Boelsterli, et al. RESEARCH COMMUNICA-TIONS IN CHEMICAL PATHOLOGY AND PHARMACOLOGY. 36(2):299-318, May 1982

Effect of menstrual cycle and method of contraception on recovery of neisseria gonorrhoeae, by W. M. McCormack, et al. JAMA: JOURNAL OF THE AMERICAN MEDICAL ASSOCIATION. 247(9):1292-1294, 1982

Effect of nonoxynol-9, a detergent with spermicidal activity, on malignant transformation in vitro, by S. D. Long, et al. CARCINO-GENESIS. 3(5):553-557, 1982

Effect of an operation for artificial abortion on the female body and reproductive function, by I. B. Frolov. AKUSHERSTVO I GINEKOLO-GIIA. (4):6-8, April 1982

Effect of oral contraceptive agents on ascorbic acid metabolism in the rhesus monkey, by J. Weininger, et al. AMERICAN JOURNAL OF CLINICAL NUTRITION. 35(6):1408-1416, June 1982

The effect of oral contraceptive on serum bile acids and liver func-tion routine tests, by R. Ferraris, et al. PANMINERVA MEDICA. 23(2):89-92, April-June 1981

Effect of oral contraceptives and epsilon-aminocaproic acid on preg-nant female rats and their fetuses. Histopathologic study, by M. J. Niznikowska-Marks, et al. PATOLOGIA POLSKA. 32(1):37-42, 1981

The effect of oral contraceptives on antiaggregatory prostacyclin and proaggregatory thromboxane A_2 in humans, by O. Ylikorkala, et al. AMERICAN JOURNAL OF OBSTETRICS AND GYNECOLOGY. 142(5):573-576, 1982

Effect of oral contraceptives on antithrombin III, by M. P. McEntee, et al. THROMBOSIS RESEARCH. 24(1-2):13-20, October 1-15, 1981

Effect of oral contraceptives on reproductive function during semi-chronic exposure to ethanol in the female rat, by C. D. Lox, et al. GENERAL PHARMACOLOGY. 13(1):53-56, 1982

Effect of progesterone withdrawal in sheep during late pregnancy, by M. J. Taylor, et al. JOURNAL OF ENDOCRINOLOGY. 92(10:85-93, Jan-uary 1982

The effect of progestins in combined oral contraceptives on serum lipids with special reference to high-density lipoproteins, by V. Wynn, et al. AMERICAN JOURNAL OF OBSTETRICS AND GYNECOLOGY. 142(6 Pt 2):766-771, March 15, 1982

The effect of prolonged oral contraceptive steroid use on erythrocyte glutathione peroxidase activity, by I. D. Capel, et al. JOURNAL OF STEROID BIOCHEMISTRY. 14(8):729-732, August 1981

Effect of psychological stress states in women with spontaneous abor-tions, by I. Vasileva. AKUSHERSTVO I GINEKOLOGIIA. 20(4):275-279,

Effect of reflexotherapy on normalizing autonomic endocrine regulation in threatened abortion, by A. F. Zharkin, et al. AKUSHERSTVO I GINEKOLOGIIA. (5):21-23, May 1981

The effect of 6-chloro-6-deoxysugrs on adenine nucleotide concentrations in and motility of rat spermatozoa, by W. C. Ford, et al. JOURNAL OF REPRODUCTIVE FERTILITY. 63(1):75-79, September 1981

The effect of some long acting steroid contraceptives on some enzymes in goats and rabbits, by M. M. Kader, et al. EGYPTIAN JOURNAL OF VETERINARY SCIENCE. 16(1/2):151-158, 1981

The effect on fecundity of pill acceptance during postpartum amenorrhea in rural Bangladesh, by S. Bhatia, et al. STUDIES IN FAMILY PLANNING. 13(6-7):200-207, June-July 1982

The effect on lipids and lipoproteins of a contraceptive vaginal ring containing levonorgestrel and estradiol, by S. Roy, et al. CONTRACEPTION. 24(4):429-449, October 1981

The effectiveness of contraceptive programs for teenagers, by P. B. Namerow, et al. JOURNAL OF ADOLESCENT HEALTH CARE. 12(3):189-198, March 1982

Effectiveness of the sympto-thermal method of natural family planning: an international study, by F. J. Rice, et al. INTERNATIONAL JOURNAL OF FERTILITY. 26(3):222-230, 1981

Effects in vitro of medroxyprogesterone acete on steroid metabolizing enzymes in the rat: selective inhibition of 3 alpha-hydroxysteroid oxidoreductase activity, by A. Sunde, et al. JOURNAL OF STEROID BIOCHEMISTRY. 17(2):197-203, August 1982

The effects of ampicillin oral contraceptive steroids in women, by D. J. Back, et al. BRITISH JOURNAL OF CLINICAL PHARMACOLOGY. 14(1): 43-48, July 1982

Effects of antiandrogens on glycogen metabolism of spermatozoa from caput epididymidis, by G. T. Panse. INDIAN JOURNAL OF EXPERIMENTAL BIOLOGY. 19(9):872-873, September 1981

Effects of antifertility drugs on epididymal protein secretion, acquisition of sperm surface proteins and fertility in male rats, by A. Y. Tsang, et al. INTERNATIONAL JOURNAL OF ANDROLOGY. 4(6): 703-712, December 1981

Effects of calmodulin-binding drugs on the guinea pig spermatozoon acrosome reaction and the use of these drugs as vaginal contraceptive agents in rabbits, by R. W. Lenz, et al. ANNALS OF THE NEW YORK ACADEMY OF SCIENCES. 383:85-97, 1982

Effects of the estrogenicity of levonorgestrel/ethinylestradiol combinations of the lipoprotein status, by U. Larsson-Cohn, et al. ACTA OBSTETRICIA ET GYNECOLOGICA SCANDINAVICA. SUPPLEMENT. 105:37-40, 1982

Effects of estrogens and progestogens on lipid metabolism, by P. Oster, et al. AMERICAN JOURNAL OF OBSTETRICS AND GYNECOLOGY.

142(6 Pt 2):773-775, March 15, 1982

Effects of hydroxysteroid dehydrogenase inhibitors on in-vitro and in-vivo steroidogenesis in the ovine adrenal gland, by P. Singh-Asa, et al. JOURNAL OF ENDOCRINOLOGY. 92(2):205-212, February 1982

Effects of low doses of cyproterone acete on sperm morphology and some other parameters of reproduction in normal men, by B. Fredricsson, et al. ANDROLOGIA. 13(4):369-375, July-August 1981

Effects of medroxyprogesterone acete on socio-sexual behavior of stumptail macaques, by H. D. Steklis, et al. PHYSIOLOGY AND BEHAVIOR. 28(3):535-544, March 1982

The effects of microcomputer assisted instruction on the contraceptive knowledge attitudes, and behavior of college students, by L. G. DeSonier. DISSERTATION ABSTRACTS INTERNATIONAL. A. p. 399, 1982

Effects of neonatal exposure to progesterone on sexual behavior of male and female rats, by E. M. Hull. PHYSIOLOGY AND BEHAVIOR. 26(3):401-405, March 1981

Effects of oral contraceptive combinations containing levonorgestrel or desogestrel on serum proteins and androgen binding, by E. W. Bergink, et al. SCANDINAVIAN JOURNAL OF CLINICAL AND LABORATORY INVESTIGATION. 41(7):663-668, November 1981

Effects of oral contraceptive steroids on serum lipid and aortic glycosaminoglycans levels in iron-deficient rats, by Y. Kanke, et al. INTERNATIONAL JOURNAL FOR VITAMIN AND NUTRITION RESEARCH. 51(4):416-420, 1981

Effects of oral contraceptives on lipoprotein triglyceride and cholesterol: relationships to estrogen and progestin potency, by R. H. Knopp, et al. AMERICAN JOURNAL OF OBSTETRICS AND GYNECOLOGY. 142(6 Pt 2):725-731, March 15, 1982

Effects of the Philippine family planning outreached project on contraceptive prevalence: a multivariate analysis, by J. E. Laing. STUDIES IN FAMILY PLANNING. 12(11):367, November 1981

Effects of progestogens on the cardiovascular system, by T. W. Meade. AMERICAN JOURNAL OF OBSTETRICS AND GYNECOLOGY. 142(6 Pt 2):776-780, March 15, 1982

Effects of 17 beta-hydroxy-7 alpha-methylandrost-5-en-3-one on early pregnancy in the rat, by S. Saksena, et al. ACTA ENDOCRINOLOGICA. 98(4):614-618, December 1981

Effects of 6-chloro-6-deoxysugars on glucose oxidation in rat spermatozoa, by W. C. Ford, et al. JOURNAL OF REPRODUCTIVE FERTILITY. 63(1):67-73, September 1981

Effects of 16,16-dimethyl-trans-delta 2-PGE1 methyl ester (ONO-802) on reproductive function, by K. Matsumoto, et al. NIPPON YAKURI-GAKU ZASSHI. 79(1):15-22, January 1982

Effects of smoking and the pill on the blood count, by H. Dodsworth, et al. BRITISH JOURNAL OF HAEMATOLOGY. 49(3):484-488, November 1981

The effects of termination of pregnancy: a follow-up study of psychiatric referrals, by R. Schmidt, et al. BRITISH JOURNAL OF MEDICAL
PSYCHOLOGY. 54(Pt 3):267-276, September 1981

Efficacy of antibodies generated by Pr-beta-hCG-TT to terminate pregnancy in baboons: its reversibility and rescue by medroxyprogesterone acetate, by A. Tandon, et al. CONTRACEPTION. 24(1):83-95,
July 1981

Efficacy of different contraceptive methods, by M. Vessey, et al.
LANCET. 1(8276):841-842, April 10, 1982

The efficacy of gestoden (delta 15-d-norgestrel) as ovulation inhibitor, by W. H. Schneider, et al. WIENER KLINISCHE WOCHENSCHRIFT.
93(19):601-604, October 16, 1981

"Effort thrombosis" of the subclavian vein associated with oral contraceptives ... [case report], by S. J. Stricker, et al. ANNALS OF
EMERGENCY MEDICINE. 10(11):596-599, November 1981

El Paso church, United Way split, by A. B. Sparke. NATIONAL CATHOLIC
REPORTER. 18:4, March 26, 1982

Elaboration and development of a family planning program for pharmacists in Mexico, by C. Gutierrez Martinez, et al. SPM: SALUD
PUBLICA DE MEXICO. 23(4):405-411, July-August 1981

Electric activity of the brain in women undergoing acupuncture for
threatened abortion, by N. M. Tkachenko, et al. AKUSHERSTVO I
GINEKOLOGIIA. (1):28-29, January 1982

Elisabeth, supervisory nurse: patients must be supported irrespective
of what we ourselves think about abortion [interview], by E. Ronnberg. VARDFACKET. 6(10):44-45, May 28, 1982

Embryo transfer, ectopic pregnancy, and preliminary tubal occlusion
[letter], by I. Craft, et al. LANCET. 2(8260-8261):1421, December
19-26, 1981

Embryonic Rhesus-positive red cells stimulating a secondary response
after early abortion [letter], by J. Eklund. LANCET. 2(8249):748,
October 3, 1981

Emotional reaction to female sterilization: a prospective study, by
S. Aribarg, et al. JOURNAL OF THE MEDICAL ASSOCIATION OF THAILAND.
65(4):167-171, April 1982

An empirical assessment of a decision making model of contraceptive
use and nonuse among adolescent girls, by N. B. Peacock. DISSER-
TATION ABSTRACTS INTERNATIONAL. A. p. 3774, 1982

Endocrine abortions and their treatment, by U. Gaspard. REVUE
MEDICALE DE LIEGE. 37(4):118-119, February 15, 1982

Endocrine profile of patients with post-tubal-ligation syndrome, by
J. T. Hargrove, et al. JOURNAL OF REPRODUCTIVE MEDICINE. 26(7):
359-362, July 1981

Endocrinological changes in depression caused by oral contraceptives, by T. Namba, et al. JOURNAL OF THE MEDICAL SOCIETY OF TOKO UNIVERSITY. 28(4):594-599, 1981

Endometrial cancer, epidemiology, and medical practice [editorial], by K. J. Ryan. JAMA: JOURNAL OF THE AMERICAN MEDICAL ASSOCIATION. 247(4):496, January 22-29, 1982

Endometrial morphology and peripheal steroid levels in women with and without intermenstrual bleeding during contraception with the 300 microgram norethisteone minipill, by E. Johannisson, et al. CONTRACEPTION. 25(1):13-30, 1982

Endometrial pathological changes after fallopian ring tubal ligation, by D. de Cristofaro, et al. ENDOSCOPY. 14(4):139-140, July 1982

Endometrial patterns in women on chronic luteinizing hormone-releasing hormone agonist treatment for contraception, by C. Bergquist, et al. FERTILITY AND STERILITY. 36(3):339-342, September 1981

Endometriosis and spontaneous abortion [letter], by W. P. Dmowski. OBSTETRICS AND GYNECOLOGY. 58(6):763-764, December 1981

Endometriosis and tuboperitoneal fistulas after tubal ligation [letter], by J. B. Massey. FERTILITY AND STERILITY. 36(3):417-418, September 1981

Endosalpingosis ('endosalpingoblastosis') following laparoscopic tubal coagulation as an etiologic factor of ectopic pregnancy, by A. McCausland. AMERICAN JOURNAL OF OBSTETRICS AND GYNECOLOGY. 143(1):12-24, May 1, 1982

Endoscopic salpingectomy, by J. C. Tarasconi. JOURNAL OF REPRODUCTIVE MEDICINE. 26(10):541-545, October 1981

The enzyme inducing effect of rifampicin in the rhesus monkey (Macaca mulatta) and its lack of interaction with oral contraceptive steroids, by D. J. Back, et al. CONTRACEPTION. 25(3):307-317, 1982

An epidemiologic study of spontaneous abortions and fetal wastage in Oklahoma City, by C. C. Anokute. DISSERTATION ABSTRACTS INTERNATIONAL. B. p. 393, 1982

Epidemiological and clinical aspects of voluntary interruption of pregnancy 2 years after passing of Law 194, by M. G. Ricci, et al. RIVISTA ITALIANA DI GINECOLOGIA. 59(4-5):405-419, 1980

Epidemiology of abortion, by C. W. Tyler, Jr. JOURNAL OF REPRODUCTIVE MEDICINE. 26(9):459-469, Sepember 1981

The epidemiology of abortion services, by K. R. O'Reilly, et al. FAMILY COMMUNITY HEALTH. 5(1):29-39, May 1982

Epidemiology of hospitalized abortion in Valdivia, Chile, by R. Guzman Serani, et al. REVISTA MEDICA DE CHILE. 109(11):1099-1106, November 1981

Epistaxis secondary to oral contraceptive, by A. Man, et al. ACTA OTO-LARYNGOLOGICA. 92(3-4):383-384, September-October 1981

Epithelial ovarian cancer and combination oral contraceptives, by L.
Rosenberg, et al. JAMA: JOURNAL OF THE AMERICAN MEDICAL ASSOCIA-
TION. 247(23):3210-3212, 1982

Equitable jurisdiction to order sterilizations, by C. L. McIvor.
WASHINGTON LAW REVIEW. 57(2):373-387, 1982

Establishment, characteristics and experience of an abortion clinic,
by F. Bottiglioni, et al. ARCHIVES OF OBSTETRICS AND GYNECOLOGY.
85(6):511-529, November-December 1980

Estradiol-17 beta cyclopentylpropionate and prostaglandin F for induction of abortion during the first trimester of pregnancy in
feedlot heifers, by K. R. Refsal, et al. JOURNAL OF THE AMERICAN
VETERINARY MEDICAL ASSOCIATION. 179(7):701-703, October 1, 1981

Estradiol treatment and precopulatory behavior in ovariectomized
female rats, by Z. Hlinak, et al. PHYSIOLOGY AND BEHAVIOR. 26(2):
171-176, February 1981

Estrogens and hypertension, by M. H. Weinberger. COMPREHENSIVE
THERAPY. 8(6):71-75, June 1982

Estrogens in oral contraceptives: historical perspectives, by J. W.
Goldzieher. JOHNS HOPKINS MEDICAL JOURNAL. 150(5):165-169, May
1982

Ethical issues in nursing: your responses to JPN's fourth annual survey, by E. Rosen, et al. JOURNAL OF PRACTICAL NURSING. 31:29-33+,
November-December 1981

The ethics of abortion, by M. A. Gellman. DISSERTATION ABSTRACTS
INTERNATIONAL. A. p. 4032, 1982

Ethics of amniocentesis and selective abortion for sickle cell
disease [letter], by F. I. Konotey-Ahulu. LANCET. 1(8262):38-39,
January 2, 1982

Etiology of delivery during the 2nd trimester and performance in subsequent pregnancies, by G. J. Patten. MEDICAL JOURNAL OF AUSTRAL-
IA. 68-2(12/13):654-656, 1981

Europe: abortion (from article by Marge Berer in "Spare Rib and Women
in Spain," a publication of the Commission of the European Communities). OFF OUR BACKS. 12:8, July 1982

Evaluating fetomaternal hemorrhage by alpha-fetoprotein and Kleihauer
test following therapeutic abortions, by D. L. Hay, et al. INTER-
NATIONAL JOURNAL OF GYNAECOLOGY AND OBSTETRICS. 20(1):1-4, 1982

Evaluation of contemporary female sterilization methods, by W. E.
Brenner. JOURNAL OF REPRODUCTIVE MEDICINE. 26(9):439-453, September 1981

Evaluation of falope ring sterilization by hysterosalpingogram, by C.
L. Cook. JOURNAL OF REPRODUCTIVE MEDICINE. 27(5):243-248, May
1982

Evaluation of family planning communications in El Salvador, by J. T.
Bertrand, et al. INTERNATIONAL JOURNAL OF HEALTH EDUCATION.

24(3):183-194, 1982

Evaluation of sex education outreach, by K. F. Darabi, et al.
ADOLESCENCE. 17:57-64, Spring 1982

Evaluation of the spring coil and Dalkon shield, by H. A. Kisnisci.
ACTA REPRODUCTION TURCICA. 3(2):67-72, 1981

Evaluation of sulprostone for second trimester abortions and its effects on liver and kidney function, by V. Ranjan, et al. CONTRA-
CEPTION. 25(2):175-184, February 1982

Evaluation of 2236 tubectomies, by M. Raghav, et al. JOURNAL OF THE
INDIAN MEDICAL ASSOCIATION. 77(7):115-117, October 1, 1981

An evaluation of the use-effectiveness of fertility awareness methods
of family planning, by J. R. Weeks. JOURNAL OF BIOSOCIAL SCIENCE.
14(1):25-32, January 1982

Evidence against oral contraceptives as a cause of neural-tube defects, by H. S. Cuckle, et al. BRITISH JOURNAL OF OBSTETRICS AND
GYNAECOLOGY. 89(7):547-549, July 1982

Evolution of design and achievement of inhibitors of the LHRH as
inhibitors of ovulation, by K. Folkers, et al. ZEITSCHRIFT FUR
NATURFORSCHUNG TEIL B. 37(2):246-259, 1982

Examination of products of conception from previable human pregnancies, by D. I. Rushton. JOURNAL OF CLINICAL PATHOLOGY. 34(8):819-
835, August 1981

Experience acquired in application of Law No. 194 for a period of 18
months, by A. Canfora, et al. MINERVA GINECOLOGIA. 33(12):1167-
1172, December 1981

Experience from use of new cervix dilatator, by H. G. Muller. ZEN-
TRALBLATT FUR GYNAEKOLOGIE. 103(19):1155-1157, 1981

Experience in obstetrics with intracervical pellets of prostaglandin
FZ alpha, by M. Herrera, et al. REVISTA CHILENA DE OBSTETRICIA Y
GINECOLOGIA. 45(3):147-155, 1980

Experience with PGF2 alpha in mid-trimester pregnancy termination
in Ibadan, by O. A. Ojo, et al. AFRICAN JOURNAL OF MEDICINE AND
MEDICAL SCIENCES. 8(3-4):103-107, September-December 1979

Experimental observation and clinical application on the occlusion of
fallopian tubes by silver clips, by S. L. Ding. CHUNG HUA FU CHAN
KO TSA CHIH. 17(2):105-107, April 1982

Experimental study of the effect of rabbits on the injectable contraceptive medroxyprogesterone acetate, cholesterol feeding and drug-
atherogenic diet combination, by T. H. Al-Shebib, et al. LABORA-
TORY ANIMALS. 16(1):78-83, January 1982

Extragenital changes caused by intake of hormonal contraceptives--
marginal periodontium, by M. Arnold, et al. ZENTRALBLATT FUR
GYNAEKOLOGIE. 103(14):827-834, 1981

Extramarital sexual attitudes and norms of an undergraduate student

46

population, by N. P. Medora, et al. ADOLESCENCE. 16:251-262, Summer 1981

Factors affecting adolescents' use of family planning clinics [research], by M. Chamie, et al. FAMILY PLANNING PERSPECTIVES. 14: 126-127+, May-June 1982

Factors affecting riboflavin requirements of oral contraceptive users and nonusers, by D. A. Roe, et al. AMERICAN JOURNAL OF CLINICAL NUTRITION. 35(3):495-501, March 1982

Factors associated with family planning acceptance in Bangkok metropolis health clinic areas (MHCs), by T. Chumnijarakij, et al. CONTRACEPTION. 23(5):517-525, May 1981

Factors influencing the acceptance of family planning by blacks in Salisbury, Zimbabwe, by D. S. MacDonald. SOUTH AFRICAN MEDICAL JOURNAL. 61(12):437-439, March 20, 1982

Faculty cell replication: abortion, congenital abnormalities, by J. F. Nunn. INTERNATIONAL ANESTHESIOLOGY CLINICS. 19(4):77-97, Winter 1981

Failure of contraceptive steroids to modify human chorionic gonadotrophin secretion by hydatidiform mole tissue and choriocarcinoma cells in culture, by D. Gal, et al. STEROIDS. 37(6):663-671, June 1981

Failure of p-pills and anticonvulsants, by L. Gram. UGESKRIFT FOR LAEGER. 143(37):2364-2365, September 7, 1981

Failure of yoon ring tubal sterilization, by P. Chenevart. REVUE MEDICALE DE LA SUISSE ROMANDE. 101(11):907-912, November 1981

Failure rates higher for postpartum sterilizations than for interval procedures. FAMILY PLANNING PERSPECTIVES. 14:100-101, March-April 1982

Failure with the new triphasic oral contraceptive Logynon [letter]. BRITISH MEDICAL JOURNAL. 284(6313):422-423, February 6, 1982

--[letter], by R. A. Fay. BRITISH MEDICAL JOURNAL. 284(6308):17-18, June 2, 1982

Failures with the tubal ligation with the Bleier-secuclips, by A. R. Schurz, et al. GEBURTSHILFE UND FRAUENHEILKUNDE. 42(5):376-378, May 1982

The fallacy of the postpill amenorrhea syndrome, by D. F. Archer, et al. CLINICAL OBSTETRICS AND GYNECOLOGY. 24(3):943-950, September 1981

Family planning, by R. Munoz, et al. NUEVA ENFERMERIA. (11):11-12, May 1980

--, by P. Stoll. LEBENSVERSICHERUNGSMEDIZIN. 34(2):42-45, February 11, 1982

--, by Z. Wei-sen, et al. AMERICAN JOURNAL OF PUBLIC HEALTH. 72:24-26, September 1982

Family planning and abortion: have they affected fertility in Tennessee?, by H. K. Atrash, et al. AMERICAN JOURNAL OF PUBLIC HEALTH. 72(6):608-610, June 1982

Family planning and contraception, by D. Fock. KATILOLEHTI. 87(3): 91-93, March 1982

Family planning and increased fitness of the child to survive, by J. R. Kumari, et al. JOURNAL OF FAMILY WELFARE. 28:77, March 1982

Family planning and sex education, by C. Bailey. NURSING. 2:32-33, June 1982

Family planning attitudes in urban Indonesia: findings from focus group research, by H. Suyono, ete al. STUDIES IN FAMILY PLANNING. 12(12 Pt 1):433, December 1981

Family planning: 'Billing's' ovulation method, by M. S. Bhering, et al. REVISTA ESPANOLA DE LAS ENFERMEDADES DEL APARATO DIGESTIVO. 14(3):257-263, December 1980

Family planning by tribals, by N. Y. Naidu. THE EASTERN ANTHROPOLO-GIST. 32(3):205-207, July-September 1979

Family planning clinics: cure or cause of teenage pregnancy?, by M. C. Schwartz, et al. LINACRE QUARTERLY. 49:143-164, May 1982

Family planning communications and contraceptive use in Guatemala, El Salvador, and Panama, by J. T. Bertrand, et al. STUDIES IN FAMILY PLANNING. 13(6-7):190-191, June-July 1982

The family planning component, by U. Bhandari, et al. NURSING JOUR-NAL OF INDIA. 73:141-143, May 1982

Family planning concept, by J. B. Dumindin. NEWSETTE. 21:9-13, April-June 1981

Family planning. Contraception, sterilization, abortion, by H. Lud-wig. FORTSCHRITTE DER MEDIZIN. 100(16):721-722+, April 29, 1982

Family planning: fundamental to care, by A. Cowper. NURSING MIRROR AND MIDWIVE'S JOURNAL. 154:58, June 23, 1982

Family planning in primary health care. NUEVA ENFERMERIA. (17):28, January 1981

Family planning in the nursing curriculum, by M. B. Agostino. PRO-FESSIONI INFERMIERISTICHE. 35(1):14-19, January-March 1982

Family planning in a suburban development of Mexico City, by J. H. Gutierrez Avila, et al. SPM: SALUD PUBLICA DE MEXICO. 24(1): 39-47, January-February 1982

Family planning--paragraph 218 StGB, by E. Jakob. OEFFENTLICHE GESUNDHEITSWESEN. 43(9):421-422, September 1981

Family planning practices among Anglo and Hispanic women in U.S. counties bordering Mexico, by R. W. Rochat, et al. FAMILY PLANNING PERSPECTIVES. 13(4):176-180, July-August 1981

The family planning program in Pakistan: what went wrong?, by W. C. Robinson, et al. INTERNATIONAL FAMILY PLANNING PERSPECTIVES. 7: 85-92, September 1981

Family planning services for Southeast Asian refugess, by J. Kubota, et al. FAMILY COMMUNITY HEALTH. 5:19-28, May 1982

The family planning 'turntable': the counsellor in the face of a wide range of requests, by N. Meregaglia, et al. THERAPEUTISCHE UMSCHAU. 38(11):1103-1106, November 1981

Family planning visits by teenagers: United States, 1978, by J. Foster, et al. VITAL HEALTH STATISTICS. 13(58):1-24, August 1981

Family size preferences and sexual permissiveness as factors differentiating abortion activists, by D. Granberg. SOCIAL PSYCHOLOGY QUARTERLY. 45(1):15-23, March 1982

Family, state, and God: ideologies of the right-to-life movement, by M. J. Neitz. SOCIOLOGICAL ANALYSIS. 42(3):265-276, 1981

Family welfare and child health: a reappraisal of community based postpartum programme, by S. Kumari, et al. INDIAN JOURNAL OF PEDIATRICS. 18(9):619-623, September 1981

Fatal amniotic fluid embolism during legally induced abortion, United States, 1972 to 1978, by R. J. Guidotti, et al. AMERICAN JOURNAL OF OBSTETRICS AND GYNECOLOGY. 141(3):257-261, October 1, 1981

Fatal subarachnoid haemorrhage in young women: role of oral contraceptives, by M. Thorogood, et al. BRITISH MEDICAL JOURNAL. 283(6294):762, September 19, 1981

Father of birth control; make posters, not babies, by S. Fraser. FAR EASTERN ECONOMIC REVIEW. 112:77-78, June 26-July 2, 1981

Father's (lack of) right and responsibilities in the abortion decision: an examination of legal-ethical implications, by M. B. Knapp. OHIO NORTHERN UNIVERSITY LAW REVIEW. 9:369-383, July 1982

Federal court largely upholds abortion clinic regulations. FAMILY LAW REPORTER: COURT OPINIONS. 7(21):2348-2349, March 31, 1981

Federal court reaffirms injunction against city hospital's abortion ban. FAMILY LAW REPORTER: COURT OPINIONS. 8(14):2197-2198, February 9, 1982

Female phase fazer: new birth control? (luteinizing hormone releasing factor agonist shortens luteal phase; work of S. C. Yen and others), by L. Garmon. SCIENCE NEWS. 121:21, January 9, 1982

Female sterilization by falope ring ligation, by A. B. Lalonde. CANADIAN MEDICAL ASSOCIATION JOURNAL. 126(2):140-144, January 15, 1982

Female sterilization. Comparative study of 3 laparoscopic technics, by L. C. Uribe Ramirez, et al. GINECOLOGIA Y OBSTETRICIA DE MEXICO. 49(295):311-324, May 1981

Female sterilization--a follow-up report, by M. Ross, et al. SOUTH

AFRICAN MEDICAL JOURNAL. 61(13):476-479, March 27, 1982

Female sterilization: guidelines for the development of services [second edition]. WHO OFFSET PUBLICATIONS. (26):1-47, 1980

Female sterilization in Costa Rica, by M. G. Barrantes, et al. STUDIES IN FAMILY PLANNING. 13(1):3, January 1982

Feminine hygiene: the news in napkins. PROGRESSIVE GROCER. 61:98-99, March 1982

Feminism and abortion arguments, by M. B. Mahowald. KINESIS: GRADU-ATE JOURNAL OF PHILOSOPHY. 11:57-68, Spring 1982

Feminist perspective and population stability, by P. Ross. HUMANIST. 42:35-36, May-June 1982

Fertility after discontinuation of levo-norgestrel-releasing intra-uterine devices, by C. G. Nilsson. CONTRACEPTION. 25(3):273-278, 1982

Fertility and family planning in Haiti, by J. Allman. STUDIES IN FAMILY PLANNING. 13:237-245, August-September 1982

Fertility and family planning in the Irish Republic 1975, by K. Wilson-Davis. JOURNAL OF BIOSOCIAL SCIENCE. 14:343-358, July 1982

Fertility and family planning in the 1970s: the National Survey of Family Growth, by W. D. Mosher. FAMILY PLANNING PERSPECTIVES. 14:314-340, November-December 1982

Fertility and family planning in the South Pacific, by D. Lucas, et al. STUDIES IN FAMILY PLANNING. 12(8-9):303-315, August-September 1981

Fertility control and the voluntarily childless: an exploratory study, by E. Carlisle. JOURNAL OF BIOSOCIAL SCIENCE. 14(2):203-212, April 1982

Fertility regulation in nursing women. II. Comparative performance of progesterone implants versus placebo and copper T, by H. B. Croxatto, et al. AMERICAN JOURNAL OF OBSTETRICS AND GYNECOLOGY. 144(2):201-208, September 15, 1982

Fertility-related state laws enacted in 1981 (laws affecting abor-tion, services to minors, pregnancy-related insurance, family-planning services, sterilization, sex education and propulation commissions), by P. Donovan. FAMILY PLANNING PERSPECTIVES. 14(2): 63-67, March-April 1982

Fetal diagnosis and medical ethics, by N. Shimada. JOSANPU ZASSHI. 35(8):640, August 1981

Fetal growth delay in threatened abortion: an ultrasound study, by M. Mantoni, et al. BRITISH JOURNAL OF OBSTETRICS AND GYNAECOLOGY. 89(7):525-527, July 1982

Fetal law, by S. Speights. PLAYBOY. 29(1):62, March 1982

Fetal loss, gravidity and pregnancy order: is the truncated cascade analysis valid?, by J. Golding, et al. EARLY HUMAN DEVELOPMENT. 6(1):71-76, January 1982

Fetal organ donors: pregnancy termination to acquire organs?, by H. Piechowiak. MEDIZINISCHE WELT. 32(47):1799-1801, November 20, 1981

Fetal rights? It depends, by A. E. Doudera. TRIAL. 18(4):38-44+, April 1982

Fewer abortions--certainly, but how?, by U. Lindqvist, et al. JORDE-MODERN. 94(6):231-234, June 1981

Fibrinolytic activity of uterine fluid in oral contraceptive users, by B. Casslen. CONTRACEPTION. 25(5):515-521, May 1982

15 senators back Hatch proposal, NCR poll finds, by M. Meehan. NATIONAL CATHOLIC REPORTER. 18(2):1+, December 11, 1981

Fincoid: a new copper intrauterine device [a preliminary report], by E. Hirvonen, et al. CONTRACEPTIVE DELIVERY SYSTEMS. 3(2):83-90, 1982

Find patients at Oxford clinic have very few contraceptive failures. FAMILY PLANNING PERSPECTIVES. 14:150-151, May-June 1982

The first abortion--and the last? A study of the personality factors underlying repeated failure of contraception, by P. Niemela, et al. INTERNATIONAL JOURNAL OF GYNAECOLOGY AND OBSTETRICS. 19(3):193-200, June 1981

First and midtrimester abortion with intramuscular injections of sulprostone, by C. A. Ballard. CONTRACEPTION. 24(2):145-150, August 1981

Five years' experience of a 'prepregnancy' clinic for insulin-dependent diabetics, by J. M. Steel, et al. BRITISH MEDICAL JOURNAL. 285(6338):353-356, July 31, 1982

Flow properties of blood in women on oral contraceptives, by L. Heilmann, et al. ZENTRALBLATT FUR GYNAEKOLOGIE. 103(12):678-686, 1981

Focus group and survey research on family planning in Mexico, by E. Folch-Iyon, et al. STUDIES IN FAMILY PLANNING. 12(12 Pt 1):409, December 1981

Focus group research (reports on the use of focus group research in evaluating family planning programs in Mexico and Indonesia). STUDIES IN FAMILY PLANNING. 12(Pt 1):407-456, December 1981

Focus on social questions pt 2: celebrating the 400th anniversary of the BOOK OF CONCORD with a view to happenings in Australian society, by D. C. Overduin. LUTHERAN THEOLOGICAL JOURNAL. 14:80-87, August 1980

Follicular stimulating hormone and estrogen levels before and after female sterilization, by T. Sørensen, et al. ACTA OBSTETRICIA ET GYNECOLOGICA SCANDINAVICA. 60(6):559-561, 1981

For pro-lifers there is still a long, tough road ahead, by L. H.

Pumphrey. OUR SUNDAY VISITOR. 70:8, February 14, 1982

The formulation of oral contraceptives: does the amount of estrogen make any clinical difference?, by L. Speroff. JOHNS HOPKINS MEDICAL JOURNAL. 150(5):170-176, May 1982

Four-day birth control pill, by S. Katz. CHATELAINE. 55:16, October 1982

The four-day pill (work of Etienne-Emile Baulieu), by R. Mason. HEALTH. 14:20, July 1982

Frank estrogenic action of 1,2-diethyl-1,3-bis-(p-methoxyphenyl)-1-propene: a new oral contraceptive, by A. O. Prakash, et al. INDIAN JOURNAL OF EXPERIMENTAL BIOLOGY. 20(3):253-254, 1982

Free norethisterone as reflected by saliva concentrations of norethisterone during oral contraceptive use, by V. Odinod, et al. ACTA ENDOCRINOLOGICA. 98(3):470-476, November 1981

Free-standing abortion clinics: services, structure and fees, by S. K. Henshaw. FAMILY PLANNING PERSPECTIVES. 14:248-256, September-October 1982

Frequency of Langdon-Down disease in newborn infants in the Neubrandenburg district after the introduction of the abortion law of 9/3/1972, by I. Goetze. ZEITSCHRIFT FUR ARZTLICHE FORTBILDUNG. 75(3):107-108, February 1, 1981

Frequency of rare electrophoretic protein variants among spontaneous human abortuses, by I. P. Altukhov, et al. DOKLADY AKADEMII NAUK SSSR. 262(4):982-985, 1982

Frequency of unwanted pregnancies among women on waiting lists for sterilization, by U. Høding, et al. UGESKRIFT FOR LAEGER. 144(12):875-876, March 22, 1982

From contraception to cancer: a review of the therapeutic applications of LHRH analogues as antitumor agents, by A. Corbin. YALE JOURNAL OF BIOLOGY AND MEDICINE. 55(1):27-47, January-February 1982

Frontlines: shot felt around the world (FDA will decide whether depo-provera should be approved for use in U.S.), by K. Brannan. MOTHER JONES. 7:10+, May 1982

Functional and biochemical aspects of laminaria use in first-trimester pregnancy termination, by B. L. Ye, et al. AMERICAN JOURNAL OF OBSTETRICS AND GYNECOLOGY. 142(1):36-39, January 1, 1982

Further studies on pituitary and ovarian function in women receiving hormonal contraception, by B. L. Cohen, et al. CONTRACEPTION. 24(2):159-172, August 1981

GPs and government clinics provide free family planning to over 70 percent of all UK women. FAMILY PLANNING PERSPECTIVES. 13:272-273, November-December 1981

Galactorrhea in oral contraceptive users, by G. Holtz. JOURNAL OF

REPRODUCTIVE MEDICINE. 27(4):210-212, April 1982

Gallbladder function in the human female: effect of the ovulatory cycle, pregnancy, and contraceptive steroids, by G. T. Everson, et al. GASTROENTEROLOGY. 82(4):711-719, April 1982

Genital mycoplasmas and chlamydiae in infertility and abortion, by E. Cracea, et al. ARCHIVES ROUMAINES DE PATHOLOGIE EXPERIMENTALE ET DE MICROBIOLOGIE. 40(2):107-112, April-June 1981

Gestational trophoblastic emboli as possible cause of an acute respiratory distress syndrome, by G. Hoflehner, et al. WIENER MEDIZINISCHE WOCHENSCHRIFT. 131(19):475-477, October 15, 1981

Given good information, public backs pro-life view. OUR SUNDAY VISITOR. 70:7, December 20, 1981

God will forgive even she who aborts her child, by P. Cullen. OUR SUNDAY VISITOR. 71:4-5, September 19, 1982

The gospel of prevention, by B. Harrison. TIMES LITERARY SUPPLEMENT. p. 1252, November 12, 1982

Gossypol: a potential male contraceptive?, by S. V. Lawrence. AMERICAN PHARMACY. 21(11):57-59, November 1981

Grady, In re (NJ) 426 A 2d 467. JOURNAL OF FAMILY LAW. 20:374-377, January 1982

Gregory Pincus and steroidal contraception revisited, by E. Diczfalusy. ACTA OBSTETRICIA ET GYNECOLOGICA SCANDINAVICA. 105:7-15, 1982

Guidelines issued on court-ordered sterilization of retarded minors. FAMILY LAW REPORTER: COURT OPINIONS. 8(8):2102-2104, December 22, 1981

Gunilla, nurse anesthetist in gyn operating room: finds much left to do where prevention is concerned [interview], by G. Sjoborg. VARD-FACKET. 6(10):42-43, May 28, 1982

Gynecology in the young, by S. J. Emans. EMERGENCY MEDICINE. 14:92-96+, April 30, 1982

H.L. v. Matheson, 101 S Ct 1164. JOURNAL OF FAMILY LAW. 20:153-157, September 1981

--: and the right of minors to seek abortions, by M. H. Wolff. CALIFORNIA WESTERN LAW REVIEW. 19:74-106, Fall 1982

--: can parental notification be required for minors seeking abortions?. UNIVERSITY OF RICHMOND LAW REVIEW. 16:429-447, Winter 1982

--: parental notice prior to abortion. ST. LOUIS UNIVERSITY LAW JOURNAL. 26:426-446, January 1982

--: where does the court stand on abortion and parental notification?. AMERICAN UNIVERSITY LAW REVIEW. 31(2):431-469, Winter 1982

Habitual abortion: diagnositcs and therapy in gynaecological practice, by I. Gerhard, et al. GEBURTSHILFE UND FRAUENHEILKUNDE.
41(11):797-803, November 1981

The Halakhic status of the fetus with respect to abortion, by R. S.
Kirschner. CONSERVATIVE JUDAISM. 34(6):3-16, 1981

Half-life and metabolism of 3H-folic acid in oral contraceptive
treated rats, by N. Lakshmaiah, et al. HORMONE AND METABOLIC
RESEARCH. 13(7):404-407, July 1981

Half a loaf: a new antiabortion strategy, by P. Donovan. FAMILY
PLANNING PERSPECTIVES. 13(6):262, November-December 1981

A hard pill to swallow? (proposal to require Federally funded family-
planning clinics to notify parents when their adolescents receive
contraceptives), by B. Brophy. FORBES. 129:99, May 10, 1982

Harris v. McRae (100 S Ct 2671): clash of a nonenumerated right with
legislative control of the purse, by D. T. Hardy. CASE WESTERN
RESERVE LAW REVIEW. 31:465-508, Spring 1981

--: cutting back abortion rights. COLUMBIA HUMAN RIGHTS LAW REVIEW.
12:113-136, Spring-Summer 1980

Hatch Amendment report hailed by pro-life director. OUR SUNDAY
VISITOR. 71:7, June 27, 1982

Hatch Amendment still splits pro-life camp, by J. Castelli. OUR
SUNDAY VISITOR. 70:6, January 17, 1982

Hatch Bill vote demanded, by M. Meehan. NATIONAL CATHOLIC REPORTER.
18:8, July 30, 1982

Headache and oral contraceptives, by W. Farias da Silva, et al.
NEUROBIOLOGIA. 41(1):29-42, January-March 1978

Health group cites multiple violations of Medicaid sterilization
rules, by M. F. Docksai. TRIAL. 17:10, October 1981

Health law--abortions. FAMILY LAW REPORTER. 7(20):3021-3036, March
24, 1981

The health of sterilized women, by B. W. McGuinness. PRACTITIONER.
226(1367):925-928, May 1982

Health services in Shanghai County: family planning, by W. S. Zheng,
et al. AMERICAN JOURNAL OF PUBLIC HEALTH. 72(9 Suppl):24-25,
September 1982

Helms bill calculated to foster pro-life unity, by C. A. Savitskas,
Jr. OUR SUNDAY VISITOR. 70:3, April 11, 1982

Helms bill stalled by Senate vote, by M. Meehan. NATIONAL CATHOLIC
REPORTER. 18:26, September 17, 1982

Hepatic adenoma associated with oral contraceptives, by A. B.
Woodyer. JOURNAL OF THE ROYAL COLLEGE OF SURGEONS OF EDINBURGH.
27(1):59-60, January 1982

Hepatic lesions caused by anabolic and contraceptive steroids, by K. G. Ishak. SEMINARS IN LIVER DISEASE. 1(2):116-128, May 1981

Hepatocellular carcinoma in women: probable lack of etiologic association with oral contraceptive steroids, by Z. D. Goodman, et al. HEPATOLOGY. 2(4):440-444, July-August 1982

Here's what you had to say about abortion (adolescents' opinions). TEEN. 26:75, February 1982

High court strikes down ad circular ban. ADVERTISING AGE. 53:73, May 24, 1982

High density lipoprotein choleteron and apolipoprotein A-I levels in 32-33-year-old women on steroid contraceptive-differences between two frequently used low-estrogen pills, by L. Havekes, et al. CLINICA CHIMICA ACTA. 116(2):223-229, October 26, 1981

Histology of the rat vas deferens after injection of a non-occlusive chemical contraceptive, by K. Verma, et al. JOURNAL OF REPRODUCTIVE FERTILITY. 63(2):539-542, November 1981

"Honeymoon" over in DC for action on abortion bills, by C. McKenna. NEW DIRECTIONS FOR WOMEN. 11:19, March-April 1982

Hormonal contraception and hearing disorders, by K. Kvorak. CESKOSLOVENSKA GYNEKOLOGIE. 45(9):653-655, November 1980

Hormonal contraception and hypertension, by K. M. Hamann, et al. ZEITSCHRIFT FUR ARZTLICHE FORTBILDUNG. 76(5):198-201, March 1, 1982

Hormonal contraceptive therapy and thromboembolic disease, by M. J. Narvaiza, et al. REVISTA DE MEDICINA DE LA UNIVERSIDAD DE NAVARRA. 24(4):49-53, December 1980

Hormonal factors in fertility, infertility and contraception. JOURNAL OF STEROID BIOCHEMISTRY. 14(11):i-xxxvii, November 1981

Hormonal levels following sterilization and hysterectomy, by S. L. Corson, et al. JOURNAL OF REPRODUCTIVE MEDICINE. 26(7):363-370, July 1981

Hormonal profile during termination of midtrimester pregnancy by extraovular instillation of saline: plasma levels of prostaglandins, progesterone and human chorionic gonadotropin, by S. Bauminger, et al. PROSTAGLANDINS LEUKOTRIENES AND MEDICINE. 8(1):83-92, January 1982

Hormone content in the plasma of women with threatened abortion treated by acupuncture, by G. M. Vorontsova, et al. AKUSHERSTVO I GINEKOLOGIIA. (5):19-20, May 1981

Hormone replacement treatment and benign intracranial hypertension [letter], by K. L. Woods. BRITISH MEDICAL JOURNAL. 285(6336):215, July 1982

Hormone therapy in threatened abortion. Retrospective evaluation of a clinical caseload, by E. Revelli, et al. MINERVA GINECOLOGIA. 34(4):277-282, April 1982

Hospitalization for medical-legal and other abortions in the United States 1970-1977 [research], by M. B. Bracken, et al. AMERICAN JOURNAL OF PUBLIC HEALTH. 72(1):30-37, January 1982

Hospitalization for tubal sterilization [letter], by H. P. Brown, et al. JAMA: JOURNAL OF THE AMERICAN MEDICAL ASSOCIATION. 246(22): 2576, December 4, 1981

Hospitals, clinics, agencies sponsor adolescent pregnancy projects [interview], by M. E. Mecklenburg. HOSPITAL PROGRESS. 63(9):46-49, September 1982

Housewives' depression: the debate over abortion and birth control in the 1930's, by B. Brookes. NEW ZEALAND JOURNAL OF HISTORY. 15: 115-134, October 1981

How do you feel about abortion?. FAMILY CIRCLE. 95:39, February 2, 1982

How many?. ECONOMIST. 294:47-48, July 3, 1982

How women felt about their sterilization--a follow-up of 368 patients in a general practice, by A. F. Wright. JOURNAL OF THE ROYAL COLLEGE OF GENERAL PRACTITIONERS. 31(231):598-604, October 1981

Human action, natural rhythms, and contraception: a response to Noonan, by J. Boyle. AMERICAN JOURNAL OF JURISPRUDENCE. 26:32-46, 1981

Human extra-embryonic membranes: role of trophoblast in normal and abnormal pregnancies, by W. P. Faulk. INTERNATIONAL JOURNAL ON TISSUE REACTIONS. 3(3-4):139-146, December 1981

Human Life Amendment hearings: Schmitz fears "bulldykes" (Senator John Schmitz's anti-Semitic and anti-female remarks), by L. Noble. UNION W.A.G.E. (68):5, January-February 1982

Human Life Bill: personhood revisited, or Congress takes aim at Roe v. Wade (93 S Ct 705). HOFSTRA LAW REVIEW. 10:1269-1295, Summer 1982

--: protecting the unborn through congressional enforcement of the fourteenth amendment, by B. J. Uddo. LOYOLA LAW REVIEW. 27:1079-1097, Fall 1981

Human life federalism amendment [an assessment], by W. R. Caron. CATHOLIC LAWYER. 27:87-111, Spring 1982

--: its language, effects, by D. J. Horan. HOSPITAL PROGRESS. 62(12):12-14, December 1981

Human life symposium: a synopsis and critique, by S. Taub. LAW, MEDICINE AND HEALTH CARE. 10(3):129-134, June 1982

Humanae vitae and the ovutektor. Making "rhythm" safe: a breakthrough, by J. Tracy. MONTH. 15:6-9, January 1982

Husband challenges wife's right to abortion (Maryland Court of Appeals to hear case in January 1983 to decide if Judge Daniel Moylan was correct in permitting Chris Fritz to veto abortion decision of

Bonnie Fritz). OFF OUR BACKS. 12:13, November 1982

Hyde amendment: an infringement upon the free exercise clause?. RUT-
GERS LAW REVIEW. 33:1054-1075, Summer 1981

Hypersensitivity reaction to depo-Provera [letter], by R. Zacest, et
al. MEDICAL JOURNAL OF AUSTRALIA. 1(1):12, January 9, 1982

Hypophyseal reaction state during oral contraception, by E. Gitsch,
et al. WIENER KLINISCHE WOCHENSCHRIFT. 93(19):599-601, 1981

Hysterectomy after interval laparoscopic sterilisation [letter], by
I. C. Chi, et al. LANCET. 1(8276):848-849, April 10, 1982

Hysterectomy and depression [a clinical study], by D. Raglianti.
BOLLETINO DI PSICOLOGIA APPLICATA. (155-156):206-211, July-December 1980

Hysterectomy and psychiatric disorder: I. Levels of psychiatric morbidity before and after hysterectomy, by D. Gath, et al. BRITISH
JOURNAL OF PSYCHIATRY. 140:335-342, April 1982

--II. Demographic psychiatric and physical factors in relation to
psychiatric outcome, by D. Gath, et al. BRITISH JOURNAL OF PSY-
CHIATRY. 140:343-350, April 1982

Hysterectomy and reliving the castration fantasy, by B. Teitelroit.
PSICO. 1(2):11-33, July-December 1980

The hysterophore: a new instrument for uterine manipulation during
laparoscopy, by F. B. Lammes. EUROPEAN JOURNAL OF OBSTETRICS,
GYNECOLOGY AND REPRODUCTIVE BIOLOGY. 12(4):243-246, October 1981

IPPF international medical advisory panel meetings May and October
1981 and policy statements on contraceptives. IPPF: INTERNATIONAL
PLANNED PARENTHOOD FEDERATION MEDICAL BULLETIN. 15(6):6, December
1981

IUD under the aspects of sexual medicine, by J. M. Wenderlein, et al.
GEBURTSHILFE UND FRAUENHEILKUNDE. 42(2):115-117, February 1982

Ideal family size, fertility, and population policy in Western
Europe, by A. Girard, et al. POPULATION AND DEVELOPMENT REVIEW.
8:323-345, June 1982

Ideal family size in Northern Ireland, by J. Coward. JOURNAL OF
BIOSOCIAL SCIENCE. 13(4):443-454, October 1981

Ileitis (probable Crohn's disease) and oral contraceptives, by J.
Husson. SEMAINES DES HOPITAUX DE PARIS. 57(41-42):1750-1751,
November 8-25, 1981

Illegal-abortion deaths in the United States: why are they still
occuring?, by N. Binkin, et al. FAMILY PLANNING PERSPECTIVES.
14:163-167, May-June 1982

Illegitimacy in England and Wales in 1911, by N. F. R. Crafts.
POPULATION STUDIES. 36:327-331, July 1982

Illinois bishop blasts senators for votes on abortion. OUR SUNDAY

VISITOR. 71:8, October 10, 1982

I'm a criminal and proud of it: an abortion outlaw speaks up (protest during the Senate hearings on the Human Life Bill), by L. Smith. MADEMOISELLE. 88:266-267, August 1982

An immune dependency of trophoblastic growth implied by the antithetic difference in immunology between spontaneous abortion and hydatidiform mole, by S. Takeuchi. PROGRESS IN CLINICAL AND BIOLOGICAL RESEARCH. 70:245-257, 1981

Immune reactivity and the vascular risk in oral contrace[tove users, by J. L. Beaumont, et al. AMERICAN JOURNAL OF REPRODUCTIVE IMMUNOLOGY. 1(3):119-125, 1981

Immunocontraception: consideration of the zona pellucida as a target antigen, by A. G. Sacco. OBSTETRICS AND GYNECOLOGY ANNUAL. 10:1-26, 1981

Immunologic contraception, by O. I. Polevaia, et al. AKUSHERSTVO I GINEKOLOGIIA. (2):3-5, February 1982

Immunologic interruption of pregnancy, by G. P. Talwar, et al. PROGRESS IN CLINICAL AND BIOLOGICAL RESEARCH. 70:451-459, 1981

Immunological control of male fertility, by G. P. Talwar, et al. ARCHIVES OF ANDROLOGY. 7(2):177-185, September 1981

Immunological studies of toxoplasmosis in case of abortion, by R. C. Mahajan, et al. INDIAN JOURNAL OF PATHOLOGY AND MICROBIOLOGY. 24(3):165-169, July 1981

Immunological studies of the vaginal secretion in women using contraceptive preparations, by B. Nalbanski, et al. AKUSHERSTVO I GINEKOLOGIIA. 20(4):337-340, 1981

Immunology of abortion and preeclampsia, by M. G. Dodson. COMPREHENSIVE THERAPY. 8(6):59-65, June 1982

Immunology of spontaneous abortion and hydatidiform mole, by S. Takeuchi. AMERICAN JOURNAL OF REPRODUCTIVE IMMUNOLOGY. 1(1):23-28, 1980

The impact of breastfeeding and pregnancy status on household contraceptive distribution in rural Haiti, by A. Bordes, et al. AMERICAN JOURNAL OF PUBLIC HEALTH. 72:835-838, August 1982

Impact of family planning programs on fertility in developing countries: a critical evaluation, by J. J. Hernandez. SOCIAL SCIENCE RESEARCH. 10:63-66, March 1981

The impact of legal abortion on marital and nonmarital fertility in upstate New York, by E. J. Tu, et al. FAMILY PLANNING PERSPECTIVES. 14(1):37-46, January-February 1982

Impact of synthetic sexual steroids on blood volume, by G. Klinger, et al. ZENTRALBLATT FUR GYNAEKOLOGIE. 104(6):343-348, 1982

The impact on breastfeeding and pregnancy status of household contraceptive distribution in rural Haiti [research], by A. Bordes, et al. AMERICAN JOURNAL OF PUBLIC HEALTH. 72(8):835-838, August 1982

Impaired reproductive performance of the unicornuate uterus; intra-uterine growth retardation, inferitlity, and recurrent abortion in five cases, by M. C. Andrews, et al. AMERICAN JOURNAL OF OBSTE-TRICS AND GYNECOLOGY. 144(2):173-176, September 15, 1982

Impairment of diazepam metabolism by low-dose estrogen-containing oral-contraceptive steroids, by D. R. Abernethy, et al. NEW ENG-LAND JOURNAL OF MEDICINE. 306(13):791-792, April 1, 1982

Implementing a permissive policy: hospital abortion services after Roe v. Wade, by J. R. Bond, et al. AMERICAN JOURNAL OF POLITICAL SCIENCE. 26:1-24, February 1982

Les implications morales de certaines dispositions legislatives con-cernant l'avortement, by M. T. Giroux. CAHIERS DE DROIT. 23:21-83, March 1982

Importance of echography in assessing the nature of the development of the pregnancy in threatened abortion, by A. M. Stygar. AKU-SHERSTVO I GINEKOLOGIIA. (5):16-18, May 1981

Improvement in cervical dysplasia associated with folic acid therapy in users of oral contraceptives, by C. E. Butterworth, Jr., et al. AMERICAN JOURNAL OF CLINICAL NUTRITION. 35(1):73-82, January 1982

In Norway's state church, a pastor's abortion protest has wide impli-cations (Boerre Knudson) [news], by H. Genet, et al. CHRISTIANITY TODAY. 26:58+, April 9, 1982

In re CDM [627 P 2d 607 (Alaska)]: should involuntary sterilization be within the general jurisdiction of a court?. DETROIT COLLEGE OF LAW REVIEW. 1982:719-736, Fall 1982

In re Grady [426 A 2d 467 (NJ)]--voluntary sterilization and the retarded. RUTGERS LAW REVIEW. 34:567-590, Spring 1982

--: the mentally retarded individual's right to choose sterilization, by D. Lachance. AMERICAN JOURNAL OF LAW AND MEDICINE. 6(4):559-590, Winter 1981

In search of health history, Margaret Higgins Sanger: health educa-tor, by P. A. Reagan. HEALTH EDUCATION. 13:5-7, July-August 1982

In vitro method for evaluation of spermicides by hemolytic potency, by M. M. Dolan. FERTILITY AND STERILITY. 36(2):248-249, 1981

In vitro studies of the abortogenic potential of antisrum to alpha-fetoprotein, by G. J. Mizejewski, et al. INTERNATIONAL JOURNAL OF IMMUNOPHARMACOLOGY. 3(1):87-95, 1981

In vitro study of comparative immunosuppressive activity of sera from pregnant women on an in vitro celluar cytotoxic reaction, by F. Fizet, et al. COMPTES RENDUS DES SEANCES DE L ACADEMIE DES SCI-ENCES. 293(10):583-588, November 16, 1981

In vitro testing for potency of various spermicidal agents, by H. P. Lee. SEOUL JOURNAL OF MEDICINE. 22(4):525-540, 1981

In vivo production of nucleolar channel system in human endocervical
secretory cells, by G. Yasuzumi, et al. JOURNAL OF SUBMICROSCOPIC
CYTOLOGY. 13(4):639-647, October 1981

Inadvertent injuries during gynecologic endoscopy [letter], by G. M.
Grunert. FERTILITY AND STERILITY. 37(2):284-285, February 1982

Incentives, reproductive behavior, and integrated community development in Asia, by H. P. David. STUDIES IN FAMILY PLANNING. 13(5):
159-173, May 1982

The incidence of congenital abnormalities following gestagen administration in early pregnancy, by W. H. Schneider, et al. WIENER
KLINISCHE WOCHENSCHRIFT. 93(23):711-712, December 1981

Incidence of listeriosis in spontaneous abortion, by C. Balbi, et al.
ARCHIVES OF OBSTETRICS AND GYNECOLOGY. 85(3):203-208, May-June
1980

Incidence of ovarian cancer in relation to the use of oral contraceptives, by N. S. Weiss, et al. INTERNATIONAL JOURNAL OF CANCER.
28(6):669-671, December 1981

Incidence rate of late complications in legally induced abortion
in the Federal Republic of Germany, by H. H. Brautigam, et al.
ZEITSCHRIFT FUR GEBURTSCHILFE UND PERINATOLOGIE. 185(4):193-199,
August 1981

Increased frequencies of chromosomal abnormalities in families with a
history of fetal wastage, by I. Nordenson. CLINICAL GENETICS.
19(3):168-173, March 1981

Increased frequency of associations of acrocentric chromosomes
brought about by the LDH virus in infertile women, by B. Mejsnarova, et al. SBORNIK LEKARSKY. 83(11-12):332-336, 1981

Increased oral activity of a new class of non-hormonal pregnancy
terminating agents, by G. Galliani, et al. JOURNAL OF PHARMACOBIO-
DYNAMICS. 5(1):55-61, January 1982

Indira Gandhi calls for revitalization of India's family planing
program. FAMILY PLANNING PERSPECTIVES. 14:149-150, May-June 1982

Induced abortion and ectopic pregnancy in subsequent pregnancies, by
C. S. Chung, et al. AMERICAN JOURNAL OF EPIDEMIOLOGY. 115(6):879-
887, June 1982

Induced abortion and placenta previa [letter], by S. Fribourg.
AMERICAN JOURNAL OF OBSTETRICS AND GYNECOLOGY. 143(7):850, August
1, 1982

Induced abortion and spontaneous fetal loss in subsequent pregnancies, by C. S. Chung, et al. AMERICAN JOURNAL OF PUBLIC HEALTH.
72(6):548-554, June 1982

Induced abortion as a risk factor for cervical pregnancy [letter], by
S. Shinagawa, et al. AMERICAN JOURNAL OF OBSTETRICS AND GYNECOL-
OGY. 143(7):853-854, August 1, 1982

Induced abortion in the hospital--the role of nursing, by E. Ketting, et al. TIJDSCHRIFT VOR ZIEKENVERPLEGING. 34(17):750-753, August 25, 1981

Induced abortion in maternal and child health centres in a general family planning programme in Cap Bon, Tunisia, by I. de Schamphe-leire. TROPICAL DOCTOR. 12(2):77-80, April 1982

Induced abortion in the Netherlands: a decade of experience, 1970-80, by E. Ketting, et al. STUDIES IN FAMILY PLANNING. 11(12):385-394, December 1980

Induced abortion. A prospective comparative study of 2 vacuum aspira-tion methods: the Vabra-ab aspirator and conventional methods, by H. K. Poulsen. UGESKRIFT FOR LAEGER. 144(2):89-92, January 11, 1982

--: a risk factor for placenta previa, by J. M. Barrett, et al. AMERICAN JOURNAL OF OBSTETRICS AND GYNECOLOGY. 141(7):769-772, December 1, 1981

Induction for termination of pregnancy in the second trimester and for delivery of babies dead in utero using intramuscular injections of 15-methyl-PGF2 alpha, by B. Kunz, et al. JOURNAL DE GYNECOLO-GIE, OBSTETRIQUE ET BIOLOGIE DE LA REPRODUCTION. 10(4):375-384, 1981

The induction of abortion and the priming of the cervix with prosta-glandin F2 alpha and prostaglandin E2 by intra-amniotic, extra-amniotic and intra-cervical application, by W. Schmidt, et al. GEBURTSHILFE UND FRAUENHEILKUNDE. 42(2):118-122, February 1982

Induction of abortion by intra-amniotic administration of prosta-glandin F2 alpha in patients with intrauterine fetal death and missed abortion, by A. Antsaklis, et al. INTERNATIONAL SURGERY. 64(5):41-43, August-October 1979

Induction of abortion in feedlot heifers with a combination of cloprostenol and dexamethasone, by A. D. Barth, et al. CANADIAN VETERINARY JOURNAL. 22(3):62-64, March 1981

The induction of abortion in the second trimester by combined ad-ministration of minprostin and sulproston, compared with the use of sulproston alone, by H. Ponnath, et al. GEBURTSHILFE UND FRAUEN-HEILKUNDE. 41(12):849-852, December 1981

Induction of abortion using prostaglandins, by R. H. Schultz, et al. ACTA VETERINARIA SCANDINAVICA. SUPPLEMENT. 77:353-361, 1981

Induction of second trimester abortion with intra-amniotic prosta-glandin F2 alpha, by A. P. Lange, et al. UGESKRIFT FOR LAEGER. 144(13):946-949, March 29, 1982

Infanticide, arsenic, phosphorus and probes used in abortion during past centuries, by U. Hogberg. LAKARTIDNINGEN. 78(35):2951-2952, August 26, 1981

Infectious complications of cervical cerclage, by D. Charles, et al. AMERICAN JOURNAL OF OBSTETRICS AND GYNECOLOGY. 141(8):1065-1071, December 15, 1981

Inferior vena cava stenosis and Budd-Chiari syndrome in a woman
taking oral contraceptives, by G. Lalonde, et al. GASTROENTEROL-
OGY. 82(6):1452-1456, June 1982

Infertility trends among U.S. couples: 1965-1976, by W. D. Mosher.
FAMILY PLANNING PERSPECTIVES. 14(1):22, January-February 1982

Inflammatory disease associated with oral contraceptive use [letter],
by S. H. Swan. LANCET. 2(8250):809, October 10, 1981

Influence of contraceptive pill and menstrual cycle on serum lipids
and high-density lipoprotein cholesterol concentrations, by P. N.
Demacker, et al. BRITISH MEDICAL JOURNAL. 284(6324):1213-1215,
April 24, 1982

Influence of estrogen content of oral contraceptives and consumption
of sucrose on blood parameters, by K. E. M. Behall. DISSERTATION
ABSTRACTS INTERNATIONAL. B. p. 1437, 1982

Influence of metabolism on the activity of a new anti-fertility
agent, 2-(3-ethoxyphenyl)-5,6-dihydro-s-triazolo [5,1-a]isouinoline
(DL 204-IT), in the rat and the hamster, by A. Assandri, et al.
ARZNEIMITTEL-FORSCHUNG. 31(12):2104-2111, 1981

The influence of oral contraception on the sex life of adolescents,
by B. Bourrit, et al. THERAPEUTISCHE UMSCHAU. 38(11):1098-1102,
November 1981

Influence of oral contraceptive therapy on the activity of systemic
lupus erythematosus, by P. Jungers, et al. ARTHRITIS AND RHEUMA-
TISM. 25(6):618-623, June 1982

The influence of oral contraceptive therapy on the periodontium--
duration of drug therapy, by C. L. Pankhurst, et al. JOURNAL OF
PERIODONTOLOGY. 52(10):617-620, October 1981

The influence of oral contraceptives on the composition of bile, by
P. Brockerhoff, et al. KLINISCHE WOCHENSCHRFIT. 60(3):153-157,
February 1, 1982

The influence of oral contraceptives on lipoprotein status, by H.
Wieland, et al. DEUTSCHE MEDIZINISCHE WOCHENSCHRIFT. 107(17):649-
653, April 30, 1982

Influence of oral hormonal contraceptives on multiple pregnancy, by
I. Halmos. MEDICINSKI RAZGLEDI. 20(2):131-136, 1981

The influence of pregnancy and contraceptive pills upon oxygen consumption during phagocytosis by human leukocytes, by B. Kvarstein,
et al. ACTA OBSTETRICIA ET GYNECOLOGICA SCANDINAVICA. 60(5):505-
506, 1981

Influence of sex and oral contraceptive steroids on antipyrine metabolite formation, by M. W. Teunissen, et al. CLINICAL PHARMA-
COLOGY AND THERAPEUTICS. 32(2):240-246, August 1982

Influence of sex difference and oral contraceptives on forearm reactive hyperemia, by R. C. Webb, et al. BLOOD VESSELS. 18(4-5):
161-170, 1981

Influence of sex, menstrual cycle and oral contraception on the disposition of nitrazepam, by R. Jochemsen, et al. BRITISH JOURNAL OF
CLINICAL PHARMACOLOGY. 13(3):319-324, March 1982

Informed consent and contraceptive order, by E. T. Wimberley. DIS-
SERTATION ABSTRACTS INTERNATIONAL. A. p. 1683, 1982

Inga, midwife: without the new abortino legislation illegal abortions
would increase [interview], by I. Abelson. VARDFACKET. 6(10):43-
44, May 28, 1982

Inherent parens patriae authority empowers court of general jurisdiction in order sterilization of incompetents. WASHINGTON UNIVERSITY
LAW QUARTERLY. 11:77-96, Fall 1982

An initial comparison of coagulation techniques of sterilization, by
H. H. Riedel, et al. JOURNAL OF REPRODUCTIVE MEDICINE. 27(5):261-
267, May 1982

Initiation of uterine contractions by purely mechanical stretching of
the uterus at midpregnancy, by Y. Manabe, et al. INTERNATIONAL
JOURNAL OF BIOLOGICAL RESEARCH IN PREGNANCY. 2(2):63-69, 1981

Injectable contraception, by P. E. Hall, et al. WORLD HEALTH. pp.
2-4, May 1982

--. Depo Provera, by G. Howard. LISTENER. 107:4-5, March 4, 1982

Injectable hormonal contraceptives: technical and safety aspects.
WHO OFFSET PUBLICATIONS. (65):1-45, 1982

Innervation of the vas deferons and its importance for vasectomy and
vasovasostomy, by P. C. Esk, et al. UROLOGIA INTERNATIONALIS.
37(1):26-33, 1982

Integrated family planning activities in maternal and child health
centres in Cap Bon, Tunisia. I: Methodology and results, by I. De
Schampheleire, et al. JOURNAL OF TROPICAL PEDIATRICS. 27(4):190-
195, August 1981

--II: Use of a family planning technical card in an integrated maternal and child health program, by I. De Schampheleire. JOURNAL
OF TROPICAL PEDIATRICS. 27(4):196-198, August 1981

--III. Impact on some maternal and child health indicators, by I. De
Schampheleire. JOURNAL OF TROPICAL PEDIATRICS. 27(6):304-307,
December 1981

Intensified electro-acupuncture in induced abortion. CHUNG HUA FU
CHAN KO TSA CHIH. 14(2):107-110, April 1979

The interaction of cigarette smoking, oral contraceptive use, and
cardiovascular risk factor variables in children: the Bogalusa
Heart Study, by L. S. Webber, et al. AMERICAN JOURNAL OF PUBLIC
HEALTH. 72(3):266-274, March 1982

Interactions between antibiotics and oral contraceptives [letter], by
R. J. True. JAMA: JOURNAL OF THE AMERICAN MEDICAL ASSOCIATION.
247(10):1408, March 12, 1982

Interactions between contraceptive pills and other drugs, by L. Nir, et al. HAREFUAH. 100(12):590-591, June 15, 1981

Interactions with the p-pill [letter], by M. B. Kristensen. UGES-KRIFT FOR LAEGER. 143(11):698, March 15, 1981

Interference with epididymal physiology as possible site of male contraception, by A. Reyes, et al. ARCHIVES OF ANDROLOGY. 7(2): 159-168, September 1981

Intermediate variables and educational differentials in fertility in Korea and the Philippines, by L. Bumpass, et al. DEMOGRAPHY. 14(2):63-67, March-April 1982

The international medicolegal status of sterilization for mentally handicapped people, by B. Gonzales. JOURNAL OF REPRODUCTIVE MEDI-CINE. 27(5):257-258, May 1982

Interruption of pregnancy by vacuum aspiration or uterotomy. Intra-and postoperative complications, by J. Kunz, et al. FORTSCHRITTE DER MEDIZIN. 100(16):749-753, April 29, 1982

Interruzione della gravidanza e legislazione: un'indagine in Tunisia, by G. Giumelli. REVISTRA DI SERVIZIO SOCIALE. 21(3):146-156, 1981

Interruzione volantaria della gravidanza in Liguria: un'esperienza sul territorio, by S. Morano. SOCIOLOGIA DEL DIRITTO. 7(3):177-180, 1980

Intramuscular administration of 15-methyl prostaglandin F2alpha in mid-trimester termination of pregnancy, by K. Bhalla, et al. JOURNAL OF INTERNATIONAL MEDICAL RESEARCH. 10(1):32-34, 1982

Intrauterine contraception from the viewpoint of an ambulatorty gynecologic department, by P. Hagen. ZEITSCHRIFT FUR ARZTLICHE FORTBILDUNG. 75(17):800-804, September 1, 1981

Intrauterine device usage and fetal loss, by H. Foreman, et al. OBSTETRICS AND GYNECOLOGY. 58(6):669-677, December 1981

Intrauterine devices: mechanism and management of uterine bleeding, by K. Srivastava. JOURNAL OF FAMILY WELFARE. 28:26-33, March 1982

Intrauterine diagnosis and management of fetal polycystic kidney disease, by L. Shenker, et al. OBSTETRICS AND GYNECOLOGY. 59(3): 385-389, March 1982

Intrauterine mummified fetus in a rhesus monkey (Macaca mulatta), by M. M. Swindle, et al. JOURNAL OF MEDICAL PRIMATOLOGY. 10(4-5): 269-273, 1981

Intravaginal administration of 9-deoxo-9-methylene-16,16-dimethyl PGE2 for cervical dilation prior to suction curettage, by A. G. Shapiro, et al. INTERNATIONAL JOURNAL OF GYNAECOLOGY AND OBSTE-TRICS. 20(2):137-140, April 1982

An intravasal non-occlusive contraceptive device in rats, by M. M. Misro, et al. JOURNAL OF REPRODUCTIVE FERTILITY. 65(1):9-14, May 1982

An investigation into the quality of service provided by telephone hotlines for family planning services [research], by D. Baxter, et al. CANADIAN JOURNAL OF PUBLIC HEALTH. 73:194-199, May-June 1982

Iowa Family Planning Program, by C. S. Adams. JOURNAL OF THE IOWA MEDICAL SOCIETY. 72(4):165-168, April 1982

Ireland: abortion vote debated (Women's Right to Choose, Dublin, fighting anti-abortion amendment to Constitution), by G. Horgan. OFF OUR BACKS. 12:6, July 1982

--: pro-life, pro-uniformity, by M. Holland. NEW STATESMAN. pp. 12-13, May 21, 1982

Is the American medical commuinity anti-life?, by R. R. Holton. OUR SUNDAY VISITOR. 71:4-5, October 17, 1982

Is every life worth living?. CHRISTIANITY TODAY. 26:12-13, March 19, 1982

--: to take a human life is to take what belongs to God [editorial]. CHRISTIANITY TODAY. 26:12-13, March 19, 1982

Is hormonal therapy still justified in imminent abortion?, by P. Berle, et al. ZEITSCHRIFT FUR GEBURTSCHILFE UND PERINATOLOGIE. 184(5):353-358, October 1980

Is it better to know the worst? ... amniocentesis confirmed Tay-Sachs disease. RN. 45:48-49+, March 1982

Is it really abortion?, by E. Peters. SOCIAL JUSTICE REVIEW. 73:24-25, January-February 1982

Is Mendelson's syndrome a 'public health hazard'? [letter], by M. J. Johnstone. ANAESTHESIA. 36(12):1145-1146, December 1981

Is prognostic information obtainable from serum pregnancy zone protein level with imminent abortion, by G. Stranz, et al. ZENTRAL-BLATT FUR GYNAEKOLOGIE. 103(13):758-762, 1981

Is there good news about the pill?, by C. Safran. MADEMOISELLE. 88:150-151+, December 1982

Isolation of human alpha-1 fetoprotein (AFP) from induced abortion material, by G. Haller, et al. INTERNATIONAL JOURNAL OF BIOLOGICAL RESEARCH IN PREGNANCY. 3(2):69-72, 1982

The issue of sterilization and the mentally retarded, by P. S. Appelbaum. HOSPITAL AND COMMUNITY PSYCHIATRY. 33(7):523-524, July 1982

Issues in family planning clinic management, by A. A. Hudgins, et al. FAMILY COMMUNITY HEALTH. 5(1):47-59, May 1982

Jerry Falwell is right, by M. Meehan. INQUIRY. 4(3):6-8, November 2, 1981

Jews and the abortion debate. JEWISH FRONTIER. 49:7-9, March 1982

Joyce's prophylactic paralysis: exposure in Dubliners, by Z. Bowen. JAMES JOYCE QUARTERLY. 19:257-273, Spring 1983

Judge hopes to combine Dalkon suits, by R. L. Rundle. BUSINESS IN-
SURANCE. 15:1+, December 28, 1981

Judgement and counter judgement ... England, by A. Langslow. AUS-
TRALIAN NURSES JOURNAL. 11:28-30, March 1982

Judges not chosen for abortion views as party platform urged, by M.
Meehan. NATIONAL CATHOLIC REPORTER. 18:1+, May 14, 1982

Judicial doors open a little more: law and life, by W. Monopoli.
FINANCIAL POST. 75:9, December 12, 1981

Just when you thought you were safe ... today's contraceptive controversy (spermicides and birth defects), by D. Weinberg. MADEMOI-
SELLE. 88:159-161, March 1982

Justifying abortion, by J. Burtchaell. SIGN. 61:18-22+, February
1982

Kinetic studies of the human renin and human substrate reaction, by
A. B. Gould, et al. BIOCHEMICAL MEDICINE. 24(3):321-326, December
1980

Kinship dependence and contraceptive use among Navaho women, by S. J.
Kunitz, et al. HUMAN BIOLOGY. 53(3):439-452, September 1981

Knowledge and attitudes toward Tay-Sachs disease among a college
student population, by C. F. Austein, et al. YALE JOURNAL OF
BIOLOGY AND MEDICINE. 54(5):345-354, September-October 1981

Knowledge concerning the family-planning clinic among the female population of Milan: studies of a group of 959 puerperas, by A. Bouzin, et al. ANNALI DI OSTETRICIA GINECOLOGIA, MEDICINA PERINATALE.
103(1):60-67, January-February 1982

Knowledge of contraceptives: an assessment of World Fertility Survey
data collection procedures, by M. Vaessen. POPULATION STUDIES.
35(3):357-373, November 1981

LH, FSH, estradiol and progesterone levels after discontinuation of
hormonal contraception, by A. Balogh, et al. ACTA UNIVERSITATIS
PALACKIANAE OLOMUCENSIS FACULTATIS MEDICAE. 101:95-101, 1981

L'abortion du crime d'avortement dans la perspective de la reforme du
droit criminel, by H. Dumont. LA REVUE JURIDIQUE THEMES. 15:149-
192, 1980-1981

Laminaria as an adjuvant in the induction of abortion [editorial], by
D. Schneider, et al. HAREFUAH. 101(7-8):180-181, October 1981

Laminaria in induction of abortion in the 2d trimester. Case of
uterine rupture, by G. Menaldo, et al. MINERVA GINECOLOGIA.
33(6):599-601, June 1981

Laparoscopic bladder injury, by A. S. Deshmukh. UROLOGY. 19(3):306-
307, March 1982

Laparoscopic removal of translocated intrauterine contraceptive devices, by P. J. McKenna, et al. BRITISH JOURNAL OF OBSTETRICS AND
GYNAECOLOGY. 89(2):163-165, 1982

Laparoscopic sterilisation using Hulka-Clemens clips, with or without termination of pregnancy. A study of 544 cases, by A. Tadjerouni, et al. JOURNAL DE GYNECOLOGIE, OBSTETRIQUE ET BIOLOGIE DE LA REPRODUCTION. 10(8):851-856, 1981

Laparoscopic sterilization with fallope rings--a Malaysian experience, by A. A. Rahman, et al. MEDICAL JOURNAL OF MALAYSIA. 36(2): 92-99, June 1981

--(a preliminary report of 200 cases), by X. J. Zhang. CHUNG HUA FU CHAN KO TSA CHIH. 17(1):60-62, January 1982

Laparoscopic sterilization with the falope-ring technique, by J. B. Hertz. ACTA OBSTETRICIA ET GYNECOLOGICA SCANDINAVICA. 61(1):13-15, 1982

Laparoscopic sterilization with thermocoagulation, by P. K. Buchhave, et al. UGESKRIFT FOR LAEGER. 144(3):147-149, January 18, 1982

Laparoscopic sterilizations requiring laparotomy, by I. C. Chi, et al. AMERICAN JOURNAL OF OBSTETRICS AND GYNECOLOGY. 142(6 Pt 1): 712-713, March 15, 1982

Laparoscopy: a retrospective study with two or more years follow-up of patients in a small community hospital, by J. D. Chapman. JAOA: JOURNAL OF THE AMERICAN OPTOMETRIC ASSOCIATION. 81(6 Suppl): 429-435, 1982

Late complications after application of different sterilization techniques--a comparison between the monopolar HF-sterilization and the endocoagulation method, by H. H. Riedel, et al. GEBURTSHILFE UND FRAUENHEILKUNDE. 42(4):273-279, April 1982

Late complications of sterilization according to method, by H. H. Riedel, et al. JOURNAL OF REPRODUCTIVE MEDICINE. 26(7):353-358, July 1981

Late spontaneous abortion associated with mycoplasma hominis infection of the fetus, by K. Christensen, et al. SCANDINAVIAN JOURNAL OF INFECTIOUS DISEASES. 14(1):73-74, 1982

The latest NFP books, by M. Kambic, et al. MARRIAGE. 64:21-22, August 1982

Latina attitudes towards abortion, by H. Amaro. NUESTRO. 5:43-44, August-September 1981

Law, abortion and rights, by R. W. Schmude. LINACRE QUARTERLY. 49:215-221, August 1982

The law and sterilization or permanent contraception, by G. Brenner. GEBURTSHILFE UND FRAUENHEILKUNDE. 42(3):226-230, March 1982

The law of human reproduction [an overview], by D. G. Warren. JOURNAL OF LEGAL MEDICINE. 3(1):1-57, March 1982

Law of the land, by H. Seiden. TODAY. p. 23, November 28, 1981

The law of menstrual therapies [editorial]. LANCET. 2(8295):422-423, August 21, 1982

Law professors explore legal meaning of proposed anti-abortion amendments. FAMILY LAW REPORTER: COURT OPINIONS. 8(4):2051-2054, November 24, 1981

Legal abortion in Italy, 1978-1979, by M. Filicori, et al. FAMILY PLANNING PERSPECTIVES. 13(5):228-231, September-October 1981

Legal abortion in Switzerland; some numbers and evolution, by P. A. Gloor, et al. PRAXIS. 71(6):225-229, February 9, 1982

Legal abortion: the public health record, by W. Cates, Jr. SCIENCE. 215(4540):1586-1590, March 26, 1982

Legal aspects of research and practice in fertility control, by J. Stepan. CESKOSLOVENSKA GYNEKOLOGIE. 46(3):212-216, April 1981

Legal assessment: human life federalism amendment, by W. R. Carron. ORIGINS. 11:495-500, January 14, 1982

Legal clout without a trial (abortions halted at Moose Jew Union Hospital due to demands of pro-life groups), by D. Eisler. MACLEAN'S. 95:17, January 28, 1982

--(therapeutic abortion), by D. Eisler. MACLEAN'S. 95:17, June 28, 1982

Legal status of the fetus (views of M. H. Shapirol). USA TODAY. 111:12-14, December 1982

Legal trends and issues in voluntary sterilization. POPULATION REPORTS. (6):E73-102, March-April 1981

Legalized abortion and profile of women in New Delhi, by R. Singh. HIROSHIMA JOURNAL OF MEDICAL SCIENCES. 30(1):43-46, March 1981

Legally speaking. Assisting at abortions: can you really say no?, by W. A. Regan. RN. 45(6):71, June 1982

Leptospirosis in porcine livestock. Second serological survey in outbreaks of infectious abortion, by A. Pumarola Busquets, et al. REVISTA DE SANIDAD E HIGIENE PUBLICA. 53(1-2):51-55, January-February 1979

Let's face the facts on abortion, by K. Hepburn. FAMILY CIRCLE. 95(12):112+, November 1981

Letting intrauterine devices lie [research review], by M. Pollock. BRITISH MEDICAL JOURNAL. 6339:395-396, August 7, 1982

Levonorgestrel and estradiol release from an improved contraceptive vaginal ring, by T. M. Jackanicz. CONTRACEPTION. 24(4):323-339, October 1981

Life amendment: abortion and the Irish constitution, by P. Kirby, et al. GUARDIAN. p. 17, November 6, 1982

Ligation of the fallopian tubes by means of minilaprotomy (our modification of Pomeroy's method) and using a laparoscope (falope ring), by K. Kuczewski. GINEKOLOGIA POLSKA. 52(1):57-62, January 1981

The limits of judicial intervention in abortion politics, by R. Tatalovich, et al. CHRISTIAN CENTURY. 99(1):16-20, 1982

Lipid metabolic effects induced by two estradiol/norgestrel combinations in women around forty, by A. Hagstad, et al. ACTA OBSTETRICIA ET GYNECOLOGICA SCANDINAVICA. SUPPLEMENT. 106:57-62, 1981

Lipoprotein patterns in women in Santo Domingo using a levonorgestrel/estradiol contraceptive ring, by D. N. Robertson, et al. CONTRACEPTION. 24(4):469-480, October 1981

Liver adenoma with granulomas. The appearance of granulomas in oral contraceptive-related hepatocellular adenoma and in the surrounding nontumorous liver, by D. A. Malatjalian, et al. ARCHIVES OF PATHOLOGY AND LABORATORY MEDICINE. 106(5):244-246, May 1982

The liver and the 'pill'. 1: Disorders of bile secretion and vessel changes, by J. Eisenburg. FORTSCHRITTE DER MEDIZIN. 99(37):1479-1483, October 1, 1981

--2: Liver tumors, by J. Eisenburg. FORTSCHRITTE DER MEDIZIN. 99(38):1527-1532, October 8, 1981

Liver diseases when using hormonal contraceptives, by T. S. Lie. MMW: MUENCHENER MEDIZINISCHE WOCHENSCHRIFT. 124(20):489-494, May 21, 1982

Liver lesions and oral contraceptives [letter], by A. N. Freedman. CANADIAN MEDICAL ASSOCIATION JOURNAL. 126(10):1149-1150, May 15, 1982

Liver regeneration after partial hepatectomy in oral contraceptive-treated female rats, by M. A. Mukundan, et al. BIOCHEMICAL MEDICINE. 26(2):222-230, October 1981

Liver tumours in pregnancy, following previous intake of hormonal contraceptives, by P. Pietsch, et al. ZENTRALBLATT FUR GYNAEKOLOGIE. 103(13):772-780, 1981

Living without the pill, by L. McQuaig. MACLEAN'S. 95:40-42+, March 15, 1982

Locus of control as related to birth control knowledge, attitudes and practices, by J. J. Lieberman. ADOLESCENCE. 16:1-10, Spring 1981

Locus of control of increasing specificity reinforcement value and contraceptive use among sexually experienced college females who are knowledgeable about contraception, by S. J. Albano. DISSERTATION ABSTRACTS INTERNATIONAL. A. p. 5058, 1982

The logic of abortion: how "quality of life" killed Infant Doe, by M. S. Evans. HUMAN EVENTS. 42:7, May 1, 1982

The long struggle for reproductive rights, by L. Gordon. RADICAL AMERICAN. 15(1-2):75-88, 1981

Long-term intracervical contraception with a levonorgestrel device, by S. El Mahgoub. CONTRACEPTION. 25(4):357-374, April 1982

Long-term intranasal luteinizing hormone-releasing hormone agonist

treatment for contraception in women, by C. Bergquist, et al. FER-
RTILITY AND STTERILITY. 38(2):190-193, August 1982

Lost genius, by R. Baker. NEW YORK TIMES MAGAZINE. p. 15, January
17, 1982

Lovesick: the birth control blues without the pill, couples choose no
sex over safe sex, by S. Levy. ROLLING STONE. pp. 25+, March 4,
1982

Low dosage oral contraception in women with previous gestational
diabetes, by S. O. Skouby, et al. OBSTETRICS AND GYNECOLOGY.
59(3):325-328, March 1982

A low-dose combination oral contraceptive. Experience with 1,700
women treated for 22,489 cycles, by T. B. Woutersz. JOURNAL OF
REPRODUCTIVE MEDICINE. 26(12):615-620, December 1981

Low-dose enflurane does not increase blood loss during therapeutic
abortion, by M. S. Sidhu, et al. ANESTHESIOLOGY. 57(2):127-129,
August 1982

Low dose rhesus immunoprophylaxis after early induced abortions, by
P. Gjøde, et al. ACTA OBSTETRICIA ET GYNECOLOGICA SCANDINAVICA.
61(2):105-106, 1982

A low power magnification technique for reanastomosis of the vas, by
D. Urquhart-Hay. BRITISH JOURNAL OF UROLOGY. 53(5):466-469,
October 1981

'Lupus' anticoagulant and inhibition of prostacyclin formation in
patients with repeated abortions, intrauterine growth retardation
and intrauterine death, by L. O. Carreras, et al. BRITISH JOURNAL
OF OBSTETRICS AND GYNAECOLOGY. 88(9):890-894, September 1981

Luteal phase defects induced by an agonist of luteinizing hormone-
releasing factor: a model for fertility control, by K. L. Sheehan,
et al. SCIENCE. 215(4529):170-172, January 8, 1982

Luteal phase pregnancies in female sterilization patients, bu I. Chi,
et al. CONTRACEPTION. 23(6):579-589, June 1981

The luteolytic and abortifacient potential of an estrogen-bromergocryptine regimen in the baboon, by V. D. Castracane, et al. FER-
TILITY AND STERILITY. 37(2):258-262, February 1982

Luteolytic effect of azastene in the nonhuman primate, by R. H. Asch,
et al. OBSTETRICS AND GYNECOLOGY. 59(3):303-308, March 1982

Lymphocyte blast transformation indices in abortion and their clinical significance, by S. D. Bulienko, et al. AKUSHERSTVO I GINE-
KOLOGIIA. (5):10-13, May 1981

Macroscopic vasovasostomy, by P. Kessler, et al. FERTILITY AND
STERILITY. 36(4):531-532, October 1981

Magnesium sulfate treatment of threatened late abortions and premature labor, by I. Penev, et al. AKUSHERSTVO I GINEKOLOGIIA.
20(4):265-268, 1981

Mahgoub'd reversible sterilization, by S. Ballas. HAREFUAH. 100(9): 415-416, May 1, 1981

Major histocompatibility complex antigens, maternal and paternal immune responses, and chronic habitual abortions in humans, by A. E. Beer, et al. AMERICAN JOURNAL OF OBSTETRICS AND GYNECOLOGY. 141(8):987-999, Decemer 15, 1981

Malignant hypertension and oral contraceptives: four cases, with two due to the 30 micrograms oestrogen pill, by G. P. Hodsman, et al. EUROPEAN HEART JOURNAL. 3(3):255-259, June 1982

Malignant mammary tumors in beagle dogs dosed with investigational oral contraceptive steroids, by R. P. Kwapien, et al. JNCI: JOURNAL OF THE NATIONAL CANCER INSTITUTE. 65(1):137-144, July 1980

Man, problems of values and a discussion of abortion, by G. Straass. ZEITSCHRIFT FUR ARZTLICHE FORTBILDUNG. 75(8):391-396, April 15, 1981

Management of amenorrhea due to contraceptive injectables by temporary intrauterine device insertion, by M. Toppozada, et al. CONTRACEPTIVE DELIVERY SYSTEMS. 3(2):127-132, 1982

Marchers were of one mind--abortions must be halted. OUR SUNDAY VISITOR. 70:7, February 7, 1982

Margareta Callersten, participant in abortion research: don't choose abortion because it appears a better solution [interview by Monica Trozell], by M. Callersten. VARDFACKET. 6(10):41-42, May 28, 1982

Marital relations and fertility control decisions among Lebanese couples, by M. Chamie, et al. POPULATION AND ENVIRONMENT. 4(3): 189, Fall 1981

Marital secrets: the emerging issue of abortion spousal notification laws. JOURNAL OF LEGAL MEDICINE. 3:461-482, September 1982

Marriage and family counseling, by A. P. Kiriushchenkov. FEL'DSHER I AKUSHERKA. 47(1):59-60, 1982

Massachusetts Medicaid Program must fund medically necessary abortions. FAMILY LAW REPORTER: COURT OPINIONS. 7(18):2291-2294, March 10, 1981

Massive, painful hepatomegaly, sinusoidal dilation and prolonged use of estroprogestational agents [letter], by D. Fischer, et al. GASTROENTEROLOGIE CLINIQUE ET BIOLOGIQUE. 6(3):302-304, March 1982

Maternal and abortion related deaths in Bangladesh, 1978-1979, by R. W. Rochat, et al. INTERNATIONAL JOURNAL OF GYNAECOLOGY AND OBSTETRICS. 19(2):155-164, April 1981

Maternal and child health and family planning in an island village locality, by S. R. Mehta. JOURNAL OF FAMILY WELFARE. 28:66-77, June 1982

Maternal and child health and family planning in Nigeria, by M. A. Oyediran. PUBLIC HEALTH. 95(6):344-346, November 1981

Maternal and public health benefits of menstrual regulation in
Chittagong, by S. N. Bhuiyan, et al. INTERNATIONAL JOURNAL OF
GYNAECOLOGY AND OBSTETRICS. 20(2):105-109, April 1982

Maternal nutrition, breast feeding, and contraception [editorial], by
J. Dobbing. BRITISH MEDICAL JOURNAL. 284(6331):1725-1726, June
12, 1982

Maternal serum hormone changes during abortion induced with 16,16-
dimethyl-trans-delta 2-PGE1 methyl ester, by K. Bremme, et al.
PROSTAGLANDINS LEUKOTRIENES AND MEDICINE. 8(6):647-651, June 1982

The maternal serum levels of human chorionic gonadotropin, beta-human
chorionic gonadotropin and human prolactin in normal pregnancy and
in patients with threatened abortion within the 1st 12 weeks of
pregnancy, by P. P. Busacchi, et al. RIVISTA ITALIANA DI GINE-
COLOGIA. 59(6):471-479, 1982

The matron and sex education. NUEVA ENFERMERIA. (11):11, May 1980

A matter of forms: Peter Huntingford, the doctor who forced a show-
down on moves to restrict the abortion law, by J. Nicholls. SUNDAY
TIMES. p. 36, February 14, 1982

Matters of life and death: social, political, and religious correlates of attitudes on abortion, by R. K. Baker. AMERICAN POLITICAL
QUARTERLY. 9(1):89-102, 1981

Measurement issues involved in examining contraceptive use among
young single women, by E. S. Herold. POPULATION AND ENVIRONMENT.
4(2):128, Summer 1981

Measurement of serum activity in short and long-term application of
various hormonal contraceptives, by G. Klinger, et al. ZEITSCHRIFT
FUR DIE GESAMTE INNERE MEDIZIN. 36(17):611-620, September 1, 1981

Measuring family planning acceptance by the criterion of excess children, by H. M. Rajyaguru. JOURNAL OF FAMILY WELFARE. 28:34-45,
March 1982

The mechanism of action of intrauterine contraceptive devices, by J.
Lippes. MIDWIFE, HEALTH VISITOR AND COMMUNITY NURSE. 17:518-521,
December 1981

The mechanism of action of vacation pills, by Z. Y. Hu. CHUNG HUA FU
CHAN KO TSA CHIH. 16(2):73-77, April 1981

Mechanism of the action of Yuanhuacine to induce labor during mid
pregnancy, by B. Y. Yang. CHUNG-KUO YAO LI HSUEH PAO. 61(10):613-
616, October 1981

Medicaid funding of family planning clinic services, by M. T. Orr, et
al. FAMILY PLANNING PERSPECTIVES. 13(6):280-287, November-December 1981

Medicaid sterilization rules violated: group, by M. Magar. AMERICAN
BAR ASSOCIATION JOURNAL. 67:1249, October 1981

Medical examination of patients before referral for termination of
pregnancy [letter], by R. E. Coles. LANCET. 2(8294):380-381,

August 14, 1982

Medical intervention in the field of human reproduction, by J. Cruz y Hermida. ANALES DE LA ACADEMIA NACIONAL DE MEDICINA. 98(3):369-394, 1981

Medium term complications after termination of pregnancy, by R. B. Hunton, et al. AUSTRALIAN AND NEW ZEALAND JOURNAL OF OBSTETRICS AND GYNAECOLOGY. 21(2):99-102, May 1981

Meeting boosts Hatch proposal, by M. Meehan. NATIONAL CATHOLIC RE-PORTER. 18(1):6, December 18, 1981

Megadose vitamin C and metabolic effects of the pill [letter], by M. H. Briggs. BRITISH MEDICAL JOURNAL. 283(6305):1547, December 5, 1981

Meleney's gangrene following sterilisation by salpingectomy [case report], by D. F. Badenoch. BRITISH JOURNAL OF OBSTETRICS AND GYNAECOLOGY. 88(10):1061-1062, 1981

Memo suggests Hatch aide expects abortion bill's defeat, by M. Meehan. NATIONAL CATHOLIC REPORTER. 18(1):4, January 1, 1982

'Menarcheal age and spontaneous abortion: a causal connection', by J. T. Casagrande, et al. AMERICAN JOURNAL OF EPIDEMIOLOGY. 115(3): 481-483, March 1982

Menopausal age and spontaneous abortion in a group of women working in a Swedish steel works, by B. Kolmodm-Hedman, et al. SCANDINA-VIAN JOURNAL OF SOCIAL MEDICINE. 10(1):17-22, 1982

Menstrual behaviour with steroid implant, by M. N. Pal, et al. JOUR-NAL OF THE INDIAN MEDICAL ASSOCIATION. 77(1):16-17, July 1, 1981

Menstrual cycle and oral contraceptive effects on alcohol pharmaco-kinetics in caucasian females, by A. R. Zeiner, et al. CURRENTS IN ALCOHOLISM. 8:47-56, 1981

Menstrual extraction in the adolescent, by T. C. Key, et al. JOURNAL OF ADOLESCENT HEALTH CARE. 1(2):127-131, December 1980

Menstrual pattern and blood loss with U-coil inert progesterone-re-leasing intrauterine devices, by F. Hefnawi, et al. CONTRACEPTIVE DELIVERY SYSTEMS. 3(2):91-98, 1982

Menstrual pattern changes following laparoscopic sterilization: a comparative study of electrocoagulation and the tubal ring in 1,025 cases, by P. P. Bhiwandiwala, et al. JOURNAL OF REPRODUCTIVE MEDI-CINE. 27(5):249-255, May 1982

Menstrual regulation at University College Hospital, Ibadan, Nigeria, by O. A. Ojo, et al. INTERNATIONAL SURGERY. 66(3):247-249, July-September 1981

Menstrual regulation with prostaglandin analogues, by K. Hagenfeldt, et al. REPRODUCCION. 5(3):195-201, July-September 1981

The mental health professional, the mentally retarded, and sex, by E. J. Saunders. HOSPITAL AND COMMUNITY PSYCHIATRY. 32(10):717-721,

October 1981

Messing with Mother Nature: fleck and the omega pill, by J. A. Montmarquet. PHILOSOPHICAL STUDIES. 41:407-420, May 1982

Metabolic clearance rates of luteinizing hormone in women during different phases of the menstrual cycle and while taking an oral contraceptive, by R. E. Wehmann, et al. JOURNAL OF CLINICAL ENDOCRINOLOGY AND METABOLISM. 55(4):654-659, October 1982

Metabolic effects of the birth control pill, by S. Sondheimer. CLINICAL OBSTETRICS AND GYNECOLOGY. 24(3):927-941, September 1981

Metabolic studies in gestational diabetic women during contraceptive treatment: effects on glucose tolerance and fatty acid composition of serum lipids, by T. Radberg, et al. GYNECOLOGIC AND OBSTETRIC INVESTIGATION. 13(1):17-29, 1982

Metabolism of (6, 7-3H) norethisterone enanthate in rats, by G. W. Sang, et al. CHUNG-KUO YAO LI HSUEH PAO. 2(1):37-41, March 1981

Methods of contraception. Educational chart at the University Gynecological Clinic, Mannheim. FORTSCHRITTE DER MEDIZIN. 100(16): 743-745, April 29, 1982

Methods used in induced abortion in Bangladesh: an anthropological perspective, by P. C. Sarker. SOCIAL SCIENCE AND MEDICINE. 15(4): 483-487, October 1981

Metoprolol pharmacokinetics and the oral contraceptive pill, by M. J. Kendall, et al. BRITISH JOURNAL OF CLINICAL PHARMACOLOGY. 14(1): 120-122, July 1982

Metronidazole and prostaglandin induced abortion, by Z. O. Amarin, et al. INTERNATIONAL JOURNAL OF GYNAECOLOGY AND OBSTETRICS. 19(2): 165-168, April 1981

The Mexican plant zoapatle (Montanoa tomentosa) in reproductive medicine. Past, present, and future, by S. D. Levine, et al. JOURNAL OF REPRODUCTIVE MEDICINE. 26(10):524-528, October 1981

Microbial presence in the uterine cavity as affected by varieties of intrauterine contraceptive devices, by M. Skangalils, et al. FERTILITY AND STERILITY. 37(2):263-269, 1982

Microcirculation and oral contraceptives, by J. F. Merlen. PHLEBOLOGIE. 35(2):631-637, April-June 1982

Microsurgical reanastomosos of the fallopian tube: increasingly successful outcome for reversal of previous sterilization procedures, by M. P. Diamond, et al. SOUTHERN MEDICAL JOURNAL. 75(4):443-445, April 1982

Mid-cycle contraception with LHRH in women, by H. Maia, Jr., et al. REPRODUCCION. 5(4):251-260, October-December 1981

Midtrimester abortion, by W. M. Hern. OBSTETRICS AND GYNECOLOGY ANNUAL. 10:375-422, 1981

Midtrimester abortion experience in a community hospital, by G. A.

West. JOURNAL OF THE NATIONAL MEDICAL ASSOCIATION. 73(11):1069-1071, November 1981

Midtrimester abortion induced by radix trichosanthis: morphologic observations in placenta and the fetus, by C. Kuo-Fen. OBSTETRICS AND GYNECOLOGY. 59(4):494-498, April 1982

Midtrimester abortion patients, by L. D. White, et al. AORN JOURNAL: ASSOCIATION OF OPERATING ROOM NURSES. 34(4):756-768, October 1981

Midtrimester abortion with intravenous administration of 15 methyl prostaglandin F_2alpha, by M. K. Mapa, et al. INTERNATIONAL JOURNAL OF GYNAECOLOGY AND OBSTETRICS. 20(2):125-128, April 1982

Midwives as counselors, by P. Woo. JORDEMODERN. 95(20:55-59, February 1982

Miffed mizzes: pro-choice vs. pro-life. ALBERTA REPORT. 8:31-32, December 4, 1981

Migrant-nonmigrant differentials in socioeconomic status, fertility and family planning in Nepal, by J. M. Tuladhar, et al. INTERNATIONAL MIGRATION REVIEW. 16:197-205, Spring 1982

Minigest--a new Czechoslovak contraceptive and its side-effects, by E. Zizkovska, et al. CESKOSLOVENSKA GYNEKOLOGIE. 45(9):649-652, November 1980

Minilaparotomy or laparoscopy for sterilization: a multicenter, multinational randomized study. AMERICAN JOURNAL OF OBSTETRICS AND GYNECOLOGY. 143(6):645-652, July 15, 1982

Minilaparotomy tubal sterilization: a comparison between normal and high-risk patients, by M. E. Domenzain, et al. OBSTETRICS AND GYNECOLOGY. 59(2):199-201, February 1982

Minimizing the risk of postabortion thrombosis. NURSES DRUG ALERT. 6:25, April 1982

Minor women obtaining abortions: a study of parental notification in a metropolitan area [research], by F. Clary. AMERICAN JOURNAL OF PUBLIC HEALTH. 72(3):283-285, March 1982

A miscarraige with a difference [letter], by J. J. de Villiers. SOUTH AFRICAN MEDICAL JOURNAL. 61(1):4, January 2, 1982

Mismating and termination of pregnancy, by V. M. Shille. VETERINARY CLINICS OF NORTH AMERICA. SMALL ANIMAL PRACTICE. 12(1):99-106, February 1982

Missed abortion treated with intramuscular 15-(S)-15-methyl-prostaglandin F2 alpha, by G. Tsalacopoulos, et al. SOUTH AFRICAN MEDICAL JOURNAL. 61(22):828-830, May 29, 1982

Model for effective contraceptive counseling on campus, by G. A. Bachmann. JOURNAL OF THE AMERICAN COLLEGE HEALTH ASSOCIATION. 30(3):119-121, December 1981

Modern methods of regulating generative function, by I. A. Manuilova. SOVETSKAIA MEDITSINA. (12):105-107, 1981

Modern, transitional, and traditional demographic and contraceptive patterns among Kenyan women, by T. E. Dow, Jr., et al. STUDIES IN FAMILY PLANNING. 13(1):12, January 1982

Mommy, what does abortion mean?, by M. Popson. LIGUORIAN. 70:30-31, January 1982

Monica was reported when she refused to give depo-provera [interview by Susanne Gare], by M. Blomster. VARDFACKET. 6(7):53, April 8, 1982

Moral development and reconstructive memory: recalling a decision to terminate an unplanned pregnancy, by G. Blackburne-Stover, et al. DEVELOPMENTAL PSYCHOLOGY. 18:862-870, November 1982

Moral philosophy and political problems, by A. Guttmann. POLITICAL THEORY. 10:33-48, February 1982

Morality, legality and abortion, by G. Dworkin. SOCIETY. 19(4):51-53, 1982

More pastoral reflections on humanae vitae, by B. Cole. PRIEST. 38:28-32, January 1982

More than 1,000,000 voluntary sterilizations performed in United States in 1980. FAMILY PLANNING PERSPECTIVES. 14:99-100, March-April 1982

Morgentaler tests the law (plan for abortion clinics), by A. Finlayson. MACLEAN'S. 95:55, November 29, 1982

Morning-after pills [editorial], by S. Rowlands. BRITISH MEDICAL JOURNAL. 285(6338):322-323, July 31, 1982

Mortality from abortion and childbirth. Are the populations comparable?, by S. A. LeBolt, et al. JAMA: JOURNAL OF THE AMERICAN MEDICAL ASSOCIATION. 248(2):188-191, July 9, 1982

---. Are the statistics biased?, by W. Cates, Jr., et al. JAMA: JOURNAL OF THE AMERICAN MEDICAL ASSOCIATION. 248(2):192-196, July 9, 1982

Mortality, legality and abortion, by G. Dworkin. SOCIETY. 19:51-53, May-June 1982

Mortality risk associated with tubal sterilization in United States hospitals, by H. B. Peterson, et al. AMERICAN JOURNAL OF OBSTETRICS AND GYNECOLOGY. 143(2):125-129, May 15, 1982

Most Americans in the middle on abortion, shun pro-extremes and anti-extremes. FAMILY PLANNING PERSPECTIVES. 14:102-106, March-April 1982

Mucosal disease virus as a cause of enzootic abortion in cattle in Czechoslovakia, by J. Mensik, et al. VETERINARNI MEDICINA. 26(8): 457-468, August 1981

A multicenter clinical investigation employing ethinyl estradiol combined with dl-norgestrel as postcoital contraceptive agent, by A. A. Yuzpe, et al. FERTILITY AND STERILITY. 37(4):508-513, April

1982

A multicenter study of levonorgestrel-estradiol contraceptive vaginal rings. I. Use effectiveness. An international comparative trial, by I. Sivin, et al. CONTRACEPTION. 24(4):341-358, October 1981

--II. Subjective and objective measures of effects. An international comparative trial, by I. Sivin, et al. CONTRACEPTION. 24(4):359-376 October 1981

--III. Menstrual patterns. An international comparative trial, by I. Sivin, et al. CONTRACEPTION. 24(4):377-392, October 1981

The multiload intra-uterine contraceptive device: comparison of 4 different models, by W. A. A. Van Os, et al. SOUTH AFRICAN MEDICAL JOURNAL. 60(24):938-940, 1981

Multiple dose extraamniotic prostaglandin gel for second trimester termination of pregnancy, by M. A. Quinn, et al. AUSTRALIAN AND NEW ZEALAND JOURNAL OF OBSTETRICS AND GYNAECOLOGY. 21(2):96-98, May 1981

Multiple pregnancy and fetal abnormalities in association with oral contraceptive usage, by D. C. Macourt, et al. AUSTRALIAN AND NEW ZEALAND JOURNAL OF OBSTETRICS AND GYNAECOLOGY. 22(1):25-28, February 1982

Multiple pregnancy, or should 2 babies be given up to save 3? [letter], by J. Breheret. NOUVELLE PRESSE MEDICALE. 11(3):210, January 23, 1982

Muslim juridical opinions concerning the status of women as demonstrated by the case of 'azi (coitus interruptus), by D. L. Bowen. JOURNAL OF NEAR EASTERN STUDIES. 40(4):323-328, October 1981

Mutagenic evaluation of two male contraceptives: 5-thio-d-glucose and gossypol acetic acid, by S. K. Majumdar, et al. JOURNAL OF HEREDITY. 73(1):76-77, January-February 1982

My abortion: why it was the most difficult decision I may ever have to make, by N. Mitchell. GLAMOUR. 80:248-249+, March 1982

My doctor said I should have an abortion. GOOD HOUSEKEEPING. 194:32+, March 1982

Mycoplasma hominis as a possible cause of spontaneous abortions and premature labor, by I. Tanev, et al. AKUSHERSTVO I GINEKOLOGIIA. 20(3):197-201, 1981

Myocardial infarction in a man handling oral contraceptives. Immunologic study [letter], by B. Ponge, et al. NOUVELLE PRESSE MEDICALE. 10(37):3076, October 17, 1981

Myths and assumptions of antiabortionists. JOURNAL OF THE AMERICAN MEDICAL WOMEN'S ASSOCIATION. 37(3):74-76, March 1982

NAS attacks evidence of anti-abortion lobby, by C. Cookson. TIMES HIGHER EDUCATIONAL SUPPLEMENT. 445:6, May 15, 1981

N.C. funding of elective abortions upheld against taxpayer challenge.

FAMILY LAW REPORTER: COURT OPINIONS. 7(22):2362, April 7, 1981

NRC launches sexuality series, by A. Jones. NATIONAL CATHOLIC RE-
PORTER. 18:1+, October 1, 1982

National College of French Gynecologists and Obstetricians. Report on
legislation on tubal sterilization, by M. F. Lerat, et al. JOURNAL
DE GYNECOLOGIE, OBSTETRIQUE ET BIOLOGIE DE LA REPRODUCTION. 11(1):
183-188, 1982

The National Inventory of Family Planning Services: 1978 survey results, by E. Graves. VITAL HEALTH STATISTICS. 14(26):1-34, February 1982

Natural birth control (breast feeding). SCIENCE DIGEST. 90:100,
January 1982

Natural family planning, by W. Fijalkowski. PIELEGNIARKA I POLOZNA.
(9):1-2, 1981

--[review], by H. Klaus. OBSTETRICAL AND GYNECOLOGICAL SURVEY.
37(2):128-150, February 1982

--: an analysis of change in procreative intention, by H. Klaus, et
al. JOURNAL OF THE AMERICAN MEDICAL WOMEN'S ASSOCIATION. 37:231-
237+, September 1982

--: postpartum period, by A. Perez. INTERNATIONAL JOURNAL OF FER-
TILITY. 26(3):219-221, 1981

--: when other contraceptive methods won't do, by J. J. McCarthy.
CONSULTANT. 21:109-110+, December 1981

Natural family planning and instructor training, by M. C. Martin.
NURSING AND HEALTH CARE. 2:554-556+, December 1981

Natural family planning at the grassroots, by V. L. Enright. PRIEST.
38:30-32, September 1982

Natural family planning basis for a happy married life, by V. J.
Dunigan. PRIEST. 38:12-17, January 1982

Natural family planning methods [letter], by J. J. Billings. AMERI-
CAN JOURNAL OF OBSTETRICS AND GYNECOLOGY. 143(1):114-115, May 1,
1982

The natural history of the retained dead fetus, by M. E. Foley.
IRISH MEDICAL JOURNAL. 74(8):237-238, August 1981

Need for family planning services among Anglo and Hispanic women in
the United States countries bordering Mexico, by S. E. Holck, et
al. FAMILY PLANNING PERSPECTIVES. 14:155-162, May-June 1982

Nelation catheter versus laminaria for a safe and gradual cervical
dilatation, by Y. Manabe, et al. CONTRACEPTION. 24(1):53-60, July
1981

Neonatal malformations and hormone therapy during pregnancy, by L.
Pacilli, et al. MINERVA GINECOLOGIA. 33(7-8):659-665, July-August
1981

Neoplasia and hormonal contraception, by G. R. Huggins. CLINICAL
OBSTETRICS AND GYNECOLOGY. 24(3):903-925, September 1981

Neurologic and cerebrovascular pathology during treatment with oral
contraceptives, by V. Sbarbaro, et al. RIVISTA DI NEUROBIOLOGIA.
26(4):453-462, October-December 1980

Neurotic psychosexual and emotional disorders after artificial termination of pregnancy, by W. Mikrut. WIADOMOSCI LEKARSKIE. 34(5):
389-393, March 1, 1981

The neurotoxicity and antifertility properties of 6-chloro-6-deoxy-
glucose in the mouse, by J. M. Jacobs, et al. NEUROTOXICOLOGY.
2(3):405-417, November 1981

Never-pregnant adolescents and family planning programs: contraception, continuation, and pregnancy risk, by E. W. Freeman, et al.
AMERICAN JOURNAL OF PUBLIC HEALTH. 72(8):815-822, August 1982

A new class of contraceptives? [news], by H. M. Fraser. NATURE.
296(5856):391-392, April 1, 1982

The new danger: a three-step abortion plan (Senator O. G. Hatch's
Human Life Amendment), by L. C. Wohl. MS. 10:87-88, February 1982

A new delivery system for metals as contraceptives in animals, by S.
S. Riar, et al. INDIAN JOURNAL OF EXPERIMENTAL BIOLOGY. 19(12):
1124-1126, December 1981

New form for termination of pregnancy [letter]. BRITISH MEDICAL
JOURNAL. 284(6317):738, March 6, 1982

New hope for the puppy problem (vaccination). TODAY. p. 6, February
27, 1982

A new key to the use of hormonal contraception, by C. Berger.
PRAXIS. 70(51):2312-2315, December 15, 1981

New light on natural family planning, by K. Banet. LIGUORIAN. 70:
34-38, August 1982

A new look at contraception, by P. M. Brunetti. ECOLOGIST. 11(4):
174, 1981

A new prostaglandin E2-gel for pretreatment of the cervix in nulliparous patients having a late first trimester terminatin of pregnancy, by L. Wingerup, et al. ARCHIVES OF GYNECOLOGY. 231(1):1-6,
1981

New sponge contraceptive, by S. Katz. CHATELAINE. 55:26, August
1982

New studies of malignant melanoma, gallbladder and heart disease
help further define pill risk. FAMILY PLANNING PERSPECTIVES. 14:
95-97, March-April 1982

A new technique for female sterilization, by D. Muzsnai, et al.
OBSTETRICS AND GYNECOLOGY. 58(4):508-512, October 1981

Nine Thai women had cancer--none of them took Depo-provera; therefore, depo-provera is safe, by S. Minkin. MOTHER JONES. 6:34+, November 1981

1979 AAGL membership survey, by J. M. Philips, et al. JOURNAL OF REPRODUCTIVE MEDICINE. 26(10):529-533, October 1981

No atherosclerosis risk in vasectomized men, preliminary studies find. FAMILY PLANNING PERSPECTIVES. 13:276-277, November-December 1981

No increased risk of spontaneous abortion found among women with a previous induced abortion. FAMILY PLANNING PERSPECTIVES. 13:238-239, September-October 1981

The noncontraceptive health benefits from oral contraceptive use, by H. W. Ory. FAMILY PLANNING PERSPECTIVES. 14:182-184, July-August 1982

Noncontraceptive health benefits of oral steroidal contraceptives, by D. R. Mishell, Jr. AMERICAN JOURNAL OF OBSTETRICS AND GYNECOLOGY. 142(6 Pt 2):809-816, March 15, 1982

Noncontraceptive uses of the pill, by D. R. Halbert. CLINICAL OBSTETRICS AND GYNECOLOGY. 24(3):987-993, September 1981

Nonmicroscopic vasovasostomy, by B. Fallon, et al. JOURNAL OF UROLOGY. 126(3):361-362, September 1981

Norethisterone, a major ingredient of contraceptive pills, is a suicide inhibitor of estrogen biosynthesis (inhibitor of estrogen synthetase), by Y. Osawa, et al. SCIENCE. 215(4537):1249-1251, March 5, 1982

Normal sister-chromatid exchanges in oral contraceptive users, by B. Husum, et al. MUTATION RESEARCH. 103(2):161-164, February 1982

Normalization of testosterone levels using a low polycystic ovary syndrome, by S. G. Raj, et al. OBSTETRICS AND GYNECOLOGY. 60(1):15-19, July 1982

The NORPLANT contraceptive method: a report on three years of use, by I. Sivin, et al. STUDIES IN FAMILY PLANNING. 13:258-261, August-September 1982

Not while you live in my house: the Supreme Court upholds mandatory parental notification of the dependent minor's abortion decision in H.L. v. Matheson (101 S Ct 1164). THE UNIVERSITY OF TOLEDO LAW REVIEW. 13:115-148, Fall 1981

A note on measuring the independent impact of family planning programs on fertility declines, by D. J. Hernadez. DEMOGRAPHY. 18(4):627-634, November 1981

Notes on the application of the law on voluntary interruption of pregnancy at a provincial general hospital, by P. Trompeo, et al. MINERVA GINECOLOGIA. 33(11):1049-1052, November 1981

Novel mode of contraception using polymeric hydrogels, by H. Singh, et al. JOURNAL OF BIOMEDICAL MATERIALS RESEARCH. 16(1):3-9, January 1982

Nuns' group rejects Hatch proposal, by R. J. McClory. NATIONAL CATHOLIC REPORTER. 18:5, July 16, 1982

The nurse and the law: judgement and counter-judgement, by A. Langslow. AUSTRALIAN NURSES' JOURNAL. 11(8):28-30, March 1982

The nurse listening to the adolescent. Contraception problems in adolescents, by A. Perron. NURSING MONTREAL. 6(3):4, June 1982

Nurse refused to assist in abortion: demoted!. REGAN REPORT ON NURSING LAW. 22:4, November 1981

Nursing care of clients in an abortion clinic, by J. Corstiaensen, et al. TIJDSCHRIFT VOR ZIEKENVERPLEGING. 34(17):739-744, August 25, 1981

Nutrition, family planning, and health promotion: the Guatemalan program of primary health care, by A. Lechtig, et al. BIRTH. 9:97-104, Summer 1982

OCs do not add to risk of birth defects. NURSES DRUG ALERT. 6:3, January 1982

Observations during the treatment of antithrombin-III deficient women with heparin and antithrombin concentrate during pregnancy, parturition, and abortion, by P. Brandt. THROMBOSIS RESEARCH. 22(1-2):15-24, April 1-15, 1981

Observations on female sterilization in Chile, by D. Menanteau-Horta. BULLETIN OF THE PAN AMERICAN HEALTH ORGANIZATION. 16(2):101, 1982

Observations with a combined oral contraceptive (Rigevidon) containing minimum oestrogen dose, by K. Karsay. THERAPIE HUNAGIRCA. 28(1):17-20, 1980

Occasional essay: Jewish perspective on prenatal diagnosis and selective abortion of affected fetuses, including some comparisons with prevailing Catholic beliefs, by R. M. Fineman, et al. AMERICAN JOURNAL OF MEDICAL GENETICS. 12(3):355-360, July 1982

Occupational hazards in the United Kingdom, by A. A. Spence. INTERNATIONAL ANESTHESIOLOGY CLINICS. 19(4):165-176, Winter 1981

Occurrence and histological structure of adenocarcinoma of the endocervix after long-term use of oral contraceptives, by G. Dallenbach-Hellweg. GEBURTSHILFE UND FRAUENHEILKUNDE. 42(4):249-255, April 1982

Oestrogenic activity of cyproterone acetate in female mice, by N. K. Lohiya, et al. ENDOKRINOLOGIE. 78(1):21-27, October 1981

Oestrogens and hypertension, by J. M. Roberts. CLINICAL ENDOCRINOLOGY. 10(3):489-512, November 1981

Of menses--pills and IUDs--neisseria--and flings--(with apologies to Lewis Carroli) [editorial], by J. C. Hume. JAMA: JOURNAL OF THE AMERICAN MEDICAL ASSOCIATION. 247(9):1321-1322, March 5, 1982

On oral contraceptive safety: cardiovascular problems [editorial], by R. A. Edgren. INTERNATIONAL JOURNAL OF FERTILITY. 26(4):241-244,

On the track of a new fertility control?, by J. Grinsted, et al.
NORDISK MEDICIN. 96(11):280-281, November 1981

One child makes sense (fertility trends in 10 Asian countries, 1950-
75), by K. Srinivasan. POPULI. 9(1):27-35, 1982

One doctor's view of abortion, by W. Savage. NEW SOCIETY. 59(1004):
224-226, 1982

One is enough, by L. R. Brown. ACROSS THE BOARD. 19:27-28, March
1982

--: the Chinese way of population control, by L. R. Brown. ACROSS
THE BOARD. 19:27-28, March 1982

1000m people, 800m peasants (population policies; China), by L.
Zheng. POPULI. 8(3):36-43, 1981

A one-sided view of natural family planning; reprint from the International Federation for Family Life Promotion Asia-Oceania Region
Newsletter, December 1981. LINACRE QUARTERLY. 49:2341-239, August
1982

The open letter to Katharine Hepburn, by P. Kaler. LIGUORIAN. 70:
34-39, April 1982

Operating techniques for voluntary interruption of pregnancy: clinical results, by A. Fantoni, et al. ARCHIVIO PER LA SCIENZE MEDI-
CHE. 138(4):483-486, 1981

Operative complicatons of laparoscopic tubal sterilization with
Bleier clips, by E. Schneller, et al. GEBURTSHILFE UND FRAUENHEIL-
KUNDE. 42(5):379-384, May 1982

Operative technics for voluntary interruption of pregancy. Clinical
results, by A. Fantoni, et al. ARCHIVIO PER LA SCIENZE MEDICHE.
138(4):483-486, October-December 1981

Optic nerve drusen and pseudopapilledema, by I. F. Gutteridge. AMER-
ICAN JOURNAL OF OPTOMETRY AND PHYSIOLOGICAL OPTICS. 58(8):671-676,
August 1981

Opting for the right to end life, by M. Engel. MACLEAN'S. 95:8,
March 8, 1982

Oral and vaginal Candida colonization under the influence of hormonal
contraception, by G. Klinger, et al. ZAHN-, MUND-, UND KIEFERHEIL-
KUNDE MIT ZENTRALBLATT. 70(2):120-125, 1982

Oral contraception and breast pathology, by N. Ragni, et al. ACTA
EUROPAEA FERTILITATIS. 12(2):141-163, June 1981

Oral contraception and cancer risk, by C. Y. Genton. SCHWEIZERISCHE
MEDIZINISCHE WOCHENSCHRIFT. 111(46):1742-1748, November 14, 1981

Oral contraception and cerebrovascular accidents, by J. Nick, et al.
BULLETIN DE L'ACADEMIE NATIONALE DE MEDICINE. 165(6):723-730, June
1981

Oral contraception and myocardial infarction revisited: the effects
of new preparations and prescribing patterns, by P. Bye. BRITISH
JOURNAL OF OBSTETRICS AND GYNAECOLOGY. 88(11):1167-1168, November
1981

Oral contraception and some debatable side effects, by B. Astedt.
ACTA OBSTETRICIA ET GYNECOLOGICA SCANDINAVICA. SUPPLEMENT. 105:17-
23, 1982

Oral contraception as a risk factor for preeclampsia, by M. B.
Bracken, et al. AMERICAN JOURNAL OF OBSTETRICS AND GYNECOLOGY.
142(2):191-196, January 15, 1982

Oral contraception, circulating immune complexes, antiethinylestradiol antibodies, and thrombosis, by V. Beaumont, et al. AMERICAN
JOURNAL OF REPRODUCTIVE IMMUNOLOGY. 2(1):8-12, February 1982

Oral contraception in diabetic women. Diabetes control, serum and
high density lipoprtein lipids during low-dose progestogen, combined oestrogen/progestogen and non-hormonal contraception, by
Radberg, et al. ACTA ENDOCRINOLOGICA. 98(2):246-21, October 1981

Oral contraception in patients with hyperprolactinaemia, by P. J.
Moult, et al. BRITISH MEDICAL JOURNAL. 284(6319):868, March 20,
1982

Oral contraception: mechanism of action, by R. A. Bronson. CLINICAL
OBSTETRICS AND GYNECOLOGY. 24(3):869-877, September 1981

Oral contraception today. Three dialogues, by D. R. Mishell, et al.
JOURNAL OF REPRODUCTIVE MEDICINE. 27(4 Suppl):235-295, April 1982

Oral contraceptive and cardiovascular disease: some questions and
answers, by M. P. Vessey. BRITISH MEDICAL JOURNAL. 6316:615-616,
February 27, 1982

Oral contraceptive and platelet lipid biosynthesis in female rats:
dose-response relationship, by M. Ciavatti, et al. LIPIDS. 17(2):
111-114, February 1982

Oral contraceptive and postmenopausal estrogen effects on lipoprotein
triglyceride and cholesterol in an adult female population: relationships to estrogen and progestin potency, by R. H. Knopp, et al.
JOURNAL OF CLINICAL ENDOCRINOLOGY AND METABOLISM. 53(6):1123-1132,
December 1981

Oral contraceptive during lactation: a global survey of physician
practice, by L. T. Strauss, et al. INTERNATIONAL JOURNAL OF GYNAE-
COLOGY AND OBSTETRICS. 19(3):169-175, June 1981

Oral contraceptive exposure of amenorrheic women with and without
prolactinomas, by J. R. Jones, et al. INTERNATIONAL JOURNAL OF
GYNAECOLOGY AND OBSTETRICS. 19(5):381-387, October 1981

Oral contraceptive: past, present and future use, by J. J. Speidel,
et al. JOHN HOPKINS MEDICAL JOURNAL. 150(5):161-164, May 1982

Oral contraceptive steroid concentrations in smokers and nonsmokers,
by F. E. Crawford, et al. BRITISH MEDICAL JOURNAL. 282(6279):
1824, 1981

Oral contraceptive steroids and malignancy, by E. Grant. CLINICAL ONCOLOGY. 8(2):97-102, June 1982

Oral contraceptive use and abortion before first term pregnancy in relation to breast cancer risk, by M. P. Vessey, et al. BRITISH JOURNAL OF CANCER. 45(3):327-331, March 1982

Oral contraceptive use and malignant melanoma, by C. Bain, et al. JNCI: JOURNAL OF THE NATIONAL CANCER INSTITUTE. 68(4):537-539, April 1982

Oral contraceptives and blood coagulation [a critical review], by E. F. Mammen. AMERICAN JOURNAL OF OBSTETRICS AND GYNECOLOGY. 142(6 Pt 2):781-790, March 15, 1982

Oral contraceptives and cancer of the liver: a review with two additional cases, by T. S. Helling, et al. AMERICAN JOURNAL OF GASTROENTEROLOGY. 77(7):504-508, July 1982

Oral contraceptives and cardiovascular disease [letter], by H. Ratner. NEW ENGLAND JOURNAL OF MEDICINE. 306(17):1052-1053, April 29, 1982

--: some questions and answers [editorial], by M. P. Vessey. BRITISH MEDICAL JOURNAL. 284(6316):615-616, February 27, 1982

Oral contraceptives and circulatory disease [letter]. FERTILITY AND STERILITY. 36(3):412-417, September 1981

Oral contraceptives and depression: impact, prevalence and cause, by G. B. Slap. JOURNAL OF ADOLESCENT HEALTH CARE. 2(1):53-64, September 1981

Oral contraceptives and diabetes mellitus, by L. M. Pedersen. UGESKRIFT FOR LAEGER. 144(4):261-263, January 25, 1982

Oral contraceptives and hepatic tumors, by J. H. Wilson. AGRES-SOLOGIE. 23(A):21-23, January 1982

Oral contraceptives and hepatocellular carcinoma, by S. R. Shar, et al. CANCER. 49(2):407-410, January 15, 1982

Oral contraceptives and nonfatal vascular disease--recent experience, by J. B. Porter, et al. OBSTETRICS AND GYNECOLOGY. 59(3):299-302, March 1982

Oral contraceptives and postoperative venous thrombosis, by F. DeStefano, et al. AMERICAN JOURNAL OF OBSTETRICS AND GYNECOLOGY. 143(2):227-228, May 15, 1982

Oral contraceptives and prolactinomas [a case-control study], by R. Maheux, et al. AMERICAN JOURNAL OF OBSTETRICS AND GYNECOLOGY. 143(2):134-138, May 15, 1982

Oral contraceptives and the risk of myocardial infarction [letter]. NEW ENGLAND JOURNAL OF MEDICINE. 305(25):1530-1531, December 17, 1981

Oral contraceptives and risk of ovarian cancer, by W. C. Willett, et al. CANCER. 48(7):1684-1687, October 1, 1981

Oral contraceptives and venous thromboembolism, by A. Bergqvist, et al. BRITISH JOURNAL OF OBSTETRICS AND GYNAECOLOGY. 89(5):381-386, May 1982

Oral contraceptives, clotting factors, and thrombosis, by T. W. Meade. AMERICAN JOURNAL OF OBSTETRICS AND GYNECOLOGY. 142(6 Pt 2):758-761, March 15, 1982

Oral contraceptives: effect of folate and vitamin B12 metabolism, by A. M. Shojania. CANADIAN MEDICAL ASSOCIATION JOURNAL. 126(3):244-247, February 1, 1982

Oral contraceptives in the 1980s. POPULATION REPORTS. 10(3): , May-June 1982

Oral contraceptives: technical and safety aspects. WHO OFFSET PUB-LICATIONS. (64):1-45, 1982

Oral contraceptives: where are the excess deaths?, by R. P. Shearman. MEDICAL JOURNAL OF AUSTRALIA. 1(13):698-700, June 27, 1981

--[letter], by M. P. Vessey, et al. MEDICAL JOURNAL OF AUSTRALIA. 2(8):390, October 17, 1981

An oral fertility test, by L. Lang. HEALTH. 14:18-19, March 1982

Oral hormonal contraceptives and benign liver tumors, by J. Giedl, et al. FORTSCHRITTE DER MEDIZIN. 99(6):165-170, February 12, 1981

Order to sterilize incompetent minor must be based on medical neces-sity. FAMILY LAW REPORTER: COURT OPINIONS. 8(40):2598-2600, Au-gust 17, 1982

Organic changes as affected by oral steroid contraception in female inbred Buffalo rats, by C. Markuszewski. PATOLOGIA POLSKA. 32(4):487-503, October-December 1981

An organizational and behavioral analysis of the contraceptive com-pliance process, by D. F. Winokur. DISSERTATION ABSTRACTS INTERNA-TIONAL. A. p. 4950, 1982

Organizational impediments to development assistance: the World Bank's population program, by B. B. Crane, et al. WORLD POLITICS. 33:516-553, July 1981

Our first experience with and considerations on the legal provisions of Law 194/78, by E. Martella, et al. ARCHIVES OF OBSTETRICS AND GYNECOLOGY. 85(6):557-566, November-December 1980

Our foundlings' fathers: let paternity flourish (the last straw), by K. Lindskoog. OTHER SIDE. 129:38, June 1982

Outcome of pregnancy in women who were refused an abortion by a secondary medical board, by M. Lekin, et al. MEDICINSKI PREGLED. 34(5-6):247-249, 1981

The outcome of pregnancy resulting from clomiphene-induced ovulation, by J. F. Correy, et al. AUSTRALIAN AND NEW ZEALAND JOURNAL OF OB-STETRICS AND GYNAECOLOGY. 22(1):18-21, February 1982

Outpatient laparoscopic sterilization, by H. Arshat, et al. MEDICAL
JOURNAL OF MALAYSIA. 36(1):20-23, March 1981

Outpatient termination of pregnancy: experience in a family practice
residency, by J. H. Marshall, et al. JOURNAL OF FAMILY PRACTICE.
14(2):245-248, February 1982

Ovarian-Hypophyseal relations in women susceptible to habitual abortion during the early stages of pregnancy, by E. S. Kononova, et
al. AKUSHERSTVO I GINEKOLOGIIA. (1):25-27, January 1982

Ovarian pregnancy: association with IUD, pelvic pathology and recurrent abortion, by J. Reichman, et al. EUROPEAN JOURNAL OF OBSTE-
TRICS, GYNECOLOGY AND REPRODUCTIVE BIOLOGY. 12(6):333-337, December 1981

An overview of studies on estrogens, oral contraceptives and breast
cancer, by V. A. Drill. PROGRESS IN DRUG RESEARCH. 25:159-187,
1981

The P pill and liver disease, by L. Ranek, et al. UGESKRIFT FOR
LAEGER. 144(3):165-166, January 18, 1982

P-pills [letter]. UGESKRIFT FOR LAEGER. 143(12):768-769, March 16,
1981

P-pills and hypertension, by K. Rasmussen. UGESKRIFT FOR LAEGER.
144(7):491-492, February 15, 1982

P-pills and inflammatory intestinal disease, by J. N. Sørensen, et
al. UGESKRIFT FOR LAEGER. 143(37):2365-2366, September 7, 1981

Parens patriae: judicial authority to order the sterilization of
mental incompetents, by N. J. West. JOURNAL OF LEGAL MEDICINE.
2(4):523-542, December 1981

Parent versus child: H.L. v. Matheson (101 S Ct 1164) and the new
abortion litigation. WISCONSIN LAW REVIEW. 1982:75-116, 1982

Parental chromosomal rearrangements associated with repetitive
spontaneous abortions, by J. L. Simpson, et al. FERTILITY AND
STERILITY. 36(5):584-590, November 1981

Parental chromosome translocations and fetal loss, by C. Tsenghi, et
al. OBSTETRICS AND GYNECOLOGY. 58(4):456-458, October 1981

Parental involvement: selling family planning clinics short [re-
esearch], by F. F. Furstenberg, Jr., et al. FAMILY PLANNING PER-
SPECTIVES. 14:140-144, May-June 1982

Parental notification: is it settled? (possible effects of the U.S.
Supreme Court decision in H.L. v. Matheson, upholding a Utah state
law requiring that all minors notify their parents before obtaining
an abortion), by P. Donovan. FAMILY PLANNING PERSPECTIVES. 13:
243-246, September-October 1981

--: a state-created obstacle to a minor woman's right of privacy.
GOLDEN GATE UNIVERSITY LAW REVIEW. 12:579-603, Summer 1982

Parental rights. AMERICA. 146:143-144, February 27, 1982

Parent's attitudes toward sterilization of their mentally retarded children, by L. Wolf, et al. AMERICAN JOURNAL OF MENTAL DEFICIEN-CY. 87:122-129, September 1982

Parts of Massachusetts abortion law deemed of doubtful constitution-ality. FAMILY LAW REPORTER: COURT OPINIONS. 7(17):2272-2274, March 3, 1981

Patentex-Oval: contraceptive intrauterine device, by B. Horoszko-Husiatynska, et al. WIADOMOSCI LEKARSKIE. 34(12):985-989, 1982

The pattern of sterilisation [editorial]. NEW ZEALAND MEDICAL JOUR-NAL. 94(689):92-93, August 12, 1981

Patterns of IUD acceptance and removals in a geographically defined urban slum area in Ludhiana, Punjab, by P. S. Zachariah, et al. JOURNAL OF FAMILY WELFARE. 28:70-76, March 1982

Peliosis hepatis, oral contraceptives and hepatic carcinoma: a case treated surgically, by J. Tocornal, et al. REVISTA MEDICA DE CHILE. 109(3):236-238, March 1981

Pelvic infection after abortion associated with chlamydia tracho-matis, by B. R. Møller, et al. OBSTETRICS AND GYNECOLOGY. 59(2):210-213, 1982

Pelvic infection after elective abortion associated with chlamydia trachomatis, by B. R. Møller, et al. OBSTETRICS AND GYNECOLOGY. 59(2):210-213, February 1982

Pelvic inflammatory disease among women using copper intrauterine de-vices, progestasert, oral contraceptive pills or vaginal contracep-tive pills. A 4-year prospective investigation, by B. Larsson, et al. CONTRACEPTIVE DELIVERY SYSTEMS. 2(3):237-242, 1981

Pensioners threatened by abortion. SOCIAL JUSTICE REVIEW. 72:215-216, November-December 1981

A people's movement for health and family planning, by I. Gandhi. INDIAN JOURNAL OF PEDIATRICS. 48(393):389-394, July-August 1981

Peptid contraception—new principles for family planning, by S. J. Nillius. LAKARTIDNINGEN. 78(34):2845-2848, August 19, 1978

Perceived physician humaneness, patient atitude, and satisfaction with the pill as a contraceptive, by D. J. Kallen, et al. JOURNAL OF HEALTH AND SOCIAL BEHAVIOR. 22(3):256-267, September 1981

Perceived versus computed change: can perceived measures tell us something that computed measures cannot?, by E. S. Herold, et al. EDUCATION AND PSYCHOLOGICAL MEASUREMENT. 41:701-707, Autumn 1981

Percentage of deaths caused by contraception increases. OUR SUNDAY VISITOR. 71:7, June 13, 1982

Perception of methods of contraception: a semantic differential study, by P. K. Kee, et al. JOURNAL OF BIOSOCIAL SCIENCE. 13(2):209-218, April 1981

Pericentric inversion of chromosome 9 in couples with repeated spon-

taneous abortion, by M. G. Tibiletti, et al. ACTA EUROPAEA FER-
TILITATIS. 12(3):245-248, September 1981

A perilous paradox: the contraceptive behavior of college students,
by K. D. Rindskopf. JOURNAL OF THE AMERICAN COLLEGE HEALTH ASSO-
CIATION. 30(3):113-118, December 1981

Periodic abstinence: how well do new approaches work?. POPULATION
REPORTS. (3):133-171, September 1981

--, by L. S. Liskin, et al. POPULATION REPORTS. 9(4):33, September
1981

Permanent decision making: counselling women for sterilization, by J.
R. Goodman, et al. SOCIAL CASEWORK. 63(2):73-81, February 1982

Personal and socio-economic variables in relation with attitudes
toward planned family, by M. Bhargava, et al. INDIAN JOURNAL OF
CLINICAL PSYCHOLOGY. 8(1):35-38, March 1981

Personal computer for birth control (computer being developed that
would tell a woman when she is fertile). PERSONAL COMPUTING. 6:
15, March 1982

Personality factors related to black teenage pregnancy and abortion,
by R. Falk, et al. PSYCHOLOGY OF WOMEN QUARTERLY. 5(5 Suppl):737-
746, 1981

Personhood, abortion and the law, by B. J. Verkamp. AMERICA.
146(3):46-48, January 23, 1982

A perspective multicentre trial of the ovulation method of natural
family planning. II. The effectiveness phase. FERTILITY AND
STERILITY. 36(5):591-598, November 1981

A perspective on progestogens in oral contraceptives, by W. N.
Spellacy. AMERICAN JOURNAL OF OBSTETRICS AND GYNECOLOGY. 142(6 Pt
2):717, March 15, 1982

Pharmacokinetic and pharmacodynamic studies with vaginal devices
releasing norethisterone at a constant, near zero order, by B. M.
Landgren, et al. CONTRACEPTION. 24(1):29-44, July 1981

Pharmacologic control of estrus in bitch and queen, by T. J. Burke.
VETERINARY CLINICS OF NORTH AMERICA. SMALL ANIMAL PRACTICE. 12(1):
79-84, February 1982

Pharmacological study of the effect of radix trichosanthis on terminating early pregnancy, by M. H. Zhou, et al. CHUNG-KUO YAO LI
HSUEH PAO. 17(3):176-181, March 1982

Pharmacological study on chemically induced tubal occlusion in
rabbits. CHUNG HUA FU CHAN KO TSA CHIH. 14(2):87-90, April 1979

Philosophical ethical aspects of the interruption of pregnancy, by G.
Henning, et al. DEUTSCHE ZEITSCHRIFT FUR PHILOSOPHIE. 30:892-902,
1982

Philosophical perspectives of iatrogenic abortion, by C. W. de
Muelenaere. SOUTH AFRICAN MEDICAL JOURNAL. 61(25):959-961, June

19, 1982

Philosophy of medicine in the United Kingdom, by D. Lamb. META-
MEDICINE. 3:3-34, February 1982

Phlegmasia cerulea dolens as a complication of short-course oral
contraceptives for dysfunctional bleeding, by C. C. Coddington.
SOUTHERN MEDICAL JOURNAL. 75(3):377-378, March 1982

Pill and breast cancer; few answers yet. NEW SCIENTIST. 91:7, July
2, 1981

Pill & diazepam, by S. Katz. CHATELAINE. 55:26, August 1982

Pill and IUD use at PPFA clinics decline: diaphragm use rises.
FAMILY PLANNING PERSPECTIVES. 14:152-153, May-June 1982

The pill and the thoracic outlet and bilateral carpal tunnel syndromes, by J. C. Chisholm. JOURNAL OF THE NATIONAL MEDICAL ASSO-
CIATION. 73(10):995-996, October 1981

Pill does not increase risk of breast cancer, even after years of
use. FAMILY PLANNING PERSPECTIVES. 14:216-219, July-August 1982

The pill: an evaluation of recent studies, by A. Rosenfield. JOHNS
HOPKINS MEDICAL JOURNAL. 150(5):177-180, May 1982

Pill-induced disability (information from interview with Susan
Odgers), by A. Fugh-Berman. OFF OUR BACKS. 12:11+, January 1982

The pill: the lowest possible dosage [interview by Werner Bauch], by
M. H. Briggs, et al. ZFA: ZEITSCHRIFT FUR ALLGEMEINMEDIZIN.
58(12):703-705, April 30, 1982

Pill use in twenty developing countries. JOURNAL OF FAMILY WELFARE.
28:93, June 1982

Pill users protected against PID if they have used OCs for longer
than one year. FAMILY PLANNING PERSPECTIVES. 14:32-33, January-
February 1982

Pituitary and gonadal function during the use of progesterone- or
progesterone-estradiol-releasing vaginal rings, by J. Toivonen.
INTERNATIONAL JOURNAL OF FERTILITY. 25(2):106-111, 1980

Pituitary and ovarian function during contraception with one subcutaneous implant releasing a progestin, St-1435, by P. Lahteenmaki, et al. CONTRACEPTION. 25(3):299-306, March 1982

Pituitary-ovarian function after tubal ligation, by F. Alvarez-
Sanchez, et al. FERTILITY AND STERILITY. 36(5):606-609, November
1981

Pituitary response to LHRH stimulation in women on oral contraceptives: a followup dose rsponse study, by L. S. Wan, et al. CONTRA-
CEPTION. 24(3):229-234, September 1981

Pituitary responsiveness to gonadotropin-releasing hormone (GnRH)
and thyrotropin-releasing hormone (TRH) during different phases of
the same cycle of oral contraceptive steroid therapy, by F. R.

Perez-Lopez, et al. FERTILITY AND STERILITY. 37(6):767-772, June 1982

Placental changes as a consequence of the interruption of midtrimeter pregnancies by prostaglandin F2 alpha. A study of 23 cases, by A. Ornoy, et al. ISRAEL JOURNAL OF MEDICAL SCIENCES. 18(2):235-240, February 1982

Placental findings in spontaneous abortions and stillbirths, by A. Ornoy, et al. TERATOLOGY. 24(3):243-252, December 1981

Plan casts doubts on abortion aid, by N. Brozan. NEW YORK TIMES MAGAZINE. p. A1, February 8, 1982

Planificaria familiei in perspectiva sociologica, by V. Trebici. VIITORUL SOCIAL. 8(1):171-176, January-March 1981

The planned family is a misconception (Catholic view), by J. McGowan. US CATHOLIC. 47:31-32, November 1982

Planned parenthood ads to fight anti-abortionists. MARKETING AND MEDIA DECISIONS. 17:32, May 1982

Planned parenthood: ideas for the 1980s, by C. W. Tyler, Jr. FAMILY PLANNING PERSPECTIVES. 14:221-223, July-August 1982

Planned Parenthood League of Massachusetts v. Bellotti, 40 U S L W 2532. AMERICAN JOURNAL OF TRIAL ADVOCACY. 5:166-171, Summer 1981

--, 641 F 2d 1006. JOURNAL OF FAMILY LAW. 20:158-161, September 1981

Planning the family way, by Z. Pauncefort. NURSING MIRROR AND MID-WIVE'S JOURNAL. 154(Community Forum #2):ii+, February 10, 1982

Plants of Haiti used as antifertility agents, by B. Weniger, et al. JOURNAL OF ETHNOPHARMACOLOGY. 6(1):67-84, July 1982

Plasma and erythrocyte membrane fatty acids in oral contraceptive users, by A. M. A. Fehily, et al. CLINICA CHIMICA ACTA. 120(1): 41-48, March 26, 1982

Plasma concentrations of oestrone, oestradiol, oestriol and proge-sterone during mechanical stretch-induced abortion at mid-trimes-ter, by Y. Manabe, et al. JOURNAL OF ENDOCRINOLOGY. 91(3):385-389, December 1981

Plasma levels of ethinylestradiol (EE) during cyclic treatment with combined oral contraceptives, by J. M. Kaufman, et al. CONTRACEP-TION. 24(5):589-602, November 1981

Plasma levels of medroxyprogesterone acetate, sex-hormone binding globulin, gonadal steroids, gonadotropins and prolactin in women during long-term use of depo-medroxy-progesterone acetate (depo-provera) as a contraceptive agent, by S. Jeppsson, et al. ACTA ENDOCRINOLOGICA. 99(3):339-343, March 1982

Plasminogen, fibrinogen, alpha 2-antiplasmin and antithrombin-III levels during a single cycle of a combined oral contraceptive regime, by G. Baele, et al. ACTA CLINICA BELGICA. 36(6):280-285,

1981

Platelet aggregation in response to 5-HT in migraine patients taking oral contraceptives [letter], by E. Hanington, et al. LANCET. 1(8278):967-968, April 24, 1982

Point of view: D & E midtrimester abortion: a medical innovation, by S. Lewit. WOMEN AND HEALTH. 7:49-55, September 1982

Political economy of sexism in industrial health [with discussion], by M. Felker. SOCIAL SCIENCE AND MEDICINE. 16(1):3-18, 1982

Politics of contraception, by A. Charney. CHATELAINE. 55:57+, April 1982

The politics of fertility. How the population situation affects political institutions. Part 1, by J. A. Loraine. MIDWIFE, HEALTH VISITOR AND COMMUNITY NURSE. 17:498-499+, December 1981

Polygyny and family planning in Sub-Saharan Africa, by J. E. Brown. STUDIES IN FAMILY PLANNING. 12(8-9):322, August-September 1981

Polyurethane contraceptive vaginal sponge: product modifications resulting from user experience, by R. Aznar, et al. CONTRACEPTION. 24(3):235-244, September 1981

The Pope and sexuality, by R. Modras. NATIONAL CATHOLIC REPORTER. 18:20+, January 15, 1982

Pope sees need for special considerations for women. OUR SUNDAY VISITOR. 70:7, December 20, 1981

Population and birth planning in the People's Republic of China. POPULATION REPORTS. 10(1):   , January-February 1982

--, by P. C. Chen, et al. POPULATION REPORTS. (25):J577-618, January-February 1982

Population-based lipoprotein lipid reference values for pregnant women compared to nonpregnant women classified by sex hormone usage, by R. H. Knopp, et al. AMERICAN JOURNAL OF OBSTETRICS AND GYNE-COLOGY. 143(6):626-637, July 15, 1982

The population debate: a survey of opinions of a professional organization's membership, by M. B. Toney, et al. POPULATION AND EN-VIRONMENT. 4(3):156, Fall 1981

Population growth and contraception in Africa [editorial]. BRITISH MEDICAL JOURNAL. 284(6325):1333-1334, May 1, 1982

--[letter], by P. V. Cosgrove. BRITISH MEDICAL JOURNAL. 284(6319): 900-901, March 20, 1982

--[letter], by A. R. Walker, et al. BRITISH MEDICAL JOURNAL. 284(6316):657-659, February 27, 1982

Population studies and population policy in China, by J. S. Aird. POPULATION AND DEVELOPMENT REVIEW. 8:267-297, June 1982

Porphyria cutanea tarda in female patients with speical regard to

hormonal contraception, by H. Fiedler, et al. DERMATOLOGISCHE
MONATSSCHRIFT. 167(8):481-485, 1981

Portal and superior mesenteric venous thrombosis secondary to oral
contraceptive trreatment, by D. Abet, et al. JOURNAL DES MALADIES
VASCULAIRES. 7(1):59-63, 1982

Portal vein thrombosis and fatal pulmonary thromboembolism associated
with oral contraceptive treatment, by J. P. Capron, et al. JOURNAL
OF CLINICAL GASTROENTEROLOGY. 3(3):295-298, September 1981

La posizione di S. Thommaso Sull'aborto, by Giovanni. REVISTA DOCTOR
COMNIS. 34:296-311, September-October 1981

Possible interactions of antihistamines and antibiotics with oral
contraceptive effectiveness, by E. A. DeSano, Jr., et al. FERTIL-
ITY AND STERILITY. 37(6):853-854, June 1982

Possible interference of synthetic estroprogestins with thyroid
hormone production, by A. Paggi, et al. CLINICAL THERAPEUTICS.
98(4):349-363, August 31, 1981

Possible relationship between circulating anticoagulants and recurrent abortion, by J. R. Duran-Suarez, et al. HAEMATOLOGICA.
67(2):320-321, April 1981

Post-bill amenorrhea following hormonal contraceptive therapy in
adolescence, by M. Brandt, et al. ARZTLICHE JUGENDKUNDE. 72(4):
241-245, 1981

Postcoital antifertility effect of mentha arvensis, by D. Kanjanapothi, et al. CONTRACEPTION. 24(5):559-567, November 1981

Post-family planning acceptance experience in the Caribbean: St.
Kitts-Nevis and St. Vincent, by J. Bailey, et al. STUDIES IN
FAMILY PLANNING. 13(2):44-58, February 1982

Postligation tubal pregnancy, by S. K. Chaudhuri, et al. JOURNAL OF
THE INDIAN MEDICAL ASSOCIATION. 78(3):50-51, February 1, 1982

Postpartum contraception, by D. A. Edelman, et al. INTERNATIONAL
JOURNAL OF GYNAECOLOGY AND OBSTETRICS. 19(4):305-311, August 1981

--, by P. A. Hillard. PARENTS. 57:82+, December 1982

Post-partum development of a mesenteric venous infarct and portal
thrombosis in a young woman taking an oral contraceptive, by X.
Quancard, et al. JOURNAL DES MALADIES VASCULAIRES. 6(4):307-311,
1981

Postpartum sterilization by operating-room nurses in Thailand, by S.
Koetsawang, et al. INTERNATIONAL JOURNAL OF GYNAECOLOGY AND OB-
STETRICS. 19(3):201-204, June 1981

Postpartum sterilization in cesarean section and non-cesarean section
deliveries: United States, 1970-75 [research], by P. J. Placek, et
al. AMERICAN JOURNAL OF PUBLIC HEALTH. 71(11):1258-1261, November
1981

Post-partum sterilization in Sao Paulo state, Brazil, by B. Janowitz, et al. JOURNAL OF BIOLOGICAL SCIENCE. 14(2):179-187, April 1982

Post-pill amenorrhea [a causal study], by M. G. Hull, et al. FER-
  TILITY AND STERILITY. 36(4):472-476, October 1981

Postpill pregnancies last longer. NURSES DRUG ALERT. 6:10, February
  1982

The post-pill secondary amenorrhea: etiology and treatment, by J. Del
  Olmo, et al. ACTA EUROPAEA FERTILITATIS. 12(2):133-139, June 1981

Post-tubal ligation hysterectomy, by A. S. Gupta, et al. JOURNAL OF
  THE INDIAN MEDICAL ASSOCIATION. 76(11):208-210, June 1, 1981

Post-tubal ligation syndrome or iatrogenic hydrosalpinx, by M. G.
  Gregory. JOURNAL OF THE TENNESSEE MEDICAL ASSOCIATION. 74(10):
  712-714, October 1981

Potential constitutional issues raised by the proposed amendments to
  the Georgia abortion statute, by R. N. Berg. JOURNAL OF THE MEDI-
  CAL ASSOCIATION OF GEORGIA. 71(20:128-131, February 1982

Potential demand for voluntary female sterilization in the 1980s: the
  compelling need for a nonsurgical method, by E. Kessel, et al.
  FERTILITY AND STERILITY. 37(6):725-733, June 1982

Potential persons and murder: a reply to John Woods "Engineered
  Death", by J. C. Moskop. DIALOGUE. 21:307-315, June 1982

Potential use of male antifertility agents in developed countries, by
  G. Bialy, et al. CHEMOTHERAPY. 27(Suppl 2):102-106, 1981

Pour ou contre l'avortement--pour assainir le debat, by L. Ducharme.
  RELATIONS. 42:96-99, April 1982

Pour ou contre une politique nataliste au Quebec (eight papers presented at the 49th meeting of the Association canadienne-francaise
  pour l'avancement des sciences, Sherbrooke, May 13-15, 1981).
  CAHIERS QUEBECOIS DE DEMOGRAPHIE. 10(2):139-303, 1981.

Power of Congress to change constitutional decisions of the Supreme
  Court: the Human Life Bill, by T. I. Emerson. NORTHWESTERN UNIVER-
  SITY LAW REVIEW. 77:129-142, April 1982

Practising prevention. Contraception, by M. J. Bull. BRITISH MEDICAL
  JOURNAL. 284(6328):1535-1536, May 22, 1982

Pregnancy abnormalities among personnel at a virological laboratory,
  by G. Axelsson, et al. AMERICAN JOURNAL OF INDUSTRIAL MEDICINE.
  1(2):129-137, 1980

Pregnancy after reproductive failure, by C. C. Floyd. AMERICAN
  JOURNAL OF NURSING. 81(11):2050-2053, November 1981

Pregnancy, contraception and the family-planning clinic: from the
  woman's point of view (studies of 3635 puerperas in 6 Lombard
  hospital obstetrical departments), by G. Remotti, et al. ANNALI DI
  OSTETRICIA GINECOLOGIA, MEDICINA PERINATALE. 103(1):7-47, January-
  February 1982

Pregnancy rates during long-term use of copper intrauterine devices, by A. Huber, et al. CONTRACEPTIVE DELIVERY SYSTEMS. 3(2):99-102, 1982

Pregnancy roulette (taking chances with birth control), by L. Draegin. MADEMOISELLE. 88:122-123+, October 1982

Pregnancy termination in dogs with novel non-hormonal compounds. Studies of 2-(3-ethoxy-phenyl)-5,6-dihydro-s-triazole [5,1-a] isoquinoline (DL 204-IT), by G. Galliani, et al. ARZNEIMITTEL-FORSCHUNG. 32(2):123-127, 1982

Pregnancy termination in patients with pregnancy-induced hypertension or eclampsia at less than 22 weeks' gestation, by M. B. Sampson, et al. AMERICAN JOURNAL OF OBSTETRICS AND GYNECOLOGY. 143(4):474-475, June 15, 1982

Preliminary experience with a family planning risk-scoring system, by W. N. Spellacy, et al. FERTILITY AND STERILITY. 36(4):527-528, October 1981

Preliminary findings of personality differences between nulliparas and repeated aborters along the dimensions of locus of control and impulsivity, by G. D. Gibb, et al. PSYCHOLOGICAL REPORTS. 49(2): 413-414, October 1981

A preliminary pharmacologicl trial of the monthly injectable contraceptive cycloprovera, by K. Fotherby, et al. CONTRACEPTION. 25(3):261-272, March 1982

A preliminary report on the intracervical contraceptive device--its effect on cervical mucus, by H. A. Pattinson, et al. ADVANCES IN EXPERIMENTAL MEDICINE AND BIOLOGY. 144:289-291, 1982

A preliminary report on the relationship between serum anti-thrombin III concentration in pre- and post-operative patients and in women on oral contraceptives, by S. H. Ton, et al. MEDICAL JOURNAL OF MALAYSIA. 36(4):212-214, December 1981

A preliminary study on the mechanism of uterine excitant action of rivanol in guinea-pigs, by W. Q. Liu, et al. CHUNG-KUO YAO LI HSUEH PAO. 17(1):58-60, January 1982

Premature labor after three miscarriages, by N. H. Lauersen. HOSPITAL PRACTICE. 17(5):199+, May 1982

Premenstrual complaints: II. Influence of oral contraceptives, by B. Andersch, et al. ACTA OBSTETRICIA ET GYNECOLOGICA SCANDINAVICA. 60(6):579-583, 1981

Prenatal diagnosis [letter]. JOURNAL OF THE AMERICAN ACADEMY OF DERMATOLOGY. 5(6):700-702, December 1981

Prenatal diagnosis and genetic counseling in 21 trisomy: its impact on family planning, by G. Evers-Keilbooms, et al. JOURNAL DE GENETIQUE HUMAINE. 28(5):147-159, February 1981

Prenatal illness as a marker of prenatal individuality, by H. Berger. PAEDIATRIE UND PAEDOLOGIE. 17(2):133-139, 1982

The Prentif contraceptive cervical cap: acceptability aspects and
their implications for future cap design, by J. P. Koch. CONTRA-
CEPTION. 25(2):161-173, February 1982

--: a contemporary study of its clinical safety and effectiveness, by
J. P. Koch. CONTRACEPTION. 25(2):135-159, February 1982

Prescribing for unlawful sexual intercourse, by D. Brahams. PRAC-
TITIONER. 226(1368):1025-1026, June 1982

Prescribing the 'pill' for minors [letter], by P. Gerber. MEDICAL
JOURNAL OF AUSTRALIA. 1(11):483, May 29, 1982

Present sakes and future prospects: the status of early abortion, by
P. Bassen. PHILOSOPHY AND PUBLIC AFFAIRS. 11:314-337, August 1982

President Reagan stands firm on pro-life views. OUR SUNDAY VISITOR.
71:8, August 1, 1982

Prevention of adolescent pregnancy: a developmental perspective, by
W. G. Cobliner. BIRTH DEFECTS. 17(3):34-47, 1981

Prevention of oestrus and/or pregnancy in dogs by methods other than
ovariohysterectomy, by A. C. Okkens, et al. TIJDSCHRIFT VOOR DIER-
GENEESKUNDE. 106(23):1215-1225, December 1981

Primary malignant nephrosclerosis (PMN)--a case of an irreversible
renal failure following septic abortion, by M. Belicza, et al.
LIJECNICKI VJESNIK. 102(7-8):432-435, July-August 1980

Private cause of action for abortion expenses under state paternity
statutes, by G. Schachter. WOMEN'S RIGHTS LAW REPORTER. 7:63-90,
Winter 1982

Pro-, anti-choice groups square off in New Jersey, by L. Hamilton.
NEW DIRECTIONS FOR WOMEN. 11:22, September-October 1982

Probate courts have power to order mental incompetent's sterilization. FAMILY LAW REPORTER: COURT OPINIONS. 8(24):2344-2347, April
20, 1982

The problem of abortion in the light of clinical statistics, by R.
Schwarz. ZEITSCHRIFT FUR DIE GESAMTE HYGIENE. 27(7):533-534, July
7, 1981

Problems in adolescent contraception, by L. Aresin. ZEITSCHRIFT FUR
DIE GESAMTE HYGIENE. 27(7):560-561, July 7, 1981

Problems of contraception in adolescents, by P. O. Hubinont. REVUE
MEDICALE DE BRUXELLES. 3(6):425-430, June 1982

Problems of contraception in sexually active female adolescents. Results of an empirical study, by S. Rehpenning. ZEITSCHRIFT FUR DIE
GESAMTE HYGIENE. 27(7):556-559, July 7, 1981

Problems of interpreting socially controverisal legislation, by J. K.
Bentil. THE SOLICITORS' JOURNAL. 125:786-788, November 20,
1981

Problems posed by the decision to perform therapeutic abortions in

the current practice of the prenatal diagnosis of fetal malformations, by A. Choiset, et al. ACQUISITIONS MEDICALES RECENTES.
198:137-147, 1981

Professional norms, personal attitudes, and medical practice: the
case of abortion, by C. A. Nathanson, et al. JOURNAL OF HEALTH AND
SOCIAL BEHAVIOR. 22(3):198-211, September 1981

Profile compassion or crusade?, by J. Evans. AMERICA. 147:373-374,
December 11, 1982

Progesterone-binding globulin and progesterone in guinea-pigs after
ovariectomy, abortion and parturition, by J. J. Evans, et al.
JOURNAL OF STEROID BIOCHEMISTRY. 16(2):171-173, February 1982

Progestogen effects and their relationship to lipoprotein changes. A
report from the Oral Contraception Study of the Royal College of
General Practitioners, by S. J. Wingrave. ACTA OBSTETRICIA ET
GYNECOLOGICA SCANDINAVICA. SUPPLEMENT. 105:33-36, 1982

Progestogens and arterial disease--evidence from the Royal College of
General Practitioners' study, by C. R. Kay. AMERICAN JOURNAL OF
OBSTETRICS AND GYNECOLOGY. 142(6 Pt 2):762-765, March 15, 1982

Progestogens in cardiovascular diseases: an introduction to the epidemiologic data, by J. I. Mann. AMERICAN JOURNAL OF OBSTETRICS AND
GYNECOLOGY. 142(6 Pt 2):752-757, March 15, 1982

Prognostic value of human chorionic gonadotropin, progesterone, 17-
beta estradiol and the echoscopic examination in threatened abortion during the 1st trimester, by I. Stoppelli, et al. CLINICAL
AND EXPERIMENTAL OBSTETRICS AND GYNECOLOGY. 8(1):6-11, 1981

Pro-life unity could be crucial to Hatch action, by R. B. Shaw. OUR
SUNDAY VISITOR. 70:3, March 28, 1982

Pro-life versus pro-choice: another look at the abortion controversy
in the U.S., by D. Granberg, et al. SOCIOLOGY AND SOCIAL RESERACH.
65(4):424-434, July 1981

Pro-lifers claim senator blocks Hatch amendment. OUR SUNDAY VISITOR.
71:3, July 18, 1982

Pro-lifers director raps magazine's abortion survey. OUR SUNDAY
VISITOR. 71:8, September 19, 1982

Pro-lifers strong in U.S. agency, by M. Meehan. NATIONAL CATHOLIC
REPORTER. 18(1):23, December 11, 1981

Pro-lifers, unions pose Catholic hospitals' dilemma, by L. H. Pumphrey. OUR SUNDAY VISITOR. 71:5, October 10, 1982

Pro-lifers urged to work for common goal, by M. Meehan. NATIONAL
CATHOLIC REPORTER. 18:5, April 23, 1982

A prolonged chloroprocaine epidural block in a postpartum patient
with abnormal pseudocholinesterase, by B. R. Kuhnert, et al.
ANESTHESIOLOGY. 56(6):477-478, June 1982

Prolonged in utero retention and mummification of a Macaca mulatta

fetus, by E. Mueller-Heubach, et al. JOURNAL OF MEDICAL PRIMATOLO-
GY. 10(4-5):265-268, 1981

Prolonged use of a diaphragm and toxic shock syndrome, by E. A.
Baehler, et al. FERTILITY AND STERILITY. 38(2):248-250, August
1982

Promoting N F P: who is responsible?, by P. Marx. HOMILETIC AND
PASTORAL REVIEW. 82:25-31, April 1982

Prophylactic antibiotic therapy in induced abortion. A cost benefit
analysis, by S. Sonne-Holm, et al. UGESKRIFT FOR LAEGER. 143(14):
881-883, March 30, 1981

Proposed law, court ruling spotlight parents' rights, by R. B. Shaw.
OUR SUNDAY VISITOR. 70:8, April 25, 1982

Proposed rule on teen-age birth control draws some surprising public
opposition [Reagan administration proposals that federally supported clinics notify parents of girls who seek birth control help], by
B. Schorr. WALL STREET JOURNAL. 199:25, April 2, 1982

A prospective cohort study of oral contraceptives and brast cancer,
by E. J. Trapido. JNCI: JOURNAL OF THE NATIONAL CANCER INSTITUTE.
67(5):1011-1015, November 1981

Prospective studies on pregnancy following induced and spontaneous
abortion of primigravidae and assessment of fertility. IV. Report,
by G. Schott, et al. ZENTRALBLATT FUR GYNAEKOLOGIE.
104(7):397-404, 1982

Prospects for planning in the global family. NEW SCIENTIST. 94:291,
April 29, 1982

Prostaglandin E and F2 alpha levels in plasma and amniotic fluid
during mid-trimester abortion induced by trichosanthin, by Y. F.
Wang, et al. PROSTAGLANDINS. 22(2):289-294, August 1981

Prostaglandin E_2 pessaries to facilitate first trimester aspiration
termination, by I. Z. MacKenzie, et al. AMERICAN JOURNAL OF OB-
STETRICS AND GYNECOLOGY. 88(10):1033-1037, October 1981

Prostaglandin-oxytocin induced rupture of the posterior fornix. A
complication after induced abortion, by J. Molin. UGESKRIFT FOR
LAEGER. 143(29):1841, July 13, 1981

Prostaglandins from bedside observation to a family of drugs, by S.
Bergstrom. PROGRESS IN LIPID RESEARCH. 20:7-12, 1981

Prostaglandins in human reproduction, by M. P. Embrey. BRITISH
MEDICAL JOURNAL. 283(6306):1563-1566, December 12, 1981

Protection against endometrial carcinoma by combination-product oral
contraceptives, by B. S. Hulka, et al. JAMA: JOURNAL OF THE
AMERICAN MEDICAL ASSOCIATION. 247(4):475-477, January 22-29, 1982

--[letter], by J. R. Evrard. JAMA: JOURNAL OF THE AMERICAN MEDICAL
ASSOCIATION. 248(6):647-648, August 13, 1982

Protection of ovarian function by oral contraceptives in women receiving chemotherapy for Hodgkin's disease, by R. M. Chapman, et al. BLOOD. 58(4):849-851, October 1981

Provision of rubella immunization in general practitioner family planning services, by N. A. Black. JOURNAL OF THE ROYAL COLLEGE OF GENERAL PRACTITIONERS. 31(231):593-595, October 1981

Prudence since the pill, by H. Chappell. NEW SOCIETY. pp. 372-374, September 2, 1982

Psychiatric aspects of therapeutic abortion, by B. K. Doane, et al. CANADIAN MEDICAL ASSOCIATION JOURNAL. 125(5):427-432, September 1, 1981

Psychiatric complications of progesterone and oral contraceptives, by I. D. Glick, et al. JOURNAL OF CLINICAL PSYCHOPHARMACOLOGY. 1(6): 350-367, November 1981

Psychic attitude of women to irreversible contraception, by R. Sudik, et al. ZENTRALBLATT FUR GYNAEKOLOGIE. 103(20):1242-1254, 1981

Psychic reactions of adolescent girls after legal abortion, by M. Merz. THERAPEUTISCHE UMSCHAU. 39(6):490-491, June 1982

Psychological and physical outcome after elective tubal steriliza-tion, by P. Cooper, et al. JOURNAL OF PSYCHOSOMATIC RESEARCH. 25(5):357-360, 1981

Psychological and social aspects of induced abortion, by J. A. Handy. BRITISH JOURNAL OF CLINICAL PSYCHOLOGY. 21(Pt 1):29-41, February 1982

Psychological aspects in counseling for preventive agents, by H. Sjorstrom. JORDEMODERN. 94(1):14-22, January 1981

Psychological aspects of contraception with the multiload Cu250, by U. Rauchfleisch. GYNAEKOLOGISCHE RUNDSCHAU. 21(3):159-165, 1981

Psychological condition of the desire to have children and its ful-fillment (empirical report), by A. Geissler. ZEITSCHRIFT FUR DIE GESAMTE HYGIENE. 27(7):522-525, July 7, 1981

A psychological investigation of contraceptive behavior, by V. A. Byron. DISSERTATION ABSTRACTS INTERNATIONAL. B. p. 242, 1982

Psychological preparation for surgery: patient recall of information, by A. E. Reading. JOURNAL OF PSYCHOSOMATIC RESEARCH. 25(1):57-62, 1981

Psychological problems of hysterectomy for patients, gynecologists, and psychiatrists: investigations on 75 women, by M. V. Costantini, et al. PSICHIATRIA GENERALE E DELL ETA EVOLUTIVA. 18(3):229-245, 1980

Psychological sequelae to elective sterilisation: a prospective study, by P. Cooper, et al. BRITISH MEDICAL JOURNAL. 284(6314): 461-464, February 13, 1982

--[letter], by M. Thiery, et al. BRITISH MEDICAL JOURNAL. 284(6328):1557, May 22, 1982

Psychosexual attitudes in the female following sterilization, by H. H. Wynter, et al. INTERNATIONAL SURGERY. 64(5):31-33, August-October 1979

Psychosocial aspects of early pregnancy termination [research], by R. A. Brown. NEW ZEALAND NURSING FORUM. 10(1):8-10, 1982

Psychosocial maturity and teenage contraceptive use: an investigation of decision-making and communication skills, by G. Cvetkovich, et al. POPULATION AND ENVIRONMENT: BEHAVIORAL AND SOCIAL ISSUES. 4(4):211-226, Winter 1981

Psychosomatic aspects of gynecological conditions: psychiatric disorder after hysterectomy, by D. Gath, et al. JOURNAL OF PSYCHO-SOMATIC RESEARCH. 25(5):347-355, 1981

Public funded abortions in FY 1980 and FY 1981, by R. B. Gold. FAMILY PLANNING PERSPECTIVES. 14:204-207, July-August 1982

Public funding of contraceptive services, 1980-1982 (United States) [research], by B. Nestor. FAMILY PLANNING PERSPECTIVES. 14:198-203, July-August 1982

Public opinion bombshell: prochoice majority vows to vote, by L. C. Wohl. MS. 11:70-71+, July-August 1982

Public school programs for adolescent pregnancy and parenthood [an assessment], by G. L. Zellman. FAMILY PLANNING PERSPECTIVES. 14(1):15, January-February 1982

Publicly funded abortions in FY 1980 and FY 1981, by R. B. Gold. FAMILY PLANNING PERSPECTIVES. 14:204-207, July-August 1982

Pulmonary embolism in a 14-year-old following an elective abortion, R. Nudelman, et al. PEDIATRICS. 68(4):584-586, October 1981

Quantitative analysis of ethynodiol diacetate and ethinyl estradiol/ mestranol in oral contraceptive tablets by high-performance liquid chromatography, by G. Carignan, et al. JOURNAL OF PHARMACEUTICAL SCIENCES. 71(2):264-266, February 1982

Quantitative analysis of some decision rules for famiy planning in an oriental society, by T. N. Goh. INTERFACES. 11:31-37, April 1981

The quest for a magic bullet, by M. Potts, et al. FAMILY PLANNING PERSPECTIVES. 13(6):269-271, November-December 1981

RIA of insulin in the determination of aberrations in the glycide metabolism in women using steroidal contraceptive preparations, by V. Dvorak, et al. ACTA UNIVERSITATIS PALACKIANAE OLOMUCENSIS FACULTATIS MEDICAE. 101:149-154, 1981

Race-specific patterns of abortion use by American teenagers [research], by N. V. Ezzard, et al. AMERICAN JOURNAL OF PUBLIC HEALTH. 72(8):809-814, August 1982

Radioimmunologic evaluation of the concentration of placental lacto-gen in threatened abortions, by W. Szymanski, et al. ACTA UNIVER-SITATIS PALACKIANAE OLOMUCENSIS FACULTATIS MEDICAE. 101:57-63, 1981

Radioimmunologic methods of determination of hormones in the blood in
pregnancy and in abortion and premature labor, by S. D. Bulienko,
et al. ACTA UNIVERSITATIS PALACKIANAE OLOMUCENSIS FACULTATIS MEDI-
CAE. 101:11-14, 1981

A randomized double-blind study of two combined and two progestogen-
only oral contraceptives, by A. Sheth, et al. CONTRACEPTION.
25(3):243-252, March 1982

A randomized, double-blind study of six combined oral contraceptives,
by S. Koetsawang, et al. CONTRACEPTION. 25(3):231-241, March 1982

Randomized prospective studies on metabolic effects of oral contraceptives, by M. H. Briggs, et al. ACTA OBSTETRICIA ET GYNECOLOGICA
SCANDINAVICA. SUPPLEMENT. 105:25-32, 1982

A randomized prospective study of the use-effectiveness of two methods of natural family planning, by M. E. Wade, et al. AMERICAN
JOURNAL OF OBSTETRICS AND GYNECOLOGY. 14(4):368-376,, October 15,
1981

A randomized study of metabolic effects of four low-estrogen oral
contraceptives: I. Results after 6 cycles, by M. Briggs, et al.
CONTRACEPTION. 23(5):463-471, May 1981

Randomized trial of one versus two days of laminaria treatment prior
to late midtrimester abortion by uterine evacuation [a pilot
study], by P. G. Stubblefield, et al. AMERICAN JOURNAL OF OBSTE-
TRICS AND GYNECOLOGY. 143(4):481-482, June 15, 1982

Ransoming the doomed, by J. Rasmussen. ALBERTA REPORT. 8:45,
November 13, 1981

Rap session on birth control, by T. A. O'Hara. LIGUORIAN. 70:45-48,
October 1982

Rape and abortion in America (dismissal of teacher and rape victim J.
Eckmann for deciding to keep her baby in McHenry County, Ill.), by
L. M. Delloff. CHRISTIAN CENTURY. 99:1037-1038, October 20, 1982

Rare combination of septic abortion and splenic rupture, by K.
Kurveniashki. AKUSHERSTVO I GINEKOLOGIIA. 21(1):89-90, 1982

Readers' position against induced abortion. TIJDSCHRIFT VOR ZIEKEN-
VERPLEGING. 34(17):754-757, August 25, 1981

Reagan appointee dismays right-to-life proponents, by M. Meehan.
NATIONAL CATHOLIC REPORTER. 18:4, June 4, 1982

Reagan: la grande croisade dans les chambres a coucher [adoles-
centes], by L. Wiznitzer. L'ACTUALITE. 7:26, September 1982

Reagan must address key social issues, by C. Thomas. CONSERVATIVE
DIGEST. 8:48, May 1982

Reagan wants parents to be told when teens get contraceptives.
CHRISTIANITY TODAY. 26:41, April 23, 1982

Real-time echography in the diagnosis of threatened abortion: diagnositc and prognostic evaluation compared with urinary HCG determi-

nation, by A. Raimondo, et al. ARCHIVES OF OBSTETRICS AND GYNE-
COLOGY. 85(5):411-421, September-October 1980

Reasoning in the personal and moral domains: adolescent and young
adult women's decision-making regarding abortion, by J. Smentana.
JOURNAL OF APPLIED DEVELOPMENTAL PSYCHOLOGY. 2(3):211-226, December 1981

Recent changes in predictors of abortion attitudes, by S. N.
Barnartt, et al. SOCIOLOGY AND SOCIAL RESEARCH. 66(3):320-334,
April 1982

Recommendations for abortion technics, by E. Ehrig, et al. ZEIT-
SCHRIFT FUR ARZTLICHE FORTBILDUNG. 75(7):305-308, April 1, 1981

Recurrent hemolytic uremic syndrome during oral contraception, by D.
Hauglustaine, et al. CLINICAL NEPHROLOGY. 15(3):148-153, March
1981

Recurrent miscarriage and preterm labour, by G. Chamberlain. CLINI-
CAL OBSTETRICS AND GYNECOLOGY. 9(1):115-130, April 1982

Recurring inflammation of optic nerve after long-time therapy with
hormonal contraceptive anacyclin 28, by H. Huismans. KLINISCHE
MONATSBLAETTER FUR AUGENHEILKUNDE. 180(2):173-175, February 1982

Reduction of fertility of mice by the intrauterine injection of
prostaglandin antagonists, by J. D. Biggers, et al. JOURNAL OF
REPRODUCTIVE FERTILITY. 63(2):365-372, November 1981

Reduction of total and free triiodothyronine in serum after abortion,
by D. Rajkovic, et al. ENDOKRINOLOGIE. 79(1):44-48, February 1982

Reform of penal regulations on abortion in the FRG. In: Topics of
crime research. WISSENSCHAFTLICHE SCHRIFTENREIHE DER HUMBOLDT-
UNIVERSITAT. pp. 57-66, 1980

Refusing to participate in abortions, by H. Creighton. NURSING
MANAGEMENT. 13:27-28, April 1982

Regional dimensions of abortion-facility services, by N. F. Henry.
PROFESSIONAL GEOGRAPHER. 34:65-70, February 1982

Regression of liver cell adenoma. A follow-up study of three consecutive patients after discontinuation of oral contraceptive use,
by H. Buhler, et al. GASTROENTEROLOGY. 82(4):775-782, April 1982

Rejecting scientific advice [editorial]. BRITISH MEDICAL JOURNAL.
284(6372):1426, May 15, 1982

The relation between oral contraceptive use and subsequent development of hyperprolactinemia, by S. Z. Badawy, et al. FERTILITY AND
STERILITY. 36(4):464-467, October 1981

The relation of static muscle function to use of oral contraceptives,
by J. C. Wirth, et al. MEDICINE AND SCIENCE IN SPORTS AND EXER-
CISE. 14(1):16-20, 1982

Relationship between women's attitudes and choice of birth control,
by K. I. Hunter, et al. PSYCHOLOGICAL REPORTS. 49(2):372-374,

The relationship of abortion attitudes and contraceptive behavior among young single women [research], by E. S. Herold. CANADIAN JOURNAL OF PUBLIC HEALTH. 73(2):101-104, March-April 1982

The relationship of celibacy and humanae vitae, by H. Klaus. SISTERS TODAY. 53:541-544, May 1982

The relationship of intrauterine device dimensions to event rates, by N. D. Goldstuck. CONTRACEPTIVE DELIVERY SYSTEMS. 3(2):103-106, 1982

The relationship of static muscle function to use of oral contraceptives, by J. C. Wirth, et al. MEDICINE AND SCIENCE IN SPORTS AND EXERCISE. 14(1):16-20, 1982

Relationship of weight change to required size of vaginal diaphragm [research], by K. Fiscella. NURSE PRACTITIONER. 7:21+, July-August 1982

Relative risks in fertility control and reproduction: individual choice and medical practice, by S. Teper. PROCEEDINGS OF THE ANNUAL SYMPOSIUM OF EUGENICS SOCIETY. 16:59-101, 1981

Religion and abortion, by J. R. Nelson. CENTER MAGAZINE. 14:51-55, July-August 1981

Religion, ideal family size, and abortion extending Renzi's hypothesis, by W. V. D'Antonio, et al. JOURNAL OF THE SCIENTIFIC STUDY OF RELIGION. 19(4):397-408, December 1980

Religion, law and public policy in America, by C. E. Curran. JURIST. 42:14-28, 1982

Repeated suboptimal pregnancy outcome, by J. L. Simpson. BIRTH DEFECTS. 17(1):113-142, 1981

Report from an international symposium about advantages and risks of oral contraceptives, Amsterdam, March 1982, by K. Andersson. JORDEMODERN. 95(7-8):244-251, July-August 1982

Reproductive failure. A survey of pathogenic mechanisms with emphasis on mechanisms for repeated failures, by J. M. Kissane. MONOGRAPHS IN PATHOLOGY. (22):369-381, 1981

Reproductive health care: delivery of services and organizational structure, by J. M. Johnson. FAMILY COMMUNITY HEALTH. 5(1):41-46, May 1982

Reproductive histories in a Norwegian twin population: evaluation of the maternal effect in early spontaneous abortion, by W. L. Golden. ACTA GENETICAE MEDICAE ET GEMELLOLOGIAE. 30(2):91-95, 1981

--DISSERTATION ABSTRACTS INTERNATIONAL. B. p. 1365, 1982

Reproductive mortality in the United States, by B. P. Sachs, et al. JAMA: JOURNAL OF THE AMERICAN MEDICAL ASSOCIATION. 247(20):2789-2792, May 28, 1982

Reproductive Rights National Network (R2N2) meets in San Francisco, by S. Schulman. OFF OUR BACKS. 12:10, January 1982

Requirements applicable to projects for family planning services: Public Health Service. Proposed rule. FEDERAL REGISTER. 47(35): 7699-7701, February 22, 1982

Research activities in the field of oral contraceptives in the People's Republic of China, by Z. De-Wei. ACTA OBSTETRICIA ET GYNE-COLOGICA SCANDINAVICA. SUPPLEMENT. 105:51-60, 1982

Research activity on systemic contraceptive drugs by the U.S. pharmaceutical industry, 1963-1976, by J. DiRaddo, et al. CONTRACEPTION. 23(4):345-365, April 1981

Research on the determinants of fertility: a note on priorites. POPULATION AND DEVELOPMENT REVIEW. 7(2):311, June 1981

Research on repeated abortion: state of the field: 1973-1979, by G. D. Gibb. PSYCHOLOGICAL REPORTS. 48(2):415-424, April 1981

Researchers confirm induced abortion to be safer for women than childbirth: refute claims of critics. FAMILY PLANNING PERSPEC-TIVES. 14:271-272, September-October 1982

Response of unmarried adolescents to contraceptive advice and service in Nigeria, by M. Ezimokhai, et al. INTERNATIONAL JOURNAL OF GYN-AECOLOGY AND OBSTETRICS. 19(6):481-485, December 1981

Response to rubella immunisation education in health authority family planning clinics: a controlled clinical trial, by N. A. Black. HEALTH EDUCATION JOURNAL. 40(4):111-118, 1981

Restoration of the ovarian response to gonadotropins in patients after molar abortions, by A. Miyake, et al. OBSTETRICS AND GYNE-COLOGY. 58(5):566-568, 1981

Restriction of Medicaid funding of abortion [letter], by M. C. Reilly. NEW ENGLAND JOURNAL OF MEDICINE. 307(13):827, September 23, 1982

Results of cervical cerclage operations in pregnant women during a five-year period, by H. Malmstrom, et al. ANNALES CHIRURGIAE ET GYNAECOLOGIAE. 70(2):75-78, 1981

Results of clinical trials with the new prostaglandin E2-derivative Nalador (sulproston), by H. D. Hodicke. THERAPIE DER GEGENWART. 121(5):312-324, May 1982

Results with laparoscopic tubal sterilization, by R. Burmucic. WIENER KLINISCHE WOCHENSCHRIFT. 94(3):77-80, February 5, 1982

Reversal of female sterilization, by P. A. Gantt, et al. SOUTHERN MEDICAL JOURNAL. 75(2):161-163, February 1982

Reversal of vasectomy with microsurgery, by M. C. Ferreira. AMB: REVISTA DA ASSOCIACAO MEDICA BRASILEIRA. 27(3):80-82, March 1981

Reversible inhibition of testicular steroidogenesis and spermato-genesis by a potent gonadotropin-releasing hormone agonist in nor-

mal men: an approach toward the development of a male contraceptive, by R. Linde, et al. NEW ENGLAND JOURNAL OF MEDICINE.
305(12):663-667, September 17, 1981

Reversible sterilization with a physiological solution in the rat:
preliminary note, by L. Gianaroli, et al. BOLLETTINO DELLA SOCIETA
ITALIANA DE BIOLOGIA SPERIMENTALE. 58(3-4):135-141, February 1982

Review and prospect of gossypol research, by H. P. Lei. YAO HSUEH
HSUEH PAO: ACTA PHARMACEUTICA SINICA. 17(1):1-4, January 1982

A review of enzyme changes in serum and urine due to treatment with
drugs (tuberculostatics, contraceptive medication, diagnostics and
drugs in real diseases), by R. J. Hashen. FOLIA MEDICA CRACOVIEN-
SIA. 22(3-4):279-291, 1980

A review of midwife training programs in Tamil Nadu, by S. B. Mani.
STUDIES IN FAMILY PLANNING. 11(12):395-400, December 1980

A review of problems of bias and confounding in epidemiologic studies
of cervical neoplasia and oral contraceptive use, by S. H. Swan, et
al. AMERICAN JOURNAL OF EPIDEMIOLOGY. 115(1):10-18, January 1982

Review: oral contraceptives and menopausal estrogens in relation to
breast neoplasia, by A. Brzezinski, et al. ISRAEL JOURNAL OF MEDI-
CAL SCIENCES. 18(4):433-438, April 1982

Right to abortion limited: the Supreme Court upholds the constitutionality of parental notification statutes. LOYOLA LAW REVIEW.
28:281-296, Winter 1982

Right to abortion under attack in Pennsylvania, Louisiana, Michigan
and Congress, by T. Dejanikus. OFF OUR BACKS. 12:8-9+, January
1982

Right to life: absolute or relative? [editorial]. RECONSTRUCTIONIST.
47:5-6, February 1982

Right-to-Life bible (handbook on abortion), by A. J. Fugh-Berman.
OFF OUR BACKS. 12:7, Decemer 1982

A right-to-life kidnapping? (kidnapping of abortion clinic doctor and
his wife by Army of God), by T. Morganthau. NEWSWEEK. 100:29-30,
August 30, 1982

Right-to-lifers close ranks on legislation, by J. Soriano. NATIONAL
CATHOLIC REPORTER. 18:25, July 30, 1982

Rights and desires, by G. E. Jones. ETHICS. 92:52-56, October 1981

Rise in antiabortion terrorism (tactics of right to life groups), by
L. C. Wohl. MS. 11:19, November 1982

Risk factors for benign breast disease [letter], by D. Glebatis.
AMERICAN JOURNAL OF EPIDEMIOLOGY. 115(5):795-797, May 1982

Risk factors in breast cancer, by R. Scolozzi, et al. RECENTI PRO-
GRESSI IN MEDICINA. 70(5):463-486, May 1981

Risk of death from abortion sterilization is three times greater

with hysterotomy or hysterectomy. FAMILY PLANNING PERSPECTIVES.
14:147-148, May-June 1982

The risk of death from combined abortion-sterilization procedures:
can hysterotomy or hysterectomy be justified?, by H. K. Atrash, et
al. AMERICAN JOURNAL OF OBSTETRICS AND GYNECOLOGY. 142(3):269-
274, February 1, 1982

Risk of ectopic pregnancy following tubectomy, by S. Ghatnagar.
INDIAN JOURNAL OF MEDICAL RESEARCH. 75:47-49, January 1982

The risk of myocardial infarction in former users of oral contraceptives, by P. M. Layde, et al. FAMILY PLANNING PERSPECTIVES.
14(2):78-80, March-April 1982

Risk of myocardial infarction in relation to current and discontinued
use of oral contraceptives, by D. Slone, et al. NEW ENGLAND JOUR-
NAL OF MEDICINE. 305:420-424, August 20, 1981

Risk-taking and contraceptive behavior among unmarried college
students, by J. R. Foreit, et al. POPULATION AND ENVIRONMENT.
4:174-188, Fall 1981

The risks and benefits of oral contraceptives in the developing
world. Past experiences and future perspectives, by M. A. Belsey.
ACTA OBSTETRICIA ET GYNECOLOGICA SCANDINAVICA. SUPPLEMENT. 105:61-
70, 1982

Risks and perspectives of steroid contraceptives, by J. Presl.
CESKOSLOVENSKA GYNEKOLOGIE. 46(1):50-58, February 1981

The role of augmented Hageman factor (factor XII) titers in the cold-
promoted activation of factor VII and spontaneous shortening of the
prothrombin time in women using oral contraceptives, by E. M.
Gordon, et al. JOURNAL OF LABORATORY AND CLINICAL MEDICINE.
99(3):363-369, March 1982

Role of copper irons in contraception, by E. Kobylec, et al. GINE-
KOLOGIA POLSKA. 52(8):751-754, August 1981

The role of estrogens as a risk factor for stroke in postmenopausal
women, by S. H. Rosenberg, et al. WESTERN JOURNAL OF MEDICINE.
133(4):292-296, October 1980

Role of hormones including diethylstibestrol (DES) in the pathogene-
sis of cervical and vaginal intraepithelial neoplasia, by S. J.
Robboy, et al. GYNECOLOGIC ONCOLOGY. 12(2 Pt 2):S98-110, October
1981

The role of maternal diabetes in repetitive spontaneous abortion, by
J. P. Crane, et al. FERTILITY AND STERILITY. 36(4):477-479,
October 1981

The role of recanalization in tubal pregnancy after sterilization, by
S. Badawy, et al. INTERNATIONAL SURGERY. 64(5):49-51, August-
October 1979

Role of retention in avoiding expulsion of intrauterine devices:
measuring devices for basic research, by K. H. Kurz. CONTRACEPTIVE
DELIVERY SYSTEMS. 3(2):107-116, 1982

Role-specific patterns use by American teenagers, by N. V. Eggard, et al. AMERICAN JOURNAL OF PUBLIC HEALTH. 72;809-8 14, August 1982

The Rov v. Wade and Doe v. Bolton decisions on abortion: an analysis critique, and examination of related issues, by A. P. Smith. DIS-SERTATION ABSTRACTS INTERNATIONAL. A. p. 4037, 1982

Rubella vaccine--therapeutic abortion, by L. R. Yen, et al. DRUG INTELLIGENCE AND CLINICAL PHARMACY. 15(11):885, November 1981

Rupture of the cervix during prostaglandin termination of pregnancy, by E. K. El-Etriby, et al. POSTGRADUATE MEDICAL JOURNAL. 57(666): 265-266, April 1981

Rupture of the posterior fornix induced by prostaglandin. Report of a complication of termination of pregnancy, by J. Molin. UGESKRIFT FOR LAEGER. 143(29):1841, 1981

Rwanda: too many people too little land, by J. Hammand. WORLD HEALTH. pp. 12-15, June 1982

Salpingoclasia by minilaparotomy following spontaneous abortion, by A. Alvardo Duran, et al. GINECOLOGIA Y OBSTETRICIA DE MEXICO. 49(294):239-253, April 1981

Scheinberg v. Smith (482 F Supp 529): toward recognition of minors' constitutional right to privacy in abortion decisions. NOVA LAW JOURNAL. 6:475-487, Spring 1982

--(659 F 2d 476). JOURNAL OF FAMILY LAW. 20:551-554, May 1982

The search for male contraception reveals exciting photographs too, by D. M. Phillips. LABOUR WORLD. 32:48-51, August 1981

Searching for an ideal contraceptive method, by L. B. Tyrer. USA TODAY. 110:31-33, March 1982

Seasonal conception by women in various age groups compared with the season of menarche, by F. Ronnike. DANISH MEDICAL BULLETIN. 28(4):148-153, September 1981

The second victory of Anthony Comstock, by R. Polenberg. SOCIETY. 19(4):32-38, 1982

Secondary hyperparathyroidism caused by oral contraceptives, by A. M. Moses, et al. ARCHIVES OF INTERNAL MEDICINE. 142(1):128-129, January 1982

Self-administration of prostaglandin for termination of early preg-nancy, by M. Bygdeman, et al. CONTRACEPTION. 24(1):45-52, July 1981

Self-help birth control study, by T. Land. TIMES HIGHER EDUCATIONAL SUPPLEMENT. 498:7, May 21, 1982

Senate committee passes anti-abortion amendment [March 10th approval by Senate Judiciary Committee of Hatch Amendment], by T. Dejanikus. OFF OUR BACKS. 12:17, April 1982

Senate debate on abortion turns into procedural tussle. CONGRESSION-

Senate panel begins consideration of constitutional amendment on abortion. FAMILY LAW REPORTER: COURT OPINIONS. 7(48):2759-2761, October 13, 1981

Senate poll: 16 of 67 for Hatch, by M. Meehan. NATIONAL CATHOLIC REPORTER. 18:1+, March 19, 1982

The Senate threat to our lives, by L. C. Wohl. MS. 10:21, January 1982

Senator Helms introduces unifying pro-life initiative. OUR SUNDAY VISITOR. 70:7, March 21, 1982

Sense and sensitivity ... intra-amniotic prostaglandin termination of pregnancy, by C. Bichard, et al. NURSING MIRROR AND MIDWIVE'S JOURNAL. 154(Clin Forum):xiii-xvi, April 14, 1982

The sensibility of the hypophysis, the gonads and the thyroid of adolescents before and after the administration of oral contraceptives [a resume], by I. Rey-Stocker, et al. PEDIATRIC ANNALS. 10(12):15-20, December 1981

Sequelae of mid-trimete abortions induced by extra-amniotic drip infusion of normal saline, by M. Blum. INTERNATIONAL SURGERY. 64(5):45-47, August-October 1979

Sequences of events following adoption of contraception: an exploratory analysis of 1973 United States fertility history data, by G. Pickens, et al. SOCIAL BIOLOGY. 28:111-125, Spring-Summer 1981

Serenely silent no longer, two angry nuns battle their bishops over the issue of abortion (opposition to Hatch Amendment). PEOPLE WEEKLY. 18:90, August 16, 1982

Serum alkaline phosphatase activity in threatened abortion, prolonged pregnancy and late pregnancy toxemia, by W. Nikodem. POLSKI TYGOD-NIK LEKARSKI. 36(37):1429-1431, September 14, 1981

Serum antibody to radix trichosanthin after its use for termination of midterm pregnancy, by L. Q. Zhuang. CHUNG HUA FU CHAN KO TSA CHIH. 14(2):122-124, April 1979

Serum bile acids during biphasic contraceptive treatment with ethinyl estradiol and norgestrel, by J. Heikkinen, et al. CONTRACEPTION. 25(1):89-95, January 1982

Serum iron concentrations in women applying Angravid (Polfa) preparation as contraceptive means, by R. Mierzwinski, et al. GINEKOLOGIA POLSKA. 52(8):747-750, 1981

Serum lactate dehydrogenase (LDH) activity in threatened abortion prolonged pregnancy and late pregnancy toxemia, by W. Nikodem. GINEKOLOGIA POLSKA. 52(1):33-37, January 1981

Serum polyamine oxidase activity in spontaneous abortion, by G. Illei, et al. BRITISH JOURNAL OF OBSTETRICS AND GYNAECOLOGY. 89(3):199-201, March 1982

Serum relaxin and human chorionic gonadotropin concentrations in spontaneous abortions, by J. Quagliarello, et al. FERTILITY AND STERILITY. 36(3):399-401, September 1981

Serum 25-hydroxycholecalciferol levels in women using oral contraceptives, by W. H. Schreurs, et al. CONTRACEPTION. 23(4):399-406, April 1981

A severe case of hyperemesis gravidarum, by A. Chatwani, et al. AMERICAN JOURNAL OF OBSTETRICS AND GYNECOLOGY. 143(8):964-965, August 15, 1982

Severe pelvic inflammatory disease and peritonitis following falope ring tubal ligation. Case report and review of the literature, by C. LoBue. JOURNAL OF REPRODUCTIVE MEDICINE. 26(11):581-584, November 1981

Sex and contraceptive behavior among young single persons, by E. Garcia Hassey, et al. GINECOLOGIA Y OBSTETRICIA DE MEXICO. 49(296):343-357, June 1981

Sex: chastity belts next?. ECONOMIST. 281:32, October 3, 1981

Sex conference--planning--sexually transmitted diseases, by M. Barrette, et al. NURSING MONTREAL. 6(3):7-8, June 1982

Sex differences in correlates of abortion attitudes among college students, by B. A. Finlay. JOURNAL OF MARRIAGE AND THE FAMILY. 43(571-582, August 1981

Sex education, by J. Spray. NURSING. 1:1508-1509, March 1982

Sex education and contraceptive education in U.S. public high schools, by M. T. Orr. FAMILY PLANNING PERSPECTIVES. 14:304-313, November-December 1982

Sex education and its association with teenage sexual activity, pregnancy and contraceptive use [research], by M. Zelnik, et al. FAMILY PLANNING PERSPECTIVES. 14:117-119+, May-June 1982

Sex education of pregnant women and its relationship with their knowledge and attitude to sex, by N. Ishimatsu, et al. JOSANPU ZASSHI. 36(6):481-489, June 1982

Sex education outreach from a family planning agency, by E. Rosen, et al. HEALTH EDUCATION. 13(2):13-15, March-April 1982

Sex guilt and the use of contraception among unmarried women, by J. F. Keller, et al. CONTRACEPTION. 25(4):387-393, April 1982

Sex hormone binding globulin: effect of synthetic steroids on the assay and effect of oral contraceptives, by S. M. Bowles, et al. ANNALS OF CLINICAL BIOCHEMISTRY. 18(Pt 4):226-231, July 1981

Sex hormone binding globulin levels in hirsuite patients: the effect of combined oral contraceptives, by O. F. Giwa-Osagie, et al. CONTRACEPTIVE DELIVERY SYSTEMS. 3(2):155-160, 1982

Sex hormones and gynaecological cancer [editorial], by J. S. Scott. BRITISH MEDICAL JOURNAL. 284(6330):1657-1658, June 5, 1982

Sex hormones and liver cancer, by G. M. Williams. LABORATORY IN-
VESTIGATION. 46(3):352-353, March 1982

Sex of offspring of women using oral contraceptives, rhythm, and
other methods of birth control around the time of conception, by P.
H. Shiono, ete al. FERTILITY AND STERILITY. 37(3):367-372, March
1982

Sex, sex guilt, and contraceptive use, by M. Gerrard. JOURNAL OF
PERSONALITY AND SOCIAL PSYCHOLOGY. 42(1):153-158, January 1982

Sexual abstinence, by V. Fecher. PRIEST. 38:4-6, April 1982

Sexual and contraceptive behavior on a college campus. A five-year
follow-up, by R. W. Hale, et al. CONTRACEPTION. 25(2):125-134,
February 1982

Sexual behavior of castrated sex offenders, by N. Heim. ARCHIVES OF
SEXUAL BEHAVIOR. 10(1):11-19, February 1981

Sexual practice and the use of contraception, by J. Bell. HIGH
SCHOOL JOURNAL. 65:241-244, April 1982

Sexuality, femininity and fertility control, by A. Woodhouse. WO-
MEN'S STUDIES INTERNATIONAL FORUM. 5(1):1-15, 1982

The sexually liberated college student--fact or fancy, by P. Murphy,
et al. JOURNAL OF THE AMERICAN COLLEGE HEALTH ASSOCIATION. 30(2):
87-89, October 1981

The shape of babies to come, by A. Ferriman, et al. OBSERVER. p. 9,
November 21, 1982

Should contraceptives be advertised on television?, by R. Horowitz.
CHANNELS. 1(3):64-66, October-November 1981

Should we have children? A decision-making group for couples, by K.
K. Kimball, et al. PERSONNEL AND GUIDANCE JOURNAL. 60(3):153-156,
November 1981

Should your conscience be your guide? ... a nurse-anesthetist refused
to participate in a tubal ligation. NURSINGLIFE. 1:15, July-August 1981

Side effects of hormonal contraception, by W. Carol, et al. ZEIT-
SCHRIFT FUR DIE GESAMTE INNERE MEDIZIN. 36(8):253-260, April 15,
1981

The significance of cultural tradition for contraceptive change: a
study of rural Indian women, by C. K. Vlassoff. DISSERTATION AB-
STRACTS INTERNATIONAL. A. p. 1702, 1982

Significance of SP1 beta-1-glycoprotein in threatened abortion, by G.
Iannotti, et al. MINERVA GINECOLOGIA. 32(12):1115-1119, December
1980

The silent holocaust, by W. Brennan. LIGUORIAN. 70:14-19, September
1982

The silent holocaust exposed, by W. Odell. OUR SUNDAY VISITOR. 71:

12-13, June 20, 1982

Silicone plugs (plugging the fallopian tubes), by C. SerVaas. SATUR-
DAY EVENING POST. 254:108, May-June 1982

A single intercourse [letter], by A. Viliunas. MEDICAL JOURNAL OF
AUSTRALIA. 2(11):578, November 28, 1981

Sixty-nine percent of United States adults now approve legal abortion
for six specified reasons: up since 1980. FAMILY PLANNING PERSPEC-
TIVES. 14:214-215, July-August 1982

Size distribution, forms and variations of glandular tissue of the
breast. Histometric examination on the question of the effect of
contraceptives on the lobular parenchyma, by C. Theele, et al.
PATHOLOGE. 2(4):208-219, August 1981

Skin changes caused by oral contraceptives. Interview with Dr. H.
Zaun, Director of the University Skin Clinic, Homburg/Saar [inter-
view by M. Minker], by H. Zaun. THERAPIE DER GEGENWART. 121(3):
146-151, March 1982

Smoking, oral contraceptives, and serum lipid and lipoprotein levels
in youths, by A. W. Voors, et al. PREVENTIVE MEDICINE. 11(1):1-
12, January 1982

Smoking, oral contraceptives, and thromboembolic disease, by F. M.
Sturtevant. INTERNATIONAL JOURNAL OF FERTILITY. 27(1):2-26, 1982

Social and affective factors associated with adolescent pregnancy, by
P. B. Smith, et al. JOURNAL OF SCHOOL HEALTH. 52(2):90-93, February 1982

Social, spatial and political determinants of U.S. abortion rates, by
N. F. Henry, et al. SOCIAL SCIENCE AND MEDICINE. 16(9):987-996,
1982

Social structure and population change: a comparative study of
Tokugawa Japan and Ch'ing China, by J. I. Nakamura, et al. ECO-
NOMIC DEVELOPMENT AND CULTURAL CHANGE. 30:229-269, January 1982

Social support for contraceptive utilization in adolescence, by J. A.
Shea. DISSERTATION ABSTRACTS INTERNATIONAL. B. p. 4008, 1982

The socio-economic determinants of recourse to legal abortion, by J.
Humphries. WOMEN'S STUDIES INTERNATIONAL QUARTERLY. 3(4):377-393,
1980

Sociologia de al poblacion y controlde la natalidad en Espana, by J.
M. de Miguel. REVISTA ESPANOLA DE INVESTIGACIONES SOCIOLOGICAS.
10:15-47, April-June 1980

Socio-psychological aspects of voluntary abortion at the Obstetrical
and Gynecological Clinic of Catania, by S. Di Leo, et al. ARCHIVES
OF OBSTETRICS AND GYNECOLOGY. 85(6):531-544, November-December
1980

Some biological insights into abortion, by G. Hardin. BIOSCIENCE.
32:720+, October 1982

Some long term problems with the pill [editorial]. NEW ZEALAND
MEDICAL JOURNAL. 94(689):92, August 12, 1982

Some metabolic effects of long-term use of the injectable contraceptive norethisterone enanthate, by G. Howard, et al. LANCET.
1(8269):423-425, February 20, 1982

Some problems concerning operations for reconstruction of tubal
patency, by Q. B. Chen. CHUNG HUA FU CHAN KO TSA CHIH. 14(2):93-
96, April 1979

Sonographic index for prognosis of early pregnancy, by J. E. Tapia,
et al. ZENTRALBLATT FUR GYNAEKOLOGIE. 103(20):1255-1259, 1981

Sources of family size attitudes and family planning knowledge among
rural Turkish youth, by C. E. Carpenter-Yaman. STUDIES IN FAMILY
PLANNING. 13(5):149-158, May 1982

Southern Baptist Convention resolutions on the family, by R. Herring.
BAPTIST HISTORY AND HERITAGE. 17:36-45, January 1982

Spastic diplegia and the significance of mothers' previous reproductive loss, by P. S. Spiers, et al. DEVELOPMENTAL MEDICINE AND
CHILD NEUROLOGY. 24(1):20-29, February 1982

Special considerations in pregnancy prevention for the mentally subnormal adolescent female, by K. Hein, et al. JOURNAL OF ADOLESCENT
HEALTH CARE. 1(1):46-49, September 1980

Spermatogenesis and SRBC haemolysin formation in various inbred mouse
strains treated with cyproterone acetate, by Z. Pokorna, et al.
FLORIDA STATE UNIVERSITY LAW REVIEW. 27(5):354-359, 1981

Spermicide use and Down's syndome, by K. J. Rothman. AMERICAN JOUR-
NAL OF PUBLIC HEALTH. 72(4):399-401, April 1982

Sponatneous abortion after intra-uterine transfer of an ovum fecundated in vitro, by R. Frydman, et al. NOUVELLE PRESSE MEDICALE.
10(42):3475-3476, November 21, 1981

Spontaneous abortion incidence in the treatment of infertility, by R.
P. Jansen. AMERICAN JOURNAL OF OBSTETRICS AND GYNECOLOGY. 143(4):
451-473, June 15, 1982

Spontaneous abortion over time: comparing occurrence in two cohorts
of women a generation apart, by A. J. Wilcox, et al. AMERICAN
JOURNAL OF EPIDEMIOLOGY. 114(4):548-553, October 1981

Spontaneous abortion. A study of 1,961 women and their conceptuses,
by B. J. Poland, et al. ACTA OBSTETRICIA ET GYNECOLOGICA SCANDI-
NAVICA. SUPPLEMENT. 102:1-32, 1981

Spontaneous abortions as an index of occupational hazards, by K.
Hemminke, et al. GIGIENA TRUDA I PROFESSIONALNYE ZABOLEVANIA.
(1):41-43, January 1982

Spontaneous occurrence of atypical hyperplasia and adenocarcinoma of
the uterus in androgen-sterilized SD rats, by S. Morikawa, et al.
JNCI: JOURNAL OF THE NATIONAL CANCER INSTITUTE. 69(1):95-101, July
1982

Spousal notice and consultation requirement: a new approach to state regulation of abortion. NOVA LAW JOURNAL. 6:457-474, Spring 1982

Spousal notification requirement is constitutionally permissible burden on woman's right to privacy in abortion decision: Scheinberg v. Smith, 659 F 2d 476. TEXAS TECH LAW REVIEW. 13:1495-1511, 1982

Spying on Right to Life (National Convention, Cherry Hill, New Jersey, July 17, 1982), by A. J. Fugh-Berman. OFF OUR BACKS. 12:18-19, August-September 1982

The squeak squawk (proposed regulations requiring birth control clinics to notify parents when minors receive contraceptives), by A. Shales. NEW REPUBLIC. 187:18-20, August 9, 1982

The 'squeal rule': government and confidentiality, by D. M. Prout. AMERICAN COLLEGE OF PHYSICIANS. 2(3):3+, April 1982

Staffing a contraceptive service for adolescents: the importance of sex, race, and age, by S. G. Philliber, et al. PUBLIC HEALTH REPORTS. 97(2):165-169, March-April 1982

Stalemated on abortion, Congress sent new bill, by M. Meehan. NATIONAL CATHOLIC REPORTER. 18:3, March 12, 1982

Starting a family in Aberdeen 1961-79: the significance of illegitimacy and abortion, by C. Pritchard, et al. JOURNAL OF BIOSOCIAL SCIENCE. 14(2):127-139, April 1982

State ordered to pay for indigents' medically necessary abortions. FAMILY LAW REPORTER: COURT OPINIONS. 8(1):2006-2008, November 3, 1981

Statistical data on abortions performed in 1979 in a Belgian out-patient clinic, by M. Vekemans, et al. REVUE MEDICALE DE BRUXELLES. 2(9):851-864, November 1981

Status of family planning among the patients visiting our clinic, by Y. Miyagawa, et al. JOSANPU ZASSHI. 36(6):500-503, June 1982

Status of the reproductive system in women taking oral contraceptive for a long time, by A. G. Khomasuridze, et al. AKUSHERSTVO I GINEKOLOGIIA. (12):17-20, December 1981

Statutes and ordinances--contraceptives and sex aids. CRIMINAL LAW REPORTER: COURT DECISIONS AND PROCEEDINGS. 30(4):2086, October 28, 1981

Sterilization and the birth rate, by D. L. Nortman. STUDIES IN FAMILY PLANNING. 11(9-10):286-300, September-October 1980

Sterilization-attributable deaths in Bangladesh, by D. A. Grimes, et al. INTERNATIONAL JOURNAL OF GYNAECOLOGY AND OBSTETRICS. 20(2):149-154, April 1982

Sterilization by occlusion of the fallopian tubes with mulcilago phenol (a seven years' clinical observation). CHUNG HUA FU CHAN KO TSA CHIH. 14(2):79-83, April 1979

Sterilization: don't count on (tubal ligation) reversal, warns a Calgary doctor, by M. McKinely. ALBERTA REPORT. 9:34-35, March 22, 1982

Sterilization failure. An analysis of 27 pregnancies after a previous sterilization procedure, by V. P. De Villiers. SOUTH AFRICAN MEDICAL JOURNAL. 61(16):589-590, April 17, 1982

Sterilization in Pennsylvania, by P. W. Beck, et al. TEMPLE LAW QUARTERLY. 54:213-236, 1981

Sterilization of the developmentally disabled: shedding some myth-conceptions. FLORIDA STATE UNIVERSITY LAW REVIEW. 9:599-643, Fall 1981

Sterilization of incompetents: the quest for legal authority, by A. H. Bernstein. HOSPITALS. 56(3):13-15, February 1, 1982

Sterilization of the male dog and cat by laparoscopic occlusion of the ductus deferens, by D. E. Wildt, et al. AMERICAN JOURNAL OF VETERINARY RESERACH. 42(11):1888-1897, November 1981

Sterilization of the mentally retarded: a decision for the courts, by G. J. Annas. HASTINGS CENTER REPORT. 11(4):18-19, August 1981

--: who decides?, by M. S. Lottman. TRIAL. 18:61-64, April 1982

Sterilization of the mentally retarded adult: the Eve case [Eve, In re (1980, 1981) 115 D L R (3d) 283], by B. Starkman. McGILL LAW JOURNAL. 26:931-950, 1981

Sterilization of women, by P. Fylling. SYKEPLEIEN. 68(8):11+, May 5, 1981

Sterilization rate rose most for women 15-24 between 1976 and 1978 (United States). FAMILY PLANNING PERSPECTIVES. 13:236-237, September-October 1981

Sterilization reversal for more women. MEDICAL WORLD NEWS. 23:18, March 29, 1982

Sterilization rights of mental retardates. WASHINGTON AND LEE LAW REVIEW. 39:207-221, Winter 1982

Sterilization without surgery, by M. Klitsch. FAMILY PLANNING PERSPECTIVES. 14:324-326, November-December 1982

--: the "ovary plug" is simplicity, by L. Lang. HEALTH. 14:19, March 1982

--(silicon plug that blocks the Fallopian tubes), by L. Lang. HEALTH. 14:13, March 1982

Sterilizing the retarded: constitutional, statutory and policy alternatives, by R. K. Sherlock, et al. NORTH CAROLINA LAW REVIEW. 60:943-983, June 1982

Steroidal contraceptives and the immune system, by J. Presl. CESKO-SLOVENSKA GYNEKOLOGIE. 47(2):143-148, March 1982

Stopping rules for family planning in an oriental society, by V. M. Ng. INTERFACES. 12:82-84, February 1982

Storm over Washington: the parental notification proposal (requiring family planning clinics to notify the parents of minors when prescription contraceptives are provided), by A. M. Kenney, et al. FAMILY PLANNING PERSPECTIVES. 14:185+, July-August 1982

Structural abnormalities of the uterus as a cause of prematurity, by G. Allocca, et al. ARCHIVES OF OBSTETRICS AND GYNECOLOGY. 85(5): 457-462, September-October 1980

Structural variations of cervical cancer and its precursors under the influence of exogenous hormones, by G. Dallenbach-Hellweg. CURRENT TOPICS IN PATHOLOGY. 70:143-170, 1981

Structure and biological function of 16a,17a-cycloprogesterones (Pregna-D'-pentarans), by V. I. Simonov, et al. BIOORGANICHESKAYA KHIMIYA. 7(6):920-926, 1981

Student-parent rapport and parent involvement in sex, birth control, and venereal disease education, by S. M. Bennett, et al. JOURNAL OF SEX RESEARCH. 16(2):114-130, May 1980

Studies continue to explore possible association between pill and breast cancer; most find none. FAMILY PLANNING PERSPECTIVES. 13:232-235, September-October 1981

Studies of the attitudes of a group of puerapas of the Brianza region toward contraception and the services offered for such purposes of the public health organizations, by G. Remotti, et al. ANNALI DI OSTETRICIA GINECOLOGIA, MEDICINA PERINATALE. 103(1):68-92, January-February 1982

Studies of humoral immunological response on the aborted trophoblasts, by A. Tokunaga. NIPPON SANKA FUJINKA GAKKAI ZASSHI. 33(12):2125-2132, December 1981

Studies of synthetic contraceptives. III. Stereospecific total synthesis of racemic prostaglandin F2 alpha, by G. D. Han, et al. YAO HSUEH HSUEH PAO: ACTA PHARMACEUTICA SINICA. 16(2):114-121, February 1981

Studies on the mechanism of action of the abortive effect of 6-hydroxydopamine in rats, by E. MacDonald, et al. MEDICAL BIOLOGY. 59(2):111-115, April 1981

Studies on the mechanism of action of me-quingestanol on fertility in the rabbit, by Y . M. Wei. CHUNG HUA FU CHAN KO TSA CHIH. 14(2): 73-78, April 1979

Studies on the role of oral contraceptive use in the etiology of benign and malignant liver tumors, by C. Mettlin, et al. JOURNAL OF SURGICAL ONCOLOGY. 18(1):73-85, 1981

Study finds lactation has no adverse effect on IUD performance. FAMILY PLANNING PERSPECTIVES. 14:338-339, November-December 1982

A study of adolescent aborters and adolescent expectant mothers regarding their perceptions of their mothers' and fathers' parenting behavior, by K. Sweeney. DISSERTATION ABSTRACTS INTERNATIONAL. A. 42(2):158, 1981

A study of the characteristics of acceptors of the Copper-T device, by V. B. Jalagar, et al. JOURNAL OF FAMILY WELFARE. 28:54-61, June 1982

A study of contraceptive choice and use in Bangkok Metropolis Health Clinics, by T. Chumnijarakij, et al. CONTRACEPTION. 24(3):245-258, September 1981

Study of 500 cases of sterilization by tubal ligation, by R. J. Leke, et al. UNION MEDICALE DU CANADA. 110(9):807-809, September 1981

Study of sociocultural aspect of tubectomy subjects, by R. Ram, et al. JOURNAL OF THE INDIAN MEDICAL ASSOCIATION. 77(8):130-133, October 16, 1981

A study on the pathogenic change and cause of death of fetus in middle pregnancy terminated with alcoholic extract of Yuanhua, by Z. F. He. CHUNG HUA FU CHAN KO TSA CHIH. 17(2):116-118, April 1982

A study on toxicity of bakuchiol to mice's kidney, by Y. S. Zhang. CHUNG-KUO YAO LI HSUEH PAO. 6(3):30-32, May 1981

Subcommittee passes Hatch bill, by. M. Meehan. NATIONAL CATHOLIC REPORTER. 18:25, December 25, 1981

The subfertile couple, by M. P. McCusker. JOGN NURSING: JOURNAL OF OBSTETRIC GYNECOLOGIC AND NEONATAL NURSING. 11(3):157-162, May-June 1982

Subjective assessment and cardiovasallar response to ischemic pain in young healthy women users and nonusers of oral contraceptives, by E. J. Stein, et al. JOURNAL OF PSYCHOSOMATIC RESEARCH. 25(6):579-586, 1981

Subsequent pregnancy among adolescent mothers, by E. Peabody, et al. ADOLESCENCE. 16:563-568, Fall 1981

Sudden circulation collapse after intra-amniotic injection of prostaglandin F2 alpha, by E. Egense, et al. UGESKRIFT FOR LAEGER. 144(13):949-950, March 29, 1982

Suppression of ovulation in the rat by an orally active antagonist of luteinizing hormone-releasing hormone, by M. V. Nekola, et al. SCIENCE. 218:160-162, October 8, 1982

The Supreme Court 1980-81 term: abortion. CRIMINAL LAW REPORTER: COURT DECISIONS AND PROCEEDINGS. 29(23):4171-4172, September 9, 1981

Supreme Court on abortion funding: the second time around, by D. J. Horan, et al. ST. LOUIS UNIVERSITY LAW JOURNAL. 25:411-427, 1981

Supreme Court report: abortion ... parental notification, by R. L. Young. AMERICAN BAR ASSOCIATION JOURNAL. 67:630-632, May 1981

Supreme Court roundup: 1980 term, by R. J. Regan. THOUGHT. 56:491-502, December 1981

The Supreme Court, the states, and social change: the case of abortion, by S. B. Hansen. PEACE AND CHANGE. 6(3):20-32, 1980

Survey of childbearing women in Qi-yi Commune, by E. S. Gao, et al. AMERICAN JOURNAL OF PUBLIC HEALTH. 72(9 Suppl):27-29, September 1982

Survey of personal habits, symptoms of illness, and histories of disease in men with and without vasectomies, by D. B. Petitti, et al. AMERICAN JOURNAL OF PUBLIC HEALTH. 72:476-480, May 1982

Sweden approved of Depo-Provera sales promotion in developing countries [interview by Elisabeth Magnusson], by B. Rubensson. VARD-FACKET. 6(7):54, April 8, 1982

The sympto-thermal methods, by S. Parenteau-Carreau. INTERNATIONAL JOURNAL OF FERTILITY. 26(3):170-181, 1981

A symptom-complex during artificial abortion. CHUNG HUA FU CHAN KO TSA CHIH. 14(2):111-115, April 1979

Symptomatic intrauterine retention of fetal bones, by F. A. Chervenak, et al. OBSTETRICS AND GYNECOLOGY. 59(6 Suppl):58S-61S, June 1982

Synthesis and evaluation of the male antifertility properties of a series of N-unsubstituted sulfamates, by A. F. Hirsch, et al. JOURNAL OF MEDICINAL CHEMISTRY. 24(7):901-903, July 1981

Synthetic laminaria for cervical dilatation prior to vacuum aspiration in midtrimester pregnancy, by W. E. Brenner, et al. AMERICAN JOURNAL OF OBSTETRICS AND GYNECOLOGY. 143(4):475-477, June 15, 1982

TV update: Washington (National Abortion Rights Action League recently refused commercial time by several TV stations), by R. Lee. TV GUIDE. 30:A14, April 17, 1982

Taking liberties with women: abortion, sterilization, and contraception, by W. Savage. INTERNATIONAL JOURNAL OF HEALTH SERVICES. 12(2):293-308, 1982

Talking to parents about sex does not affect teens' contraceptive use. FAMILY PLANNING PERSPECTIVES. 14:279-280, September-October 1982

Taxpayer attack on abortion funding repelled by Maryland's high court. FAMILY LAW REPORTER: COURT OPINIONS. 7(22):2360-2361, April 7, 1981

Teen sex hazards discussed, by M. Meehan. NATIONAL CATHOLIC REPORTER. 18:4, April 30, 1982

Teenage women and contraceptive behavior: focus on self-efficacy in sexual and contraceptive situations, by R. A. Levinson. DISSERTATION ABSTRACTS INTERNATIONAL. A. p. 151, 1982

Teenagers and interruption of pregnancy, by C. Revaz. THERAPEUTISCHE UMSCHAU. 39(6):487-489, June 1982

Teenagers who use organized family planning services: United States, 1978, by E. Eckard. VITAL HEALTH STATISTICS. 13(57):1-18, August 1981

Teens and contraception (parental notification proposal), by A. J. Fugh-Berman. OFF OUR BACKS. 12:13, June 1982

Telltale birth control (proposal to require federally funded family-planning clinics to notify parents when their teen-agers receive contraceptives), by M. Beck. NEWSWEEK. 99:33, April 5, 1982

Temporal relationship between the abortifacient effects of GnRH antagonists and hormonal secretion, by C. Rivier, et al. BIOLOGICAL REPRODUCTION. 24(5):1061-1067, June 1981

Ten years of evidence on therapeutic abortion: the jury is still out [editorial], by B. K. Doane. CANADIAN MEDICAL ASSOCIATION JOURNAL. 125(5):413-415, September 1, 1981

Teratogenic hazards of oral contraceptives [letter], by M. Labbok. AMERICAN JOURNAL OF OBSTETRICS AND GYNECOLOGY. 142(8):1066, April 15, 1982

Teratology study of intravaginally administered nonoxynol-9-containing contraceptive cream in rats, by D. Abrutyn, et al. FERTILITY AND STERILITY. 37(1):113-117, January 1982

Termination of early first trimester pregnancy with 16,16-dimethyl trans delta 2 prostaglandin E1 methyl ester, by O. Reiertsen, et al. PROSTAGLANDINS LEUKOTRIENES AND MEDICINE. 8(1):31-35, January 1982

Termination of early gestation with (15S)-15-methyl prostaglandin F2 alpha methyl ester vaginal suppositories, by R. P. Marrs, et al. CONTRACEPTION. 24(6):617-630, December 1981

Termination of midtrimester missed abortion by extraovular instillation of normal saline, by H. Abramovici, et al. BRITISH JOURNAL OF OBSTETRICS AND GYNAECOLOGY. 88(9):931-933, September 1981

Termination of midtrimester pregnancies induced by hypertonic saline and prostaglandin F2 alpha: 116 consecutive cases, by E. Bostofte, et al. ACTA OBSTETRICIA ET GYNECOLOGICA SCANDINAVICA. 60(6):575-578, 1981

Termination of mid-trimester pregnancy with intramuscular 15-(S)-15-, methyl-prostaglandin F2 alpha, by G. Tsalacopoulos, et al. SOUTH AFRICAN MEDICAL JOURNAL. 61(22):822-824, May 29, 1982

Termination of pregnancy by intramuscular administration of 15-(S)-15-methyl-prostaglandin in F2 alpha, by W. Parewijck, et al. ZEITSCHRIFT FUR GEBURTSCHILFE UND PERINATOLOGIE. 184(5):366-370, October 1980

Termination of pregnancy in Papua New Guinea: the traditional and contemporary position, by I. A. McGoldrick. PAPAU NEW GUINEA MEDICAL JOURNAL. 24(2):113-120, June 1981

Termination of pregnancy: a prospective comparative investigation of 2 vacuum aspiration methods: vibra ab aspirator and the conventional method, by H. K. Poulsen. UGESKRIFT FOR LAEGER. 144(2):89-92, 1981

Termination of pregnancy with cloprostenol and dexamethasone in intact or ovariectomized cows, by W. H. Johnson, et al. CANADIAN VETERINARY JOURNAL. 22(9):288-290, September 1981

Termination of second trimester pregnancy with laminaria and intramuscular 16 phenoxy-omega-17, 18, 19, 20 tetranor PGE2 methylsulfonylamide (sulprostone)-A randomized study, by S. M. Karim, et al. PROSTAGLANDINS. 23(2):257-263, February 1982

Termination of very early pregnancy by vaginal suppositories-(15S)-15-methyl prostaglandin F2 alpha methyl ester, by L. S. Wan, et al. CONTRACEPTION. 24(6):603-615, December 1981

Terminology and core curricula in natural family planning, by J. J. Brennan, et al. FERTILITY AND STERILITY. 38(1):117-118, July 1982

--LINACRE QUARTERLY. 48:313-315, November 1981

A test of the Luker theory of contraceptive risk-taking, by P. V. Crosbie, et al. STUDIES IN FAMILY PLANNING. 13:67-78, March 1982

Testing a better birth-control pill. NEWSWEEK. 99:85, May 3, 1982

Thailand's family planning program: an Asian success story, by A. Rosenfield, et al. INTERNATIONAL FAMILY PLANNING PERSPECTIVES. 8:43-51, June 1982

Thailand's reproductive revolution [update], by P. Kamnuansilpa, et al. INTERNATIONAL FAMILY PLANNING PERSPECTIVES. 8:51-56, June 1982

Theoretical framework for studying adolescent contraceptive use, by K. A. Urberg. ADOLESCENCE. 17:527-540, Fall, 1982

The theory of reasoned action and health belief model applied to contraception of college women, by S. McCammon. DISSERTATION ABSTRACTS INTERNATIONAL. B. p. 72, 1982

Therapeutic abortion and chlamydia trachomatis infection, by E. Qvigstad, et al. BRITISH JOURNAL OF VENEREAL DISEASES. 58(3):182-183, June 1982

Therapeutic abortion: a difficult choice, by F. Gratton-Jacob. NURSING QUEBEC. 2(1):7-15, November-December 1981

Therapeutic and prophylactic care in habitual abortion in women with genital infantilism, by N. T. Gudakova, et al. AKUSHERSTVO I GINE-KOLOGIIA. (5):26-27, May 1981

There is no place in gynecological endoscopy for unipolar of bipolar high frequency current, by H. H. Riedel, et al. ENDOSCOPY. 14(2): 51-54, March 1982

Thinking twice about fertility, by K. Holman. GUARDIAN. p. 11, November 3, 1982

The third S.K. & F. Prize lecture, University of London, December

1981. The clinical pharmacology of oral contraceptive steroids, by
M. L. Orme. BRITISH JOURNAL OF CLINICAL PHARMACOLOGY. 14(1):31-
42, July 1982

Third world policies. USA TODAY. 110:4-5, December 1981

A thirty-month clinical experience in natural family planning, by R.
Kambic, et al. AMERICAN JOURNAL OF PUBLIC HEALTH. 7(11):1255-
1258, November 1981

This is what you thought about ... men's rights (results of survey).
GLAMOUR. 80:21, July 1982

Thousands rally for pro-life amendment (in Washington, D.C. on Jan
22). HUMAN EVENTS. 42:8, February 6, 1982

The threat of miscarriage. Etiologic research, by R. Lambotte. REVUE
MEDICALE DE LIEGE. 37(4):109-114, February 15, 1982

The threat of numbers, by R. W. Peterson. AUDUBON. 84:107, July
1982

3 cases of acute pulmonary edema in pregnant women treated with
tocolytics and betamethasone, by F. Coggiola, et al. MINERVA
GINECOLOGIA. 34(3):191-194, March 1982

Thrombosis and oral contraception [letter], by P. Armitage. BRITISH
JOURNAL OF HOSPITAL MEDICINE. 26(2):185-186, August 1981

Thrombotic disorders associated with pregnancy and the pill, by J. E.
Tooke, et al. CLINICS IN HAEMOTOLOGY. 10(2):613-630, June 1981

A throw-away diaphragm, by R. Kall. HEALTH. 14:18, March 1982

The time has come for pastoral work in natural family planning, by A.
Zimmerman. PRIEST. 38:12-15, July-August 1982

Time of application of intrauterine devices in women with prior voluntary abortions, by C. Balbi, et al. ARCHIVES OF OBSTETRICS AND
GYNECOLOGY. 85(3):195-198, May-June 1980

A time series of instrumental fertility variables, by N. B. Ryder.
DEMOGRAPHY. 18(4):487-509, November 1981

Toledo doctor wages compaign against the pill, by A. Jones. NATIONAL
CATHOLIC REPORTER. 18:1+, October 15, 1982+

Topical contraceptives, by V. I. Alipov, et al. AKUSHERSTVO I GINE-
KOLOGIIA. (2):5-7, February 1982

Total cholesterol level in human placenta, by S. Narahari, et al.
HUMAN HEREDITY. 31(5):276-278, 1981

Toward a closer integration of population in development policies in
Taiwan [conference paper], by P. K. C. Liu. INDUSTRY OF FREE
CHINA. 56:9-28, August 1981

Toward a male contraceptive [letter], by J. S. Morrill. NEW ENGLAND
JOURNAL OF MEDICINE. 306(3):177, January 21, 1982

Toward a taxonomy of contraceptive behaviors and attitudes of single
college men, by D. B. Stephen. DISSERTATION ABSTRACTS INTERNATION-
AL. A. p. 1431, 1982

Toxic-shock syndrome associated with diaphragm use [letter]. NEW
ENGLAND JOURNAL OF MEDICINE. 305(26):1585-1586, December 24, 1981

Toxic-shock syndrome associated with diaphragm use for only nine
hours [letter], by D. V. Alcid, et al. LANCET. 1(8285):1363-1364,
June 12, 1982

Toxoplasmosis and habitual abortion. Our experience, by F. L.
Giiorgino, et al. CLINICAL AND EXPERIMENTAL OBSTETRICS AND
GYNECOLOGY. 8(3):132-134, 1981

Training of doctors in conducting M.T.P. and tubectomy--an experimental approach, by M. Arundhathi, et al. JOURNAL OF FAMILY WEL-
FARE. 28:62-65, June 1982

Transabdominal cervicoisthmic cerclage for the management of repetitive abortion and premature delivery, by M. J. Novy. AMERICAN
JOURNAL OF OBSTETRICS AND GYNECOLOGY. 143(1):44-54, May 1, 1982

Transfer of contraceptive steroids in milk of women using long-acting
gestagens, by S. Koetsawang, et al. CONTRACEPTION. 25(4):321-331,
April 1982

The transition in Korean family planning behavior, 1935-1976: a
retrospective cohort analysis, by J. R. Foreit. STUDIES IN FAMILY
PLANNING. 13:227-236, August-September 1982

Translocations involving chromosome 12. I. A report of a 12,21 translocation in a woman with recurrent abortions, and a study of the
breakpoints and modes of ascertainment of translocations involving
chromosome 12, by J. H. Ford, et al. HUMAN GENETICS. 58(2):144-
148, 1981

Transposition of the great vessels in an infant exposed to massive
doses of oral contraceptives, by R. W. Redline, et al. AMERICAN
JOURNAL OF OBSTETRICS AND GYNECOLOGY. 141(4):468-469, October 15,
1981

Treatment of cervix and isthmus insufficiency with cerclage using the
McDonald method, by C. Balbi, et al. ARCHIVES OF OBSTETRICS AND
GYNECOLOGY. 85(3):179-184, May-June 1980

The trend toward delayed parenthood, by J. R. Wilkie. JOURNAL OF
MARRIAGE AND THE FAMILY. 43(3):583-591, August 1981

Trends and patterns in the attitudes of the public toward legal abortion in the United States, 1972-1978, by S. A. Moldando. DISSERTA-
TION ABSTRACTS INTERNATIONAL. B. p. 1054, 1982

Trends in contraceptive practice: United States, 1965-1976, by W. D.
Mosher, et al. VITAL HEALTH STATISTICS. 23(10):1-47, February
1982

Triquilar/trinordiol. A new pill with 3 sequences, by E. B. Obel.
UGESKRIFT FOR LAEGER. 143(25):1610-1611, June 15, 1981

Trophoblastic disease: a bridge between pregnancy and malignancy, by L. Deligdisch. PROGRESS IN CLINICAL AND BIOLOGICAL RESEARCH. 70: 323-337, 1981

Tubal anastomosis following unipolar cautery, by J. A. Rock, et al. FERTILITY AND STERILITY. 37(5):613-618, May 1982

Tubal occlusion with silicone rubber. Update, 1980, by T. P. Reed, et al. JOURNAL OF REPRODUCTIVE MEDICINE. 26(10):534-537, October 1981

Tubal plugs bar pregnancy (tubal occlusion: silicone plugs block fallopian tubes). SCIENCE DIGEST. 90:89, November 1982

Tubal sterilization and hysterectomy, by J. H. Johnson. FAMILY PLANNING PERSPECTIVES. 14(1):28-30, January-February 1982

Tubal sterilization. Characteristics of women most affected by the option of reversibility, by R. N. Shain, et al. SOCIAL SCIENCE AND MEDICINE. 16(10):1067-1077, 1982

Tubal sterilization with silver clips--clinical observation and follow-up of 1,182 cases. CHUNG HUA FU CHAN KO TSA CHIH. 16(1):52-54, January 1981

Twelve years of legal abortion in England and Wales, by F. Munoz-Perez. POPULATION. 36:1105-1140, November-December 1981

25 years of hormonal contraception, by M. Sas. ORVOSI HETILAP. 123(4):195-200, January 24, 1982

Twenty years progress in oral contraception. Based on the symposium arranged by Shering Nordiska AB in Stockholm on March 21, 1981. ACTA OBSTETRICIA ET GYNECOLOGICA SCANDINAVICA. SUPPLEMENT. 105:1-71, 1982

Twin pregnancy, abortion of one fetus with Down's syndrome by sectio parva, the other delivered mature and healthy, by L. Beck, et al. EUROPEAN JOURNAL OF OBSTETRICS, GYNECOLOGY AND REPRODUCTIVE BIOLOGY. 12(5):267-269, November 1981

Twin pregnancy with operative removal of one fetus with chromosomal mosaicism 46,XX/45,XO and term delivery of a healthy baby, by U. Gigon, et al. ZEITSCHRIFT FUR GEBURTSCHILFE UND PERINATOLOGIE. 185(6):365-366, December 1981

Twinning following oral contraceptive discontinuation, by D. Hemon, et al. INTERNATIONAL JOURNAL OF EPIDEMIOLOGY. 10(4):319-328, December 1981

Two competing "pro-life" measures split the anti-abortion lobby: one faction supports an outright ban on abortions, while another favors a constitutional amendment that would turn the issue largely over to the states, by T. Miller. NATIONAL JOURNAL. 14:511-513, March 20, 1982

A two-year follow-up study of women sterilized in India, by R. V. Ghatt, et al. CONTRACEPTION. 23(6):603-619, June 1981

US bishops on abortion, by J. G. Deedy. TABLET. 235:1222-1223,

121

December 12, 1981

U.S. population policies, development, and the rural poor of Africa, by E. Green. JOURNAL OF MODERN AFRICAN STUDIES. 20:45-67, March 1982

USCC backs proposed parental notice legislation. OUR SUNDAY VISITOR. 70:8, April 25, 1982

Ultrastructural study of placentas in yellow daphne (Wikstroemia chmamedaphne Meisn) induced labor, by Z. H. Wang. CHUNG HUA FU CHAN KO TSA CHIH. 14(2):125-126, April 1979

Ultrastructure of cervical mucus and sperm penetration during use of a triphasic oral contraceptive, by M. Ulstein, et al. ACTA OBSTE-TRICIA ET GYNECOLOGICA SCANDINAVICA. SUPPLEMENT. 105:45-49, 1982

Unexpected encounters in cytogenetics: repeated abortions and paren-tal sex chromosome mosaicism may indicte risk of nondisjunction [editorial], by F. Hecht. AMERICAN JOURNAL OF HUMAN GENETICS. 34(3):514-516, May 1982

Unlikely role of tryptophan metabolites in glucose tolerance and gluconeogenesis in oral contraceptive and pyridoxine treated rats, by S. Safaya, et al. INDIAN JOURNAL OF MEDICAL RESEARCH. 74:236-243, August 1981

Unmarried black adolescent father's attitudes toward abortion, con-traception, and sexuality [a preliminary report], by L. E. Hen-dricks. JOURNAL OF ADOLESCENT HEALTH CARE. 2(3):199-203, March 1982

Unplanned pregnancies in a midwestern community, by D. Hilliard, et al. JOURNAL OF FAMILY PRACTICE. 15(2):259-263, August 1982

Update on oral contraception. CLINICAL OBSTETRICS AND GYNECOLOGY. 24(30:867-996, September 1981

The urchins of summer, by G. Weissmann. HOSPITAL PRACTICE. 16(10): 69+, October 1981

Urine free dopamine in normal primigravid pregnancy and women taking oral contraceptives, by C. M. Perkins, et al. CLINICAL SCIENCE. 61(4):423-428, October 1981

The use of birth control pills in women with medical disorders, by A. H. Decherney. CLINICAL OBSTETRICS AND GYNECOLOGY. 24(3):965-975, September 1981

Use of cloprostenol with dexamethasone in the termination of advanced pregnancy in heifers, by R. D. Murray, et al. VETERINARY RECORD. 108(17):378-380, April 25, 1981

Use of a contraceptive suppository as chemoprophylaxis against sex-ually-transmitted diseases, by G. Marion-Landais. SPM: SALUD PUB-LICA DE MEXICO. 23(4):345-352, July-August 1981

Use of dacron cervical sutures for correction of the abnormal posi-tiion of the chorion frondosum and the placenta, by A. I. Liubi-mova, et al. AKUSHERSTVO I GINEKOLOGIIA. (1):39-41, January 1982

The use of a drug combination in anesthesia for voluntary interruption of pregnancy. Medical considerations and social and economic repercussions, by G. De Angelis, et al. MINERVA ANESTESIOLOGICA. 47(6):287-290, June 1981

Use of electrorelaxation of the uterus in the treatment of threatened abortion, by A. Z. Khasin, et al. AKUSHERSTVO I GINEKOLOGIIA. (1):30-32, January 1982

Use of fallopian ring with laparoscopy for closure of oviduct, by F. Zabransky. ZENTRALBLATT FUR GYNAEKOLOGIE. 103(20):1228-1234, 1981

The use of hospital resources to treat incomplete abortions: examples from Latin America, by J. A. Fortney. PUBLIC HEALTH REPORTS. 96(6):574-579, November-December 1981

Use of mepregenol diacetate (Diamol), a gestagen preparation, for estrus synchronization in caracul sheep during mating season, by IuD. Klinskii, et al. ARCHIV FUR EXPERIMENTELLE VETERINARMEDIZIN. 36(1):159-162, January 1982

Use of a new synthetic prostaglandin (sulprostone) in various obstetrical conditions, by G. B. Melis, et al. MINERVA GINECOLOGIA. 34(3):183-190, March 1982

Use of prostaglandin F_2alpha gel prior to termination of pregnancy of primigravidae for cervix maturation, by G. Koehler, et al. ZENTRALBLATT FUR GYNAEKOLOGIE. 103(14):818-822, 1981

Use of services for family planning and infertility: United States, by G. E. Hendershot, et al. VITAL HEALTH SERVICES. 23(8):1-41, December 1981

Use of trilene and sombrevin anesthesia in minor gynecologic operations, by A. V. Mishenin, et al. MEDITSINSKAIA SESTRA. 40(10):16-17, October 1981

Use of turinal in the combined treatment of threatened abortion and its effect on placental hormone function, by N. G. Kosheleva, et al. AKUSHERSTVO I GINEKOLOGIIA. (5):23-25, May 1981

Use of turinal in the treatment of habitual abortion, by K. R. Alimova. AKUSHERSTVO I GINEKOLOGIIA. (1):55-56, January 1982

User preferences for contraceptive methods in India, Korea, The Philippines, and Turkey. STUDIES IN FAMILY PLANNING. 11(9-10):267-273, September-October 1980

Using local anesthesia for 1st-trimester abortion cuts mortality sharply. FAMILY PLANNING PERSPECTIVES. 14:332-334, November-December 1982

Using model projects to introduce change into family planning programs, by M. H. Bernhart. STUDIES IN FAMILY PLANNING. 12(10):346, October 1981

Uterine cornual cauterization as a sterilization method, by M. Ishikawa, et al. JAPANESE JOURNAL OF FERTILITY AND STERILITY. 27(1):122-125, 1982

--REPRODUCCION. 5(3):157-162, July-September 1981

Uterine leiomyomas, serum cholesterol, and oral contraceptives. A preliminary study of epidemiologic differences in Los Angeles, California and Albany, New York, by H. Ratech, eet al. DIAGNOSTIC GYNECOLOGY AND OBSTETRICS. 4(1):21-24, Spring 1982

Uterine malformations and pregnancy, by V. Giustolisi, et al. MINERVA GINECOLOGIA. 34(1-2):47-55, January-February 1982

Uterine rupture occurring during midtrimester abortion, by D. Graham. OBSTETRICS AND GYNECOLOGY. 59(6 Suppl):62S-4S, June 1982

Utilitarianism and children, by D. S. Hutchinson. CANADIAN JOURNAL OF PHYSIOLOGY AND PHARMACOLOGY. 12:61-73, March 1982

Utilization of contralateral fallopian tube segments in tubal reanastomosis, by A. F. Haney. FERTILITY AND STERILITY. 37(5):701-703, May 1982

Utilizing research to manage a family planning project, by N. E. Williamson. STUDIES IN FAMILY PLANNING. 11(9-10):301-307, September-October 1980

The vaginal administration of 9-deoxo-16,16-dimethyl-9-methylene PGE2 for second trimester abortion, by C. A. Ballard. CONTRACEPTION. 24(2):151-157, August 1981

Vaginal application agent before legal abortion: a way of reducing infectious complication?, by O. Meirik, et al. ACTA OBSTETRICIA ET GYNECOLOGICA SCANDINAVICA. 60(3):233-235, 1981

Vaginal prostaglandin F2 alpha gel before first trimester termination of pregnancy, by M. A. Quinn, et al. AUSTRALIAN AND NEW ZEALAND JOURNAL OF OBSTETRICS AND GYNAECOLOGY. 21(2):93-95, May 1981

Vaginal spermicidal activity of gossypol in Macaca arctoides, by S. M. Cameron, et al. FERTILITY AND STERILITY. 37(2):273-274, 1982

Vaginal spermicides and outcome of pregancy: findings in a large cohort study, by G. Huggins, et al. CONTRACEPTION. 25(3):219-230, 1982

The value of children and the costs of contraception: predictors of reproductive ideals and contraceptive practice in Egypt, by R. Vernon-Carter. DISSERTATION ABSTRACTS INTERNATIONAL. A. p. 938, 1982

Various aspects of voluntary abortion at the Obstetrical and Gynecological Clinic of the University of Modena, by M. G. Lucchi, et al. ARCHIVES OF OBSTETRICS AND GYNECOLOGY. 85(6):567-587, November-December 1980

Vascular effects of hormonal contraception, by L. C. Huppert. CLINICAL OBSTETRICS AND GYNECOLOGY. 24(3):951-963, September 1981

Vascular thrombosis related to oral contraceptives and antiethinylestradiol antibodies--epidemiology and prevention, by V. Beaumont, et al. THERAPEUTISCHE UMSCHAU. 39(2):109-113, 1982

Vasecotomy reversal: use of microsurgical technique, by F. C. Derrick, Jr., et al. JOURNAL OF THE SOUTH CAROLINA MEDICAL ASSOCIATION. 78(2):90-91, February 1982

Vasectomy: it's simple, it works, but it has drawbacks, too. CHANGING TIMES. 35:63-65, February 1981

Vasectomy reversal: technique and results, by S. S. Schmidt. INFECTION CONTROL AND UROLOGICAL CARE. 6(1):13-16, 1981

Vasovasostomy-microscopy versus macroscopic techniques, by H. Fenster, et al. ARCHIVES OF ANDROLOGY. 7(2):201-204, September 1981

Vasovasostomy. Refertilization after vasectomy illustrated by a questionnaire study, by J. Eldrup, et al. UGESKRIFT FOR LAEGER. 144(16):1160-1162, April 19, 1982

Vasovasostomy with use of intraoperative vasography, by P. R. Hartig, et al. UROLOGY. 19(4):404-406, April 1982

Vatican on amniocentesis ultrasound scanning and abortion, by W. F. Jenks. PRIEST. 38:7-8, January 1982

Ventilatory response of humans to chronic contraceptive pill administration, by C. A. Smith, et al. RESPIRATION. 43(3):179-185, May-June 1982

Vestibular side effects of contraceptives, by F. Nagymajtenyi, et al. ORVOSI HETILAP. 122(8):455-457, February 22, 1981

A victory for women? The abortion referendum in Italy, by M. Bosworth. REFRACTORY GIRL. (23):17-19, March 1982

Visits to family planning clinics: United States, 1979, by B. Bloom. ADVANCE DATA. (74):1-7, September 4, 1981

Visits to family planning service sites: United States, 1978, by B. L. Hudson. ADVANCE DATA. (72):1-7, June 29, 1981

Voluntary childlessness and contraception: problems and practices, by F. Baum. JOURNAL OF BIOSOCIAL SCIENCE. 14(1):17-23, January 1982

Voluntary interruption of pregnancy: social aspects and psychological motivation, by F. Leone. ARCHIVES OF OBSTETRICS AND GYNECOLOGY. 85(6):545-556, November-December 1980

Voluntary sterilization for persons with mental disabilities: the need for legislation, by B. A. Burnett. SYRACUSE LAW REVIEW. 32:913-955, Fall 1981

Voluntary sterilization of the non-institutionalized mentally incompetent individual: judicial involvement or abstention?. NEW ENGLAND LAW REVIEW. 17:527-547, 1981-1982

Voting on abortion, by J. Wale. SUNDAY TIMES. p. 15, August 1, 1982

WHO special programme of research, development and research training in human reproduction. Task force on long-acting agents for the regulation of fertility. CONTRACEPTION. 25(1):1-11, January 1982

Wanted and unwanted fertility: Victoria 1971 to 1975, by K. Betts.
AUSTRALIAN JOURNAL OF SOCIAL ISSUES. 15(3):194-208, 1980

What does it mean to be "pro-life"?, by D. Granberg. CHRISTIAN CEN-
TURY. 99(17):562-566, May 12, 1982

What happens at conception?, by G. H. Ball. CHRISTIANITY AND CRISIS.
41:274+, October 19, 1981

What legalized abortion has meant to America, by R. P. Lockwood. OUR
SUNDAY VISITOR. 70:16, January 17, 1982

What the Supreme Court heard on abortion, by T. Gest. US NEWS AND
WORLD REPORT. 93:83, December 13, 1982

What value (risks) do today's modern possibilities of contraception
have?. MEDIZINISCHE WELT. 32(39):1456-1459, September 25, 1981

Whatever happend to new methods of birth control?. ECONOMIST. 279:
75-77, May 30, 1981

What's new in the law: constitutional law ... abortions. by A.
Ashman. AMERICAN BAR ASSOCIATION JOURNAL. 67:644-645, May 1981

--: constitutional law ... discriminatory funding, by A. Ashman.
AMERICAN BAR ASSOCIATION JOURNAL. 67:917-918, July 1981

--: courts ... authority to sterilize, by A. Ashman. AMERICAN BAR
ASSOCIATION JOURNAL. 67:1044+, August 1981

--: mentally impaired ... sterilization, by A. Ashman. AMERICAN BAR
ASSOCIATION JOURNAL. 67:918-919, July 1981

When life begins [symposium]. SOCIETY. 19:32-72, May-June 1982

When teens want contraceptives, should their parents know? Two impassioned advocates face off (views of M. Mecklenburg and F. Wattleton), by K. Huff, et al. PEOPLE WEEKLY. 17:44-45, May 24, 1982

Where abortion is for export only, by M. Holland. TIMES (London).
p. 12, November 24, 1982

Who asks for vasectomy reversal and why?, by G. Howard. BRITISH
MEDICAL JOURNAL. 6340:490-492, August 14, 1982

Who does speak for human life? (debate on Hatch Amendment by National
Conference of Catholic Bishops), by W. F. Buckley. NATIONAL RE-
VIEW. 34:381, April 2, 1982

Who has the responsibility for the unborn?. LAKARTIDNINGEN. 78(37):
3131-3141, September 9, 1981

Whose freedom of choice? (effect of abortion on men), by J. Paterson.
PROGRESSIVE. 46:42-45, April 1982

Why the diaphragm doesn't work, by G. Berkowitz. SAN FRANCISCO.
23(4):72-75, December 1981

Why I ended my baby's life (Klinefelter's syndrome), by J. K. Ivey.
GLAMOUR. 80:134+, May 1982

Why they delay: a study of teenage family planning clinic patients [research], by L. S. Zabin, et al. FAMILY PLANNING PERSPECTIVES. 13(5):205-207+, September-October 1982

Will consumption or oral contraceptives enhance the gastrointestinal absorption of lead, by E. J. Calabrese. MEDICAL HYPOTHESES. 8(1): 11-15, January 1982

Win 32,729, a new, potent interceptive agent in rats and rhesus monkeys, by J. E. Creange, et al. CONTRACEPTION. 24(3):289-299, September 1981

With friends like these (Senate debate). COMMONWEAL. 109:483-485, September 24, 1982

Woman's reaction to spantaneous abortion, by M. C. Turcotte-Lamou-reux. INFIRMIERE CANADIENNE. 23(8):38+, September 1981

Women and the pill: from panacea to catalyst, by S. C. M. Scrimshaw. FAMILY PLANNING PERSPECTIVES. 13(6):254-256+, November-December 1981

Women and sterilization: the after effects, by S. Katz. CHATELAINE. 55:16, October 1982

Women as teachers of violence, by A. O'Donnell. HOMILETIC AND PAS-TORAL REVIEW. 82:54-58, June 1982

Women doctors talk about birth control, by M. Abrams. LADIES HOME JOURNAL. 99:64+, September 1982

Women saying no to pill, by M. Neilson. NATIONAL CATHOLIC REPORTER. 18(1):23, January 15, 1982

Women seeking abortion, by J. L. E. Thomas. ETHICAL ISSUES IN SOCIAL WORK. pp. 208-231, 1982

Women who have had abortions. Part 2. FAMILY PLANNING PERSPECTIVES. 14:60-62, March-April 1982

Women who never used pill are twice as likely as users to develop endometrial or ovarian cancer. FAMILY PLANNING PERSPECTIVES. 14: 145-146, May-June 1982

Women who use organized family planning services: United States, 1979, by E. Eckard. VITAL HEALTH STATISTICS. 13(62):1-28, January 1982

Women's employment and fertility in Quebec, by N. Kyriazis, et al. POPULATION STUDIES. 36:431-440, November 1982

Women's health care: approaches in delivery to physically disabled women, by L. Peters. NURSE PRACTITIONER. 7(1):34-37+, January 1982

Women's involvement in socioeconomic projects related to family plan-ning, by A. Duza. POPULATION STUDIES. pp. 3-30, July-September 1981

World fertility survey: charting global childbearing, by R. Lightbourne, Jr., et al. POPULATION BULLETIN. 37:2-54, March 1982

Wrongful birth. What is the damage?, by V. R. Greenfield. JAMA: JOURNAL OF THE AMERICAN MEDICAL ASSOCIATION. 248(8):926-927, August 27, 1982

Yoruba traditional healers' knowledge of contraception, abortion and infertility, by D. D. Oyebola. EAST AFRICAN MEDICAL JOURNAL. 58(10):777-784, October 1981

A Young People's Advisory Service, by N. Harrison, et al. HEALTH BULLETIN. 40(3):133-139, May 1982

Your parents or the judge: Massachusetts' new abortion consent law, by P. Donovan. FAMILY PLANNING PERSPECTIVES. 13(5):224-228, September-October 1981

Zona pellucida composition: species cross reactivity and contraceptive potential of antiserum to a purified pig zona antigen (PPZA), by A. G. Sacco, et al. BIOLOGICAL REPRODUCTION. 25(5):997-1008, December 1981

PERIODICAL LITERATURE

SUBJECT INDEX

ABORTION: GENERAL
Abortion. NEW ZEALAND MEDICAL JOURNAL. 94(698):472-473,
December 23, 1981

--, by R. H. Bube. JOURNAL OF THE AMERICAN SCIENTIFIC AFFILIA-
TION. 33(3):158-165, 1981

--[letter], by V. J. Hartfield. NEW ZEALAND MEDICAL JOURNAL.
95(700):57-58, January 27, 1982

--[letter], by A. Simpson, et al. NEW ZEALAND MEDICAL JOURNAL.
94(697):433-434, December 9, 1981

Abortion alarms, by C. Tietze. AMERICAN JOURNAL OF PUBLIC
HEALTH. 72:534-535, June 1982

Abortion and the rhetoric of individual rights, by L. R.
Churchill. HASTINGS CENTER REPORT. 12(1):9-12, 1982

Abortion attitudes, by C. Doyle. OBSERVER. p. 27, July 13,
1982

Abortion: exercise in biomedical ethics, by D. G. Jones.
JOURNAL OF THE AMERICAN SCIENTIFIC AFFILIATION. 34(1):6-17,
1982

Abortion for fetal abnormalities [letter], by J. E. McArthur.
NEW ZEALAND MEDICAL JOURNAL. 94(698):473, December 23,
1981

Abortion--restrictions. FAMILY LAW REPORTER: COURT OPINIONS.
7(35):2567, July 14, 1981

Abortion strategies for 1983, by T. Dejanikus. OFF OUR BACKS.
13:10, January 1983

Abortions and moles, by K. Benirschke. MONOGRAPHS IN PATHOLOGY.
(22):23-48, 1981

Abortions because of unavailability of prenatal diagnosis [let-
ter], by E. B. Hook, et al. LANCET. 2(8252):936, October 24,
1981

Abortions preventable by contraceptive practice, by C. F. Westoff, et al. FAMILY PLANNING PERSPECTIVES. 13(5):218-223,
September-October 1981

The acceptability of day stay for termination of pregnancy, by
J. M. Cundy, et al. BRITISH JOURNAL OF CLINICAL PRACTICE.
35(6):215-218, June 1981

Adoption wins tax break, by M. Meehan. NATIONAL CATHOLIC RE-
PORTER. 18:2, February 19, 1982

Aetiology of delivery during the second trimester and performance in subsequent pregnancies, by G. J. Ratten. MEDICAL
JOURNAL OF AUSTRALIA. 2(12-13):654-656, December 12-26, 1981

Amniocentesis and the apotheosi of human quality control, by J.
M. Nolan-Haley. JOURNAL OF LEGAL MEDICINE. 2(3):347-363,
September 1981

Ancora in materia di pianificazione familiare e di interruzione
volontaria della gravidanzam, by V. Segre. SOCIOLOGIA DEL
DIRITTO. 7(3):159-176, 1980

Anti-abortion march marks out ruling, by M. Holahan. NATIONAL
CATHOLIC REPORTER. (1):18-24, January 29, 1982

Apostle of abortion, by G. Epps. SCIENCE. 3(2):70, March 1982

Aspects of reproduction related to human rights. II. Contraception, by J. Martinez-Manautou. GACETA MEDICA DE MEXICO.
117(7):266-268, July 1981

--III. Artificial termination of pregnancy, by L. Castelazo-
Ayala. GACETA MEDICA DE MEXICO. 117(7):268-272, July 1981

Assisting at abortions: can you really say no?, by W. A. Regan.
RN. 45:71, June 1982

Behind the anti-abortion lines, by L. Bush. THE VILLAGE VOICE.
26(4):18+, November 25, 1981

A case of porcine abortion caused by nocardia asteroides [let-
ter], by R. W. Mason. AUSTRALIAN VETERINARY JOURNAL. 57(8):
398-399, August 1981

Contradiction isn't unreasonableness, by C. Sureau. ACQUISI-
TIONS MEDICALES RECENTES. 198:173-178, 1981

Diphyllobothriasis in Americans and Asians [letter]. JAMA:
JOURNAL OF THE AMERICAN MEDICAL ASSOCIATION. 247(16):2230,
April 23, 1982

Early fetal loss, by Z. Stein. BIRTH DEFECTS. 17(1):95-111,
1981

Effect of an operation for artificial abortion on the female
body and reproductive function, by I. B. Frolov. AKUSHERSTVO
I GINEKOLOGIIA. (4):6-8, April 1982

The effects of termination of pregnancy: a follow-up study of
psychiatric referrals, by R. Schmidt, et al. BRITISH JOURNAL
OF MEDICAL PSYCHOLOGY. 54(Pt 3):267-276, September 1981

Family planning and abortion: have they affected fertility in Tennessee?, by H. K. Atrash, et al. AMERICAN JOURNAL OF PUBLIC HEALTH. 72(6):608-610, June 1982

Family planning. Contraception, sterilization, abortion, by H. Ludwig. FORTSCHRITTE DER MEDIZIN. 100(16):721-722+, April 29, 1982

Fetal organ donors: pregnancy termination to acquire organs?, by H. Piechowiak. MEDIZINISCHE WELT. 32(47):1799-1801, November 20, 1981

The Halakhic status of the fetus with respec to abortion, by R. S. Kirschner. CONSERVATIVE JUDAISM. 34(6):3-16, 1981

Immunologic interruption of pregnancy, by G. P. Talwar, et al. PROGRESS IN CLINICAL AND BIOLOGICAL RESEARCH. 70:451-459, 1981

Lost genius, by R. Baker. NEW YORK TIMES MAGAZINE. p. 15, January 17, 1982

Maternal and public health benefits of menstrual regulation in Chittagong, by S. N. Bhuiyan, et al. INTERNATIONAL JOURNAL OF GYNAECOLOGY AND OBSTETRICS. 20(2):105-109, April 1982

Medical examination of patients before referral for termination of pregnancy [letter], by R. E. Coles. LANCET. 2(8294):380-381, August 14, 1982

Midtrimester abortion, by W. M. Hern. OBSTETRICS AND GYNECOLOGY ANNUAL. 10:375-422, 1981

Midtrimester abortion patients, by L. D. White, et al. AORN JOURNAL: ASSOCIATION OF OPERATING ROOM NURSES. 34(4):756-768, October 1981

Muslim juridical opinions concerning the status of women as demonstrated by the case of 'azi (coitus interruptus), by D. L. Bowen. JOURNAL OF NEAR EASTERN STUDIES. 40(4):323-328, October 1981

Potential persons and murder: a reply to John Woods "Engineered Death", by J. C. Moskop. DIALOGUE. 21:307-315, June 1982

Prenatal diagnosis [letter]. JOURNAL OF THE AMERICAN ACADEMY OF DERMATOLOGY. 5(6):700-702, December 1981

Present sakes and future prospects: the status of early abortion by P. Bassen. PHILOSOPHY AND PUBLIC AFFAIRS. 11:314-337, August 1982

Ransoming the doomed, by J. Rasmussen. ALBERTA REPORT. 8:45, November 13, 1981

The risk of death from combined abortion-sterilization procedures: can hysterotomy or hysterectomy be justified?, by H. K. Atrash, et al. AMERICAN JOURNAL OF OBSTETRICS AND GYNECOLOGY.

142(3):269-274, February 1, 1982

A single intercourse [letter], by A. Viliunas. MEDICAL JOURNAL OF AUSTRALIA. 2(11):578, November 28, 1981

Starting a family in Aberdeen 1961-79: the significance of illegitimacy and abortion, by C. Pritchard, et al. JOURNAL OF BIOSOCIAL SCIENCE. 14(2):127-139, April 1982

Taking liberties with women: abortion, sterilization, and contraception, by W. Savage. INTERNATIONAL JOURNAL OF HEALTH SERVICES. 12(2):293-308, 1982

Third world policies. USA TODAY. 110:4-5, December 1981

Thousands rally for pro-life amendment (in Washington, D.C. on Jan 22). HUMAN EVENTS. 42:8, February 6, 1982

The urchins of summer, by G. Weissmann. HOSPITAL PRACTICE. 16(10):69+, October 1981

Women seeking abortion, by J. L. E. Thomas. ETHICAL ISSUES IN SOCIAL WORK. pp. 208-231, 1982

Women's health care: approaches i delivery to physically disabled women, by L. Peters. NURSE PRACTITIONER. 7(1):34-37+, January 1982

AFRICA
   Avoiding shame: the ethical context of abortion in Ghana, by W. Bleek. ANTHROPOLOGICAL QUARTERLY. 54:203-209, October 1981

AUSTRALIA
   Abortion--an industrial issue (ACTU Congress, 1981 [Australian trade union]), by D. Hague, et al. REFRACTORY GIRL. (23): 15-16, March 1982

BANGLADESH
   Case studies of indigenous abortion practitioners in rural Bangladesh, by S. Islam. STUDIES IN FAMILY PLANNING. 13(3):86, March 1982

   Maternal and abortion related deaths in Bangladesh, 1978-1979, by R. W. Rochat, et al. INTERNATIONAL JOURNAL OF GYNAECOLOGY AND OBSTETRICS. 19(2):155-164, April 1981

   Methods used in induced abortion in Bangladesh: an anthropological perspective, by P. C. Sarker. SOCIAL SCIENCE AND MEDICINE. 15(4):483-487, October 1981

BELGIUM
   Statistical data on abortions performed in 1979 in a Belgian out-patient clinic, by M. Vekemans, et al. REVUE MEDICALE DE BRUXELLES. 2(9):851-864, November 1981

CHILE
   Epidemiology of hospitalized abortion in Valdivia, Chile, by

R. Guzman Serani, et al. REVISTA MEDICA DE CHILE. 109(11): 1099-1106, November 1981

CHINA
Abortion and birth control in Canton, China, by M. Vink. WALL STREET JOURNAL. 198:26, November 30, 1981

CZECHOSLOVAKIA
Mucosal disease virus as a cause of enzootic abortion in cattle in Czechoslovakia, by J. Mensik, et al. VETERINARNI MEDICINA. 26(8):457-468, August 1981

DANISH
Abortion and accident proneness: a Danish validation study, by R. L. Somers. JOURNAL OF BIOLOGICAL SCIENCE. 13(4):425-429, October 1981

ENGLAND
Illegitimacy in England and Wales in 1911, by N. F. R. Crafts. POPULATION STUDIES. 36:327-331, July 1982

Judgement and counter judgement ... England, by A. Langslow. AUSTRALIAN NURSES JOURNAL. 11:28-30, March 1982

Twelve years of legal abortion in England and Wales, by F. Munoz-Perez. POPULATION. 36:1105-1140, November-December 1981

EUROPE
Eastern Europe: pronatalist policies and private behavior, by H. P. David. POPULATION BULLETIN. 36(6):48, February 1982

Europe: abortion (from article by Marge Berer in "Spare Rib and Women in Spain," a publication of the Commission of the European Communities). OFF OUR BACKS. 12:8, July 1982

GERMANY
Incidence rate of late complications in legally induced abortion in the Federal Republic of Germany, by H. H. Brautigam, et al. ZEITSCHRIFT FUR GEBURTSCHILFE UND PERINATOLOGIE. 185(4):193- 199, August 1981

GREAT BRITAIN
Abortion: British conference [National Abortion Campaign (NAC) national conference, May 22-23, 1981], by A. Henry. OFF OUR BACKS. 12:5, July 1982

HONG KONG
Abortion in single girls in Hong Kong, by G. W. Tang. JOURNAL OF ADOLESCENT HEALTH CARE. 2(3):213-216, March 1982

INDIA
Attitudes of rural Bangladesh physicans toward abortion, by M. J. Rosenberg, et al. STUDIES IN FAMILY PLANNING. 12(8-9): 318, August-September 1981

Case studies of indigenous abortion practitioners in rural Bangladesh, by S. Islam. STUDIES IN FAMILY PLANNING. 13:

86-93, March 1982

Clinical reprography of women seeking medical termination of
pregnancy at AIIMS Hospital, New Delhi, by R. Singh, et al.
JOURNAL OF FAMILY WELFARE. 28:3-17, June 1982

IRELAND
Babies and bishops, by M. Holland. NEW STATESMAN. pp. 8-9,
July 30, 1982

Criminal liability for complicity in abortions committed outside Ireland, by M. J. Findlay. IRISH JURIST. 15:88-98,
Summer 1980

Ireland: abortion vote debated (Women's Right to Choose, Dublin, fighting anti-abortion amendment to Constitution), by
G. Horgan. OFF OUR BACKS. 12:6, July 1982

Ireland: pro-life, pro-uniformity by M. Holland. NEW STATES-
MAN. pp. 12-13, May 21, 1982

Voting on abortion, by J. Wale. SUNDAY TIMES. p. 15, August
1, 1982

ITALY
Conoscenza dell'aborto e organizzazione del lavoro consultoriale by A. Capodilupo. REVISTRA DI SERVIZIO SOCIALE.
21(2):74-81, 1981

Contributo all'analisi del ruolo dell'operatore in un consultori pubblico di fronte alla richiesta di interruzione di
gravidanza, by M. Ghezzi. REVISTRA DI SERVIZIO SOCIALE.
21(1):82- 90, 1981

Interruzione volantaria della gravidanza in Liguria: un'esperienza sul territorio, by S. Morano. SOCIOLOGIA DEL DIRIT-
TO. 7(3):177-180, 1980

Legal abortion in Italy, 1978-1979, by M. Filicori, et al.
FAMILY PLANNING PERSPECTIVES. 13(5):228, September-October
1981

A victory for women? The abortion referendum in Italy, by M.
Bosworth. REFRACTORY GIRL. (23):17-19, March 1982

KOREA
Abortion and contraception in the Korean fertility transition,
by P. J. Donaldson, et al. POPULATION STUDIES. 36:227-236,
July 1982

LATIN AMERICA
Latin attitudes towards abortion, by H. Amaro. NUESTRO.
5:43- 44, August-September 1981

The use of hospital resources to treat incomplete abortions:
examples from Latin America, by J. A. Fortney. PUBLIC
HEALTH REPORTS. 96:574-579, November-December 1981

ABORTION: GENERAL (continued)

THE NETHERLANDS
Induced abortion in the Netherlands: a decade of experience,
1970-80, by E. Ketting, et al. STUDIES IN FAMILY PLANNING.
11(12):385-394, December 1980

NEW GUINEA
Termination of pregnancy in Papua New Guinea: the traditional
and contemporary position, by I. A. McGoldrick. PAPAU NEW
GUINEA MEDICAL JOURNAL. 24(2):113-120, June 1981

NEW ZEALAND
Congenital defects and miscarriages among New Zealand 2, 4,
5-T sprayers, by A. H. Smith, et al. ARCHIVES OF ENVIRON-
MENTAL HEALTH. 37(4):197-200, July-August 1982

Housewives' depression: the debate over abortion and birth
control in the 1930's, by B. Brookes. NEW ZEALAND JOURNAL
OF HISTORY. 15:115-134, October 1981

NIGERIA
Adolescent induced abortion in Benin City, Nigeria, by A. E.
Omu, et al. INTERNATIONAL JOURNAL OF GYNAECOLOGY AND OBSTE-
TRICS. 19(6):495-499, December 1981

Menstrual regulation at University College Hospital, Ibadan,
Nigeria, by O. A. Ojo, et al. INTERNATIONAL SURGERY.
66(3):247-249, July-September 1981

NORWAY
In Norway's state church, a pastor's abortion protest has wide
implications (case of B. Knudson), by H. Genet. CHRISTIANI-
ITY TODAY. 26:58+, April 9, 1982

Reproductive histories in a Norwegian twin population: evaluation of the maternal effect in early spontaneous abortion,
by W. L. Golden ACTA GENETICAE MEDICAE ET GEMELLOLOGIAE.
30(2): 91-95, 1981

THE PHILIPPINES
Abortion in the Philippines: a study of clients and practitioners, by M. Gallen. STUDIES IN FAMILY PLANNING. 13(2):
35-43, February 1982

SCOTLAND
Cervical suture in Scotland; strengths and weaknesses in the
use of routine clinical summaries, by S. K. Cole. BRITISH
JOURNAL OF OBSTETRICS AND GYNAECOLOGY. 89(7):528-535, July
1982

SOUTH KOREA
Abortion and contraception in the Korean fertility transition,
by P. J. Donaldson, et al. POPULATION STUDIES. 36:227-235,
July 1982

SOUTH PACIFIC
Termination of pregnancy in Papua New Guinea: the traditional
and contemporary position, by I. A. McGoldrick. PAPAU NEW
GUINEA MEDICAL JOURNAL. 24(2):113-120, 1981

ABORTION: GENERAL (continued)

SWEDEN
Menopausal age and spontaneous abortion in a group of women
working in a Swedish steel works, by B. Kolmodm-Hedman, et
al. SCANDINAVIAN JOURNAL OF SOCIAL MEDICINE. 10(1):17-22,
1982

TAIWAN
Attitude toward and use of induced abortion among Taiwanese
women [research], by J. F. Wang. ISSUES IN HEALTH CARE OF
WOMEN. 3(3):179-202, May-June 1981

TUNISIA
Induced abortion in maternal and child health centres in a
general family planning programme in Cap Bon, Tunisia, by I.
de Schampheleire. TROPICAL DOCTOR. 12(2):77-80, April 1982

UNITED KINGDOM
Occupational hazards in the United Kingdom, by A. A. Spence.
INTERNATIONAL ANESTHESIOLOGY CLINICS. 19(4):165-176, Winter
1981

Philosophy of medicine in the United Kingdom, by D. Lamb.
METAMEDICINE. 3:3-34, February 1982

UNITED STATES
Abortion and the public opinion polls (United States), by S.
K. Henshaw, et al. FAMILY PLANNING PERSPECTIVES. 14:53-
55+, March-April 1982

Abortion attitudes, by C. Doyle. OBSERVER. p. 27, July 13,
1982

Abortion in the U.S., 1977-1978, by J. D. Forrest, et al.
FAMILY PLANNING PERSPECTIVES. 11(6):329-341, November-
December 1979

The abortion mess in Los Angeles (controversy over disposition
of dead fetuses found at defunct private pathology lab), by
D. W. Pawley. CHRISTIANITY TODAY. 26:46+, September 17,
1982

Abortion services in the United States, 1979 and 1980, by S.
K. Henshaw, et al. FAMILY PLANNING PERSPECTIVES. 14(1):5-
8+, January-February 1982

Family planning and abortion: have they affected fertility in
Tennessee, USA?, by H. K. Atrash, et al. AMERICAN JOURNAL
OF PUBLIC HEALTH. 72(6):608-610, June 1982

Hospitalization for medical legal and other abortions in the
United States 1970-1977 [research], by M. B. Bracken, et al.
AMERICAN JOURNAL OF PUBLIC HEALTH. 72(1):30-37, January
1982

Illegal abortion deaths in the United States: why are they
still occurring, by N. Binkin, et al. FAMILY PLANNING PER-
SPECTIVES. 14:163-174, May-June 1982

The impact of legal abortion on marita and nonmarital fertility in upstate New York, by E. J. Tu, et al. FAMILY PLANNING PERSPECTIVES. 14:37-46, January-February 1982

Massachusetts Medicaid Program must fund medically necessary abortions. FAMILY LAW REPORTER: COURT OPINIONS. 7(18): 2291-2294, March 10, 1981

Most Americans in the middle on abortion, shun pro-extremes and anti-extremes. FAMILY PLANNING PERSPECTIVES. 14:102-106, March-April 1982

N.C. funding of elective abortions upheld agains taxpayer challenge. FAMILY LAW REPORTER: COURT OPINIONS. 7(22): 2362, April 7, 1981

Parts of Massachusetts abortion law deemed of doubtful constitutionality. FAMILY LAW REPORTER: COURT OPINIONS. 7(17): 2272- 2274, March 3, 1981

Pro-, anti-choice groups square off in New Jersey, by L. Hamilton. NEW DIRECTIONS FOR WOMEN. 11:22, Sepember-October 1982

Pro-life versus pro-choice: another look at the abortion controversy in the U.S., by D. Granberg, et al. SOCIOLOGY AND SOCIAL RESEARCH. 65(4):424-434, July 1981

Race-specific patterns of abortion use by American teenagers [research], by N. V. Ezzard, et al. AMERICAN JOURNAL OF PUBLIC HEALTH. 72:809-814, August 1982

Rape and abortion in America (dismissal of teacher and rape victim J. Eckmann for deciding to keep her baby in McHenry County, Ill.), by L. M. Delloff. CHRISTIAN CENTURY. 99: 1037- 1038, October 20, 1982

Reproductive mortality in the United States, by B. P. Sachs, et al. JAMA: JOURNAL OF THE AMERICAN MEDICAL ASSOCIATION. 247(20):2789-2792, May 28, 1982

Social, spatial and political determinants of U.S. abortion rates, by N. F. Henry, et al. SOCIAL SCIENCE AND MEDICINE. 16(9):987-996, 1982

Trends and patterns in the attitudes of the public toward legal abortion in the United States, 1972-1978, by S. A. Moldando. DISSERTATION ABSTRACTS INTERNATIONAL. B. p. 1054, 1982

U.S.S.R.

The anti-abortion campaign (Soviet Union) by M. Ryan. BRITISH MEDICAL JOURNAL. 6303:1378-1379, November 21, 1981

Communist party of the Soviet Union and the women's question: the case of the 1936 decree in defence of mother and child, by J. Evans. JOURNAL OF CONTEMPORARY HISTORY. 16:757-775, October 1981

ABORTION: GENERAL (continued)

WALES
Illegitimacy in England and Wales in 1911, by N. F. R. Crafts.
POPULATION STUDIES. 36:327-331, July 1982

Twelve years of legal abortion in England and Wales, by F.
Munoz-Perez. POPULATION. 36:1105-1140, November-December
1981

WEST GERMANY
Incidence rate of late complications in legally induced abortion in West Germany, by H. H. Braeutigam, et al. ZEIT-
SCHRIFT FUR GEBURTSCHILFE UND PERINATOLOGIE. 185(4):193-
199, 1981

ABORTION: ATTITUDES
Abortion and American pluralism, by M. Bunson. SOCIAL JUSTICE
REVIEW. 72:198-204, November-December 1981

Abortion and the consideration of fundamental, irreconcilable
interests, by C. J. Jones. SYRACUSE LAW REVIEW. 33:565-613,
Spring 1982

Abortion and the Hatch Amendment, by E. Bryce. AMERICA. 146:
166-168, March 6, 1982

Abortion and the public opinion polls. Morality and legality.
Part I, by S. K. Henshaw, et al. FAMILY PLANNING PERSPEC-
TIVES. 14(2):53-55+, March-April 1982

Abortion and reverence for human life, by H. Kraatz, et al.
DEUTSCHES GESUNDHEITSWESEN. 36(21):ix-xiii, 1981

Abortion and the rhetoric of individual rights: why the abortion
debate isterile, by L. R. Churchill, et al. HASTINGS CENTER
REPORT. 12:9-12, February 1982

Abortion and women's health: a meeting of the National Abortion
Federation, by J. H. Johnson. FAMILY PLANNING PERSPECTIVES.
14:327-328, November-December 1982

Abortion battles, by J. McLaughlin. NATIONAL REVIEW. 34:1599,
December 24, 1982

The abortion controversy and the claim that this body is mine,
by M. R. Wicclair. SOCIAL THEORY AND PRACTICE. 7(3):337-346,
Fall 1981

Abortion death toll rises, but rate tapers off in 1980. OUR
SUNDAY VISITOR. 70:7, March 14, 1982

Abortion ethics , by M. J. Fromer. NURSING OUTLOOK. 30(4):
234-240, April 1982

Abortion is not a banner-waving issue [letter], by J. P. James.
JOGN NURSING: JOURNAL OF OBSTETRIC GYNECOLOGIC AND NEONATAL
NURSING. 10(6):458-459, November-December 1981

Abortion: a national security issue (alleged threats posed to the United States by continued world population growth; abortion as a possible solution), by S. D. Mumford. HUMANIST. 42:12-13+, September-October 1982

Abortion: one man's view, by H. Bray. ESSENCE. 12:146, April 1982

Abortion, personhood, and moral rights, by D. Algeo. THE MONIST. 64:543-549, October 1981

Abortion: a plea for moral sensitivity, by J. M. Orenduff. SOUTHWEST PHILOSOPHICAL STUDIES. 6:69-74, April 1981

Abortion practices and attitudes in cross-cultural perspective, by R. N. Shain. AMERICAN JOURNAL OF OBSTETRICS AND GYNECOLOGY. 142(3):245-251, February 1, 1982

Abortion: readers respond. COMMONWEAL. 109:75-84, February 12, 1982

Abortion: what kind of moral issue?, by L. Nicholson. JOURNAL OF VALUE INQUIRY. 15:235-242, 1981

Abortion: a woman's decision, by J. B. Conlin. HOSPITAL/HEALTH CARE TRAINING. 8(2):38, 1981

Adolescent aborters. Factors associated with gestational age, by J. Poliak, et al. NEW YORK STATE JOURNAL OF MEDICINE. 82(2): 176-179, February 1982

Ancient Greek ethical perspectives on abortion and euthanasia, by P. J. Carrick. DISSERTATION ABSTRACTS INTERNATIONAL. A. p. 5146, 1982

Anti-abortion doctors: why a former foetus killer heads a pro-life campaign, by S. McCarthy. ALBERTA REPORT. 9:34, May 17, 1982

Anti-abortion protestors had no right t necessity charge at trespass trial. CRIMINAL LAW REPORTER: COURT DECISIONS AND PROCEEDINGS. 29(22):2475-2476, Septemer 2, 1981

Un appel en faveur de la vie: pourquoi si mal recu?, by J. Harvey. RELATIONS. 42:32-37+, January-February 1982

Attitude toward and use of induced abortion among Taiwanese women [research], by J. F. Wang. ISSUES IN HEALTH CARE OF WOMEN. 3:179-202, May-June 1981

Attitudes of rural Bangladesh physicans toward abortion, by M. J. Rosenberg, et al. STUDIES IN FAMILY PLANNING. 12(8-9): 318, August-September 1981

Attitudes to pregnancy [editorial]. JOURNAL OF THE ROYAL COLLEGE OF GENERAL PRACTITIONERS. 31(229):452-453, August 1981

Choisis done in vie, by G. Huyghe. LA DOCUMENTATION CATHOLIQUE. 79:457-458, May 2, 1982

A comparison of moral and ego development in women: a quantative and qualitative study of the reconstruction of the abortion decision, by L. M. Connor. DISSERTATION ABSTRACTS INTERNA-TIONAL. A. p. 1085, 1982

Concepts of abortion and their relevance to the abortion debate, by M. B. Mahowald. SOUTHERN JOURNAL OF PHILOSOPHY. 20:195-208, Summer 1982

Conservatism, attitude to abortion and Macoby's biophilia, by J. J. Ray, et al. JOURNAL OF SOCIAL PSYCHOLOGY. 118(1):143-144, October 1982

Context effects on survey response to questions about abortion, by H. Schuman, et al. PUBLIC OPINION QUARTERLY. 45(2):216-223, Summer 1981

A contextual approach to decisions about pregnancy and abortion, by J. Lambert. FEMINISM AND PROCESS THOUGHT. pp. 106-137, 1981

Contraceptive methods and abortion: one question, by L. Bale-striere. ANNALES MEDICO-PSYCHOLOGIQUES. 139(5):513-528, May 1981

Crushing freedom in the name of life, by N. Dorsen. HUMAN RIGHTS. 10:19-21+, Spring 1982

Damage awards for wrongful birth and wrongful life, by A. H. Bernstein. HOSPITALS. 56(5):65-67, March 1, 1982

A defence of abortion: a question for Judit Jarvis Thomson. PHILOSOPHICAL INVESTIGATIONS. 5:142-145, April 1982

Deregulation and the right to life, by A. Yankauer. AMERICAN JOURNAL OF PUBLIC HEALTH. 71:797-801, August 1981

The do it yourself abortion, by G. Sherry. OUR SUNDAY VISITOR. 70:12+, March 28, 1982

Do zygotes become people?, by W. R. Carter. MIND. 91:77-95, January 1982

The dynamics of the abortion debate, by J. G. Johnson. AMERICA. 146:106-109, February 13, 1982

Eastern Europe: pronatalist policies and private behavior, by H. P. David. POPULATION BULLETIN. 36:2-47, February 1982

The effects of termination of pregnancy: a follow-up study of psychiatric referrals, by R. Schmidt, et al. BRITISH JOURNAL OF MEDICAL PSYCHOLOGY. 54(Pt 3):267-276, September 1981

Ethical issues in nursing: your responses to JPN's fourth annual survey, by E. Rosen, et al. JOURNAL OF PRACTICAL NURSING. 31:29-33+, November-December 1981

The ethics of abortion, by M. A. Gellman. DISSERTATION AB-

STRACTS INTERNATIONAL. A. p. 4032, 1982

Ethics of amniocentesis and selective abortion for sickle cell
disease [letter], by F. I. Konotey-Ahulu. LANCET. 1(8262):
38-39, January 2, 1982

Family size preferences and sexual permissiveness as factors
differentiating abortion activists, by D. Granberg. SOCIAL
PSYCHOLOGY QUARTERLY. 45(1):15-23, March 1982

Fetal diagnosis and medical ethics, by N. Shimada. JOSANPU
ZASSHI. 35(8):640, August 1981

Given good information, public backs pro-life view. OUR SUNDAY
VISITOR. 70:7, December 20, 1981

God will forgive even she who aborts her child, by P. Cullen.
OUR SUNDAY VISITOR. 71:4-5, September 19, 1982

Helms bill calculated to foster pro-life unity, by C. A.
Savitskas, Jr. OUR SUNDAY VISITOR. 70:3, April 11, 1982

How do you feel about abortion?. FAMILY CIRCLE. 95:39, February 2, 1982

How many?. ECONOMIST. 294:47-48, July 3, 1982

Human life symposium: a synopsis and critique, by S. Taub. LAW,
MEDICINE AND HEALTH CARE. 10(3):129-134, June 1982

Les implications morales de certaines dispositions legislatives
concernant l'avortement, by M. T. Giroux. CAHIERS DE DROIT.
23:21-83, March 1982

Is the American medical commuinity anti-life?, by R. R. Holton.
OUR SUNDAY VISITOR. 71:4-5, October 17, 1982

Is every life worth living?. CHRISTIANITY TODAY. 26:12-13,
March 19, 1982

Jerry Falwell is right, by M. Meehan. INQUIRY. 4(3):6-8, November 2, 1981

Justifying abortion, by J. Burtchaell. SIGN. 61:18-22+, February 1982

Latina attitudes towards abortion, by H. Amaro. NUESTRO. 5:43-
44, August-September 1981

Let's face the facts on abortion, by K. Hepburn. FAMILY CIRCLE.
95(120:112+, November 1981

The long struggle for reproductive rights, by L. Gordon. RADI-
CAL AMERICAN. 15(1-2):75-88, 1981

Man, problems of values and a discussion of abortion, by G.
Straass. ZEITSCHRIFT FUR ARZTLICHE FORTBILDUNG. 75(8):391-
396, April 15, 1981

Matters of life and death: social, political, and religious correlates of attitudes on abortion, by R. K. Baker. AMERICAN
POLITICAL QUARTERLY. 9(1):89-102, 1981

Miffed mizzes: pro-choice vs. pro-life. ALBERTA REPORT. 8:31-
32, December 4, 1981

Moral development and reconstructive memory: recalling a decision to terminate an unplanned pregnancy, by G. Blackburne-
Stover, et al. DEVELOPMENTAL PSYCHOLOGY. 18:862-870, November 1982

Most Americans in the middle on abortion, shun pro-extremes and
anti-extremes. FAMILY PLANNING PERSPECTIVES. 14:102-106,
March-April 1982

My abortion: why it was the most difficult decision I may ever
have to make, by N. Mitchell. GLAMOUR. 80:248-249+, March
1982

Myths and assumptions of antiabortionists. JOURNAL OF THE
AMERICAN MEDICAL WOMEN'S ASSOCIATION. 37(3):74-76, March 1982

The open letter to Katharine Hepburn, by P. Kaler. LIGUORIAN.
70:34-39, April 1982

Opting for the right to end life, by M. Engel. MACLEAN'S. 95:
8, March 8, 1982

Pensioners threatened by abortion. SOCIAL JUSTICE REVIEW. 72:
215-216, November-December 1981

Personhood, abortion and the law, by B. J. Verkamp. AMERICA.
146:46-48, January 23, 1982

Philosophical ethical aspects of the interruption of pregnancy,
by G. Henning, et al. DEUTSCHE ZEITSCHRIFT FUR PHILOSOPHIE.
30:892-902, 1982

Philosophical perspectives of iatrogenic abortion, by C. W. de
Muelenaere. SOUTH AFRICAN MEDICAL JOURNAL. 61(25):959-961,
June 19, 1982

Point of view: D & E midtrimester abortion: a medical innovation
by S. Lewit. WOMEN AND HEALTH. 7:49-55, September 1982

La posizione di S. Thommaso Sull'aborto, by Giovanni. REVISTA
DOCTOR COMNIS. 34:296-311, September-October 1981

President Reagan stands firm on pro-life views. OUR SUNDAY
VISITOR. 71:8, August 1, 1982

Pro-, anti-choice groups square off in New Jersey, by L. Hamilton. NEW DIRECTIONS FOR WOMEN. 11:22, September-October 1982

Problems of interpreting socially controverisal legislation, by
J. K. Bentil. THE SOLICITORS' JOURNAL. 125:786-788,
November 20, 1981

Professional norms, personal attitudes, and medical practice:
the case of abortion, by C. A. Nathanson, et al. JOURNAL OF
HEALTH AND SOCIAL BEHAVIOR. 22(3):198-211, September 1981

Profile compassion or crusade?, by J. Evans. AMERICA. 147:373-
374, December 11, 1982

Pro-life versus pro-choice: another look at the abortion controversy in the U.S., by D. Granberg, et al. SOCIOLOGY AND SO-
CIAL RESERACH. 65(4):424-434, 1981

Pro-lifers urged to work for common goal, by M. Meehan. NATION-
AL CATHOLIC REPORTER. 18:5, April 23, 1982

Psychosocial aspects of early pregnancy termination [research],
by R. A. Brown. NEW ZEALAND NURSING FORUM. 10(1):8-10, 1982

Public opinion bombshell: prochoice majority vows to vote, by L.
C. Wohl. MS. 11:70-71+, July-August 1982

Recent charges in predictors of abortion attitudes, by S. N.
Barnartt, et al. SOCIOLOGY AND SOCIAL RESEARCH. 66(3):320-
334, April 1982

Refusing to participate in abortions, by H. Creighton. NURSING
MANAGEMENT. 13:27-28, April 1982

The relationship of abortion attitudes and contraceptive behaviour among young single women, by E. S. Herold. CANADIAN
JOURNAL OF PUBLIC HEALTH. 73(2):101-104, March-April 1982

Right to life: absolute or relative? [editorial]. RECONSTRUC-
TIONIST. 47:5-6, February 1982

Right-to-Life bible (handbook on abortion), by A. J. Fugh-
Berman. OFF OUR BACKS. 12:7, Decemer 1982

Rights and desires, by G. E. Jones. ETHICS. 92:52-56, October
1981

Rise in antiabortion terrorism (tactics of right to life
groups), by L. C. Wohl. MS. 11:19, November 1982

The shape of babies to come, by A. Ferriman, et al. OBSERVER.
p. 9, November 21, 1982

The silent holocaust, by W. Brennan. LIGUORIAN. 70:14-19,
September 1982

Sixty-nine percent of United States adults now approve legal
abortion for six specified reasons: up since 1980. FAMILY
PLANNING PERSPECTIVES. 14:214-215, July-August 1982

Spying on Right to Life (National Convention, Cherry Hill, New
Jersey, July 17, 1982), by A. J. Fugh-Berman. OFF OUR BACKS.
12:18-19, August-September 1982

Taking liberties with women: abortion, sterilization, and con-

ABORTION: ATTITUDES (continued)

traception, by W. Savage. INTERNATIONAL JOURNAL OF HEALTH
SERVICES. 12(2):293-308, 1982

Utilitarianism and children, by D. S. Hutchinson. CANADIAN
JOURNAL OF PHYSIOLOGY AND PHARMACOLOGY. 12:61-73, March 1982

What does it mean to be 'pro-life'?, by D. Granberg. CHRISTIAN
CENTURY. 99(17):562-566, 1982

When life begins [symposium]. SOCIETY. 19:32-72, May-June 1982

Who has the responsibility for the unborn?. LAKARTIDNINGEN.
78(37):3131-3141, September 9, 1981

Why I ended my baby's life (Klinefelter's syndrome), by J. K.
Ivey. GLAMOUR. 80:134+, May 1982

With friends like these. COMMONWEAL. 109:483-485, September
24, 1982

Women as teachers of violence, by A. O'Donnell. HOMILETIC AND
PASTORAL REVIEW. 82:54-58, June 1982

ABORTION: COMPLICATIONS

Abortion alarums [editorial], by C. Tietze. AMERICAN JOURNAL OF
PUBLIC HEALTH. 72(6):534-535, June 1982

Abortion may sensitize the mother to HLA antigens, by A. Gelabert, et al. TISSUE ANTIGENS. 17(4):353-356, 1981

Abortion of a 5-month pregnancy caused b fistula cervicolaqueatica, by K. Pekhlivanov. AKUSHERSTVO I GINEKOLOGIIA.
20(5):418-419, 1981

Abortion or birth? Discriminators in problem pregnancy decisions
by D. Williams, et al. SOCIOLOGICAL SPECTRUM. 1(2):115-133,
April-June 1981

Abortion rights in danger, by E. Doerr. HUMANIST. 42:52-66,
May-June 1982

The after-care of abortion patients, by J. R. Ashton. JOURNAL
OF THE ROYAL COLLEGE OF GENERAL PRACTITIONERS. 31(225):217-
222, April 1981

Blood cloting defects in second-trimester D and E easy to treat,
say MDs. FAMILY PLANNING PERSPECTIVES. 13:279-280, November-
December 1981

Blood loss and side effects in day case abortion, by G. W.
Cochrane, et al. BRITISH JOURNAL OF OBSTETRICS AND GYNAECLO-
GY. 88(11):1120-1123, November 1981

A case of female pseudohermaphroditism of difficult interpretation, by T. De Toni, et al. MINERVA PEDIATRICA. 34(8):361-
365, April 30, 1982

A case report: ureterouterine fistul as a complication of elec-

tive abortion, by G. T. Keegan, et al. JOURNAL OF UROLOGY.
128(1):137-138, July 1982

Cases of abortion, premature labor and fetal anoxia after trea
ment of anovulation, by J. Krzysiek, et al. GINEKOLOGIA
POLSKA. 52(1):45-50, January 1981

Chances of abortion prophylaxis in early pregnancy, by S.
Koller. GEBURTSHILFE UND FRAUENHEILKUNDE. 42(3):204-212,
March 1982

Damaged placenta in mid-trimenon abortion, by A. Jakobovits.
JUGOSLAVENSKA GINEKOLOGIJA I OPSTETRICIJA. 21(3-40:72-74,
May-August 1981

Dermatoglyphic characteristics in abortion, by N. A. Bel'tseva
et al. AKUSHERSTVO I GINEKOLOGIIA. (3):44-47, March 1982

Embryonic Rhesus-positive red cells stimulating a secondary
response after early abortion [letter], by J. Eklund. LANCE
2(8249):748, October 3, 1981

Endocrine abortions and their treatment, by U. Gaspard. REVUE
MEDICALE DE LIEGE. 37(4):118-119, February 15, 1982

Evaluation of sulprostone for second trimester abortions and i
effects on liver and kidney function, by V. Ranjan, et al.
CONTRACEPTION. 25(2):175-184, February 1982

Fatal amniotic fluid embolism during legally induced abortion,
United States, 1972 to 1978, by R. J. Guidotti, et al. AMER
CAN JOURNAL OF OBSTETRICS AND GYNECOLOGY. 141(3):257-261,
October 1, 1981

Gestational trophoblastic emboli as possible cause of an acute
respiratory distress syndrome, by G. Hoflehner, et al. WIEN
MEDIZINISCHE WOCHENSCHRIFT. 131(19):475-477, October 15, 19

Human extra-embryonic membranes: role of trophoblast in norma
and abnormal pregnancies, by W. P. Faulk. INTERNATIONAL JOUI
NAL ON TISSUE REACTIONS. 3(3-4):139-146, December 1981

Immunology of abortion and preeclampsia, by M. G. Dodson. COM-
PREHENSIVE THERAPY. 8(6):59-65, June 1982

In vitro studies of the abortogenic potential of antisrum to
alpha-fetoprotein, by G. J. Mizejewski, et al. INTERNATIONA
JOURNAL OF IMMUNOPHARMACOLOGY. 3(1):87-95, 1981

Intrauterine diagnosis and management of fetal polycystic kidn
disease, by L. Shenker, et al. OBSTETRICS AND GYNECOLOGY.
59(3):385-389, March 1982

Is prognostic information obtainable from serum pregnancy zone
protein level with imminent abortion, by G. Stranz, et al.
ZENTRALBLATT FUR GYNAEKOLOGIE. 103(13):758-762, 1981

Leptospirosis in porcine livestock. Second serological survey outbreaks of infectious abortion, by A. Pumarola Busquets, et al. REVISTA DE SANIDAD E HIGIENE PUBLICA. 53(1-2):51-55, January-February 1979

Medium term complications after termination of pregnancy, by R. B. Hunton, et al. AUSTRALIAN AND NEW ZEALAND JOURNAL OF OB-STETRICS AND GYNAECOLOGY. 21(2):99-102, May 1981

Minimizing the risk of postabortion thrombosis. NURSES DRUG ALERT. 6:25, April 1982

Oral contraceptive use and abortion before first term pregnancy in relation to breast cancer risk, by M. P. Vessey, et al. BRITISH JOURNAL OF CANCER. 45(3):327-331, March 1982

Pelvic infection after elective abortion associated with chlamydia trachomatis, by B. R. Møller, et al. OBSTETRICS AND GYNECOLOGY. 59(2):210-213, February 1982

Pulmonary embolism in a 14-year-old following an elective abortion, by R. Nudelman, et al. PEDIATRICS. 68(4):584-586, October 1981

Research activity on systemic contraceptive drugs by the U.S. pharmaceutical industry, 1963-1976, by J. DiRaddo, et al. CONTRACEPTION. 23(4):345-365, April 1981

Restoration of the ovarian response to gonadotropins in patients after molar abortions, by A. Miyake, et al. OBSTETRICS AND GYNECOLOGY. 58(5):566-568, 1981

Rupture of the cervix during prostaglandin termination of pregnancy, by E. K. El-Etriby, et al. POSTGRADUATE MEDICAL JOUR-NAL. 57(666):265-266, April 1981

Rupture of the posterior fornix induced by prostaglandin. Report of a complication of termination of pregnancy, by J. Molin. UGESKRIFT FOR LAEGER. 143(29):1841, 1981

Spastic diplegia and the significance of mothers' previous reproductive loss, by P. S. Spiers, et al. DEVELOPMENTAL MEDI-CINE AND CHILD NEUROLOGY. 24(1):20-29, February 1982

Structural abnormalities of the uterus as a cause of prematurity by G. Allocca, et al. ARCHIVES OF OBSTETRICS AND GYNECOLOGY. 85(5):457-462, September-October 1980

Studies of humoral immunological response on the aborted tropho-blasts, by A. Tokunaga. NIPPON SANKA FUJINKA GAKKAI ZASSHI. 33(12):2125-2132, December 1981

A symptom-complex during artificial abortion. CHUNG HUA FU CHAN KO TSA CHIH. 14(2):111-115, April 1979

3 cases of acute pulmonary edema in pregnant women treated with tocolytics and betamethasone, by F. Coggiola, et al. MINERVA GINECOLOGIA. 34(3):191-194, March 1982

ABORTION: COMPLICATIONS (continued)

Total cholesterol level in human placenta, by S. Narahari, et al. HUMAN HEREDITY. 31(5):276-278, 1981

Twin pregnancy, abortion of one fetu with Down's syndrome by sectio parva, the other delivered mature and healthy, by L. Beck, et al. EUROPEAN JOURNAL OF OBSTETRICS, GYNECOLOGY AND REPRODUCTIVE BIOLOGY. 12(5):267-269, November 1981

Use of dacron cervical sutures for correction of the abnormal position of the chorion frondosum and the placenta, by A. I. Liubimova, et al. AKUSHERSTVO I GINEKOLOGIIA. (1):39-41, January 1982

Uterine malformations and pregnancy, by V. Giustolisi, et al. MINERVA GINECOLOGIA. 34(1-2):47-55, January-February 1982

Uterine rupture occurring during midtrimester abortion, by D. Graham. OBSTETRICS AND GYNECOLOGY. 59(6 Suppl):62S-4S, June 1982

Zona pellucida composition: species cross reactivity and contra-ceptive potential of antiserum to a purified pig zona antigen (PPZA), by A. G. Sacco, et al. BIOLOGICAL REPRODUCTION. 25(5):997-1008, December 1981

ABORTION: COMPLICATIONS: PSYCHOLOGICAL
Abortion: a technique for working through grief, by N. B. Buckles. JOURNAL OF THE AMERICAN COLLEGE HEALTH ASSOCIATION. 30(4):181-182, February 1982

Adolescent suicide attempts following elective abortion: a spe-cial case of anniversary reaction, by C. Tishler. PEDIATRICS. 68(5):670-671, 1981

The after-care of abortion patients, by J. R. Ashton. JOURNAL OF THE ROYAL COLLEGE OF GENERAL PRACTITIONERS. 31(225):217-222, April 1981

Effect of psychological stress states in women with spontaneous abortions, by I. Vasileva. AKUSHERSTVO I GINEKOLOGIIA. 20(4):275-279, 1981

Neurotic psychosexual and emotional disorders after artificial termination of pregnancy, by W. Mikrut. WIADOMOSCI LEKARSKIE. 34(5):389-393, March 1, 1981

Pregnancy after reproductive failure, by C. C. Floyd. AMERICAN JOURNAL OF NURSING. 81(11):2050-2053, November 1981

Psychological and social aspects of induced abortion, by J. A. Handy. BRITISH JOURNAL OF CLINICAL PSYCHOLOGY. 21(Pt 1):29-41, February 1982

Psychosocial aspects of early pregnancy termination, by R. A. Brown, et al. NEW ZEALAND NURSING FORUM. 10(1):8-10, 1982

Socio-psychological aspects of voluntary abortion at the Obste-trical and Gynecological Clinic of Catania, by S. Di Leo, et

ABORTION: COMPLICATIONS: PSYCHOLOGICAL (continued)

al. ARCHIVES OF OBSTETRICS AND GYNECOLOGY. 85(6):531-544,
November-December 1980

Voluntary interruption of pregnancy: social aspects and psychological motivation, by F. Leone. ARCHIVES OF OBSTETRICS AND
GYNECOLOGY. 85(6):545-556, November-December 1980

ABORTION: HABITUAL

Abdominal approach in cerclage for treatment of repeated abortion due to segmental cervical insufficiency, by R. Grio, et
al. MINERVA GINECOLOGIA. 33(12):1131-1136, December 1981

Anti-factor XI, direct positive Coombs's test and recurrent
abortion in a system lupus erythematosus [letter], by J. R.
Duran-Suarez, et al. HAEMATOLOGICA. 66(3):383-384, June 1981

Balanced translocation karyotypes in patients with repetitive
abortion. Case study and literature review, by J. R. Davis, et
al. AMERICAN JOURNAL OF OBSTETRICS AND GYNECOLOGY. 144(2):
229-233, September 15, 1982

Cellular and humoral immunity in habitual abortion, by K. A.
Khashimova, et al. VOPROSY OKHRANY MATERINSTVA I DETSTVA.
26(5):66-68, 1981

Cytogenetic studies in recurrent fetal loss, by M. T. Mulcahy.
AUSTRALIAN AND NEW ZEALAND JOURNAL OF OBSTETRICS AND GYNAE-
COLOGY. 22(1):29-30, February 1982

Decidual vasculopathy and extensive placental infarction in a
patient with repeated thromboembolic accidents, recurrent
fetal loss, and a lupus anticoagulant, by F. De Wolf, et al.
AMERICAN JOURNAL OF OBSTETRICS AND GYNECOLOGY. 142(7):829-
834, April 1, 1982

Early therapy for the incompetent cervix in patients with habitual abortion, by J. W. Ayers, et al. FERTILITY AND STERIL-
ITY. 38(2):177-181, August 1982

Early total occlusion of os uteri to prevent habitual abortion
and premature deliveries, by E. Saling. ZEITSCHRIFT FUR
GEBURTSCHILFE UND PERINATOLOGIE. 185(5):259-261, 1981

Habitual abortion: diagnositc and therapy in gynaecological
practice, by I. Gerhard, et al. GEBURTSHILFE UND FRAUENHEIL-
KUNDE. 41(11):797-803, November 1981

Infectious complications of cervical cerclage, by D. Charles, et
al. AMERICAN JOURNAL OF OBSTETRICS AND GYNECOLOGY. 141(8):
1065-1071, December 15, 1981

Major histocompatibility complex antigens, maternal and paternal
immune responses, and chronic habitual abortions in humans, by
A. E. Beer, et al. AMERICAN JOURNAL OF OBSTETRICS AND GYNE-
COLOGY. 141(8):987-999, Decemer 15, 1981

Ovarian-Hypophyseal relations in women susceptible to habitual
abortion during the early stages of pregnancy, by E. S.

ABORTION: HABITUAL (continued)

Kononova, et al. AKUSHERSTVO I GINEKOLOGIIA. (1):25-27, January 1982

Pericentric inversion of chromosome 9 in couples with repeated spontaneous abortion, by M. G. Tibiletti, et al. ACTA EURO-PAEA FERTILITATIS. 12(3):245-248, September 1981

Premature labor after three miscarriages, by N. H. Lauersen. HOSPITAL PRACTICE. 17(5):199+, May 1982

Recurrent miscarriage and preterm labour, by G. Chamberlain. CLINICAL OBSTETRICS AND GYNECOLOGY. 9(1):115-130, April 1982

Results of cervical cerclage operations in pregnant women during a five-year period, by H. Malmstrom, et al. ANNALES CHIRUR-GIAE ET GYNAECOLOGIAE. 70(2):75-78, 1981

The role of maternal diabetes in repetitive spontaneous abortion, by J. P. Crane, et al. FERTILITY AND STERILITY. 36(4): 477-479, October 1981

Therapeutic and prophylactic care in habitual abortion in women with genital infantilism, by N. T. Gudakova, et al. AKUSHER-STVO I GINEKOLOGIIA. (5):26-27, May 1981

Toxoplasmosis and habitual abortion. Our experience, by F. L. Giiorgino, et al. CLINICAL AND EXPERIMENTAL OBSTETRICS AND GYNECOLOGY. 8(3):132-134, 1981

Transabdominal cervicoisthmic cerclage for the management of repetitive abortion and premature delivery, by M. J. Novy. AMERICAN JOURNAL OF OBSTETRICS AND GYNECOLOGY. 143(1):44-54, May 1, 1982

Use of turinal in the treatment of habitual abortion, by K. R. Alimova. AKUSHERSTVO I GINEKOLOGIIA. (1):55-56, January 1982

ABORTION: HISTORY

The attitude toward abortion in Middle English writings: a note on the history of ideas, by R. R. Barkley. COMMUNIO. 9:176-183, Summer 1982

The gospel of prevention, by B. Harrison. TIMES LITERARY SUP-PLEMENT. p. 1252, November 12, 1982

In search of health history, Margaret Higgins Sanger: health educator, by P. A. Reagan. HEALTH EDUCATION. 13:5-7, July-August 1982

The natural history of the retained dead fetus, by M. E. Foley. IRISH MEDICAL JOURNAL. 74(8):237-238, August 1981

ABORTION: ILLEGAL

Clostridium perfringens sepsis following criminal abortion, by A. Meijernik, et al. NEDERLANDS TIJDSCHRIFT VOOR GENEESKUNDE. 126(14):613-616, April 3, 1982

Complications following the vaginal use of potassium permangan-

ate for an abortion, by A. Atanasov, et al. AKUSHERSTVO I
GINEKOLOGIIA. 20(4):355-357, 1981

Illegal abortion deaths in the United States: why are they still
occurring, by N. Binkin, et al. FAMILY PLANNING PERSPECTIVES.
14:163-174, May-June 1982

Inga, midwife: without the new abortin legislation illegal abortions would increase [interview], by I. Abelson. VARDFACKET.
6(10):43-44, May 28, 1982

ABORTION: INCOMPLETE
Arias-Stella reaction with prominent nuclear pseudoinclusins
simulating herpetic endometritis, by L. E. Dardi, et al.
DIAGNOSTIC GYNECOLOGY AND OBSTETRICS. 4(2):127-132, Summer
1982

Clostridium perfringens sepsis following criminal abortion, by
A. Meijernik, et al. NEDERLANDS TIJDSCHRIFT VOOR GENEESKUNDE.
126(14):613-616, April 3, 1982

Symptomatic intrauterine retention of fetal bones, by F. A.
Chervenak, et al. OBSTETRICS AND GYNECOLOGY. 59(6 Suppl):
58S-61S, June 1982

The use of hospital resources to treat incomplete abortions:
examples from Latin America, by J. A. Fortney. PUBLIC HEALTH
REPORTS. 96(6):574-579, November-December 1981

ABORTION: INDUCED
Abortion ethics, by M. J. Fromer. NURSING OUTLOOK. 30(4):234-
240, April 1982

Abortion induced for eugenic reasons [editorial], by K. Betke.
MMW: MUENCHENER MEDIZINISCHE WOCHENSCHRIFT. 123(39):1441-
1442, September 25, 1981

Abortion is not a banner-waving issue [letter], by J. P. James.
JOGN NURSING: JOURNAL OF OBSTETRIC GYNECOLOGIC AND NEONATAL
NURSING. 10(6):458-459, November-December 1981

Attitude toward and use of induced abortion among Taiwanese
women, by J. F. Wang. ISSUES IN HEALTH CARE OF WOMEN. 3(3):
179-202, May-June 1981

Causes of chromosome anomalies suggested by cytogenetic epidemiology of induced abortions, by M. Yamamoto, et al. HUMAN
GENETICS. 60(4):360-364, 1982

Changes in intraocular pressure during prostaglandin-induced
abortion, by M. Ober, et al. KLINISCHE MONATSBLAETTER FUR
AUGENHEILKUNDE. 180(3):230-231, March 1981

Choice of ecbolic and the morbidity of day-case terminations of
pregnancy, by D. B. Garrioch, et al. BRITISH JOURNAL OF
OBSTETRICS AND GYNAECOLOGY. 88(10):1029-1032, October 1981

Currently used methods in induced abortion, by A. A. Haspels.

TIJDSCHRIFT VOR ZIEKENVERPLEGING. 34(17):745-749, August 25, 1981

Effects of 17 beta-hydroxy-7 alpha-methylandrost-5-en-3-one on early pregnancy in the rat, by S. Saksena, et al. ACTA ENDOCRINOLOGICA. 98(4):614-618, December 1981

Experience with PGF2 alpha in mid-trimester pregnancy termination in Ibadan, by O. A. Ojo, et al. AFRICAN JOURNAL OF MEDICINE AND MEDICAL SCIENCES. 8(3-4):103-107, September-December 1979

Fewer abortions--certainly, but how?, by U. Lindqvist, et al. JORDEMODERN. 94(6):231-234, June 1981

Induced abortion and spontaneous fetal loss in subsequent pregnancies, by C. S. Chung, et al. AMERICAN JOURNAL OF PUBLIC HEALTH. 72(6):548, June 1982

Induced abortion in the hospital--the role of nursing, by E. Ketting, et al. TIJDSCHRIFT VOR ZIEKENVERPLEGING. 34(17): 750-753, August 25, 1981

Induced abortion in the Netherlands: a decade of experience, 1970-80, by E. Ketting, et al. STUDIES IN FAMILY PLANNING. 11(12):385-394, December 1980

The induction of abortion and the priming of the cervix with prostaglandin F2 alpha and prostaglandin E2 by intra-amniotic, extra-amniotic and intra-cervical application, by W. Schmidt, et al. GEBURTSHILFE UND FRAUENHEILKUNDE. 42(2):118-122, February 1982

The induction of abortion in the second trimester by combined administration of minprostin and sulproston, compared with the use of sulproston alone, by H. Ponnath, et al. GEBURTSHILFE UND FRAUENHEILKUNDE. 41(12):849-852, December 1981

Induction of second trimester abortion with intra-amniotic prostaglandin F2 alpha, by A. P. Lange, et al. UGESKRIFT FOR LAEGER. 144(13):946-949, March 29, 1982

Intensified electro-acupuncture in induced abortion. CHUNG HUA FU CHAN KO TSA CHIH. 14(2):107-110, April 1979

Isolation of human alpha-1 fetoprotein (AFP) from induced abortion material, by G. Haller, et al. INTERNATIONAL JOURNAL OF BIOLOGICAL RESEARCH IN PREGNANCY. 3(2):69-72, 1982

Low dose rhesus immunoprophylaxis after early induced abortions, by P. Gjøde, et al. ACTA OBSTETRICIA ET GYNECOLOGICA SCANDINAVICA. 61(2):105-106, 1982

Maternal serum hormone changes during abortion induced with 16, 16-dimethyl-trans-delta 2-PGE1 methyl ester, by K. Bremme, et al. PROSTAGLANDINS LEUKOTRIENES AND MEDICINE. 8(6):647-651, June 1982

Messing with Mother Nature: fleck and the omega pill, by J. A. Montmarquet. PHILOSOPHICAL STUDIES. 41:407-420, May 1982

Multiple pregnancy, or should 2 babies be given up to save 3? [letter], by J. Breheret. NOUVELLE PRESSE MEDICALE. 11(3): 210, January 23, 1982

No increased risk of spontaneous abortion found among women with a previous induced abortion. FAMILY PLANNING PERSPECTIVES. 13:238-239, September-October 1981

Prophylactic antibiotic therapy in induced abortion. A cost benefit analysis, by S. Sonne-Holm, et al. UGESKRIFT FOR LAEGER. 143(14):881-883, March 30, 1981

Prospective studies on pregnancy following induced and spontaneous abortion of primigravidae and assessment of fertility. IV. Report, by G. Schott, et al. ZENTRALBLATT FUR GYNAEKOLOGIE. 104(7):397-404, 1982

Prostaglandin E and F2 alpha levels in plasma and amniotic fluid during mid-trimester abortion induced by trichosanthin, by Y. F. Wang, et al. PROSTAGLANDINS. 22(2):289-294, August 1981

Psychological and social aspects of induced abortion, by J. A. Handy. BRITISH JOURNAL OF CLINICAL PSYCHOLOGY. 21(Pt 1):29-41, 1982

Readers' position against induced abortion. TIJDSCHRIFT VOR ZIEKENVERPLEGING. 34(17):754-757, August 25, 1981

Termination of midtrimester pregnancies induced by hypertonic saline and prostaglandin F2 alpha 116 consecutive cases, by E. Bostofte, et al. ACTA OBSTETRICIA ET GYNECOLOGICA SCANDINAVICA. 60(6):575-578, 1981

Use of trilene and sombrevin anesthesia in minor gynecologic operations, by A. V. Mishenin, et al. MEDITSINSKAIA SESTRA. 40(10):16-17, October 1981

ABORTION: INDUCED: COMPLICATIONS

Characteristics of women recruited to a long-term study of the sequelae of induced abortion. Report from a joint RCGP/RCOG Study co-ordinated by the Royal College of General Practitioners' Manchester Research Unit, by C. R. Kay, et al. JOURNAL OF THE ROYAL COLLEGE OF GENERAL PRACTITIONERS. 31(229):473-477, August 1981

Comparative risk of death from induced abortion at less than or equal to 12 weeks gestation performed with local vs. general anesthesia, by H. Peterson, et al. AMERICAN JOURNAL OF OBSTETRICS AND GYNECOLOGY. 141(7):763-768, December 1, 1981

Decreased cyclic A M P concentration in amniotic fluid during rivanol-induced abortion, by P. Bistoletti, et al. GYNECOLOGIC AND OBSTETRIC INVESTIGATION. 13(3):184-188, 1982

Demonstration of an early abortifacient effect of norethisterone

(NET) in the primate (baboon), by L. R. Beck, et al. CONTRA-
CEPTION. 25(1):97-105, January 1982

Early complications of induced abortion in primigravidae, by K.
Dalaker, et al. ANNALES CHIRURGIAE ET GYNAECOLOGIAE. 70(6):
331-336, 1981

Ectopic pregnancy and prior induced abortion [research], by A.
A. Levin, et al. AMERICAN JOURNAL OF PUBLIC HEALTH. 72(3):
253-256, March 1982

Faculty cell replication: abortion, congenital abnormalities, by
J. F. Nunn. INTERNATIONAL ANESTHESIOLOGY CLINICS. 19(4):77-
97, Winter 1981

Incidence rate of late complications in legally induced abortion
in West Germany, by H. H. Braeutigam, et al. ZEITSCHRIFT FUR
GEBURTSCHILFE UND PERINATOLOGIE. 185(4):193-199, 1981

Induced abortion and ectopic pregnancy in subsequent pregnancies
by C. S. Chung, et al. AMERICAN JOURNAL OF EPIDEMIOLOGY.
115(6):879-887, June 1982

Induced abortion and placenta previa [letter], by S. Fribourg.
AMERICAN JOURNAL OF OBSTETRICS AND GYNECOLOGY. 143(7):850,
August 1, 1982

Induced abortion and spontaneous fetal loss in subsequent pregnancies, by C. S. Chung, et al. AMERICAN JOURNAL OF PUBLIC
HEALTH. 72(6):548-554, June 1982

Induced abortion as a risk factor for cervical pregnancy [let-
ter], by S. Shinagawa, et al. AMERICAN JOURNAL OF OBSTETRICS
AND GYNECOLOGY. 143(7):853-854, August 1, 1982

Induced abortion: a risk factor for placenta previa, by J. M.
Barrett, et al. AMERICAN JOURNAL OF OBSTETRICS AND GYNECOL-
OGY. 141(7):769-772, December 1, 1981

Laminaria as an adjuvant in the induction of abortion [edi-
torial], by D. Schneider, et al. HAREFUAH. 101(7-8):180-181,
October 1981

Laminaria in induction of abortion in the 2d trimester. Case of
uterine rupture, by G. Menaldo, et al. MINERVA GINECOLOGIA.
33(6):599-601, June 1981

Midtrimester abortion induced by radix trichosanthis: morphologic observations in placenta and the fetus, by C. Kuo-Fen.
OBSTETRICS AND GYNECOLOGY. 59(4):494-498, April 1982

The outcome of pregnancy resulting from clomiphene-induced ovulation, by J. F. Correy, et al. AUSTRALIAN AND NEW ZEALAND JOUR-
NAL OF OBSTETRICS AND GYNAECOLOGY. 22(1):18-21, February 1982

Psychological and social aspects of induced abortion, by J.
Handy. BRITISH JOURNAL OF CLINICAL PSYCHOLOGY. 21(1):29-41,
February 1982

ABORTION: INDUCED: TECHNIQUES

Decreased adenosine 3'-5'-cyclic monophosphate concentration in
amniotic fluid during rivanol-induced abortion, by P. Bistoletti, et al. GYNECOLOGIC AND OBSTETRIC INVESTIGATION.
13(3):184-188, 1982

Decreased cyclic A M P concentration in amniotic fluid during
rivanol-induced abortion, by P. Bistoletti, et al. GYNECOLO-
GIC AND OBSTETRIC INVESTIGATION. 13(3):184-188, 1982

Induced abortion. A prospective comparative study of 2 vacuum
aspiration methods: the Vabra-ab aspirator and conventional
methods, by H. K. Poulsen. UGESKRIFT FOR LAEGER. 144(2):89-
92, January 11, 1982

Midtrimester abortion induced by "Radix trichosanthis": morphologic observations in placenta and fetus, by C. Kuo-Fen. OB-
STETRICS AND GYNECOLOGY. 59(4):494-498, 1982

ABORTION: JOURNALISM
Am I getting paid for this? (TV news story about a woman's
decision to have an abortion: excerpt), by B. Rollin. VOGUE.
172:308-310, August 1982

Joyce's prophylactic paralysis: exposure in Dubliners, by Z.
Bowen. JAMES JOYCE QUARTERLY. 19:257-273, Spring 1983

The latest NFP books, by M. Kambic, et al. MARRIAGE. 64:21-22,
August 1982

Pro-lifers director raps magazine's abortion survey. OUR SUNDAY
VISITOR. 71:8, September 19, 1982

ABORTION: LAWS AND LEGISLATION: GENERAL
Abortion. OUR SUNDAY VISITOR. 70:3, January 17, 1982

An abortion alternative, by J. Gilhooley. AMERICA. 147:289-
290, November 13, 1982

Abortion and the Hatch Amendment, by E. Bryce. AMERICA.
146(9):166-168, March 6, 1982

Abortion and infant mortality before and after the 1973 US
Supreme Court decision on abortion, by L. S. Robertson.
JOURNAL OF BIOLOGICAL SCIENCE. 13(3):275-280, July 1981

Abortion and informed consent requirements, by M. B. Kapp.
AMERICAN JOURNAL OF OBSTETRICS AND GYNECOLOGY. 144(1):1-4,
September 1, 1982

Abortion and international law: the status and possible extension of women's right to privacy, by A. E. Michel. JOURNAL OF
FAMILY LAW. 20(2):241-262, January 1982

Abortion and the public opinions polls: morality and legality.
Part I, by S. K. Henshaw, et al. FAMILY PLANNING PERSPEC-
TIVES. 14(2):53-54+, March-April 1982

Abortion and the rhetoric of individual rights, by L. R.

Churchill, et al. HASTINGS CENTER REPORT. 12(1):9-12,
February 1982

Abortion cases pending in Supreme Court, by N. Hunter. OFF OUR
BACKS. 12:12, October 1982

Abortion: the debate begins. NEWSWEEK. 100:29, August 30,
1982

Abortion debate in Senate. NEW DIRECTIONS FOR WOMEN. 11:1+,
September-October 1982

Abortion: first round in a long fight (Senate debate). US NEWS
AND WORLD REPORT. 93:7, August 30, 1982

Abortion--an industrial issue (ACTU Congress, 1981 [Australian
trade union]), by D. Hague, et al. REFRACTORY GIRL. (23):15-
16, March 1982

Abortion legislation. Implications for medicine, by A. Milunsky,
et al. JAMA: JOURNAL OF THE AMERICAN MEDICAL ASSOCIATION.
248(7):833-834, August 20, 1982

Abortion--legislation restricting access t abortion services
during first trimester must meet strict scru- tiny test and
may not unreasonably confine or burden aborting physician's
practice. Restrictions must be based on medical necessity and
will be voided if not narrowly tailored to meet needs asserted
or supported by medical necessity. JOURNAL OF FAMILY LAW.
19:745-750, August 1981

Abortion myths and realities: who is misleading whom?, by W.
Cates, Jr. AMERICAN JOURNAL OF OBSTETRICS AND GYNECOLOGY.
142(8):954-956, April 15, 1982

Abortion: a national security issue, by S. D. Mumford. AMERICAN
JOURNAL OF OBSTETRICS AND GYNECOLOGY. 142(8):951-953, April
15, 1982

--HUMANIST. 42:12-13, September-October 1982

Abortion: Planned Parenthood Association of Kansas City, Missouri, Inc. v. Ashcroft (655 F 2d 848): Missouri loses latest
round in battle over permissible abortion regulations. UMKC
LAW REVIEW. 50:320-339, Spring 1982

Abortion--a police response, by G. H. Kleinknecht, et al. FBI
LAW ENFORCEMENT BULLETIN. 51:20-23, March 1982

Abortion rights group opposes bill, by M. Meehan. NATIONAL
CATHOLIC REPORTER. 18:28, July 2, 1982

Abortion rights in danger, by E. Doerr. HUMANIST. 45:52-66,
May-June 1982

Abortion: stalled in Congress, trouble in the states, by T.
Dejanikus. OFF OUR BACKS. 12:21, March 1982

Abortion--State Budget Act restricting circumstances under which public funds would be authorized to pay for abortions for Medi-Cal recipients held unconstitutional. JOURNAL OF FAMILY LAW. 20:345-351, January 1982

Abortion test cases, by J. G. Deedy. TABLET. 236:1007-1008, October 9, 1982

Abortion, tuition tax credits fall short of mark, by J. Castelli. OUR SUNDAY VISITOR. 71:3, October 3, 1982

Abortions preventable by contraceptive practice, by C. F. Westoff, et al. FAMILY PLANNING PERSPECTIVES. 13(5):218-223, September-October 1981

Abortions--regulation by state and local municipalities--a municipal ordinance which requires that all abortion facilities be equipped with expensive and unnecessary equipment similar to that of a hospital operating room is an unconstitutional burden on a woman's right to choose to abort a pregnancy. CAPITAL UNIVERSITY LAW REVIEW. 10:925-930, Summer 1981

Analysis of the results and considerations on the organizatinal aspects of the implementation of the Law 194/78 in a provincial hospital, by L. Pacilli, et al. MINERVA GINECOLOGIA. 33(9):811-816, September 1981

Anti-abortion bid fails in Congress, by T. Dejanikus. OFF OUR BACKS. 12:13, October 1982

The anti-abortion campaign, by M. Ryan. BRITISH MEDICAL JOURNAL. 283(6303):1378-1379, November 21, 1981

Anti-abortion march marks court ruling by M. Holahan. NATIONAL CATHOLIC REPORTER. 18:4, January 29, 1982

Antiabortion measures loom before congress, by M. J. England. JOURNAL OF THE AMERICAN MEDICAL WOMEN'S ASSOCIATION. 37(2): 34-35, February 1982

Avortement et securite sociale; vers l'avortement gratuit?, by P. Verspieren. ETUDES. 356:321-327, March 1982

Battle over abortion moves back to high court, by R. B. Shaw. OUR SUNDAY VISITOR. 71:4, October 24, 1982

Beyond the limits of reproductive choice: the contributions of the abortion-funding cases to fundamental-rights analysis and to the welfare-rights thesis, by S. F. Appleton. COLUMBIA LAW REVIEW. 81(4):721-758, May 1981

The bishops and the Hatch Amendment, by W. F. Buckley. NATIONAL REVIEW. 34:132-133, February 5, 1982

A calm look at abortion arguments: legislation relating to abortion must hinge on the question: when does the right to life begin?, by R. Bissell. REASON. 13:27-31, September 1981

Can Congress settle the abortion issue?, by M. C. Segers.
HASTINGS CENTER REPORT. 12(3):20-28, June 1982

Cenni sulla valutazione dell'aborto hella religione islamica, by
M. Vallaro. SOCIOLOGIA DEL DIRITTO. 7(3):87-106, 1980

Changes in the legislation regulating the legal status of
artificial abortion in the world in the past 10 years, by
D. Vasilev. AKUSHERSTVO I GINEKOLOGIIA. 20(4):269-275,
1981

Child psychiatry and the law; developmental rights to privacy an
independent decision-making, by M. J. Guyer, et al. JOURNAL
OF THE AMERICAN ACADEMY OF CHILD PSYCHIATRY. 21:298-302, May
1982

Chromosomes, crime and the courts: the XX and XYY quandary, by
H. J. Grace. SOUTH AFRICAN JOURNAL OF CRIMINAL LAW AND CRIM-
INOLOGY. 5(3):223-227, 1981

City appeals overturn of abortion consent rule. NATIONAL
CATHOLIC REPORTER. 18:23, September 17, 1982

Cliff-hanger Hatch plan vote likely, by M. Meehan. NATIONAL
CATHOLIC REPORTER. 18:3, February 19, 1982

Clinical and epidemiological aspects of voluntary interruption
of pregnancy 2 years after law No. 194 on abortion, by M. G.
Ricci, et al. RIVISTA ITALIANA DI GINECOLOGIA. 59(4/5):405-
420, ?

Comments to the United States Senate Judiciary Subcommittee on
Separation of Powers. A bill to provide that human life shall
be deemed to exist from conception [editorial]. TERATOLOGY.
24(1):107-109, August 1981

Committee to Defend Reproductive Rights v. Myers: abortion funding as an unconstitutional condition, by C. W. Sherman. CALI-
FORNIA LAW REVIEW. 70:978-1013, July 1982

--[625 P 2d 779 (Cal)]: procreative choice guaranteed for all
women. GOLDEN GATE UNIVERSITY LAW REVIEW. 12:691-716, Summer
1982

Compelling state interest justifies spousal notice burden on
abortion. FAMILY LAW REPORTER: COURT OPINIONS. 8(2):2018-
2020, November 10, 1981

Congressional power and constitutional rights: reflections on
proposed "human life" legislation (whether recent U.S. Supreme
Court decisions on abortion can be undone by ordinary legislation), by S. Estreicher. VIRGINIA LAW REVIEW. 68:333-358,
February 1982

Congressional withdrawal of jurisdiction from federal courts: a
reply to Professor Uddo, by M. Vitiello. LOYOLA LAW REVIEW.
28:61-76, Winter 1982

Constitution law--right to privacy--parental notice requirements in abortion statutes. TENNESSEE LAW REVIEW. 48:974-999, Summer 1981

Constitutional law/abortion. ILLINOIS BAR JOURNAL. 70:515-519, April 1982

Constitutional law--abortion--Utah' parental notification statute held constitutional. H.L. v. Matheson (101 S Ct 1164). CUMBERLAND LAW REVIEW. 12:711-725, 1981-1982

Constitutional law--Medicaid fundin restriction does not unconstitutionally burden the right to terminate a pregnancy. TULANE LAW REVIEW. 56:435-446, December 1981

Constitutional law--the minor, parent, state triangle and the requirement of parental notification: H.L. v. Matheson (101 S Ct 1164). HOWARD LAW REVIEW. 25:299-322, 1982

Constitutional law--privacy rights--consent requirements and abortions for minors. NEW YORK STATE LAW SCHOOL LAW REVIEW. 26:837-854, 1981

Constitutional law--right of privacy--abortion--family law--parent and child--standing--as applied to immature, unemancipated and dependent minors, a state statute requiring a physician to notify a pregnant minor's parents prior to the performing of an abortion is constitutional--H.L. v. Matheson. UNIVERSITY OF CINCINNATI LAW REVIEW. 50:867-881, 1981

Constitutional law--a state statute, which requires physicians to notify the parents of immature and unemancipated minors before performing an abortion, does not violate the minors' fundamental right to have an abortion. DRAKE LAW REVIEW. 31:476-485, 1981-1982

Constitutional law--United States Supreme Court upholds the constitutionality of the Hyde Amendment, withholding Medicaid funds for therapeutic abortions unless the life of the mother is endangered. TEMPLE LAW QUARTERLY. 54:109-144, 1981

Court public college paper can't reject abortion ads (Portland Community College), by F. King. EDITOR AND PUBLISHER--THE FOURTH ESTATE. 114:20, October 10, 1981

Court upholds parental notice requirement before allowing abortions on minors, by P. A. Ewer. JOURNAL OF CRIMINAL LAW AND CRIMINOLOGY. 72(4):1461-1481

Court won't intervene to compel girl to have abortion urged by mother. FAMILY LAW REPORTER: COURT OPINIONS. 8(10):2140-2141, January 11, 1982

Criminal liability for complicity in abortions committed outside Ireland, by M. J. Findlay. IRISH JURIST. 15:88-98, Summer 1980

Critical abortion litigation, by D. J. Horan. CATHOLIC LAWYER.

26:198-208, Summer 1981

A death in a hospital (liberals silent as unwanted child is starved to death in Indiana hospital; they are busy protesting the danger of nuclear weapons to human life), by R. E. Tyrrell, Jr. AMERICAN SPECTATOR. 15:6+, June 1981

Depo-provera debate revs up at FDA. SCIENCE. 217:424-428, July 30, 1982

Down go the abortion and school prayer bills, by B. Spring. CHRISTIANITY TODAY. 26:56-58, October 22, 1982

Epidemiological and clinical aspects of voluntary interruption of pregnancy 2 years after passing of Law 194, by M. G. Ricci, et al. RIVISTA ITALIANA DI GINECOLOGIA. 59(4-5):405-419, 1980

Experience acquired in application of Law No. 194 for a period of 18 months, by A. Canfora, et al. MINERVA GINECOLOGIA. 33(12):1167-1172, December 1981

Father's (lack of) right and responsibilities in the abortion decision: an examination of legal-ethical implications, by M. B. Knapp. OHIO NORTHERN UNIVERSITY LAW REVIEW. 9:369-383, July 1982

Federal court largely upholds abortion clinic regulations. FAMILY LAW REPORTER: COURT OPINIONS. 7(21):2348-2349, March 31, 1981

Federal court reaffirms injunction against city hospital's abortion ban. FAMILY LAW REPORTER: COURT OPINIONS. 8(14):2197-2198, February 9, 1982

Fertility-related state laws enacted in 1981 (laws affecting abortion, services to minors, pregnancy-related insurance, family-planning services, sterilization, sex education and propulation commissions), by P. Donovan. FAMILY PLANNING PERSPECTIVES. 14:63+, March-April 1982

Fetal law, by S. Speights. PLAYBOY. 29(1):62, March 1982

Fetal rights? It depends, by A. E. Doudera. TRIAL. 18(4):38-44+, April 1982

Focus on social questions pt 2: celebrating the 400th anniversary of the BOOK OF CONCORD with a view to happenings in Australian society, by D. C. Overduin. LUTHERAN THEOLOGICAL JOURNAL. 14:80-87, August 1980

For pro-lifers there is still a long, tough road ahead, by L. H. Pumphrey. OUR SUNDAY VISITOR. 70:8, February 14, 1982

Frequency of Langdon-Down disease in newborn infants in the Neubrandenburg district after the introduction of the abortion law of 9/3/1972, by I. Goetze. ZEITSCHRIFT FUR ARZTLICHE FORTBILDUNG. 75(3):107-108, February 1, 1981

H.L. v. Matheson, 101 S Ct 1164. JOURNAL OF FAMILY LAW. 20: 153-157, September 1981

--: and the right of minors to seek abortions, by M. H. Wolff. CALIFORNIA WESTERN LAW REVIEW. 19:74-106, Fall 1982

--: can parental notification be required for minors seeking abortions?. UNIVERSITY OF RICHMOND LAW REVIEW. 16:429-447, Winter 1982

--: parental notic prior to abortion. ST. LOUIS UNIVERSITY LAW JOURNAL. 26:426-446, January 1982

--: where does the court stand on abortion and parental notification?, by H. N. Feldman. AMERICAN UNIVERSITY LAW REVIEW. 31(2):431-469, 1982

Half a loaf: a new antiabortion strategy, by P. Donovan. FAMILY PLANNING PERSPECTIVES. 13:262-279, November-December 1981

Harris v. McRae (100 S Ct 2671): clash of a nonenumerated right with legislative control of the purse, by D. T. Hardy. CASE WESTERN RESERVE LAW REVIEW. 31:465-508, Spring 1981

--: cutting back abortion rights. COLUMBIA HUMAN RIGHTS LAW REVIEW. 12:113-136, Spring-Summer 1980

Hatch Amendment report hailed by pro-life director. OUR SUNDAY VISITOR. 71:7, June 27, 1982

Hatch Amendment still splits pro-life camp, by J. Castelli. OUR SUNDAY VISITOR. 70:6, January 17, 1982

Hatch Bill vote demanded, by M. Meehan. NATIONAL CATHOLIC RE-PORTER. 18:8, July 30, 1982

Health law--abortions. FAMILY LAW REPORTER. 7(20):3021-3036, March 24, 1981

Helms bill stalled by Senate vote, by M. Meehan. NATIONAL CATHOLIC REPORTER. 18:26, September 17, 1982

"Honeymoon" over in DC for action on abortion bills, by C. McKenna. NEW DIRECTIONS FOR WOMEN. 11:19, March-April 1982

Hospitalization for medical legal and other abortions in the United States, 1970-1977, by M. B. Bracken, et al. AMERICAN JOURNAL OF PUBLIC HEALTH. 72:30-37, January 1982

Human Life Amendment hearings: Schmitz fears "bulldykes" (Senator John Schmitz's anti-Semitic and anti-female remarks), by L. Noble. UNION W.A.G.E. (68):5, January-February 1982

Human Life Bill: personhood revisited, or Congress takes aim at Roe v. Wade (93 S Ct 705). HOFSTRA LAW REVIEW. 10:1269-1295, Summer 1982

--: protecting the unborn through congressional enforcement of the fourteenth amendment, by B. J. Uddo. LOYOLA LAW REVIEW. 27:1079-1097, Fall 1981

Human life federalism amendment [an assessment], by W. R. Caron. CATHOLIC LAWYER. 27:87-111, Spring 1982

--: its language, effects, by D. J. Horan. HOSPITAL PROGRESS. 62(12):12-14, December 1981

Husband challenges wife's right to abortion (Maryland Court of Appeals to hear case in January 1983 to decide if Judge Daniel Moylan was correct in permitting Chris Fritz to veto abortion decision of Bonnie Fritz). OFF OUR BACKS. 12:13, November 1982

Hyde amendment: an infringement upo the free exercise clause?. RUTGERS LAW REVIEW. 33:1054-1075, Summer 1981

I'm a criminal and proud of it: an abortion outlaw speaks up (protest during the Senate hearings on the Human Life Bill), by L. Smith. MADEMOISELLE. 88:266-267, August 1982

The impact of legal abortion on marital and nonmarital fertility in Upstate New York, by E. J. C. Tu, et al. FAMILY PLANNING PERSPECTIVES. 14:37+, January-February 1982

Implementing a permissive policy hospital abortion services after Roe v. Wade, by J. R. Bond, et al. AMERICAN JOURNAL OF POLITICAL SCIENCE. 26:1-24, February 1982

Les implications morales de certaines dispositions legislatives concernant l'avortement, by M. T. Giroux. CAHIERS DE DROIT. 23:21-83, March 1982

Inga, midwife: without the new abortin legislation illegal abortions would increase [interview], by I. Abelson. VARDFACKET. 6(10):43-44, May 28, 1982

Interruzione della gravidanza e legislazione: un'indagine in tunisia, by G. Giumelli. REVISTRA DI SERVIZIO SOCIALE. 21(3):146-156, 1981

Is it really abortion?, by E. Peters. SOCIAL JUSTICE REVIEW. 73:24-25, January-February 1982

Judges not chosen for abortion views as party platform urged, by M. Meehan. NATIONAL CATHOLIC REPORTER. 18:1+, May 14, 1982

Judicial doors open a little more: law and life, by W. Monopoli. FINANCIAL POST. 75:9, December 12, 1981

Law, abortion and rights, by R. W. Schmude. LINACRE QUARTERLY. 49:215-221, August 1982

The law of human reproduction [an overview], by D. G. Warren. JOURNAL OF LEGAL MEDICINE. 3(1):1-57, March 1982

Law of the land, by H. Seiden. TODAY. p. 23, November 28, 1981

The law of menstrual therapies [editorial]. LANCET. 2(8295):
422-423, August 21, 1982

Law professors explore legal meaning of proposed anti-abortion
amendments. FAMILY LAW REPORTER: COURT OPINIONS. 8(4):2051-
2054, November 24, 1981

Legal abortion: the public health record, by W. Cates, Jr.
SCIENCE. 215(4540):1586-1590, March 26, 1982

Legal assessment: human life federalism amendment, by W. R.
Carron. ORIGINS. 11:495-500, January 14, 1982

Legal clout without a trial (abortions halted at Moose Jew Union
Hospital due to demands of pro-life groups), by D. Eisler.
MACLEAN'S. 95:17, January 28, 1982

--(therapeutic abortion), by D. Eisler. MACLEAN'S. 95:17, June
28, 1982

Legal status of the fetus (views of M. H. Shapirol). USA TODAY.
111:12-14, December 1982

Legally speaking. Assisting at abortions: can you really say
no?, by W. A. Regan. RN. 45(6):71, June 1982

The limits of judicial intevention in abortion politics (Roe v
Wade and Doe v Bolton), by R. Tatalovich, et al. CHRISTIAN
CENTURY. 99(1):16-20, January 6-13, 1982

The logic of abortion: how "quality of life" killed Infant Doe,
by M. S. Evans. HUMAN EVENTS. 42:7, May 1, 1982

Marchers were of one mind--abortions must be halted. OUR SUNDAY
VISITOR. 70:7, February 7, 1982

Marital secrets: the emerging issue of abortion spousal notification laws. JOURNAL OF LEGAL MEDICINE. 3:461-482, September
1982

Memo suggests Hatch aide expects abortion bill's defeat, by M.
Meehan. NATIONAL CATHOLIC REPORTER. 18(1):4, January 1, 1982

Morality, legality and abortion, by G. Dworkin. SOCIETY.
19(4):51-53, 1982

Morgentaler tests the law (plan for abortion clinics), by A.
Finlayson. MACLEAN'S. 95:55, November 29, 1982

NAS attacks evidence of anti-abortion lobby, by C. Cookson.
TIMES HIGHER EDUCATIONAL SUPPLEMENT. 445:6, May 15, 1981

The new danger: a three-step abortion pla (Senator O. G. Hatch's
Human Life Amendment), by L. C. Wohl. MS. 10:87-88, February
1982

New form for termination of pregnancy [letter]. BRITISH MEDICAL
JOURNAL. 284(6317):738, March 6, 1982

Not while you live in my house: the Supreme Court upholds mandatory parental notification of the dependent minor's abortion
decision in H.L. v. Matheson (101 S Ct 1164). UNIVERSITY OF
TOLEDO LAW REVIEW. (the). 13:115-148, Fall 1981

Notes on the application of the law on voluntary interruption of
pregnancy at a provincial general hospital, by P. Trompeo, et
al. MINERVA GINECOLOGIA. 33(11):1049-1052, November 1981

The nurse and the law: judgement and counter-judgement, by A.
Langslow. AUSTRALIAN NURSES' JOURNAL. 11(8):28-30, March
1982

Opting for the right to end life, by M. Engel. MACLEAN'S. 95:
8, March 8, 1982

Our first experience with and considerations on the legal provisions of Law 194/78, by E. Martella, et al. ARCHIVES OF
OBSTETRICS AND GYNECOLOGY. 85(6):557-566, November-December
1980

Outcome of pregnancy in women who were refused an abortion by a
secondary medical board, by M. Lekin, et al. MEDICINSKI
PREGLED. 34(5-6):247-249, 1981

Parent versus child: H.L. v. Matheson (101 S Ct 1164) and the
new abortion litigation. WISCONSIN LAW REVIEW. 1982:75-116,
1982

Parental notification: a state-created obstacle to a minor
woman's right of privacy. GOLDEN GATE UNIVERSITY LAW REVIEW.
12:579-603, Summer 1982

Parental rights. AMERICA. 146:143-144, February 27, 1982

Parts of Massachusetts abortion law deemed of doubtful constitutionality. FAMILY LAW REPORTER: COURT OPINIONS. 7(17):2272-
2274, March 3, 1981

Personhood, abortion and the law, by B. J. Verkamp. AMERICA.
146(3):46-48, January 23, 1982

Planned Parenthood League of Massachusetts v. Bellotti, 40 U S L
W 2532. AMERICAN JOURNAL OF TRIAL ADVOCACY. 5:166-171, Summer 1981

--, 641 F 2d 1006. JOURNAL OF FAMILY LAW. 20:158-161, September 1981

Potential constitutional issues raised by the proposed amendment
to the Georgia abortion statute, by R. N. Berg. JOURNAL OF
THE MEDICAL ASSOCIATION OF GEORGIA. 71(20:128-131, February
1982

Power of Congress to change constitutional decisions of the Supreme Court: the Human Life Bill, by T. I. Emerson. NORTH-
WESTERN UNIVERSITY LAW REVIEW. 77:129-142, April 1982

Private cause of action for abortion expenses under state paternity statutes, by G. Schachter. WOMEN'S RIGHTS LAW REPORTER. 7:63-90, Winter 1982

Problems of interpreting socially controverisal legislation, by J. K. Bentil. THE SOLICITORS' JOURNAL. 125:786-788, November 20, 1981

Progesterone-binding globulin and progesterone in guinea-pigs after ovariectomy, abortion and parturition, by J. J. Evans, et al. JOURNAL OF STEROID BIOCHEMISTRY. 16(2):171-173, February 1982

Pro-life unity could be crucial to Hatch action, by R. B. Shaw. OUR SUNDAY VISITOR. 70:3, March 28, 1982

Pro-lifers claim senator blocks Hatch amendment. OUR SUNDAY VISITOR. 71:3, July 18, 1982

Public opinion bombshell: prochoice majority vows to vote, by L. C. Wohl. MS. 11:70-71+, July-August 1982

Reagan must address key social issues, by C. Thomas. CONSERVATIVE DIGEST. 8:48, May 1982

Reform of penal regulations on abortion in the FRG. In: Topics of crime research. WISSENSCHAFTLICHE SCHRIFTENREIHE DER HUMBOLDT-UNIVERSITAT. pp. 57-66, 1980

Religion, law and public policy in America, by C. E. Curran. JURIST. 42:14-28, 1982

Reproductive Rights National Network (R2N2) meets in San Francisco, by S. Schulman. OFF OUR BACKS. 12:10, January 1982

Right to abortion limited: the Supreme Court upholds the constitutionality of parental notification statutes. LOYOLA LAW REVIEW. 28:281-296, Winter 1982

Right-to-Life bible (handbook on abortion), by A. J. Fuch-Berman. OFF OUR BACKS. 12:7, Decemer 1982

Right-to-lifers close ranks on legislation by J. Soriano. NATIONAL CATHOLIC REPORTER. 18:25, July 30, 1982

Schienberg v. Smith, 659 F 2d 476. JOURNAL OF FAMILY LAW. 20: 551-554, May 1982

The second victory of Anthony Comstock, by R. Polenberg. SOCIETY. 19(4):32-38, 1982

Senate committee passes anti-abortion amendment [March 10th approval by Senate Judiciary Committee of Hatch Amendment], by T. Dejanikus. OFF OUR BACKS. 12:17, April 1982

Senate debate on abortion turns into procedural tussle. CONGRESSIONAL QUARTERLY WEEKLY REPORT. 40:2202, September 4, 1982

Senate panel begins consideration of constitutional amendment on abortion. FAMILY LAW REPORTER: COURT OPINIONS. 7(48):2759-2761, October 13, 1981

Senate poll: 16 of 67 for Hatch, by M. Meehan. NATIONAL CATHO-LIC REPORTER. 18:1+, March 19, 1982

The Senate threat to our lives, by L. C. Wohl. MS. 10:21, January 1982

Senator Helms introduces unifying pro-life initiative. OUR SUNDAY VISITOR. 70:7, March 21, 1982

Sixty-nine percent of United States adults now approve legal abortion for six specified reasons: up since 1980. FAMILY PLANNING PERSPECTIVES. 14:214-215, July-August 1982

The socio-economic determinants o recourse to legal abortion, by J. Humphries. WOMEN'S STUDIES INTERNATIONAL QUARTERLY. 3(4): 377-393, 1980

Spousal notice and consultation requirement: a new approach to state regulation of abortion. NOVA LAW JOURNAL. 6:457-474, Spring 1982

Spousal notification requirement is constitutionally permissible burden on woman's right to privacy in abortion decision: Scheinberg v. Smith, 659 F 2d 476. TEXAS TECH LAW REVIEW. 13:1495-1511, 1982

Stalemated on abortion, Congress sent new bill, by M. Meehan. NATIONAL CATHOLIC REPORTER. 18:3, March 12, 1982

State ordered to pay for indigents' medically necessary abor-tions. FAMILY LAW REPORTER: COURT OPINIONS. 8(1):2006-2008, November 3, 1981

Storm over Washington: the parental notification proposal, by A. M. Kenney, et al. FAMILY PLANNING PERSPECTIVES. 14:185+, July-August 1982

Subcommittee passes Hatch bill, by M. Meehan. NATIONAL CATHOLIC REPORTER. 18:25, December 25, 1981

The Supreme Court 1980-81 term: abortion. CRIMINAL LAW RE-PORTER: COURT DECISIONS AND PROCEEDINGS. 29(23):4171-4172, September 9, 1981

Supreme Court report: abortion ... parental notification, by R. L. Young. AMERICAN BAR ASSOCIATION JOURNAL. 67:630-632, May 1981

Supreme Court roundup: 1980 term, by R. J. Regan. THOUGHT. 56: 491-502, December 1981

The Supreme Court, the states, and social change: the case of abortion, by S. B. Hansen. PEACE AND CHANGE. 6(3):20-32, 1980

Trends and patterns in the attitudes of the public toward legal
abortion in the United States, 1972-1978, by S. A. Moldando.
DISSERTATION ABSTRACTS INTERNATIONAL. B. p. 1054, 1982

Two competing "pro-life" measures split the anti-abortion lobby:
one faction supports an outright ban on abortions, while another favors a constitutional amendment that would turn the
issue largely over to the states, by T. Miller. NATIONAL
JOURNAL. 14:511-513, March 20, 1982

What legalized abortion has meant to America, by R. P. Lockwood.
OUR SUNDAY VISITOR. 70:16, January 17, 1982

What the Supreme Court heard on abortion, by T. Gest. US NEWS
AND WORLD REPORT. 93:83, December 13, 1982

What's new in the law: constitutional law ... abortions, by A.
Ashman. AMERICAN BAR ASSOCIATION JOURNAL. 67:644-645, May 1981

--: constitutional law ... discriminatory funding, by A. Ashman.
AMERICAN BAR ASSOCIATION JOURNAL. 67:917-918, July 1981

Who does speak for human life? (debate on Hatch Amendment by
National Conference of Catholic Bishops), by W. F. Buckley.
NATIONAL REVIEW. 34:381, April 2, 1982

With friends like these (Senate debate). COMMONWEAL. 109:483-
485, September 24, 1982

Your parents or the judge: Massachusetts' new abortion consent
law, by P. Donovan. FAMILY PLANNING PERSPECTIVES. 13(5):224-
228, September-October 1981

GREAT BRITAIN
A matter of forms: Peter Huntingford, the docto who forced a
show-down on moves to restrict the abortion law, by J.
Nicholls. SUNDAY TIMES. p. 36, February 14, 1982

INDIA
Legalized abortion and profile of women in New Delhi, by R.
Singh. HIROSHIMA JOURNAL OF MEDICAL SCIENCES. 30(1):43-46,
March 1981

IRELAND
Ireland: abortion vote debated (Women's Right to Choose,
Dublin, fighting anti-abortion amendment to Constitution),
by G. Horgan. OFF OUR BACKS. 12:6, July 1982

Life amendment: abortion and the Irish constitution, by P.
Kirby, et al. GUARDIAN. p. 17, November 6, 1982

Where abortion is for export only, by M. Holland. TIMES (London). p. 12, November 24, 1982

ITALY
Legal abortion in Italy, 1978-1979, by M. Filicori, et al.
FAMILY PLANNING PERSPECTIVES. 13:228-231, September-October
1981

ABORTION: LAWS AND LEGISLATION: GENERAL (continued)

A victory for women? The abortion referendum in Italy, by M.
Bosworth. REFRACTORY GIRL. (23):17-19, March 1982

SWITZERLAND
Legal abortion in Switzerland; some numbers and evolution, by
P. A. Gloor, et al. PRAXIS. 71(6):225-229, February 9,
1982

UNITED STATES
Abortion: winning at the state level (Pennsylvania), by T.
Sgrignoll. MS. 10:26, April 1982

Committee to Defend Reproductive Rights v. Myers [625 P 2d
119 (Cal)]: the constitutionality of conditions on public
benefits in California. THE HASTINGS LAW JOURNAL. 33:1475-
1500, July 1982

Hospitalization for medical-legal and other abortions in the
United States 1970-1977, by M. B. Bracken, et al. AMERICAN
JOURNAL OF PUBLIC HEALTH. 72(1):30, January 1982

The impact of legal abortion on marital and nonmarital fertility in upstate New York, by E. J-C. Tu, et al. FAMILY
PLANNING PESPECTIVES. 14(1):37, January-February 1982

Parental notification: is it settled? (possible effects of
the U.S. Supreme Court decision in H.L. v. Matheson, upholding a Utah state law requiring that all minors notify
their parents before obtaining an abortion), by P. Donovan.
FAMILY PLANNING PERSPECTIVES. 13:243-246, September-October
1981

Taxpayer attack on abortion funding repelled by Maryland's
high court. FAMILY LAW REPORTER: COURT OPINIONS. 7(22):
2360-2361, April 7, 1981

Your parents or the judge: Massachusetts' new abortion consent
law, by P. Donovan. FAMILY PLANNING PERSPECTIVES. 13(5):
224- 228, September-October 1981

Right to abortion under attack in Pennsylvania, Louisiana,
Michigan and Congress, by T. Dejanikus. OFF OUR BACKS.
12:8-9+, January 1982

ABORTION: MISSED
Contribution of HCG radioimmunoassay in the diagnosis of patho-
logical states in early pregnancy, by H. Fingerova, et al.
CESKOSLOVENSKA GYNEKOLOGIE. 46(9):673-680, November 1981

Induction of abortion by intra-amniotic administration of prostaglandin F2 alpha in patients with intrauterine fetal death
and missed abortion, by A. Antsaklis, et al. INTERNATIONAL
SURGERY. 64(5):41-43, August-October 1979

Missed abortion treated with intramuscular 15-(S)-15-methyl-
prostaglandin F2 alpha, by G. Tsalacopoulos, et al. SOUTH
AFRICAN MEDICAL JOURNAL. 61(22):828-830, May 29, 1982

ABORTION: MISSED (continued)

Termination of midtrimester missed abortion by extraovular instillation of normal saline, by H. Abramovici, et al. BRITISH
JOURNAL OF OBSTETRICS AND GYNAECOLOGY. 88(9):931-933, September 1981

ABORTION: MORTALITY AND MORTALITY STATISTICS
Abortion and infant mortality before and after the 1973 US
Supreme Court decision on abortion, by L. S. Robertson.
JOURNAL OF BIOLOGICAL SCIENCE. 13(3):275-280, July 1981

Behavioral factors contributing to abortion deaths: a new approach to mortality studies, by R. M. Selik, et al. OBSTE-
TRICS AND GYNECOLOGY. 58(5):631-635, November 1981

Comparative risk of death from induced abortion at less than or
equal to 12 weeks' gestation performed with local versus general anesthesia, by H. B. Peterson, et al. AMERICAN JOURNAL
OF OBSTETRICS AND GYNECOLOGY. 141(7):763-768, December 1,
1981

Deaths from second trimester abortion by dilatation and evacuation: causes, prevention, facilities, by W. Cates, Jr., et al.
OBSTETRICS AND GYNECOLOGY. 58(4):401-408, October 1981

Illegal-abortion deaths in the United States: why are they still
occuring?, by N. Binkin, et al. FAMILY PLANNING PERSPECTIVES.
14:163-167, May-June 1982

Maternal and abortion related deaths in Bangladesh, 1978-1979,
by R. W. Rochat, et al. INTERNATIONAL JOURNAL OF GYNAECOLOGY
AND OBSTETRICS. 19(2):155-164, April 1981

Mortality from abortion and childbirth. Are the populations
comparable?, by S. A. LeBolt, et al. JAMA: JOURNAL OF THE
AMERICAN MEDICAL ASSOCIATION. 248(2):188-191, July 9, 1982

---. Are the statistics biased?, by W. Cates, Jr., et al. JAMA:
JOURNAL OF THE AMERICAN MEDICAL ASSOCIATION. 248(2):192-196,
July 9, 1982

Mortality, legality and abortion, by G. Dworkin. SOCIETY. 19:
51-53, May-June 1982

Reproductive mortality in the United States, by B. P. Sachs,
et al. JAMA: JOURNAL OF THE AMERICAN MEDICAL ASSOCIATION.
247(20):2789-2792, May 28, 1982

Using local anesthesia for 1st-trimester abortion cuts mortality
sharply. FAMILY PLANNING PERSPECTIVES. 14:332-334, November-
December 1982

ABORTION: PSYCHOLOGY AND PSYCHIATRY
Counselling needs of women seeking abortions, by M. J. Hare, et
al. JOURNAL OF BIOLOGICAL SCIENCE. 13(3):269-273, July 1981

Is it better to know the worst? ... amniocentesis confirmed Tay-
Sachs disease. RN. 45:48-49+, March 1982

Preliminary findings of personality differences between nulliparas and repeated aborters along the dimensions of locus of
control and impulsivity, by G. D. Gibb, et al. PSYCHOLOGICAL
REPORTS. 49(2):413-414, October 1981

Psychiatric aspects of therapeutic abortion, by B. K. Doane, et
al. CANADIAN MEDICAL ASSOCIATION JOURNAL. 125(5):427-432,
September 1, 1981

ABORTION: REPEATED
Abdominal approach in cerclage for treatment of repeated abortion due to segmental cervical insufficieny, by R. Grio, et
al. MINERVA GINECOLOGIA. 33(12):1131-1136, December 1981

Care of a pre-eclampsia multipara with repeated pregnancy loss,
by C. H. Chou. HU LI TSA CHIH. 28:11-16, July 1981

Chromosome analyses in couples with repeated pregnancy loss, by
T. Andrews, et al. JOURNAL OF BIOLOGICAL SCIENCE. 14(1):33-
52, January 1982

Etiology of delivery during the 2nd trimester and performance in
subsequent pregnancies, by G. J. Patten. MEDICAL JOURNAL OF
AUSTRALIA. 68-2(12/13):654-656, 1981

The first abortion--and the last? A study of the personality
factors underlying repeated failure of contraception, by P.
Niemela, et al. INTERNATIONAL JOURNAL OF GYNAECOLOGY AND
OBSTETRICS. 19(3):193-200, June 1981

Increased frequencies of chromosomal abnormalities in families
with a history of fetal wastage, by I. Nordenson. CLINICAL
GENETICS. 19(3):168-173, March 1981

Increased frequency of associations of acrocentric chromosomes
brought about by the LDH virus in infertile women, by B.
Mejsnarova, et al. SBORNIK LEKARSKY. 83(11-12):332-336, 1981

'Lupus' anticoagulant and inhibition of prostacyclin formation
in patients with repeated abortions, intrauterine growth
retardation and intrauterine death, by L. O. Carreras, et al.
BRITISH JOURNAL OF OBSTETRICS AND GYNAECOLOGY. 88(9):890-894,
September 1981

Ovarian pregnancy: association with IUD, pelvic pathology and
recurrent abortion, by J. Reichman, et al. EUROPEAN JOURNAL
OF OBSTETRICS, GYNECOLOGY AND REPRODUCTIVE BIOLOGY. 12(6):
333-337, December 1981

Ovarian pregnancy: association with intrauterine device, pelvic
pathology and recurrent abortion, by J. Reichman, et al.
EUROPEAN JOURNAL OF OBSTETRICS, GYNECOLOGY AND REPRODUCTIVE
BIOLOGY. 12(6):333-338, 1981

Parental chromosomal rearrangements associated with repetitive
spontaneous abortions, by J. L. Simpson, et al. FERTILITY AND
STERILITY. 36(5):584-590, November 1981

Possible relationship between circulating anticoagulants and recurrent abortion, by J. R. Duran-Suarez, et al. HAEMATOLOG-
ICA. 67(2):320-321, April 1981

Preliminary findings of personality differences between nulliparas and repeated aborters along the dimensions of locus of
control and impulsivity, by G. D. Gibb, et al. PSYCHOLOGICAL
REPORTS. 49:413-414, October 1981

Repeated suboptimal pregnancy outcome, by J. L. Simpson. BIRTH
DEFECTS. 17(1):113-142, 1981

Reproductive failure. A survey o pathogenic mechanisms with emphasis on mechanisms for repeated failures, by J. M. Kissane.
MONOGRAPHS IN PATHOLOGY. (22):369-381, 1981

Research on repeated abortion: state of the field: 1973-1979, by
G. D. Gibb, et al. PSYCHOLOGICAL REPORTS. 48(2):415-424,
April 1981

Translocations involving chromosome 12. I. A report of a 12,21
translocation in a woman with recurrent abortions, and a study
of the breakpoints and modes of ascertainment of translocations involving chromosome 12, by J. H. Ford, et al. HUMAN
GENETICS. 58(2):144-148, 1981

Unexpected encounters in cytogenetics: repeated abortions and
parental sex chromosome mosaicism may indicte risk of nondisjunction [editorial], by F. Hecht. AMERICAN JOURNAL OF HUMAN
GENETICS. 34(3):514-516, May 1982

Women who have had abortions. Part 2. FAMILY PLANNING PERSPEC-
TIVES. 14:60-62, March-April 1982

ABORTION: RESEARCH
Abortion and the death of the fetus, by S. L. Ross. PHILOSOPHY
AND PUBLIC AFFAIRS. 11:232-245, Summer 1982

Abortions and hydatidiform mole: the genetic link [editorial],
by R. Toaff. HAREFUAH. 101(5-6):120-122, September 1981

An analysis of electrocardiographic changes during artificial
abortion in 51 cases. CHUNG HUA FU CHAN KO TSA CHIH. 14(2):
116-117, April 1979

Biologic and physical means of assessing the threat of miscarriage, by J. P. Schaaps. REVUE MEDICALE DE LIEGE. 37(4):114-
117, February 15, 1982

Cellular immunity in normal pregnancy and abortion: subpopulations of T lymphocytes bearing Fc receptors for IgG and IgM,
by Y. Sumiyoshi, et al. AMERICAN JOURNAL OF REPRODUCTIVE
IMMUNOLOGY. 1(3):145-149, 1981

Centric fission of chromosome no. 7 in three generations, by D.
Janke. HUMAN GENETICS. 60(2):200-201, 1982

Changes of gap junctions in myometrium of guinea pig at parturition and abortion, by R. E. Garfield, et al. CANADIAN JOURNAL OF PHYSIOLOGY AND PHARMACOLOGY. 60(3):335-341, 1982

Cyematopathology. Principles an recommendations for practical handling of pathologico-anatomic and histologic examinations in abortions, diseases and death of premature and full-term infants, by K. Kloos. PATHOLOGE. 3(3):121-126,

Cytogenetic examinations of married couples with obstetrical failures, by H. Kedzia, et al. GINEKOLOGIA POLSKA. 52(9):80-1804, September 1981

Detection of subclinical abortion in infertile women by beta-hCG radioimmunoassay, by T. Onoue, et al. NIPPON SANKA FUJINKA GAKKAI ZASSHI. 33(8):1255-1258, August 1981

Dietary deprivation induces fetal loss and abortion in rabbits, by T. Matsuzawa, et al. TOXICOLOGY. 22(3):255-260, 1981

Echographic examinations in 246 cases of voluntary interruption of pregnancy, by P. Rattazzi, et al. MINERVA GINECOLOGIA. 33(12):1173-1178, December 1981

Effect of progesterone withdrawal in sheep during late pregnancy by M. J. Taylor, et al. JOURNAL OF ENDOCRINOLOGY. 92(1):85-85-93, January 1982

Efficacy of antibodies generated by Pr-beta-hCG-TT to terminate pregnancy in baboons: its reversibility and rescue by medroxy-progesterone acetate, by A. Tandon, et al. CONTRACEPTION. 24(1):83-95, July 1981

Epidemiology of abortion, by C. W. Tyler, Jr. JOURNAL OF REPRO-DUCTIVE MEDICINE. 26(9):459-469, Sepember 1981

Estradiol-17 beta cyclopentylpropionat and prostaglandin F for induction of abortion during the first trimester of pregnancy in feedlot heifers, by K. R. Refsal, et al. JOURNAL OF THE AMERICAN VETERINARY MEDICAL ASSOCIATION. 179(7):701-703, October 1, 1981

Examination of products of conception from previable human preg-nancies, by D. I. Rushton. JOURNAL OF CLINICAL PATHOLOGY. 34(8):819-835, August 1981

Fetal loss, gravidity and pregnancy order: is the truncated cascade analysis valid?, by J. Golding, et al. EARLY HUMAN DEVELOPMENT. 6(1):71-76, January 1982

Immunological studies of toxoplasmosis in case of abortion, by R. C. Mahajan, et al. INDIAN JOURNAL OF PATHOLOGY AND MICRO-BIOLOGY. 24(3):165-169, July 1981

In vitro study of comparative immunosuppressive activity of sera from pregnant women on an in vitro celluar cytotoxic reaction, by F. Fizet, et al. COMPTES RENDUS DES SEANCES DE L ACADEMIE DES SCIENCES. 293(10):583-588, November 16, 1981

The incidence of congenital abnormalities following gestagen administration in early pregnancy, by W. H. Schneider, et al. WIENER KLINISCHE WOCHENSCHRIFT. 93(23):711-712, December 1981

Induction of abortion in feedlot heifers with a combination of cloprostenol and dexamethasone, by A. D. Barth, et al. CANADIAN VETERINARY JOURNAL. 22(3):62-64, March 1981

Induction of abortion using prostaglandins, by R. H. Schultz, et al. ACTA VETERINARIA SCANDINAVICA. SUPPLEMENT. 77:353-361, 1981

Infanticide, arsenic, phosphorus and probes used in abortion during past centuries, by U. Hogberg. LAKARTIDNINGEN. 78(35):2951-2952, August 26, 1981

Intrauterine mummified fetus in a rhesus monkey (Macaca mulatta) by M. M. Swindle, et al. JOURNAL OF MEDICAL PRIMATOLOGY. 10(4-5):269-273, 1981

Is prognostic information obtainable from serum PZ level with imminent abortion?, by G. Stranz, et al. ZENTRALBLATT FUR GYNAEKOLOGIE. 103(13):758-762, 1981

The luteolytic and abortifacient potential of an estrogen-bromergocryptine regimen in the baboon, by V. D. Castracane, et al. FERTILITY AND STERILITY. 37(2):258-262, February 1982

Luteolytic effect of azastene in the nonhuman primate, by R. H. Asch, et al. OBSTETRICS AND GYNECOLOGY. 59(3):303-308, March 1982

Margareta Callersten, participant in abortion research: don't choose abortion because it appears a better solution [interview by Monica Trozell], by M. Callersten. VARDFACKET. 6(10):41-42, May 28, 1982

The Mexican plant zoapatle (Montanoa tomentosa) in reproductive medicine. Past, present, and future, by S. D. Levine, et al. JOURNAL OF REPRODUCTIVE MEDICINE. 26(10):524-528, October 1981

Midtrimester abortion patients, by L. D. White, et al. AORN JOURNAL: ASSOCIATION OF OPERATING ROOM NURSES. 34:756+, October 1981

Mismating and termination of pregnancy, by V. M. Shille. VETERINARY CLINICS OF NORTH AMERICA. SMALL ANIMAL PRACTICE. 12(1):99-106, February 1982

Observations during the treatment of antithrombin-III deficient women with heparin and antithrombin concentrate during pregnancy, parturition, and abortion, by P. Brandt. THROMBOSIS RESEARCH. 22(1-2):15-24, April 1-15, 1981

Parental chromosome translocations and fetal loss, by C. Tsenghi, et al. OBSTETRICS AND GYNECOLOGY. 58(4):456-458, October 1981

Pregnancy abnormalities among personnel at a virological laboratory, by G. Axelsson, et al. AMERICAN JOURNAL OF INDUSTRIAL MEDICINE. 1(2):129-137, 1980

Pregnancy termination in dogs with novel non-hormonal compounds. Studies of 2-(3-ethoxy-phenyl)-5,6-dihydro-s-triazole [5,1-a] isoquinoline (DL 204-IT), by G. Galliani, et al. ARZNEIMIT-TEL-FORSCHUNG. 32(2):123-127, 1982

A preliminary study on the mechanism of uterine excitant action of rivanol in guinea-pigs, by W. Q. Liu, et al. CHUNG-KUO YAO LI HSUEH PAO. 17(1):58-60, January 1982

Prenatal illness as a marker of prenatal individuality, by H. Berger. PAEDIATRIE UND PAEDOLOGIE. 17(2):133-139, 1982

Prolonged in utero retention and mummification of a Macaca mulatta fetus, by E. Mueller-Heubach, et al. JOURNAL OF MEDICAL PRIMATOLOGY. 10(4-5):265-268, 1981

Psychosocial aspects of early pregnancy termination [research], by R. A. Brown. NEW ZEALAND NURSING FORUM. 10(1):8-10, 1982

Research on repeated abortion: state of the field: 1973-1979, by G. D. Gibb, et al. PSYCHOLOGICAL REPORTS. 48(2):415-424, April 1981

Researchers confirm induced abortion to be safer for women than childbirth: refute claims of critics. FAMILY PLANNING PER-SPECTIVES. 14:271-272, September-October 1982

Risk of death from abortion sterilization is three times greater with hysterotomy or hysterectomy. FAMILY PLANNING PERSPEC-TIVES. 14:147-148, May-June 1982

Some biological insights into abortion, by G. Hardin. BIO-SCIENCE. 32:720+, October 1982

Spontaneous occurrence of atypical hyperplasia and adenocarcinom of the uterus in androgen-sterilized SD rats, by S. Morikawa, et al. JNCI: JOURNAL OF THE NATIONAL CANCER INSTITUTE. 69(1):95-101, July 1982

Studies on the mechanism of action of the abortive effect of 6-hydroxydopamine in rats, by E. MacDonald, et al. MEDICAL BIOLOGY. 59(2):111-115, April 1981

A study on the pathogenic change and cause of death of fetus in middle pregnancy terminated with alcoholic extract of Yuanhua, by Z. F. He. CHUNG HUA FU CHAN KO TSA CHIH. 17(2):116-118, April 1982

Termination of pregnancy with cloprostenol and dexamethasone in intact or ovariectomized cows, by W. H. Johnson, et al. CANADIAN VETERINARY JOURNAL. 22(9):288-290, September 1981

The threat of miscarriage. Etiologic research, by R. Lambotte. REVUE MEDICALE DE LIEGE. 37(4):109-114, February 15, 1982

ABORTION: RESEARCH (continued)

Translocations involving chromosome 12:1. A report of a 12,21
translocation in a woman with recurrent abortions, and a study
of breakpoints and modes of ascertainment of translocations
involving chromosome 12, by J. Ford, et al. HUMAN GENETICS.
58(2):144-148, 1981

Trophoblastic disease: a bridge between pregnancy and malignancy
by L. Deligdisch. PROGRESS IN CLINICAL AND BIOLOGICAL RE-
SEARCH. 70:323-337, 1981

Twin pregnancy with operative removal of one fetus with chromosomal mosaicism 46,XX/45,XO and term delivery of a healthy
baby, by U. Gigon, et al. ZEITSCHRIFT FUR GEBURTSCHILFE UND
PERINATOLOGIE. 185(6):365-366, December 1981

Use of cloprostenol with dexamethasone in the termination of advanced pregnancy in heifers, by R. D. Murray, et al. VETERIN-
ARY RECORD. 108(17):378-380, April 25, 1981

Various aspects of voluntary abortion at the Obstetrical and
Gynecological Clinic of the University of Modena, by M. G.
Lucchi, et al. ARCHIVES OF OBSTETRICS AND GYNECOLOGY. 85(6):
567-587, November-December 1980

Win 32,729, a new, potent interceptive agent in rats and rhesus
monkeys, by J. E. Creange, et al. CONTRACEPTION. 24(3):289-
299, September 1981

ABORTION: SEPTIC: COMPLICATIONS
Acute renal failure. Experience over a 22-year period, by M.
Alvo, et al. REVISTA MEDICA DE CHILE. 109(5):420-427, May
1981

Anaerobic sepsis and septic shock in criminal abortion, by A.
Angelov, et al. AKUSHERSTVO I GINEKOLOGIIA. 20(3):262-264,
1981

Primary malignant nephrosclerosis (PMN)--a case of an irreversible renal failure following septic abortion, by M. Belicza, et
al. LIJECNICKI VJESNIK. 102(7-8):432-435, July-August 1980

Rare combination of septic abortion and splenic rupture, by K.
Kurveniashki. AKUSHERSTVO I GINEKOLOGIIA. 21(1):89-90, 1982

ABORTION: SPONTANEOUS
Are we ignoring the needs of the woman with a spontaneous abor-
tion?, by S. K. Wetzel. MCN: AMERICAN JOURNAL OF MATERNAL
CHILD NURSING. 7(4):258-259, July-August 1982

Endometriosis and spontaneous abortion [letter], by W. P.
Dmowski. OBSTETRICS AND GYNECOLOGY. 58(6):763-764, December
1981

Induced abortion and spontaneous fetal loss in subsequent pregnancies, by C. S. Chung, et al. AMERICAN JOURNAL OF PUBLIC
HEALTH. 72(6):548-554, June 1982

Messing with Mother Nature: fleck and the omega pill, by J. A.

Montmarquet. PHILOSOPHICAL STUDIES. 41:407-420, May 1982

No increased risk of spontaneous abortion found among women with a previous induced abortion. FAMILY PLANNING PERSPECTIVES. 13:238-239, September-October 1981

Placental findings in spontaneous abortions and stillbirths, by A. Ornoy, et al. TERATOLOGY. 24(3):243-252, 1981

Prospective studies on pregnancy following induced and spontaneous abortion of primigravidae and assessment of fertility. IV. Report, by G. Schott, et al. ZENTRALBLATT FUR GYNAEKOLOGIE. 104(7):397-404, 1982

Reproductive histories in a Norwegian twin population evaluation of the maternal effect in early spontaneous abortion, by W. L. Golden. DISSERTATION ABSTRACTS INTERNATIONAL. B. p. 1365, 1982

Serum lactate dehydrogenase (LDH) activity in threatened abortion prolonged pregnancy and late pregnancy toxemia, by W. Nikodem. GINEKOLOGIA POLSKA. 52(1):33-37, January 1981

Serum polyamine-oxidase activity in spontaneous abortion, by G. Illei, et al. BRITISH JOURNAL OF OBSTETRICS AND GYNAECOLOGY. 89(3):199-201, March 1982

Woman's reaction to spantaneous abortion, by M. C. Turcotte-Lamoureux. INFIRMIERE CANADIENNE. 23(8):38+, September 1981

ABORTION: SPONTANEOUS: COMPLICATIONS
The analysis of spontaneous abortion using a new half-sib model for qualitative traits, by W. L. Golden, et al. PROGRESS IN CLINICAL AND BIOLOGICAL RESEARCH. 69A:197-202, 1981

Are we ignoring the needs of the woman with a spontaneous abortion?, by S. K. Wetzel. MCN: AMERICAN JOURNAL OF MATERNAL CHILD NURSING. 7:258-259, July-August 1982

Association between endometriosis and spontaneous abortion: a retrospective clinical study, by D. L. Olive, et al. JOURNAL OF REPRODUCTIVE MEDICINE. 27(6):333-338, 1982

Chromosome abnormalities in 150 couples with multiple spontaneous abortions, by P. Husslein, et al. FERTILITY AND STERILITY. 37(3):379-383, March 1982

Chromosome translocations in couples with multiple spontaneous abortions, by V. V. Michels, et al. AMERICAN JOURNAL OF HUMAN GENETICS. 34(3):507-513, May 1982

A cytogenetic study of 1000 spontaneous abortions, by T. Hassold, et al. ANNALS OF HUMAN GENETICS. 44(Pt 2):151-178, October 1980

Cytogenetics of spontaneous abortions, by L. Zergollern, et al. ACTA MEDICA IUGOSLAVICA. 36(2):107-113, 1982

Effect of the blood serum from pregnant women with early and late toxicoses and threatened abortions on spontaneous contractile activity of smooth muscle, by S. Sharankov, et al. AKUSHERSTVO I GINEKOLOGIIA. 20(3):190-197, 1981

Effect of psychological stress states in women with spontaneous abortions, by I. Vasileva. AKUSHERSTVO I GINEKOLOGIIA. 20(4):275-279, 1981

An epidemiologic study of spontaneous abortions and fetal wastage in Oklahoma City, by C. C. Anokute. DISSERTATION ABSTRACTS INTERNATIONAL. B. p. 393, 1982

Frequency of rare electrophoretic protein variants among spontaneous human abortuses, by I. P. Altukhov, et al. DOKLADY AKADEMII NAUK SSSR. 262(4):982-985, 1982

An immune dependency of trophoblastic growth implied by the antithetic difference in immunology between spontaneous abortion and hydatidiform mole, by S. Takeuchi. PROGRESS IN CLINICAL AND BIOLOGICAL RESEARCH. 70:245-257, 1981

Immunology of spontaneous abortion and hydatidiform mole, by S. Takeuchi. AMERICAN JOURNAL OF REPRODUCTIVE IMMUNOLOGY. 1(1): 23-28, 1980

Incidence of listeriosis in spontaneous abortion, by C. Balbi, et al. ARCHIVES OF OBSTETRICS AND GYNECOLOGY. 85(3):203-208, May-June 1980

Induced abortion and spontaneous fetal loss in subsequent pregnancies, by C. S. Chung, et al. AMERICAN JOURNAL OF PUBLIC HEALTH. 72(6):548-554, June 1982

Late spontaneous abortion associated with mycoplasma hominis infection of the fetus, by K. K. Christensen, et al. SCANDINAVIAN JOURNAL OF INFECTIOUS DISEASES. 14(1):73-74, 1982

'Menarcheal age and spontaneous abortion: a causal connection', by J. T. Casagrande, et al. AMERICAN JOURNAL OF EPIDEMIOLOGY. 115(3):481-483, March 1982

Menopausal age and spontaneous abortion in a group of women working in a Swedish steel works, by B. Kolmodm-Hedman, et al. SCANDINAVIAN JOURNAL OF SOCIAL MEDICINE. 10(1):17-22, 1982

Mycoplasma hominis as a possible cause of spontaneous abortions and premature labor, by I. Tanev, et al. AKUSHERSTVO I GINEKOLOGIIA. 20(3):197-201, 1981

Parental chromosomal rearrangements associated with repetitive spontaneous abortions, by J. L. Simpson, et al. FERTILITY AND STERILITY. 36(5):584-590, November 1981

Pericentric inversion of chromosome 9 in couples with repeated spontaneous abortion, by M. G. Tibiletti, et al. ACTA EUROPAEA FERTILITATIS. 12(3):245-248, September 1981

Placental findings in spontaneous abortions and stillbirths, by A. Ornoy, et al. TERATOLOGY. 24(3):243-252, December 1981

Reproductive histories in a Norwegian twin population: evaluation of the maternal effect in early spontaneous abortion, by W. L. Golden ACTA GENETICAE MEDICAE ET GEMELLOLOGIAE. 30(2): 91-95, 1981

The role of maternal diabetes in repetitive spontaneous abortion, by J. P. Crane, et al. FERTILITY AND STERILITY. 36(4): 477-479, October 1981

Salpingoclasia by minilaparotomy following spontaneous abortion, by A. Alvarado Duran, et al. GINECOLOGIA Y OBSTETRICIA DE MEXICO. 49(294):239-253, April 1981

Serum polyamine oxidase activity in spontaneous abortion, by G. Illei, et al. BRITISH JOURNAL OF OBSTETRICS AND GYNAECOLOGY. 89(3):199-201, 1982

Serum relaxin and human chorionic gonadotropin concentrations in spontaneous abortions, by J. Quagliarello, et al. FERTILITY AND STERILITY. 36(3):399-401, September 1981

Spontaneous abortion after intra-uterine transfer of an ovum fecundated in vitro, by R. Frydman, et al. NOUVELLE PRESSE MEDICALE. 10(42):3475-3476, November 21, 1981

Spontaneous abortion incidence in the treatment of infertility, by R. P. Jansen. AMERICAN JOURNAL OF OBSTETRICS AND GYNECOLOGY. 143(4):451-473, June 15, 1982

Spontaneous abortion over time: comparing occurrence in two cohorts of women a generation apart, by A. J. Wilcox, et al. AMERICAN JOURNAL OF EPIDEMIOLOGY. 114(4):548-553, October 1981

Spontaneous abortion. A study of 1,961 women and their conceptuses, by B. J. Poland, et al. ACTA OBSTETRICIA ET GYNECOLOGICA SCANDINAVICA. SUPPLEMENT. 102:1-32, 1981

Spontaneous abortions as an inde of occupational hazards, by K. Hemminke, et al. GIGIENA TRUDA I PROFESSIONALNYE ZABOLEVANIA. (1):41-43, January 1982

ABORTION: STATISTICS
Abortion statistics 1980. HEALTH BULLETIN. 39(6):382-383, November 1981

Abortion surveillance, 1979--provisional statistics. MMWR: MORBIDITY AND MORALITY WEEKLY REPORT. 31(4):47-50, February 5, 1982

Anaerobic sepsis and septic shock in criminal abortion, by A. Angelov, et al. AKUSHERSTVO I GINEKOLOGIIA. 20(3):262-264, 1981

Ectopic pregnancies: rising incidence rates in northern Cali-

fornia, by P. H. Shiono, et al. AMERICAN JOURNAL OF PUBLIC
HEALTH. 72:173-175, February 1982

The effects of termination of pregnancy: a follow-up study of
psychiatric referrals, by R. Schmidt, et al. BRITISH JOURNAL
OF MEDICAL PSYCHOLOGY. 54(3):267-276, September 1981

Hypersensitivity reaction to depo-Provera [letter], by R.
Zacest, et al. MEDICAL JOURNAL OF AUSTRALIA. 1(1):12, January 9, 1982

Oral contraceptive use and abortion before first term pregnancy
in relation to breast cancer risk, by M. P. Vessey, et al.
BRITISH JOURNAL OF CANCER. 45(3):327-331, March 1982

The problem of abortion in the light of clinical statistics, by
R. Schwarz. ZEITSCHRIFT FUR DIE GESAMTE HYGIENE. 27(7):533-
534, July 7, 1981

Social, spatial and political determinants of USA abortion rates,
by N. F. Henry, et al. SOCIAL SCIENCE AND MEDICINE. 16(9):
987-996, 1982

Statistical data on abortions performed in 1979 in a Belgian
out-patient clinic, by M. Vekemans, et al. REVUE MEDICALE DE
BRUXELLES. 2(9):851-864, November 1981

ABORTION: TECHNIQUES

Abortifacient action of endotoxin on pregnant rats and its inhibitory action on placental mitochondrial Mg++-ATPase, by M.
Ema, et al. EISEI SHIKENJO HOKOKU. 99:68-73, 1981

Abortion at midpregnancy by catheter or catheter-balloon supple-
mented by intravenous oxytocin and prostaglandin F_2alpha, by
Y. Manabe, et al. INTERNATIONAL JOURNAL OF BIOLOGICAL RE-
SEARCH IN PREGNANCY. 2(2):85-89, 1981

Abortion during mid-pregnancy by rivanol-catheter supplemented
with PGF2 alpha drip-infusion or quinine hydrocholoride, by Y.
Manabe, et al. CONTRACEPTION. 23(6):621-628, June 1981

Amniocentesis and selective abortion, by T. J. Silber. PEDIA-
TRIC ANNALS. 10(10):31-34, October 1981

Antiestrogenic and antifertility actions of anordrin (2 alpha 17
alpha-diethynyl-A-nor-5 alpha-androstane-2 beta, 17 beta-diol
2,17-dipropionate), by R. R. Mehta, et al. STEROIDS. 38(6):
679-691, December 1981

Antimicrobial prophylaxis for termination of pregnancy?. DRUG
AND THERAPEUTICS BULLETIN. 20(7):28, April 2, 1982

Bacteriologic studies in second-trimester pregnancy termination:
a comparison of intra- and extra-amniotic methods, by J.
Reichman, et al. INTERNATIONAL JOURNAL OF GYNAECOLOGY AND
OBSTETRICS. 19(5):409-412, 1981

Characteristics of medical termination of pregnancy acceptors in

Pondicherry State, 1972-1976, by N. S. Rao. INDIAN JOURNAL OF MEDICAL SCIENCES. 35(3):43-46, March 1981

Choice of ecbolic and the morbidity of day-case terminations of pregnancy, by D. B. Garrioch, et al. BRITISH JOURNAL OF OB-STETRICS AND GYNAECOLOGY. 88(10):1029-1032, 1981

Clinical experience with sulprostone, by W. Brabec, et al. WIENER KLINISCHE WOCHENSCHRIFT. 93(6):193-197, March 20, 1981

Clinical experience with use of a jet injector for paracervical blocks in office practice, by A. D. Kovacs. OBSTETRICS AND GYNECOLOGY. 59(3):373-374, March 1982

A combined device of negative pressure bottle with injector for artificial abortion, by J. K. Zhou. CHUNG HUA FU CHAN KO TSA CHIH. 61(9):551, September 1981

Contribution of auxiliary sanitary personnel to the care of patients with toxico-septic abortion, by A. Koros. VITA MEDICALA. 29(6):129-133, June 1981

The course of intrauterine pregnancy with a coil in situ, by J. J. Kjer, et al. UGESKRIFT FOR LAEGER. 143(7):416-417, February 9, 1981

Death from amniotic fluid embolism and disseminated intravascular coagulation after a curettage abortion, by W. Cates, Jr., et al. AMERICAN JOURNAL OF OBSTETRICS AND GYNECOLOGY. 141(3):346-348, October 1, 1981

Deaths from 2nd trimester abortion by dilation and evacuation: causes, prevention, facilities, by W. Cates, Jr., et al. OB-OBSTETRICS AND GYNECOLOGY. 58(4):401-408, 1981

Early complications and sequence of pregnancy interruption with hypertonic saline, by R. Borenstein, et al. INTERNATIONAL JOURNAL OF FERTILITY. 25(2):88-93, 1980

Effect of intra amniotic saline and prostaglandin on fibrinolytic activity, prothrombin time and serum electrolytes [a comparative study], by V. D. Joshi, et al. INDIAN JOURNAL OF PHYSIOLOGY AND PHARMACOLOGY. 25(2):167-170, April-June 1981

Effects of hydroxysteroid dehydrogenase inhibitors on in-vitro and in-vivo steroidogenesis in the ovine adrenal gland, by P. Singh-Asa, et al. JOURNAL OF ENDOCRINOLOGY. 92(2):205-212, February 1982

Effects of 16,16-dimethyl-trans-delt 2-PGE1 methyl ester (ONO-802) on reproductive function, by K. Matsumoto, et al. NIPPON YAKURIGAKU ZASSHI. 79(1):15-22, January 1982

Experience from use of new cervix dilatator, by H. G. Muller. ZENTRALBLATT FUR GYNAEKOLOGIE. 103(19):1155-1157, 1981

First and midtrimester abortion with intramuscular injections of sulprostone, by C. A. Ballard. CONTRACEPTION. 24(2):145-150, August 1981

Functional and biochemical aspects of laminaria use in first-trimester pregnancy termination, by B. L. Ye, et al. AMERICAN JOURNAL OF OBSTETRICS AND GYNECOLOGY. 142(1):36-39, January 1, 1982

Increased oral activity of a new class of non-hormonal pregnancy terminating agents, by G. Galliani, et al. JOURNAL OF PHARMA-COBIO-DYNAMICS. 5(1):55-61, January 1982

Induction for termination of pregnancy in the second trimester and for delivery of babies dead in utero using intramuscular injections of 15-methyl-PGF2 alpha, by B. Kunz, et al. JOUR-NAL DE GYNECOLOGIE, OBSTETRIQUE ET BIOLOGIE DE LA REPRODUC-TION. 10(4):375-384, 1981

Induction of abortion by intra-amniotic administration of pro-staglandin F2 alpha in patients with intrauterine fetal death and missed abortion, by A. Antsaklis, et al. INTERNATIONAL SURGERY. 64(5):41-43, August-October 1979

Initiation of uterine contractions by purely mechanical stretch-ing of the uterus at midpregnancy, by Y. Manabe, et al. IN-TERNATIONAL JOURNAL OF BIOLOGICAL RESEARCH IN PREGNANCY. 2(2):63-69, 1981

Interruption of pregnancy by vacuum aspiration or uterotomy. Intra- and postoperative complications, by J. Kunz, et al. FORTSCHRITTE DER MEDIZIN. 100(16):749-753, April 29, 1982

Intrauterine device usage and fetal loss, by H. Foreman, et al. OBSTETRICS AND GYNECOLOGY. 58(6):669-677, December 1981

Intravaginal administration of 9-deoxo-9-methylene-16,16-dimethy PGE2 for cervical dilation prior to suction curettage, by A. G. Shapiro, et al. INTERNATIONAL JOURNAL OF GYNAECOLOGY AND OBSTETRICS. 20(2):137-140, April 1982

Lymphocyte blast transformation indices in abortion and their clinical significance, by S. D. Bulienko, et al. AKUSHERSTVO I GINEKOLOGIIA. (5):10-13, May 1981

Mechanism of the action of Yuanhuacine t induce labor during mid-pregnancy, by B. Y. Yang. CHUNG-KUO YAO LI HSUEH PAO. 61(10):613-616, October 1981

Nelation catheter versus laminaria for a safe and gradual cervi-cal dilatation, by Y. Manabe, et al. CONTRACEPTION. 24(1): 53-60, July 1981

Operative technics for voluntary interruption of pregancy. Clinical results, by A. Fantoni, et al. ARCHIVIO PER LA SCIENZE MEDICHE. 138(4):483-486, October-December 1981

Pharmacological study of the effect of radix trichosanthis on terminating early pregnancy, by M. H. Zhou, et al. CHUNG-KUO YAO LI HSUEH PAO. 17(3):176-181, March 1982

Pregnancy termination in patients with pregnancy-induced hypertension or eclampsia at less than 22 weeks' gestation, by M. B. Sampson, et al. AMERICAN JOURNAL OF OBSTETRICS AND GYNECOLOGY. 143(4):474-475, June 15, 1982

Prostaglandin E_z pessaries to facilitate 1st trimester aspiration termination, by I. Z. Mackenzie, et al. BRITISH JOURNAL OF OBSTETRICS AND GYNAECOLOGY. 88(10):1033-1037, 1981

Randomized trial of one versus two days of laminaria treatment prior to late midtrimester abortion by uterine evacuation [a pilot study], by P. G. Stubblefield, et al. AMERICAN JOURNAL OF OBSTETRICS AND GYNECOLOGY. 143(4):481-482, June 15, 1982

Recommendations for abortion technics, by E. Ehrig, et al. ZEITSCHRIFT FUR ARZTLICHE FORTBILDUNG. 75(7):305-308, April 1, 1981

Reduction of total and free triiodothyronine in serum after abortion, by D. Rajkovic, et al. ENDOKRINOLOGIE. 79(1):44-48, February 1982

Self-administration of prostaglandin for termination of early pregnancy, by M. Bygdeman, et al. CONTRACEPTION. 24(1):45-52, July 1981

Sense and sensitivity ... intra-amniotic prostaglandin termination of pregnancy, by C. Bichard, et al. NURSING MIRROR AND MIDWIVE'S JOURNAL. 154(Clin Forum):xiii-xvi, April 14, 1982

Sequelae of mid-trimete abortions induced by extra-amniotic drip infusion of normal saline, by M. Blum. INTERNATIONAL SURGERY. 64(5):45-47, August-October 1979

Serum antibody to radix trichosanthin after its use for termination of midterm pregnancy, by L. Q. Zhuang. CHUNG HUA FU CHAN KO TSA CHIH. 14(2):122-124, April 1979

Synthetic laminaria for cervical dilatation prior to vacuum aspiration in midtrimester pregnancy, by W. E. Brenner, et al. AMERICAN JOURNAL OF OBSTETRICS AND GYNECOLOGY. 143(4):475-477, June 15, 1982

Termination of early first trimester pregnancy with 16,16-dimethyl trans delta 2 prostaglandin E1 methyl ester, by O. Reiertsen, et al. PROSTAGLANDINS LEUKOTRIENES AND MEDICINE. 8(1):31-35, January 1982

Termination of early gestation with (15S)-15-methyl prostaglandin F2 alpha methyl ester vaginal suppositories, by R. P. Marrs, et al. CONTRACEPTION. 24(6):617-630, December 1981

Termination of midtrimester missed abortion by extraovular instillation of normal saline, by H. Abramovici, et al. BRITISH

JOURNAL OF OBSTETRICS AND GYNAECOLOGY. 88(9):931-933, September 1981

Termination of midtrimester pregnancies induced by hypertonic saline and prostaglandin F2alpha: 116 consecutive cases, by E. Bostofte, et al. ACTA OBSTETRICIA ET GYNECOLOGICA SCANDINAVICA. 60(6):575-578, 1981

Termination of mid-trimester pregnancy with intramuscular 15-(S)-15-,methyl-prostaglandin F2 alpha, by G. Tsalacopoulos, et al. SOUTH AFRICAN MEDICAL JOURNAL. 61(22):822-824, May 29, 1982

Termination of pregnancy by intramuscular administration of 15 (S)-15-methyl-prostaglandin in F2 alpha, by W. Parewijck, et al. ZEITSCHRIFT FUR GEBURTSCHILFE UND PERINATOLOGIE. 184(5): 366-370, October 1980

Termination of pregnancy: prospective comparative investigation of 2 vacuum aspiration methods: vibra ab aspirator and the conventional method, by H. K. Poulsen. UGESKRIFT FOR LAEGER. 144(2):89-92, 1981

Termination of second trimester pregnancy with laminaria and intramuscular 16 phenoxy-omega-17, 18, 19, 20 tetranor PGE2 methylsulfonylamide (sulprostone)-A randomized study, by S. M. Karim, et al. PROSTAGLANDINS. 23(2):257-263, February 1982

Termination of very early pregnancy by vaginal suppositories-(15S)-15-methyl prostaglandin F2 alpha methyl ester, by L. S. Wan, et al. CONTRACEPTION. 24(6):603-615, December 1981

Treatment of cervix and isthmus insufficiency with cerclage using the McDonald method, by C. Balbi, et al. ARCHIVES OF OBSTETRICS AND GYNECOLOGY. 85(3):179-184, May-June 1980

Ultrastructural study of placentas in yellow daphne (Wikstroemia chmamedaphne Meisn) induced labor, by Z. H. Wang. CHUNG HUA FU CHAN KO TSA CHIH. 14(2):125-126, April 1979

Use of prostaglandin F$_2$alpha gel prior to termination of pregnancy of primigravidae for cerivix maturation, by G. Kohler, et al. ZENTRALBLATT FUR GYNAEKOLOGIE. 103(14):818-822, 1981

The vaginal administration of 9-deoxo-16,16-dimethyl-9-methylene PGE2 for second trimester abortion, by C. A. Ballard. CONTRACEPTION. 24(2):151-157, August 1981

Vaginal application agent before legal abortion: a way of reducing infectious complication?, by O. Meirik, et al. ACTA OBSTETRICIA ET GYNECOLOGICA SCANDINAVICA. 60(3):233-235, 1981

Vaginal prostaglandin F2 alpha gel before first trimester termination of pregnancy, by M. A. Quinn, et al. AUSTRALIAN AND NEW ZEALAND JOURNAL OF OBSTETRICS AND GYNAECOLOGY. 21(2):93-95, May 1981

Activities of a commission on the termination pregnancy for medical reasons, by E. Khristzova, et al. AKUSHERSTVO I GINEKOLOGIIA. 21(1):16-20, 1982

Amount of tissue evacuated by vacuum aspiration in therapeutic abortions, by P. Rasmussen. ACTA OBSTETRICIA ET GYNECOLOGICA SCANDINAVICA. 60(5):475-479, 1981

Clinical forum 4. Gynecological nursing: sense of sensitivity, by G. Bichard, et al. NURSING MIRROR AND MIDWIVE'S JOURNAL. 154(15):xiii-xvi, April 14, 1982

Continued follow-up study of 120 persons born after refusal of application for therapeutic abortion, by H. Forssman, et al. ACTA PSYCHIATRICA SANDINAVICA. 64(2):142-149, 1981

Evaluating fetomaternal hemorrhage by alpha-fetoprotein and Kleihauer test following therapeutic abortions, by D. L. Hay, et al. INTERNATIONAL JOURNAL OF GYNAECOLOGY AND OBSTETRICS. 20(1):1-4, 1982

Intramuscular administration of 15-methyl prostaglandin F2alpha in mid-trimester termination of pregnancy, by K. Bhalla, et al. JOURNAL OF INTERNATIONAL MEDICAL RESEARCH. 10(1):32-34, 1982

Legal clout without a trial (therapeutic abortion), by D. Eisler. MACLEAN'S. 95:17, June 28, 1982

Low-dose enflurane does not increase blood loss during therapeutic abortion, by M. S. Sidhu, et al. ANESTHESIOLOGY. 57(2):127-129, August 1982

Midtrimester abortion patients, by L. D. White, et al. AORN JOURNAL: ASSOCIATION OF OPERATING ROOM NURSES. 34(4):756-768, October 1981

Problems posed by the decision to perform therapeutic abortions in the current practice of the prenatal diagnosis of fetal malformations, by A. Choiset, et al. ACQUISITIONS MEDICALES RECENTES. 198:137-147, 1981

Psychiatric aspects of therapeutic abortion, by B. K. Doane, et al. CANADIAN MEDICAL ASSOCIATION JOURNAL. 125(5):427-432, September 1, 1981

Rubella vaccine--therapeutic abortion, by L. R. Yen, et al. DRUG INTELLIGENCE AND CLINICAL PHARMACY. 15(11):885, November 1981

A severe case of hyperemesis gravidarum, by A. Chatwani, et al. AMERICAN JOURNAL OF OBSTETRICS AND GYNECOLOGY. 143(8):964-965, August 15, 1982

Ten years of evidence on therapeutic abortion: the jury is still out [editorial], by B. K. Doane. CANADIAN MEDICAL ASSOCIATION JOURNAL. 125(5):413-415, September 1, 1981

ABORTION: THERAPEUTIC (continued)

Termination of midtrimester missed abortion by extraovular instillation of normal saline, by H. Abramovici, et al. BRITISH
JOURNAL OF OBSTETRICS AND GYNAECOLOGY. 88(9):931-933, September 1981

Therapeutic abortion and chlamydia trachomatis infection, by
E. Qvigstad, et al. BRITISH JOURNAL OF VENEREAL DISEASES.
58(3):182-183, June 1982

Therapeutic abortion: a difficult choice, by F. Gratton-Jacob.
NURSING QUEBEC. 2(1):7-15, November-December 1981

ABORTION: THREATENED
Cellular and humoral factors of immunity in threatened abortion,
by V. S. Rakut, et al. ZDRAVOOKHRANENIYE BELORUSSII. (1):24-
25, 1981

Comparative study of the action of phytohemagglutinin on DNA
fluorescence in the lymphocytes of women with physiological
pregnancy and in threatened abortion, by V. S. Tolmachev, et
al. TSITOL I GENETIKA. 15(4):16-18, July-August 1981

Comparison of 2 therapeutic schemes in threatened premature
labor, by G. C. Di Renzo, et al. MINERVA GINECOLOGIA. 33(9):
841-850, September 1981

Control of the effect of treatment in late threatened abortions
using the DU-1 Dynamo-uterograph, by D. Tsenov, et al. AKU-
SHERSTVO I GINEKOLOGIIA. 21(1):11-15, 1982

Control of uterine contraction with tocolytic agents (ritodrine)
2. Use in cases of threatened abortion, cervical incontinence
and gynecologic surgery in pregnancy, by P. A. Colombo, et al.
ANNALI DI OSTETRICIA GINECOLOGIA, MEDICINA PERINATALE.
102(6):431-440, November-December 1981

Diagnostic and prognostic value of colpocytosmears in threatened
abortion in the first half of pregnancy, by S. Hristamian.
FOLIA MEDICA. 23(3-4):24-29, 1981

Effect of the blood serum from pregnant women with early and
late toxicoses and threatened abortions on spontaneous contractile activity of smooth muscle, by S. Sharankov, et al.
AKUSHERSTVO I GINEKOLOGIIA. 20(3):190-197, 1981

Effect of exogenous human chorionic gonadotropin on the endogenous hormoral milieu of serum estradiol-17 beta and progesterone in the patient with threatened abortion, by B. H.
Park, et al. CATHOLIC MEDICAL COLLEGE JOURNAL. 34(2):349-
358, 1981

Effect of reflexotherapy on normalizing autonomic endocrine
regulation in threatened abortion, by A. F. Zharkin, et al.
AKUSHERSTVO I GINEKOLOGIIA. (5):21-23, May 1981

Electric activity of the brain in women undergoing acupuncture
for threatened abortion, by N. M. Tkachenko, et al. AKU-
SHERSTVO I GINEKOLOGIIA. (1):28-29, January 1982

Fetal growth delay in threatened abortion: an ultrasound study, by M. Mantoni, et al. BRITISH JOURNAL OF OBSTETRICS AND GYNAECOLOGY. 89(7):525-527, July 1982

Hormone therapy in threatened abortion. Retrospective evaluation of a clinical caseload, by E. Revelli, et al. MINERVA GINE-COLOGIA. 34(4):277-282, April 1982

Importance of echography in assessing the nature of the development of the pregnancy in threatened abortion, by A. M. Stygar. AKUSHERSTVO I GINEKOLOGIIA. (5):16-18, May 1981

Magnesium sulfate treatment of threatened late abortions and premature labor, by I. Penev, et al. AKUSHERSTVO I GINEKOLO-GIIA. 20(4):265-268, 1981

The maternal serum levels of human chorionic gonadotropin, beta-human chorionic gonadotropin and human prolactin in normal pregnancy and in patients with threatened abortion within the 1st 12 weeks of pregnancy, by P. P. Busacchi, et al. RIVISTA ITALIANA DI GINECOLOGIA. 59(6):471-479, 1982

A miscarraige with a difference [letter], by J. J. de Villiers. SOUTH AFRICAN MEDICAL JOURNAL. 61(1):4, January 2, 1982

Prognostic value of human chorionic gonadotropin, progesterone, 17-beta estradiol and the echoscopic examination in threatened abortion during the 1st trimester, by I. Stoppelli, et al. CLINICAL AND EXPERIMENTAL OBSTETRICS AND GYNECOLOGY. 8(1):6-11, 1981

Radioimmunologic evaluation of the concentration of placental lactogen in threatened abortions, by W. Szymanski, et al. ACTA UNIVERSITATIS PALACKIANAE OLOMUCENSIS FACULTATIS MEDICAE. 101:57-63, 1981

Real-time echography in the diagnosis o threatened abortion: diagnositc and prognostic evaluation compared with urinary HCG determination, by A. Raimondo, et al. ARCHIVES OF OBSTETRICS AND GYNECOLOGY. 85(5):411-421, September-October 1980

Serum alkaline phosphatase activity in threatened abortion, prolonged pregnancy and late pregnancy toxemia, by W. Nikodem. POLSKI TYGODNIK LEKARSKI. 36(37):1429-1431, September 14, 1981

Significance of SP1 beta-1-glycoprotein in threatened abortion, by G. Iannotti, et al. MINERVA GINECOLOGIA. 32(12):1115-1119, December 1980

Sonographic index for prognosis of early pregnancy, by J. E. Tapia, et al. ZENTRALBLATT FUR GYNAEKOLOGIE. 103(20):1255-1259, 1981

Use of electrorelaxation of the uterus in the treatment of threatened abortion, by A. Z. Khasin, et al. AKUSHERSTVO I GINEKOLOGIIA. (1):30-32, January 1982

ABORTION: THREATENED (continued)

Use of turinal in the combined treatment of threatened abortion and its effect on placental hormone function, by N. G. Kosheleva, et al. AKUSHERSTVO I GINEKOLOGIIA. (5):23-25, May 1981

ABORTION: VOLUNTARY
Clinical and epidemiological aspects of voluntary interruption of pregnancy 2 years after law No. 194 on abortion, by M. G. Ricci, et al. RIVISTA ITALIANA DI GINECOLOGIA. 59(4/5):405-420, ?

Operating techniques for voluntary interruption of pregnancy: clinical results, by A. Fantoni, et al. ARCHIVIO PER LA SCIENZE MEDICHE. 138(4):483-486, 1981

ABORTION AND ACUPUNCTURE
Electric activity of the brain in women undergoing acupuncture for threatened abortion, by N. M. Tkachenko, et al. AKUSHERSTVO I GINEKOLOGIIA. (1):28-29, January 1982

ABORTION AND ADOLESCENTS
Adolescent aborters: factors associated with gestational age, by J. Poliak, et al. NEW YORK STATE JOURNAL OF MEDICINE. 82(2):176-179, 1982

Court upholds parental notice requirement before allowing abortions on minors, by P. A. Ewer. JOURNAL OF CRIMINAL LAW AND CRIMINOLOGY. 72(4):1461-1481

Minor women obtaining abortions: a study of parental notification in a metropolitan area, by F. Clary. AMERICAN JOURNAL OF PUBLIC HEALTH. 72;283-284, March 1982

Public school programs for adolescent pregnancy and parenthood [an assessment], by G. L. Zellman. FAMILY PLANNING PERSPECTIVES. 14(1):15, January-February 1982

Social and affective factors associated with adolescent pregnancy, by P. B. Smith, et al. JOURNAL OF SCHOOL HEALTH. 52(2):90-93, February 1982

A study of adolescent aborters and adolescent expectant mothers regarding their perceptions of their mothers' and fathers' parenting behavior, by K. Sweeney. DISSERTATION ABSTRACTS INTERNATIONAL. A. 42(2):158, 1981

Subsequent pregnancy among adolescent mothers, by E. Peabody, et al. ADOLESCENCE. 16:563-568, Fall 1981

ABORTION AND ANESTHESIA
Anaesthesia for outpatient termination of pregnancy. A comparison of two anaesthetic techniques, by G. H. Hackett, et al. BRITISH JOURNAL OF ANAESTHESIA. 54(8):865-870, August 1982

Anesthesia in the pregnant myasthenic patient (considerations on 2 cases of voluntary interruption of pregnancy), by M. Chiefari, et al. ARCHIVES OF OBSTETRICS AND GYNECOLOGY. 85(4):259-270, July-August 1980

ABORTION AND ANESTHESIA (continued)

Comparative risk of death from induced abortion at less than
equal to 12 weeks gestation performed with local vs. general
anesthesia, by H. Peterson, et al. AMERICAN JOURNAL OF OB-
STETRICS AND GYNECOLOGY. 141(7):763-768, 1981

Gunilla, nurse anesthetist in gyn operating room: finds much
left to do where prevention is concerned [interview], by G.
Sjoborg. VARDFACKET. 6(10):42-43, May 28, 1982

The use of a drug combination in anesthesia for voluntary interruption of pregnancy. Medical considerations and social and
economic repercussions, by G. De Angelis, et al. MINERVA
ANESTESIOLOGICA. 47(6):287-290, June 1981

Using local anesthesia for 1st-trimester abortion cuts mortality
sharply. FAMILY PLANNING PERSPECTIVES. 14:332-334, November-
December 1982

ABORTION AND COLLEGE STUDENTS
Court: public college paper can't reject abortion ads (Portland
Community College), by F. King. EDITOR AND PUBLISHER--THE
FOURTH ESTATE. 114:20, October 10, 1981

Sex differences in correlates of abortion attitudes among college students, by B. A. Finlay. JOURNAL OF MARRIAGE AND THE
FAMILY. 43(571-582, August 1981

ABORTION AND CRIMINALS
L'abortion du crime d'avortement dans la perspective de la
reforme du droit criminel, by H. Dumont. REVUE JURIDIQUE
THEMES. (la) 15:149-192, 1980-1981

ABORTION AND ERA
Abortion and women's health: a meeting of the National Abortion
Federation, by J. H. Johnson. FAMILY PLANNING PERSPECTIVES.
14:327-328, November-December 1982

Administrative, counseling and medical practices in National
Abortion Federation facilities, by U. Landy, et al. FAMILY
PLANNING PERSPECTIVES. 14:257-280, September-October 1982

Feminism and abortion arguments, by M. B. Mahowald. KINESIS:
GRADUATE JOURNAL OF PHILOSOPHY. 11:57-68, Spring 1982

Feminist perspective and population stability, by P. Ross.
HUMANIST. 42:35-36, May-June 1982

ABORTION AND FERTILITY
Genital mycoplasmas and chlamydiae in infertility and abortion,
by E. Cracea, et al. ARCHIVES ROUMAINES DE PATHOLOGIE EXPERI-
MENTALE ET DE MICROBIOLOGIE. 40(2):107-112, April-June 1981

Impaired reproductive performance of the unicornuate uterus;
intrauterine growth retardation, inferitlity, and recurrent
abortion in five cases, by M. C. Andrews, et al. AMERICAN
JOURNAL OF OBSTETRICS AND GYNECOLOGY. 144(2):173-176, September 15, 1982

The abortifacient effect of 16,16-dimethyl-trans-delta 2-PGE1 methyl ester, a new prostaglandin analogue, on mid-trimester pregnancies and long-term follow-up observations, by S. Takagi, et al. PROSTAGLANDINS. 23(4):591-601, April 1982

About the clinical value of estimations of plasma progesterone levels and urinary pregnandiol output in cases of imminent abortion during the first half of pregnancy, by I. Misinger, et al. CESKOSLOVENSKA GYNEKOLOGIE. 46(9):668-672, Novemer 1981

Action of prostaglandin F2 alpha on 1st-trimester pregnancy, by M. Talas, et al. AKUSHERSTVO I GINEKOLOGIIA. (11):52, November 1981

Antifertility effect of azastene mediated by prostaglandin, by A. Helvacioglu, et al. AMERICAN JOURNAL OF OBSTETRICS AND GYNECOLOGY. 141(2):138-144, September 15, 1981

Biophysical studies on molecular mechanism of abortificient action of prostaglandins. I. The study of molecular electrostatic potential distribution of PGF2 alpha, PGF1 beta and PGA1, by V. Kothekar, et al. JOURNAL OF THEORETICAL BIOLOGY. 93(1):7-23, November 7, 1981

--II. The study of the long and short range interaction between different fragments of PGF2 alpha, PGF1 beta and PGA1, by V. Kothekar, et al. JOURNAL OF THEORETICAL BIOLOGY. 93(10:25-40, November 7, 1981

--IV. Conformation energy calculation of PGA1, PGB1 and PGE1, by V. Kothekar. JOURNAL OF THEORETICAL BIOLOGY. 94(4):943-949, February 21, 1982

Cervical dilatation in late first trimester termination by prostaglandin, hylase and isogel, by A. V. Mandlekar, et al. PROSTAGLANDINS LEUKOTRIENES AND MEDICINE. 6(4):381-387, April 1981

Concentration of hormones in early pregnancy in response to prostaglandin-induced abortion, by B. Seifert, et al. ZENTRAL-BLATT FUR GYNAEKOLOGIE. 104(1):45-51, 1982

Effect of 15-methyl-prostaglandin F2 alpha used for dilating the cervix uteri before abortion on endogenous prostaglandin F2 alpha systhesis, by V. N. Goncharova, et al. AKUSHERSTVO I GINEKOLOGIIA. (12):37-38, December 1981

Experience in obstetrics with intracervical pellets of prostaglandin FZ alpha, by M. Herrera, et al. REVISTA CHILENA DE OBSTETRICIA Y GINECOLOGIA. 45(3):147-155, 1980

Hormonal profile during termination of midtrimester pregnancy by extraovular instillation of saline: plasma levels of prostaglandins, progesterone and human chorionic gonadotropin, by S. Bauminger, et al. PROSTAGLANDINS LEUKOTRIENES AND MEDICINE. 8(1):83-92, January 1982

Hormone content in the plasma of women with threatened abortion treated by acupuncture, by G. M. Vorontsova, et al. AKUSHER-STVO I GINEKOLOGIIA. (5):19-20, May 1981

Is hormonal therapy still justified in imminent abortion?, by P. Berle, et al. ZEITSCHRIFT FUR GEBURTSCHILFE UND PERINATOLO-GIE. 184(5):353-358, October 1980

Menstrual regulation with prostaglandin analogues, by K. Hagenfeldt, et al. REPRODUCCION. 5(3):195-201, July-September 1981

Metronidazole and prostaglandin induced abortion, by Z. O. Amarin, et al. INTERNATIONAL JOURNAL OF GYNAECOLOGY AND OBSTETRICS. 19(2):165-168, April 1981

Midtrimester abortion with intravenous administration of 15 methyl prostaglandin F_2alpha, by M. K. Mapa, et al. INTERNATIONAL JOURNAL OF GYNAECOLOGY AND OBSTETRICS. 20(2):125-128, 1982

Multiple dose extraamniotic prostaglandin gel for second trimester termination of pregnancy, by M. A. Quinn, et al. AUSTRALIAN AND NEW ZEALAND JOURNAL OF OBSTETRICS AND GYNAECOLOGY. 21(2):96-98, May 1981

A new prostaglandin E2-gel for pretreatment of the cervix in nulliparous patients having a late first trimester termination of pregnancy, by L. Wingerup, et al. ARCHIVES OF GYNECOLOGY. 231(1):1-6, 1981

Placental changes as a consequence of the interruption of midtrimeter pregnancies by prostaglandin F2 alpha. A study of 23 cases, by A. Ornoy, et al. ISRAEL JOURNAL OF MEDICAL SCIENCES. 18(2):235-240, February 1982

Plasma concentrations of estrone, estradiol, estriol and progesterone during mechanical stretch-induced abortion at midtrimester, by Y. Manabe, et al. JOURNAL OF ENDOCRINOLOGY. 91(3):385-390, December 1981

Progesterone-binding globulin and progesterone in guinea pigs after ovariectomy, abortion and parturition, by J. J. Evans, et al. JOURNAL OF STEROID BIOCHEMISTRY. 16(2):171-174, 1982

Prognostic value of hCG, progesterone, 17-beta estradiol and the echoscopic examination in threatened abortion during the first trimester, by I. Stoppelli, et al. CLINICAL AND EXPERIMENTAL OBSTETRICS AND GYNECOLOGY. 8(1):6-11, 1981

Prostaglandin E2 pessaries to facilitate first trimester aspiration termination, by I. Z. MacKenzie, et al. AMERICAN JOURNAL OF OBSTETRICS AND GYNECOLOGY. 88(10):1033-1037, October 1981

Prostaglandin-oxytocin induced rupture of the posterior fornix. A complication after induced abortion, by J. Molin. UGESKRIFT FOR LAEGER. 143(29):1841, July 13, 1981

ABORTION AND HORMONES (continued)

Prostaglandins from bedside observation to a family of drugs, by S. Bergstrom. PROGRESS IN LIPID RESEARCH. 20:7-12, 1981

Prostaglandins in human reproduction, by M. P. Embrey. BRITISH MEDICAL JOURNAL. 283(6306):1563-1566, December 12, 1981

Radioimmunologic methods of determination of hormones in the blood in pregnancy and in abortion and premature labor, by S. D. Bulienko, et al. ACTA UNIVERSITATIS PALACKIANAE OLOMUCEN-SIS FACULTATIS MEDICAE. 101:11-14, 1981

Results of clinical trials with the new prostaglandin E2-derivative Nalador (sulproston), by H. D. Hodicke. THERAPIE DER GEGENWART. 121(5):312-324, May 1982

Sense and sensitivity ... intra-amniotic prostaglandin termination of pregnancy, by C. Bichard, et al. NURSING MIRROR AND MIDWIVE'S JOURNAL. 154(Clin Forum):xiii-xvi, April 14, 1982

Sudden circulation collapse after intra-amniotic injection of prostaglandin F2 alpha, by E. Egense, et al. UGESKRIFT FOR LAEGER. 144(13):949-950, March 29, 1982

Temporal relationship between the abortifacient effects of GnRH antagonists and hormonal secretion, by C. Rivier, et al. BIO-LOGICAL REPRODUCTION. 24(5):1061-1067, June 1981

Use of a new synthetic prostaglandin (sulprostone) in various obstetrical conditions, by G. B. Melis, et al. MINERVA GINE-COLOGIA. 34(3):183-190, March 1982

ABORTION AND HOSPITALS
The abortion mess in Los Angeles (controversy over disposition of dead fetuses found at defunct private pathology lab), by D. W. Pawley. CHRISTIANITY TODAY. 26:46+, September 17, 1982

Abortion--restrictions--county hospitals. FAMILY LAW REPORTER: COURT OPINIONS. 8(4):2049, November 24, 1981

Abortions--hospitals. FAMILY LAW REPORTER: COURT OPINIONS. 7(33):2535, June 23, 1981

Clinical reprography of women seeking medical termination of pregnancy at AIIMS Hospital, New Delhi, by R. Singh, et al. JOURNAL OF FAMILY WELFARE. 28:3-17, June 1982

Federal court reaffirms injunction against city hospital's abortion ban. FAMILY LAW REPORTER: COURT OPINIONS. 8(14):2197-2198, February 9, 1982

Hospitalization for medical-legal and other abortions in the United States 1970-1977, by M. B. Bracken, et al. AMERICAN JOURNAL OF PUBLIC HEALTH. 72(1):30-37, January 1982

Implementing a permissive policy hospital abortion services after Roe v. Wade, by J. R. Bond, et al. AMERICAN JOURNAL OF POLITICAL SCIENCE. 26:1-24, February 1982

ABORTION AND HOSPITALS (continued)

Legal clout without a trial (abortions halted at Moose Jew Union Hospital due to demands of pro-life groups), by D. Eisler. MACLEAN'S. 95:17, January 28, 1982

Midtrimester abortion experience in a community hospital, by G. A. West. JOURNAL OF THE NATIONAL MEDICAL ASSOCIATION. 73(11):1069-1071, November 1981

ABORTION AND INSURANCE
Abortion--insurance. FAMILY LAW REPORTER: COURT OPINIONS. 7(50):2789, October 27, 1981

Constitutional law--Medicaid funding restriction does not uncon-stitutionally burden the right to terminate a pregnancy. TU-LANE LAW REVIEW. 56:435-446, December 1981

Constitutional law--United States Supreme Court upholds the con-stitutionality of the Hyde Amendment, withholding Medicaid funds for therapeutic abortions unless the life of the mother is endangered. TEMPLE LAW QUARTERLY. 54:109-144, 1981

ABORTION AND MALES
Abortion affects men too, by P. Black. NEW YORK TIMES MAGAZINE. pp. 76-78+, March 28, 1982

Husband challenges wife's right to abortion (Maryland Court of Appeals to hear case in January 1983 to decide if Judge Daniel Moylan was correct in permitting Chris Fritz to veto abortion decision of Bonnie Fritz). OFF OUR BACKS. 12:13, November 1982

Marital secrets: the emerging issue of abortion spousal notifi-cation laws. JOURNAL OF LEGAL MEDICINE. 3:461-482, September 1982

Private cause of action for abortion expenses under state pa-ternity statutes, by G. Schachter. WOMEN'S RIGHTS LAW REPORT-ER. 7:63-90, Winter 1982

Spousal notice and consultation requirement: a new approach to state regulation of abortion. NOVA LAW JOURNAL. 6:457-474, Spring 1982

Spousal notification requirement is constitutionally permissible burden on woman's right to privacy in abortion decision: Scheinberg v. Smith, 659 F 2d 476. TEXAS TECH LAW REVIEW. 13:1495-1511, 1982

This is what you thought about ... men's rights (results of survey). GLAMOUR. 80:21, July 1982

Whose freedom of choice? (effect of abortion on men), by J. Paterson. PROGRESSIVE. 46:42-45, April 1982

ABORTION AND NURSES
Accommodation of conscientious objection to abortion: a case study of the nursing profession, by W. C. Durham, Jr., et al. BRIGHAM YOUNG UNIVERSITY LAW REVIEW. 1982:253-370, 1982

Clinical forum 4. Gynecological nursing: sense of sensitivity, by G. Bichard, et al. NURSING MIRROR AND MIDWIVE'S JOURNAL. 154(15):xiii-xvi, April 14, 1982

The clinical nurse specialist's role in the management of gestational trophoblastic neoplasms, by A. R. Marean. MAJOR PROBLEMS IN OBSTETRICS AND GYNECOLOGY. 14:229-241, 1982

Elisabeth, supervisory nurse: patients must be supported irrespective of what we ourselves think about abortion [interview], by E. Ronnberg. VARDFACKET. 6(10):44-45, May 28, 1982

Ethical issues in nursing: your responses to JPN's fourth annual survey, by E. Rosen, et al. JOURNAL OF PRACTICAL NURSING. 31:29-33+, November-December 1981

Gunilla, nurse anesthetist in gyn operating room: finds much left to do where prevention is concerned [interview], by G. Sjoborg. VARDFACKET. 6(10):42-43, May 28, 1982

The nurse and the law: judgement and counter-judgement, by A. Langslow. AUSTRALIAN NURSES' JOURNAL. 11(8):28-30, March 1982

Nurse refused to assist in abortion: demoted!. REGAN REPORT ON NURSING LAW. 22:4, November 1981

Nursing care of clients in an abortion clinic, by J. Corstiaensen, et al. TIJDSCHRIFT VOR ZIEKENVERPLEGING. 34(17):739-744, August 25, 1981

ABORTION AND PARENTAL CONSENT
Constitution law--right to privacy--parental notice requirements in abortion statutes. TENNESSEE LAW REVIEW. 48:974-999, Summer 1981

Constitutional law--abortion--Utah' parental notification statute held constitutional. H.L. v. Matheson (101 S Ct 1164). CUMBERLAND LAW REVIEW. 12:711-725, 1981-1982

Constitutional law--the minor, parent, state triangle and the requirement of parental notification: H.L. v. Matheson (101 S Ct 1164). HOWARD LAW REVIEW. 25:299-322, 1982

Constitutional law--privacy rights--consent requirements and abortions for minors. NEW YORK STATE LAW SCHOOL LAW REVIEW. 26:837-854, 1981

Constitutional law--right of privacy--abortion--family law--parent and child--standing--as applied to immature, unemancipated and dependent minors, a state statute requiring a physician to notify a pregnant minor's parents prior to the performing of an abortion is constitutional--H.L. v. Matheson. UNIVERSITY OF CINCINNATI LAW REVIEW. 50:867-881, 1981

Constitutional law--a state statute, which requires physicians to notify the parents of immature and unemancipated minors before performing an abortion, does not violate the minors'

fundamental right to have an abortion. DRAKE LAW REVIEW.
31:476-485, 1981-1982

Father's (lack of) right and responsibilities in the abortion
decision: an examination of legal-ethical implications, by M.
B. Knapp. OHIO NORTHERN UNIVERSITY LAW REVIEW. 9:369-383,
July 1982

Fertility-related state laws enacted in 1981 (laws affecting
abortion, services to minors, pregnancy-related insurance,
family-planning services, sterilization, sex education and
propulation commissions), by P. Donovan. FAMILY PLANNING
PERSPECTIVES. 14:63+, March-April 1982

H.L. v. Matheson (101 S Ct 1164): can parental notification be
required for minors seeking abortions?. UNIVERSITY OF RICH-
MOND LAW REVIEW. 16:429-447, Winter 1982

--: parental notic prior to abortion. ST. LOUIS UNIVERSITY
LAW JOURNAL. 26:426-446, January 1982

--: where does the court stand on abortion and parental notification?, by H. N. Feldman. AMERICAN UNIVERSITY LAW REVIEW.
31(2):431-469, Winter 1982

Minor women obtaining abortions: a study of parental notification in a metropolitan area [research], by F. CLary. AMERI-
CAN JOURNAL OF PUBLIC HEALTH. 72(3):283-285, March 1982

Not while you live in my house: the Supreme Court upholds mandatory parental notification of the dependent minor's abortion
decision in H.L. v. Matheson (101 S Ct 1164). THE UNIVERSITY
OF TOLEDO LAW REVIEW. 13:115-148, Fall 1981

Parental notification: is it settled? ... obtaining an abortion,
by P. Donovan. FAMILY PLANNING PERSPECTIVES. 13:243-246,
September-October 1981

--: a state-created obstacle to a minor woman's right of privacy. GOLDEN GATE UNIVERSITY LAW REVIEW. 12:579-603, Summer
1982

Parental rights. AMERICA. 146:143-144, February 27, 1982

Right to abortion limited: the Supreme Court upholds the constitutionality of parental notification statutes. LOYOLA LAW RE-
VIEW. 28:281-296, Winter 1982

Scheinberg v. Smith (482 F Supp 529): toward recognition of
minors' constitutional right to privacy in abortion decisions.
NOVA LAW JOURNAL. 6:475-487, Spring 1982

Storm over Washington: the parental notification proposal, by A.
M. Kenney, et al. FAMILY PLANNING PERSPECTIVES. 14:185+,
July-August 1982

A study of adolescent aborters and adolescent expectant mothers
regarding their perceptions of their mothers' and fathers'

ABORTION AND PARENTAL CONSENT (continued)

>parenting behavior, by K. Sweeney. DISSERTATION ABSTRACTS INTERNATIONAL. A. 42(2):158, 1981

>Supreme Court report: abortion ... parental notification, by R. L. Young. AMERICAN BAR ASSOCIATION JOURNAL. 67:630-632, May 1981

>Unmarried black adolescent father's attitudes toward abortion, contraception, and sexuality [a preliminary report], by L. E. Hendricks. JOURNAL OF ADOLESCENT HEALTH CARE. 2(3):199-203, March 1982

>Your parents or the judge: Massachusetts' new abortion consent law, by P. Donovan. FAMILY PLANNING PERSPECTIVES. 13(5):224-228, September-October 1981

ABORTION AND PHYSICIANS

>Anti-abortion doctors: why a former foetus killer heads a pro-life campaign, by S. McCarthy. ALBERTA REPORT. 9:34, May 17, 1982

>Blood cloting defects in second-trimester D and E easy to treat, say MDs. FAMILY PLANNING PERSPECTIVES. 13:279-280, November-December 1981

>Dilatation and evacuation procedures and second-trimester abortions. The role of physician skill and hospital setting, by W. Cates, Jr., et al. JAMA: JOURNAL OF THE AMERICAN MEDICAL ASSOCIATION. 248(5):559-563, August 6, 1982

>My doctor said I should have an abortion. GOOD HOUSEKEEPING. 194:32+, March 1982

>One doctor's view of abortion, by W. Savage. NEW SOCIETY. 59(1004):224-226, 1982

>Outpatient termination of pregnancy: experience in a family practice residency, by J. H. Marshall, et al. JOURNAL OF FAMILY PRACTICE. 14(2):245-248, February 1982

ABORTION AND POLITICS

>The abortion activists, by D. Granberg. FAMILY PLANNING PERSPECTIVES. 13(4):157-163, July-August 1981

>Abortion and the Hatch Amendment, by E. Bryce. AMERICA. 146(9):166-168, 1982

>Abortion and international law: the status and possible extension of women's right to privacy, by A. E. Michel. JOURNAL OF FAMILY LAW. 20(2):241-262, 1982

>Abortion and the public opinion polls. Morality and legality. Part I, by S. K. Henshaw, et al. FAMILY PLANNING PERSPECTIVES. 14:53-55+, March-April 1982

>Abortion battles, by J. McLaughlin. NATIONAL REVIEW. 34:1599, December 24, 1982

Abortion: British conference [National Abortion Campaign (NAC) national conference, May 22-23, 1981], by A. Henry. OFF OUR BACKS. 12:5, July 1982

Abortion cases pending in Supreme Court, by N. Hunter. OFF OUR BACKS. 12:12, October 1982

Abortion debate [editorial], by M. Istona. CHATELAINE. 55:6, March 1982

Abortion: the debate begins. NEWSWEEK. 100:29, August 30, 1982

Abortion debate in Senate. NEW DIRECTIONS FOR WOMEN. 11:1+, September-October 1982

Abortion: first round in a long fight (Senate debate). US NEWS AND WORLD REPORT. 93:7, August 30, 1982

Abortion--judicial consent--children' rights--parental consultation. FAMILY LAW REPORTER: COURT OPINIONS. 7(41):2652, August 25, 1981

Abortion: a national security issue, by S. D. Mumford. HUMANIST. 42:12-13+, September-October 1982

Abortion: stalled in Congress, trouble in the states, by T. Dejanikus. OFF OUR BACKS. 12:21, March 1982

Anti-abortion bid fails in Congress, by T. Dejanikus. OFF OUR BACKS. 12:13, October 1982

Beyond abortion: the potential reach of a human life amendment, by D. Westfall. AMERICAN JOURNAL OF LAW AND MEDICINE. 8:97-135, Summer 1982

Can Congress settle the abortion issue?, by M. C. Segers. HASTINGS CENTER REPORT. 12:20-28, June 1982

Chromosomes, crime and the courts: the XX and XYY quandary, by H. J. Grace. SOUTH AFRICAN JOURNAL OF CRIMINAL LAW AND CRIMINOLOGY. 5(3):223-227, 1981

Committee to Defend Reproductive Rights v. Myers [625 P 2d 779 (Cal)]: procreative choice guaranteed for all women. GOLDEN GATE UNIVERSITY LAW REVIEW. 12:691-716, Summer 1982

Concepts of abortion and their relevance to the abortion debate, by M. B. Mahowald. SOUTHERN JOURNAL OF PHILOSOPHY. 20:195-208, Summer 1982

Congressional power and constitutional rights: reflections on proposed "human life" legislation, by S. Estreicher. VIRGINIA LAW REVIEW. 68:333-458, February 1982

Congressional withdrawal of jurisdiction from federal courts: a reply to Professor Uddo, by M. Vitiello. LOYOLA LAW REVIEW. 28:61-76, Winter 1982

A death in a hospital (liberals silent as unwanted child is starved to death in Indiana hospital; they are busy protesting the danger of nuclear weapons to human life), by R. E. Tyrrell, Jr. AMERICAN SPECTATOR. 15:6+, June 1981

Deregulation and the right to life, by A. Yankauer. AMERICAN JOURNAL OF PUBLIC HEALTH. 71:797-801, August 1981

Down go the abortion and school prayer bills, by B. Spring. CHRISTIANITY TODAY. 26:56-58, October 22, 1982

The dynamics of the abortion debate, by J. G. Johnson. AMERICA. 146:106-109, February 13, 1982

15 senators back Hatch proposal, NCR poll finds, by M. Meehan. NATIONAL CATHOLIC REPORTER. 18(2):1+, December 11, 1981

Half a loaf: a new antiabortion strategy, by P. Donovan. FAMILY PLANNING PERSPECTIVES. 13(6):262-268, November-December 1981

"Honeymoon" over in DC for action on abortion bills, by C. McKenna. NEW DIRECTIONS FOR WOMEN. 11:19, March-April 1982

Human Life Amendment hearings: Schmitz fears "bulldykes" (Senator John Schmitz's anti-Semitic and anti-female remarks), by L. Noble. UNION W.A.G.E. (68):5, January-February 1982

Human Life Bill: personhood revisited, or Congress takes aim at Roe v. Wade (93 S Ct 705). HOFSTRA LAW REVIEW. 10:1269-1295, Summer 1982

Human Life Federalism Amendment [an assessment], by W. R. Caron. CATHOLIC LAWYER. 27:87-111, Spring 1982

Hyde amendment: an infringement upo the free exercise clause?. RUTGERS LAW REVIEW. 33:1054-1075, Summer 1981

I'm a criminal and proud of it: an abortion outlaw speaks up (protest during the Senate hearings on the Human Life Bill), by L. Smith. MADEMOISELLE. 88:266-267, August 1982

Jews and the abortion debate. JEWISH FRONTIER. 49:7-9, March 1982

Legal status of the fetus (views of M. H. Shapirol). USA TODAY. 111:12-14, December 1982

The limits of judicial intervention in abortion politics (Roe v Wade and Doe v Bolton), by R. Tatalovich, et al. CHRISTIAN CENTURY. 99(1):16-20, January 6-13, 1982

Meeting boosts Hatch proposal, by M. Meehan. NATIONAL CATHOLIC REPORTER. 18(1):6, December 18, 1981

Memo suggests Hatch aide expects abortion bill's defeat, by M. Meehan. NATIONAL CATHOLIC REPORTER. 18(1):4, January 1, 1982

Moral philosophy and political problems, by A. Guttmann. PO-

LITICAL THEORY. 10:33-48, February 1982

NAS attacks evidence of anti-abortion lobby, by C. Cookson. TIMES HIGHER EDUCATIONAL SUPPLEMENT. 445:6, May 15, 1981

The new danger: a three-step abortion pla (Senator O. G. Hatch's Human Life Amendment), by L. C. Wohl. MS. 10:87-88, February 1982

Personality factors related to black teenage pregnancy and abortion, by R. Falk, et al. PSYCHOLOGY OF WOMEN QUARTERLY. 5(5 Suppl):737-746, 1981

Planned parenthood ads to fight anti-abortionists. MARKETING AND MEDIA DECISIONS. 17:32, May 1982

Power of Congress to change constitutional decisions of the Supreme Court: the Human Life Bill, by T. I. Emerson. NORTH-WESTERN UNIVERSITY LAW REVIEW. 77:129-142, April 1982

President Reagan stands firm on pro-life views. OUR SUNDAY VISITOR. 71:8, August 1, 1982

A private cause of action for abortion expenses under state paternity statutes, by G. Schachter. WOMEN'S RIGHTS LAW REPORTER. 7:63-90, Winter 1982

Pro-life versus pro-choice: another look at the abortion contro-versy in the U.S., by D. Granberg, et al. SOCIOLOGY AND SO-CIAL RESERACH. 65(4):424-434, 1981

Pro-lifers strong in U.S. agency, by M. Meehan. NATIONAL CATHO-LIC REPORTER. 18(1):23, December 11, 1981

Reagan appointee dismays right-to-life proponents, by M. Meehan. NATIONAL CATHOLIC REPORTER. 18:4, June 4, 1982

Reagan must address key social issues, by C. Thomas. CONSERVA-TIVE DIGEST. 8:48, May 1982

Reproductive Rights National Network (R2N2) meets in San Fran-cisco, by S. Schulman. OFF OUR BACKS. 12:10, January 1982

Right to abortion under attack in Pennsylvania, Louisiana, Michigan and Congress, by T. Dejanikus. OFF OUR BACKS. 12:8-9+, January 1982

Rise in antiabortion terrorism (tactics of right to life groups), by L. C. Wohl. MS. 11:19, November 1982

The second victory of Anthony Comstock, by R. Polenberg. SOCIETY. 19(4):32-38, 1982

Senate committee passes anti-abortion amendment [March 10th approval by Senate Judiciary Committee of Hatch Amendment], by T. Dejanikus. OFF OUR BACKS. 12:17, April 1982

Senate debate on abortion turns into procedural tussle. CON-

GRESSIONAL QUARTERLY WEEKLY REPORT. 40:2202, September 4,
1982

The Senate threat to our lives, by L. C. Wohl. MS. 10:21,
January 1982

Serenely silent no longer, two angry nuns battle their bishops
over the issue of abortion (opposition to Hatch Amendment).
PEOPLE WEEKLY. 18:90, August 16, 1982

The Supreme Court 1980-81 term: abortion. CRIMINAL LAW RE-
PORTER: COURT DECISIONS AND PROCEEDINGS. 29(23):4171-4172,
September 9, 1981

Supreme Court on abortion funding: the second time around, by D.
J. Horan, et al. ST. LOUIS UNIVERSITY LAW JOURNAL. 25:411-
427, 1981

Supreme Court roundup: 1980 term, by R. J. Regan. THOUGHT.
56:491-502, December 1981

The Supreme Court, the states, and social change: the case of
abortion, by S. B. Hansen. PEACE AND CHANGE. 6(3):20-32,
1980

TV update: Washington (National Abortion Rights Action League
recently refused commercial time by several TV stations), by
R. Lee. TV GUIDE. 30:A14, April 17, 1982

Voting on abortion, by J. Wale. SUNDAY TIMES. p. 15, August 1,
1982

What the Supreme Court heard on abortion, by T. Gest. US NEWS
AND WORLD REPORT. 93:83, December 13, 1982

With friends like these (Senate debate). COMMONWEAL. 109:483-
485, September 24, 1982

ABORTION AND RELIGION
Abortion and the death of the fetus, by S. L. Ross. PHILOSOPHY
AND PUBLIC AFFAIRS. 11:232-245, Summer 1982

Abortion & healing, by M. T. Mannion. MODERN MINISTRIES. 3:22-
25+, April 1982

Abortion, capital punishment and th Judco-Christian ethic, by P.
Cameron. LINACRE QUARTERLY. 48:316-332, November 1981

Abortion debate [editorial], by M. Istona. CHATELAINE. 55:6,
March 1982

Abortion, personhood, and moral rights, by D. Alego. MONIST.
64:543-549, October 1981

Anti-abortion march marks court ruling by M. Holahan. NATIONAL
CATHOLIC REPORTER. 18:4, January 29, 1982

Antiabortion movement broadens (statement signed by 200 American religious leaders). CHRISTIANITY TODAY. 26:64+, January 18, 1982

Applying humanae vitae solution, by C. W. Thomson. NATIONAL CATHOLIC REPORTER. 18:18, June 4, 1982

Babies and bishops, by M. Holland. NEW STATESMAN. pp. 8-9, July 30, 1982

The biotechnological revolution: th hidden pro-life issue, by R. McMunn. OUR SUNDAY VISITOR. 70:6-7+, January 17, 1982

The bishops and the Hatch Amendment, by W. F. Buckley. NATIONAL REVIEW. 34:132-133, February 5, 1982

C.S.C. justifying abortion, by J. Burtchaell. SIGN. 61:18-22+, February 1982

Catholic, non-Catholic clinic patients endorse abortion legality, oppose Church stand. FAMILY PLANNING PERSPECTIVES. 14: 98-99, March-April 1982

Catholics and sex, by J. Garvey. COMMONWEAL. 109:134-136, March 12, 1982

--[discussion]. COMMONWEAL. 109:412-414, July 16, 1982

The child in the silent walk, by D. De Marco. LINACRE QUARTERLY. 48:333-339, November 1981

Choices that make us whate we are; abortion and the bomb--U.S. bishops' meeting, by J. R. Roach. ORIGINS. 12:377+, November 25, 1982

Choisis done in vie, by G. Huyghe. LA DOCUMENTATION CATHOLIQUE. 79:457-458, May 2, 1982

Christian freedom and ethical inquiry, by P. H. Van Ness. CALVIN THEOLOGICAL JOURNAL. 17:26-52, April 1982

Les Christiens et le probleme social de l'avortement: tableronde, by P. Cote, et al. RELATIONS. 42:28-31, January-February 1982

Clarity can be confusing, by W. S. Coffin, Jr. CHRISTIANITY AND CRISIS. 41:274+, October 19, 1981

The debate over life, by C. M. Odell. OUR SUNDAY VISITOR. 70: 10-11+, January 17, 1982

El Paso church, United Way split, by A. B. Sparke. NATIONAL CATHOLIC REPORTER. 18:4, March 26, 1982

Family, state, and God: ideologies of the right-to-life movement, by M. J. Neitz. SOCIOLOGICAL ANALYSIS. 42(3):265-276, Fall 1981

For pro-lifers there is still a long, tough road ahead, by L. H. Pumphrey. OUR SUNDAY VISITOR. 70:8, February 14, 1982

Given good information, public backs pro-life view. OUR SUNDAY VISITOR. 70:7, December 20, 1981

Hatch amendment still splits pro-life camp, by J. Castelli. OUR SUNDAY VISITOR. 70:6, January 17, 1982

Illinois bishop blasts senators for votes on abortion. OUR SUNDAY VISITOR. 71:8, October 10, 1982

In Norway's state church, a pastor's abortion protest has wide implications (Boerre Knudson) [news], by H. Genet, et al. CHRISTIANITY TODAY. 26:58+, April 9, 1982

Is every life worth living: to take a human life is to take what belongs to God [editorial]. CHRISTIANITY TODAY. 26:12-13, March 19, 1982

Justifying abortion, by J. Burtchaell. SIGN. 61:18-22+, February 1982

Marchers were of one mind--abortions must be halted. OUR SUNDAY VISITOR. 70:7, February 7, 1982

Matters of life and death: social, political, and religious correlates of attitudes on abortion, by R. K. Baker. AMERICAN POLITICAL QUARTERLY. 9(1):89-102, 1981

Memo suggests Hatch aide expects abortion bill's defeat, by M. Meehan. NATIONAL CATHOLIC REPORTER. 18:4, January 1, 1982

Mommy, what does abortion mean?, by M. Popson. LIGUORIAN. 70:30-31, January 1982

Nuns' group rejects Hatch proposal, by R. J. McClory. NATIONAL CATHOLIC REPORTER. 18:5, July 16, 1982

Occasional essay: Jewish perspective on prenatal diagnosis and selective abortion of affected fetuses, including some comparisons with prevailing Catholic beliefs, by R. M. Fineman, et al. AMERICAN JOURNAL OF MEDICAL GENETICS. 12(3):355-360, July 1982

Our foundlings' fathers: let paternity flourish (the last straw), by K. Lindskoog. OTHER SIDE. 129:38, June 1982

Pope sees need for special considerations for women. OUR SUNDAY VISITOR. 70:7, December 20, 1981

Pour ou contre l'avortement--pour assainir le debat, by L. Ducharme. RELATIONS. 42:96-99, April 1982

Profile compassion or crusade?, by J. Evans. AMERICA. 147:373-374, December 11, 1982

Pro-lifers, unions pose Catholic hospitals' dilemma, by L. H.

Pumphrey. OUR SUNDAY VISITOR. 71:5, October 10, 1982

Religion and abortion, by J. R. Nelson. CENTER MAGAZINE. 14: 51-55, July-August 1981

Religion, ideal family size, and abortion: extending Renzi's hypothesis, by W. V. D'Antonio, et al. JOURNAL OF THE SCIEN- TIFIC STUDY OF RELIGION. 19(4):397-408, December 1980

Religion, law and public policy in America, by C. E. Curran. JURIST. 42:14-28, 1982

A right-to-life kidnapping? (kidnappin of abortion clinic doctor and his wife by Army of God), by T. Morganthau. NEWSWEEK. 100:29-30, August 30, 1982

Serenely silent no longer, two angry nuns battle their bishops over the issue of abortion (opposition to Hatch Amendment). PEOPLE WEEKLY. 18:90, August 16, 1982

The silent Holocaust exposed, by W. Odell. OUR SUNDAY VISITOR. 71;12-13, June 20, 1982

Southern Baptist Convention resolutions on the family, by R. Herring. BAPTIST HISTORY AND HERITAGE. 17:36-45, January 1982

Subcommittee passes Hatch bill, by M. Meehan. NATIONAL CATHOLIC REPORTER. 18:25, December 25, 1981

US bishops on abortion, by J. G. Deedy. TABLET. 235:1222-1223, December 12, 1981

Vatican on amniocentesis ultrasound scanning and abortion, by W. F. Jenks. PRIEST. 38:7-8, January 1982

What does it mean to be "pro-life", by D. Granberg. CHRISTIAN CENTURY. 99:562-566, May 12, 1982

What happens at conception?, by G. H. Ball. CHRISTIANITY AND CRISIS. 41:274+, October 19, 1981

Who does speak for human life? (debate on Hatch Amendment by National Conference of Catholic Bishops), by W. F. Buckley. NATIONAL REVIEW. 34:381, April 2, 1982

ABORTION AND YOUTH
Abortion in single girls in Hong Kong, by G. W. Tang. JOURNAL OF ADOLESCENT HEALTH CARE. 2(3):213-216, March 1982

Adolescent aborters. Factors associated with gestational age, by J. Poliak, et al. NEW YORK STATE JOURNAL OF MEDICINE. 82(2): 176-179, 1982

Adolescent abortions in the United States, by W. Cates, Jr. JOURNAL OF ADOLESCENT HEALTH CARE. 1(1):18-25, September 1980

Adolescent induced abortion in Benin City, Nigeria, by A. E.

Omu, et al. INTERNATIONAL JOURNAL OF GYNAECOLOGY AND OBSTE-
TRICS. 19(6):495-499, December 1981

Adolescent suicide attempts following elective abortion: a special case of anniversary reaction, by C. Tishler. PEDIATRICS.
68(5):670-671, November 1981

Age of consent to abortion [letter], by M. Colvin, et al.
LANCET. 1(8286):1418, June 19, 1982

Child psychiatry and the law; developmental rights to privacy
and independent decision-making, by M. J. Guyer, et al. JOUR-
NAL OF THE AMERICAN ACADEMY OF CHILD PSYCHIATRY. 21:298-302,
May 1982

Early adolescent childbearing: a changing morbidity?, by R. E.
Kreipe, et al. JOURNAL OF ADOLESCENT HEALTH CARE. 2(2):127-
131, December 1981

H.L. v. Matheson (101 S Ct 1164) and the right of minors to seek
abortions, by M. H. Wolff. CALIFORNIA WESTERN LAW REVIEW.
19:74-106, Fall 1982

Here's what you had to say about abortion (adolescents' opinions). TEEN. 26:75, February 1982

Menstrual extraction in the adolescent, by T. C. Key, et al.
JOURNAL OF ADOLESCENT HEALTH CARE. 1(2):127-131, December 1980

Minor women obtaining abortions: a study of parental notification in a metropolitan area [research], by F. CLary. AMERI-
CAN JOURNAL OF PUBLIC HEALTH. 72(3):283-285, March 1982

Parental notification: is it settled? (possible effects of the
U.S. Supreme Court decision in H.L. v. Matheson, upholding a
Utah state law requiring that all minors notify their parents
before obtaining an abortion), by P. Donovan. FAMILY PLANNING
PERSPECTIVES. 13:243-246, September-October 1981

Personality factors related to black teenage pregnancy and
abortion, by R. Falk, et al. PSYCHOLOGY OF WOMEN QUARTERLY.
5(5 Suppl):737-746, 1981

Psychic reactions of adolescent girls after legal abortion, by
M. Merz. THERAPEUTISCHE UMSCHAU. 39(6):490-491, June 1982

Race-specific patterns of abortion use b American teenagers [re-
search], by N. V. Ezzard, et al. AMERICAN JOURNAL OF PUBLIC
HEALTH. 72(8):809-814, August 1982

Reasoning in the personal and moral domains: adolescent and
young adult women's decision-making regarding abortion, by J.
Smentana. JOURNAL OF APPLIED DEVELOPMENTAL PSYCHOLOGY. 2(3):
211-226, December 1981

The relationship of abortion attitudes and contraceptive behavior
among young single women [research], by E. S. Herold. CANAD-
IAN JOURNAL OF PUBLIC HEALTH. 73:101-104, March-April 1982

ABORTION AND YOUTH (continued)

Role-specific patterns use by American teenagers, by N. V. Eggard, et al. AMERICAN JOURNAL OF PUBLIC HEALTH. 72;809-814,
August 1982

Scheinberg v. Smith (482 F Supp 529): toward recognition of
minors' constitutional right to privacy in abortion decisions.
NOVA LAW JOURNAL. 6:475-487, Spring 1982

Social and affective factors associated with adolescent pregnancy, by P. B. Smith, et al. JOURNAL OF SCHOOL HEALTH.
52(2):90-93, February 1982

Teenagers and interruption of pregnancy, by C. Revaz. THERA-
PEUTISCHE UMSCHAU. 39(6):487-489, June 1982

A Young People's Advisory Service, by N. Harrison, et al.
HEALTH BULLETIN. 40(3):133-139, May 1982

Your parents or the judge: Massachusetts' new abortion consent
law, by P. Donovan. FAMILY PLANNING PERSPECTIVES. 13(5):224-
228, September-October 1981

ABORTION CLINICS
Abortion clinics and the organization of work: a case study of
Charles Circle, by N. R. Aries. REVIEW OF RADICAL POLITICAL
ECONOMY. 12(2):53-62, 1980

Abortion services in the United States, 1979 and 1980, by S. K.
Henshaw, et al. FAMILY PLANNING PERSPECTIVES. 14(1):5-8+,
January-February 1982

Catholic, non-Catholic clinic patients endorse abortion legality, oppose Church stand. FAMILY PLANNING PERSPECTIVES. 14:
98-99, March-April 1982

An economic interpretation of the distribution and organization
of abortion services (Georgia; based on conference paper), by
B. J. Kay, et al. INQUIRY. 18:322-331, Winter 1981

The epidemiology of abortion services, by K. R. O'Reilly, et al.
FAMILY COMMUNITY HEALTH. 5(1):29-39, May 1982

Establishment, characteristic and experience of an abortion
clinic, by F. Bottiglioni, et al. ARCHIVES OF OBSTETRICS AND
GYNECOLOGY. 85(6):511-529, November-December 1980

Federal court largely upholds abortion clinic regulations.
FAMILY LAW REPORTER: COURT OPINIONS. 7(21):2348-2349, March
31, 1981

Free-standing abortion clinics: services structure and fees, by
S. K. Henshaw. FAMILY PLANNING PERSPECTIVES. 14:248-256,
September-October 1982

Morgentaler tests the law (plan for abortion clinics), by A.
Finlayson. MACLEAN'S. 95:55, November 29, 1982

Regional dimensions of abortion-facility services, by N. F.

ABORTION CLINICS (continued)

Henry. PROFESSIONAL GEOGRAPHER. 34:65-70, February 1982

A right-to-life kidnapping? (kidnappin of abortion clinic doctor and his wife by Army of God), by T. Morganthau. NEWSWEEK. 100:29-30, August 30, 1982

ABORTION COUNSELING
Administrative, counseling and medical practices in National Abortion Federation facilities, by U. Landy, et al. FAMILY PLANNING PERSPECTIVES. 14:257-280, September-October 1982

Context effects on survey responses to questions about abortion, by H. Schuman, et al. PUBLIC OPINION QUARTERLY. 45(2):216-223, Summer 1981

Counseling on contraception following interruption of pregnancy. Responsibility of the hospital gynecologist. Model of contraceptive counseling at the Gynecological Clinic Berlin-Neukolln, by S. Ufer, et al. FORTSCHRITTE DER MEDIZIN. 100(16): 746-748, April 29, 1982

Counselling needs of women seeking abortions, by M. J. Hare, et al. JOURNAL OF BIOLOGICAL SCIENCE. 13(3):269-273, July 1981

Divergent perspectives in abortion counseling, by G. D. Gibb, et al. PSYCHOLOGICAL REPORTS. 50(3 Pt 1):819-822, June 1982

Planned parenthood ads to fight anti-abortionists. MARKETING AND MEDIA DECISIONS. 17:32, May 1982

ABORTION FUNDING
Abortion--State Budget Act restricting circumstances under which public funds would be authorized to pay for abortions for Medi-Cal recipients held unconstitutional. JOURNAL OF FAMILY LAW. 20:345-351, January 1982

Beyond the limits of reproductive choice: the contribution of the abortion-funding cases to fundamental-rights analysis and to the welfare-rights thesis, by S. F. Appleton. COLUMBIA LAW REVIEW. 81(4):721-758, May 1981

Committee to defend reproductive rights v. Myers: abortion funding as an unconstitutional condition, by C. W. Sherman. CALIFORNIA LAW REVIEW. 70:978-1013, July 1982

Dynamics of policy politics: the cases of abortion funding and family planning in the state of Oregon, by G. L. Keiser. DISSERTATION ABSTRACTS INTERNATIONAL. A. p. 4919, 1982

An economic interpretation of th distribution and organization of abortion services, by B. J. Kay, et al. INQUIRY. 18(4): 322-331, Winter 1981

Free-standing abortion clinics: services structure and fees, by S. K. Henshaw. FAMILY PLANNING PERSPECTIVES. 14:248-256, September-October 1982

Massachusetts Medicaid Program must fund medically necessary abortions. FAMILY LAW REPORTER: COURT OPINIONS. 7(18):2291-2294, March 10, 1981

N.C. funding of elective abortions upheld agains taxpayer challenge. FAMILY LAW REPORTER: COURT OPINIONS. 7(22):2362, April 7, 1981

Plan casts doubts on abortion aid, by N. Brozan. NEW YORK TIMES MAGAZINE. p. A1, February 8, 1982

A private cause of action for abortion expenses under state paternity statutes, by G. Schachter. WOMEN'S RIGHTS LAW REPORTER. 7:63-90, Winter 1982

Publicly funded abortions in FY 1980 and FY 1981, by R. B. Gold. FAMILY PLANNING PERSPECTIVES. 14:204-207, July-August 1982

Restriction of Medicaid funding of abortion [letter], by M. C. Reilly. NEW ENGLAND JOURNAL OF MEDICINE. 307(13):827, September 23, 1982

State ordered to pay for indigents' medically necessary abortions. FAMILY LAW REPORTER: COURT OPINIONS. 8(1):2006-2008, November 3, 1981

Supreme Court on abortion funding: the second time around, by D. J. Horan, et al. ST. LOUIS UNIVERSITY LAW JOURNAL. 25:411-427, 1981

Taxpayer attack on abortion funding repelled by Maryland's high court. FAMILY LAW REPORTER: COURT OPINIONS. 7(22):2360-2361, April 7, 1981

What's new in the law: constitutional law ... discriminatory funding, by A. Ashman. AMERICAN BAR ASSOCIATION JOURNAL. 67:917-918, July 1981

BIRTH CONTROL: GENERAL
Birth control: contraception, by A. Bicego, et al. PROFESSIONI INFERMIERISTICHE. 34(3):149-159, July-September 1981

Current birth control methods: know your choices, by C. West. ESSENCE. 1:60+ March 1982

CHINA
Abortion and birth control in Canton, China, by M. Vink. WALL STREET JOURNAL. p. 26, November 30, 1981

Attitudes of Chinese women towards sexuality and birth control, by D. Ellis, et al. CANADIAN NURSE. 78(3):28-31, March 1982

Bevolkerungspolitische zielsetzungen in der volksrepublik China und ihre sozio-okonomische begrundung, by H. Schubnell. ZEITSCHRIFT FUR DIE BEVOLKERUNGSWISSENSCHAFT. 7(1): 3-57, 1981

BIRTH CONTRO: GENERAL (continued)

   Birth control: a view from a Chinese village by S. W. Mosher.
      ASIAN SURVEY. 22:356-368, April 1982

   China and the one-child family, by J. Mirsky. NEW SOCIETY.
      pp. 264-265, February 18, 1982

   China's 'one-child' population future. INTERCOM. 9(8):1, Au-
      gust 1981

   China's population policy, by K.-I. Chen. CURRENT HISTORY.
      81:251-254+, September 1982

   Father of birth control; make posters, not babies, by S.
      Fraser. FAR EASTERN ECONOMIC REVIEW. 112:77-78, June 26-
      July 2, 1981

   One is enough, by L. R. Brown. ACROSS THE BOARD. 19:27-28,
      March 1982

   Social structure and population change: a comparative study of
      Tokugawa Japan and Ch'ing China, by J. I. Nakamura, et al.
      ECONOMIC DEVELOPMENT AND CULTURAL CHANGE. 30:229-269,
      January 1982

COSTA RICA
   Dinamica demografica, planificacion familiar y politica de
      poblacion en Costa Rica, by L. Rosero Bixby. DEMOGRAFIA Y
      ECONOMIA. 15(1):59-84, 1981

DEVELOPING COUNTRIES
   Organizational impediments to development assistance: the
      World Bank's population program, by B. B. Crane, et al.
      WORLD POLITICS. 33:516-553, July 1981

JAPAN
   Social structure and population change: a comparative study of
      Tokugawa Japan and Ch'ing China, by J. I. Nakamura, et al.
      ECONOMIC DEVELOPMENT AND CULTURAL CHANGE. 30:229-269,
      January 1982

NEW ZEALAND
   Housewives' depression: the debate over abortion and birth
      control in the 1930's, by B. Brookes. NEW ZEALAND JOURNAL
      OF HISTORY. 15:115-134, October 1981

SPAIN
   Sociologia de al poblacion y controlde la natalidad en Espana,
      by J. M. de Miguel. REVISTA ESPANOLA DE INVESTIGACIONES
      SOCIOLOGICAS. 10:15-47, April-June 1980

UNITED STATES
   Childlessness in a transitional population: the U.S. at the
      turn of the century, by S. E. Tolnay, et al. JOURNAL OF
      FAMILY HISTORY. 7:200-219, Summer 1982

BIRTH CONTROL: ATTITUDES
   Attitudes of Chinese women towards sexuality and birth control,
      by D. Ellis, et al. CANADIAN NURSE. 78(3):28-31, March 1982

BIRTH CONTROL: ATTITUDES (continued)

Attitudes of Chinese women towards sexuality and birth control, by D. Ellis, et al. CANADIAN NURSE. 78(3):28-31, March 1982

The birth control blues, by S. Levy. ROLLING STONE. pp. 25-26+, March 4, 1982

Birth control: lay challenge to medical authority over child-birth, by M. J. Steckevicz. DISSERTATION ABSTRACTS INTERNATIONAL. A. p. 4168, 1982

La contraception artificielle: conflit de devoirs ou acte a double effet, by N. Hendricks. NOUVELLE REVUE THEOLOGIQUE. 204:396-413, May-July 1982

Couple to Couple League an idea whose time has come, by C. A. Savitskas, Jr. OUR SUNDAY VISITOR. 70:6, March 28, 1982

Locus of control as related to birth control knowledge, attitude and practices, by J. J. Lieberman. ADOLESCENCE. 16:1-10, Spring 1981

Lovesick: the birth control blues without the pill, couples choose no sex over safe sex, by S. Levy. ROLLING STONE. pp. 25+, March 4, 1982

Rap session on birth control, by T. A. O'Hara. LIGUORIAN. 70:45-48, October 1982

Relationship between women's attitudes and choice of birth control, by K. I. Hunter, et al. PSYCHOLOGICAL REPORTS. 49(2):372-374, October 1981

Thinking twice about fertility, by K. Holman. GUARDIAN. p. 11, November 3, 1982

BIRTH CONTROL: COMPLICATIONS
Age and birth control, by N. Mallovy. HOME MAGAZINE. 17:80X, May 1982

Birth control today: his kicks, your risks?, by C. L. Mithers. MADEMOISELLE. 88:34, November 1982

Pregnancy roulette (taking chances with birth control), by L. Draegin. MADEMOISELLE. 88:122-123+, October 1982

BIRTH CONTROL: EDUCATION
Locus of control as related to birth control knowledge, attitudes and practices, by J. J. Lieberman. ADOLESCENCE. 16:1-10, Spring 1981

BIRTH CONTROL: HISTORY
Birth-control in the West in the thirteenth and early fourteenth centuries, by P. P. A. Biller. PAST AND PRESENT. 94:3-26, February 1982

Housewives' depression: the debate over abortion and birth control in the 1930's, by B. Brookes. NEW ZEALAND JOURNAL OF

BIRTH CONTROL: HISTORY (continued)

HISTORY. 15:115-134, October 1981

BIRTH CONTROL: LAWS AND LEGISLATION
Proposed law, court ruling spotlight parents rights, by R. B.
Shaw. OUR SUNDAY VISITOR. 70:8, April 25, 1982

The squeak squawk (proposed regulations requiring birth control
clinics to notify parents when minors receive contraceptives,
by A. Shales. NEW REPUBLIC. 187:18-20, August 9, 1982

USCC backs proposed parental notice legislation. OUR SUNDAY
VISITOR. 70:8, April 25, 1982

BIRTH CONTROL: METHODS
Evolution of design and achievement of inhibitors of the LHRH as
inhibitors of ovulation, by K. Folkers, et al. ZEITSCHRIFT
FUR NATURFORSCHUNG TEIL B. 37(2):246-259, 1982

Post tubal ligation syndrome or iatrogenic hydrosalpinx, by M.
G. Gregory. JOURNAL OF THE TENNESSEE MEDICAL ASSOCIATION.
74(10):712-714, October 1981

Sex of offspring of women using oral contraceptives, rhythm and
other methods of birth control around the time of conception,
by P. H. Shiono, et al. FERTILITY AND STERILITY. 37(3):367-
372, 1982

Whatever happend to new methods of birth control?. ECONOMIST.
279:75-77, May 30, 1981

BIRTH CONTROL: NATURAL
Humanae vitae and the ovutektor. Making "rhythm" safe: a breakthrough, by J. Tracy. MONTH. 15:6-9, January 1982

Natural birth control (breast feeding). SCIENCE DIGEST. 90:
100, January 1982

Periodic abstinence: how well do new approaches work?, by L. S.
Liskin, et al. POPULATION REPORTS. 9(4):33, September 1981

BIRTH CONTROL: PSYCHOLOGY OF
Hysterectomy and psychiatric disorder: I. Levels of psychiatric
morbidity before and after hysterectomy, by D. Gath, et al.
BRITISH JOURNAL OF PSYCHIATRY. 140:335-342, April 1982

--II. Demographic psychia tric and physical factors in relation
to psychiatric outcome, by D. Gath, et al. BRITISH JOURNAL OF
PSYCHIATRY. 140:343-350, April 1982

Self-help birth control study, by T. Land. TIMES HIGHER EDUCA-
TIONAL SUPPLEMENT. 498:7, May 21, 1982

BIRTH CONTROL: RESEARCH
Basal body temperature [letter], by B. Kambic. FERTILITY AND
STERILITY. 38(1):120-121, July 1982

Better birth control pill seen. NEW YORK TIMES MAGAZINE. p.
33, January 1, 1982

BIRTH CONTROL: RESEARCH (continued)

Birth control: 4-day pill is promising in early test, by R.
Eder. NEW YORK TIMES MAGAZINE. p. C1, April 20, 1982

Effects of neonatal exposure to progesterone on sexual behavior
of male and female rats, by E. M. Hull. PHYSIOLOGY AND BE-
HAVIOR. 26(3):401-405, March 1981

Estradiol treatment and precopulatory behavior in ovariectomized
female rats, by Z. Hlinak, et al. PHYSIOLOGY AND BEHAVIOR.
26(2):171-176, February 1981

Female phase fazer: new birth control? (luteinizing hormone releasing factor agonist shortens luteal phase; work of S. C.
Yen and others), by L. Garmon. SCIENCE NEWS. 121:21, January
9, 1982

BIRTH CONTROL: STATISTICS
Birth control-sex preference and sex ratio, by M. A. Toro.
HEREDITY. 47(Pt 3):417-423, December 1981

Perceived versus computed change: can perceived measures tell us
something that computed measures cannot?, by E. S. Herold, et
al. EDUCATION AND PSYCHOLOGICAL MEASUREMENT. 41:701-707,
Autumn 1981

BIRTH CONTROL: TECHNIQUES
La contraception artificielle: conflit de devoirs ou acte a
double effet, by N. Hendricks. NOUVELLE REVUE THEOLOGIQUE.
204:396-413, May-July 1982

Personal computer for birth control (computer being developed
that would tell a woman when she is fertile). PERSONAL COM-
PUTING. 6:15, March 1982

BIRTH CONTROL AND HORMONES
A clinical trail of norethisterone oenanthate (Norigest) injected every 2 months, by G. Howard, et al. CONTRACEPTION.
25(4):333-344, 1982

Effects of neonatal exposure to progesterone on sexual behavior
of male and female rats, by E. M. Hull. PHYSIOLOGY AND BE-
HAVIOR. 26(3):401-405, March 1981

More pastoral reflections on humanae vitae, by B. Cole. PRIEST.
38:28-32, January 1982

BIRTH CONTROL AND MALES
Birth control-sex preference and sex ratio, by M. A. Toro.
HEREDITY. 47:417-423, December 1981

BIRTH CONTROL AND PARENTAL CONSENT
Adolescents, parents, and birth control by N. Brozan. NEW YORK
TIMES MAGAZINE. p. B6, March 8, 1982

Proposed law, court ruling spotlight parents rights, by R. B.
Shaw. OUR SUNDAY VISITOR. 70:8, April 25, 1982

The squeak squawk (proposed regulations requiring birth control

BIRTH CONTROL AND PARENTAL CONSENT (continued)

   clinics to notify parents when minors receive contraceptives),
   by A. Shales. NEW REPUBLIC. 187:18-20, August 9, 1982

   Student-parent rapport and parent involvement in sex, birth
   control, and venereal disease education, by S. M. Bennett, et
   al. JOURNAL OF SEX RESEARCH. 16(2):114-130, May 1980

   USCC backs proposed parental notice legislation. OUR SUNDAY
   VISITOR. 70:8, April 25, 1982

BIRTH CONTROL AND PHYSICIANS
   Women doctors talk about birth control, by M. Abrams. LADIES
   HOME JOURNAL. 99:64+, September 1982

BIRTH CONTROL AND POLITICS
   Proposed rule on teen-age birth control draws some surprising
   public opposition [Reagan administration proposals that
   federally supported clinics notify parents of girls who seek
   birth control help], by B. Schorr. WALL STREET JOURNAL. 199:
   25, April 2, 1982

BIRTH CONTROL AND RELIGION
   Birth-control in the west in the 13th and early 14th centuries,
   by P. P. A. Biller. PAST AND PRESENT. (94):3-26, February
   1982

   The Pope and sexuality, by R. Modras. NATIONAL CATHOLIC RE-
   PORTER. 18:20+, January 15, 1982

   Promoting NFP: who is responsible?, by P. Marx. HOMILETIC AND
   PASTORAL REVIEW. 82:25-31, April 1982

   The relationship of celibacy and humanae vitae, by H. Klaus.
   SISTERS TODAY. 53:541-544, May 1982

   Sexual abstinence, by V. Fecher. PRIEST. 38:4-6, April 1982

   Women's employment and fertility in Quebec, by N. Kyriazis, et
   al. POPULATION STUDIES. 36:431-440, November 1982

BIRTH CONTROL AND YOUTH
   Adolescents, parents, and birth control, by N. Brozan. NEW YORK
   TIMES MAGAZINE. p. B6, March 8, 1982

   Cognitive-behavioral prevention of adolescent pregnancy, by S.
   P. Schinke, et al. JOURNAL OF COUNSELING PSYCHOLOGY. 28(5):
   451-454, September 1981

   Prevention of adolescent pregnancy: a developmental perspective,
   by W. G. Cobliner. BIRTH DEFECTS. 17(3):34-47, 1981

   Proposed rule on teen-age birth control draws some surprising
   public opposition [Reagan administration proposals that
   federally supported clinics notify parents of girls who seek
   birth control help], by B. Schorr. WALL STREET JOURNAL. 199:
   25, April 2, 1982

   Teen sex hazards discussed, by M. Meehan. NATIONAL CATHOLIC RE-

BIRTH CONTROL AND YOUTH (continued)

PORTER. 18:4, April 30, 1982

BIRTH CONTROL CLINICS
The squeak squawk (proposed regulations requiring birth control
clinics to notify parents when minors receive contraceptives),
by A. Shales. NEW REPUBLIC. 187:18-20, August 9, 1982

BIRTH CONTROL COUNSELING
Psychological aspects in counseling for preventive agents, by H.
Sjorstrom. JORDEMODERN. 94(1):14-22, January 1981

CONTRACEPTION AND CONTRACEPTIVES: GENERAL
Abortions preventable by contraceptive practice, by C. F. West-
off, et al. FAMILY PLANNING PERSPECTIVES. 13(5):218-223,
September-October 1981

And now? OR: How not to get into trouble. Practical advice on
contraception, by E. Revelli. ANNALI DELL OSPEDALE MARIA
VITTORIA DI TORINO. 22(7-12):339-359, July-December 1979

Birth control: contraception, by A. Bicego, et al. PROFESSIONI
INFERMIERISTICHE. 34(3):149-159, July-September 1981

Community availability of contraceptives and family limitation,
by A. O. Tsui, et al. DEMOGRAPHY. 18:615-625, November 1981

Community forum. 2. Contraception, by Z. Pauncefort. NURSING
MIRROR AND MIDWIVE'S JOURNAL. 154(6 Suppl):i-xii, February
10, 1982

Contraception: yesterday & today (1979), by B. Morrison. FAMILY
RELATIONS. 30(1):141, January 1981

The efficacy of gestoden (delta 15-d-norgestrel) as ovulation
inhibitor, by W. H. Schneider, et al. WIENER KLINISCHE WO-
CHENSCHRIFT. 93(19):601-604, October 16, 1981

Family planning and contraception, by D. Fock. KATILOLEHTI.
87(3):91-93, March 1982

Gregory Pincus and steroidal contraception revisited, by E.
Diczfalusy. ACTA OBSTETRICIA ET GYNECOLOGICA SCANDINAVICA.
105:7-15, 1982

Is Mendelson's syndrome a 'public health hazard'? [letter], by
M. J. Johnstone. ANAESTHESIA. 36(12):1145-1146, December
1981

Knowledge of contraceptives: an assessment of World Fertility
Survey data collection procedures, by M. Vaessen. POPULATION
STUDIES. 35:357-373, November 1981

A low-dose combination oral contraceptive. Experience with 1,700
women treated for 22,489 cycles, by T. B. Woutersz. JOURNAL
OF REPRODUCTIVE MEDICINE. 26(12):615-620, December 1981

Modern methods of regulating generative function, by I. A.
Manuilova. SOVETSKAIA MEDITSINA. (12):105-107, 1981

Oral contraception today. Three dialogues, by D. R. Mishell, et al. JOURNAL OF REPRODUCTIVE MEDICINE. 27(4 Suppl):235-295, April 1982

Oral contraceptive: past, present and future use, by J. J. Speidel, et al. JOHN HOPKINS MEDICAL JOURNAL. 150(5):161-164, May 1982

The pill: the lowest possible dosag [interview by Werner Bauch], by M. H. Briggs, et al. ZFA: ZEITSCHRIFT FUR ALLGEMEINMEDI-ZIN. 58(12):703-705, April 30, 1982

Postpartum contraception, by D. A. Edelman, et al. INTERNA-TIONAL JOURNAL OF GYNAECOLOGY AND OBSTETRICS. 19(4):305-311, August 1981

--, by P. A. Hillard. PARENTS. 57:82+, December 1982

Practising prevention. Contraception, by M. J. Bull. BRITISH MEDICAL JOURNAL. 284(6328):1535-1536, May 22, 1982

Prevention of oestrus and/or pregnancy in dogs by methods other than ovariohysterectomy, by A. C. Okkens, et al. TIJDSCHRIFT VOOR DIERGENEESKUNDE. 106(23):1215-1225, December 1981

The quest for a magic bullet, by M. Potts, et al. FAMILY PLANNING PERSPECTIVES. 13(6):269-271, November-December 1981

Sex, sex guilt, and contraceptive use, by M. Gerrard. JOURNAL OF PERSONALITY AND SOCIAL PSYCHOLOGY. 42(1):153-158, January 1982

Taking liberties with women: abortion, sterilization, and con-traception, by W. Savage. INTERNATIONAL JOURNAL OF HEALTH SERVICES. 12(2):293-308, 1982

Yoruba traditional healers' knowledge of contraception, abortion and infertility, by D. D. Oyebola. EAST AFRICAN MEDICAL JOUR-NAL. 58(10):777-784, October 1981

AFRICA
Population growth and contraception in Africa [editorial]. BRITISH MEDICAL JOURNAL. 284(6325):1333-1334, May 1, 1982

--[letter], by P. V. Cosgrove. BRITISH MEDICAL JOURNAL. 284(6319):900-901, March 20, 1982

--[letter], by A. R. Walker, et al. BRITISH MEDICAL JOURNAL. 284(6316):657-659, February 27, 1982

BANGKOK
A study of contraceptive choice and use in Bangkok Metropolis Health Clinics, by T. Chumnijarakij, et al. CONTRACEPTION. 24(3):245-258, September 1981

BANGLADESH
The effect on fecundity of pill acceptance during postpartum amenorrhea in rural Bangladesh, by S. Bhatia, et al. STUD-

IES IN FAMILY PLANNING. 13(6-7):200-207, June-July 1982

CARIBBEAN
The impact on breastfeeding and pregnancy status of household contraceptive distribution in rural Haiti, by A. Bordes, et al. AMERICAN JOURNAL OF PUBLIC HEALTH. 72(8):835, August 1982

CHINA
Research activities in the field of oral contraceptives in the People's Republic of China, by Z. De-Wei. ACTA OBSTETRICIA ET GYNECOLOGICA SCANDINAVICA. SUPPLEMENT. 105:51-60, 1982

COLUMBIA
Correlates of contraceptive use among urban poor in Colombia, by J. T. Bertrand, et al. JOURNAL OF BIOSOCIAL SCIENCE. 13(4):431-441, October 1981

DEVELOPING COUNTRIES
Pill use in twenty developing countries. JOURNAL OF FAMILY WELFARE. 28:93, June 1982

Sweden approved of Depo-Provera sales promotion in developing countries [interview by Elisabeth Magnusson], by B. Rubensson. VARDFACKET. 6(7):54, April 8, 1982

EGYPT
The value of children and the costs of contraception: predictors of reproductive ideals and contraceptive practice in Egypt, by R. Vernon-Carter. DISSERTATION ABSTRACTS INTERNATIONAL. A. p. 938, 1982

EL SALVADOR
Family planning communications and contraceptive use in Guatemala, El Salvador, and Panama, by J. T. Bertrand, et al. STUDIES IN FAMILY PLANNING. 13(6-7):190-191, June-July 1982

GUATEMALA
Family planning communications and contraceptive use in Guatemala, El Salvador, and Panama, by J. T. Bertrand, et al. STUDIES IN FAMILY PLANNING. 13(6-7):190-191, June-July 1982

HAITI
The impact on breastfeeding and pregnancy status of household contraceptive distribution in rural Haiti, by A. Bordes, et al. AMERICAN JOURNAL OF PUBLIC HEALTH. 72(8):835-838, August 1982

INDIA
Contraceptive practice in Bangladesh: a study of mediators and differentials, by S. M. Shahidullah. DISSERTATION ABSTRACTS INTERNATIONAL. A. p. 5261, 1982

The demographic impact of the contraceptive distribution project in Matlab, Bangladesh, by W. S. Stinson, et al. STUDIES IN FAMILY PLANNING. 13(5):141, May 1982

The significance of cultural tradition for contraceptive
change: a study of rural Indian women, by C. K. Vlassoff.
DISSERTATION ABSTRACTS INTERNATIONAL. A. p. 1702, 1982

KENYA
Modern, transitional, and traditional demographic and contraceptive patterns among Kenyan women, by T. E. Dow, Jr., et
al. STUDIES IN FAMILY PLANNING. 13(1):12, January 1982

LATIN AMERICA
Acceptability of the contraceptive vaginal ring by rural and
urban population in two Latin American countries, by A.
Faundes, et al. CONTRACEPTION. 24(4):393-414, October 1981

Contraceptive sterilization in four Latin American countries,
by J. McCarthy. JOURNAL OF BIOSOCIAL SCIENCE. 14(2):189-
201, April 1982

MEXICO
Acceptability of medroxyprogesterone acetate in rural areas of
Mexico, by V. Velasco Murillo, et al. GINECOLOGIA Y OBSTE-
TRICIA DE MEXICO. 49(293):153-161, March 1981

Contraceptive use and family planning services along the U.S.-
Mexico border, by C. W. Warren, et al. INTERNATIONAL FAMILY
PLANNING PERSPECTIVES. 7:52-59, June 1981

MILAN
Contraception, pregnancy management and the clinic: opinions
of 1271 puerperas in a large hospital on the northern border
of Milan, by P. Dall'Aglio. ANNALI DI OSTETRICIA GINECOLO-
GIA, MEDICINA PERINATALE. 103(1):48-59, January-February
1982

NIGERIA
Response of unmarried adolescents to contraceptive advice and
service, by M. Ezimokhai, et al. INTERNATIONAL JOURNAL OF
GYNAECOLOGY AND OBSTETRICS. 19(6):481-485, December 1981

PANAMA
Contraceptive use and fertility in the Republic of Panama, by
R. S. Monteith, et al. STUDIES IN FAMILY PLANNING. 12:331-
340, October 1981

Family planning communications and contraceptive use in
Guatemala, El Salvador, and Panama, by J. T. Bertrand, et
al. STUDIES IN FAMILY PLANNING. 13(6-7):190-191, June-July
1982

SANTO DOMINGO
Lipoprotein patterns in women in Santo Domingo using a levo-
norgestrel/estradiol contraceptive ring, by D. N. Robertson,
et al. CONTRACEPTION. 24(4):469-480, October 1981

SOUTH KOREA
Abortion and contraception in the Korean fertility transition,
by P. J. Donaldson, et al. POPULATION STUDIES. 36:227-235,
July 1982

THAILAND
Antecedents to contraceptive innovation: evidence from rural Northern Thailand, by D. P. Hogan, et al. DEMOGRAPHY. 18(4):597-614, November 1981

Continuation of injectable contraceptives in Thailand, by T. Narkavonnakit, et al. STUDIES IN FAMILY PLANNING. 13(4): 99, April 1982

UNITED STATES
Contraceptive failure in the United States: the impact of social, economic and demographic factors [research], by A. L. Schirm, et al. FAMILY PLANNING PERSPECTIVES. 14(2):68, March-April 1982

Contraceptive method switching among American female adolescents 1979, by M. B. Hirsch. DISSERTATION ABSTRACTS INTERNATIONAL. A. p. 1303, 1982

Contraceptive use, pregnancy intentions and pregnancy outcomes among U.S. women, by J. G. Dryfoos. FAMILY PLANNING PERSPECTIVES. 14(2):81, March-April 1982

Reproductive mortality in the United States, by B. P. Sachs, et al. JAMA: JOURNAL OF THE AMERICAN MEDICAL ASSOCIATION. 247(20):2789-2792, May 28, 1982

Trends in contraceptive practice: United States, 1965-1976, by W. D. Mosher, et al. VITAL HEALTH STATISTICS. 23(10):1-47, February 1982

CONTRACEPTION AND CONTRACEPTIVES: LAWS AND LEGISLATION
Aspects of reproduction related to human rights. II. Contraception, by J. Martinez-Manautou. GACETA MEDICA DE MEXICO. 117(7):266-268, July 1981

Constitutional law--fourteenth amendment--right to privacy--contraceptives--minors--the United States Court of Appeals for the Sixth Circuit has held that a state-funded family planning cen- ter's distribution of contraceptives to minors without parental notice does not violate the parents' constitutional rights. DUSQUESNE LAW REVIEW. 20:111-121, Fall 1981

Contraceptive choice and maternal image, by M. Viglione. DISSERTATION ABSTRACTS INTERNATIONAL. B. p. 2010, 1982

High court strikes down ad circular ban. ADVERTISING AGE. 53: 73, May 24, 1982

Judge hopes to combine Dalkon suits, by R. L. Rundle. BUSINESS INSURANCE. 15:1+, December 28, 1981

Legal aspects of research and practice in fertility control, by J. Stepan. CESKOSLOVENSKA GYNEKOLOGIE. 46(3):212-216, April 1981

Prescribing for unlawful sexual intercourse, by D. Brahams. PRACTITIONER. 226(1368):1025-1026, June 1982

CONTRACEPTION AND CONTRACEPTIVES: LAWS AND LEGISLATION (continued)

A psychological investigation of contraceptive behavior, by V.
A. Byron. DISSERTATION ABSTRACTS INTERNATIONAL. B. p. 242,
1982

Role of copper irons in contraception, by E. Kobylec, et al.
GINEKOLOGIA POLSKA. 52(8):751-754, August 1981

Statutes and ordinances--contraceptives and sex aids. CRIMINAL
LAW REPORTER: COURT DECISIONS AND PROCEEDINGS. 30(4):2086,
October 28, 1981

Storm over Washington: the parental notification proposal (requiring family planning clinics to notify the parents of
minors when prescription contraceptives are provided), by A.
M. Kenney, et al. FAMILY PLANNING PERSPECTIVES. 14:185+,
July-August 1982

CONTRACEPTION AND CONTRACEPTIVES: MORTALITY AND MORTALITY STATISTICS
Percentage of deaths caused by contraception increases. OUR
SUNDAY VISITOR. 71:7, June 13, 1982

CONTRACEPTION AND CONTRACEPTIVES: RESEARCH
Activities of various 6-chloro-6-deoxysugars and (S) alpha-
chlorohydrin in producing spermatocoeles in rats and paralysis
in mice and in inhibiting glucose metabolism in bull spermatozoa in vitro, by W. C. Ford, et al. JOURNAL OF REPRODUCTIVE
FERTILITY. 65(1):177-183, May 1982

Advances in contraception (glossypol), by S. Katz. CHATELAINE.
55:36, February 1982

Alpha-difluoromethylornithine as a postcoitally effective antifertility agent in female rats, by P. R. Reddy, et al. CON-
TRACEPTION. 24(2):215-221, August 1981

Alteration in blood pressures associated with combined alcohol
and oral contraceptive use--the lipid research clinics prevalence study, by R. B. Wallace, et al. JOURNAL OF CHRONIC
DISEASES. 35(4):251-257, 1982

Antiandrogenic effects of cyproterone acetate and chloromadinone
acetate on the rat hypothalamus as revealed by electroen-
cephalographic responses, by C. Kaur, et al. PHYSIOLOGIA
BOHEMOSLOVACA. 30(4):365-373, 1981

Antiestrogenic and antifertility actions of anordrin (2 alpha, 1
alpha-diethynyl-A-nor-5 alpha-androstan-2 beta, 17 beta-diol
2,17-dipropionate), by R. R. Mehta, et al. STEROIDS. 38(6):
679-691, 1981

Anti-fertility activity of a benzene extract of hibiscus rosa-
sinensis flowers on female albino rats, by M. P. Singh, et al.
PLANTA MEDICA. 44(3):171-174, March 1982

Antifertility effects of gossypol and its impurities on male
hamsters, by D. P. Waller, et al. CONTRACEPTION. 23(6):653-
660, June 1981

At what age is contraception no longer necessary?, by J. H.
Meuwissen. NEDERLANDS TIJDSCHRIFT VOOR GENEESKUNDE. 100(16):
743-745, April 29, 1982

Attitudes toward male oral contraceptives: implications for
models of the relationship between beliefs and attitudes, by
J. Jaccard, et al. JOURNAL OF APPLIED SOCIAL PSYCHOLOGY.
11(3):181-191, May-June 1981

Back to basics ... a CAC report. CANADIAN CONSUMER. 12:10-14,
July 1982

Beyond the pill: contraceptives of the future, by E. P. Frank.
MADEMOISELLE. 88:130-132+, October 1982

Carbohydrate metabolism studies in women using Brevicon, a low-
estrogen type of oral contraceptive, for one year, by W. N.
Spellacy, et al. AMERICAN JOURNAL OF OBSTETRICS AND GYNECOLO-
GY. 142(1):105-108, January 1, 1982

Changing patterns of contraception, by J. Peel. PROCEEDINGS OF
THE ANNUAL SYMPOSIUM OF EUGENICS SOCIETY. 16:41-48, 1981

Chromosomal analysis of baboons and their mothers, following application to mothers of potentially post-ovulation fertility-
inhabiting steroids, by Z. A. Jemilev, et al. ZENTRALBLATT
FUR GYNAEKOLOGIE. 103(20):1215-1219, 1981

Clinical observations on long-acting oral contraceptives--a report of 43,373. CHUNG HUA FU CHAN KO TSA CHIH. 14(2):65-67,
April 1979

Clinical performance of a new levonorgestrel-releasing intrauterine device: a randomized comparison with a nova-T-copper
device, by C. G. Nilsson, et al. CONTRACEPTION. 25(4):345-
356, 1982

The continuing need for contraceptive research [editorial], by
J. J. Sciarra. FERTILITY AND STERILITY. 53(3):439-452,
September 1981

Contraception in the future, by H. S. Jacobs. PROCEEDINGS OF
THE ANNUAL SYMPOSIUM OF EUGENICS SOCIETY. 16:49-57, 1981

Contraceptive cover for rubella vaccination, by S. Rowlands, et
al. PRACTITIONER. 226(1368):1155-1156, June 1982

Contraceptive efficacy of 200 microgram R2323 and 10 microgram
R2858, by H. Rall. CLINICAL TRIALS JOURNAL. 18(6):395-400,
1981

Contraceptive research on the value and cost of children, by K.
Sadashivaiah. JOURNAL OF FAMILY WELFARE. 28:25-32, June 1982

Demonstration of a spirocheticidal effect by chemical contraceptives on treponema pallidum, by B. Singh, et al. BULLETIN OF
THE PAN AMERICAN HEALTH ORGANIZATION. 16(1):59-64, 1982

Development of a male contraceptive--a beginning [editorial], by W. J. Crowley, Jr. NEW ENGLAND JOURNAL OF MEDICINE. 305:695-696, September 17, 1981

Effect of aflatoxin B1 on hepatic drug-metabolizing enzymes in female rats. Interaction with a contraceptive agent, by L. Kamdem, et al. XENOBIOTICA. 11(4):275-279, April 1981

Effect of castration and oral contraceptives on hepatic ethanol and acetaldehyde metabolizing enzymes in the male rat, by F. S. Messiha, et al. SUBSTANCE AND ALCOHOL ACTIONS/MISUSE. 1(2):197-202, 1980

The effect of contraceptive steroids on the incorporation of uniformly carbon-14-labeled glucose into porcine aortic lipids, by W. C. Kent, et al. ARTERY. 9(6):425-436, 1981

The effect of high doses of 6-chloro-6-deoxyglucose on the rat, by W. C. Ford, et al. CONTRACEPTION. 24(5):577-588, November 1981

Effect of injectable norethisterone oenanthate (Norigest) on blood lipid levels, by K. Fotherby, et al. CONTRACEPTION. 25(4):435-446, April 1982

Effect of a low-protein diet on contraceptive steroid-induced cholestasis in rats, by U. A. Boelsterli, et al. RESEARCH COMMUNICATIONS IN CHEMICAL PATHOLOGY AND PHARMACOLOGY. 36(2): 299-318, May 1982

Effect of nonoxynol-9, a detergent with spermicidal activity, on malignant transformation in vitro, by S. D. Long, et al. CARCINOGENESIS. 3(5):553-557, 1982

Effect of oral contraceptive agents on ascorbic acid metabolism in the rhesus monkey, by J. Weininger, et al. AMERICAN JOURNAL OF CLINICAL NUTRITION. 35(6):1408-1416, June 1982

Effect of oral contraceptives and epsilon-aminocaproic acid on pregnant female rats and their fetuses. Histopathologic study, by M. J. Niznikowska-Marks, et al. PATOLOGIA POLSKA. 32(1): 37-42, 1981

Effect of oral contraceptives on antithrombin III, by M. P. McEntee, et al. THROMBOSIS RESEARCH. 24(1-2):13-20, October 1-15, 1981

The effect of oral contraceptives on reproductive function during semichronic exposure to ethanol by the female rat, by C. D. Lox, et al. GENERAL PHARMACOLOGY. 13(1):53-56, 1982

The effect of 6-chloro-6-deoxysugrs on adenine nucleotide concentrations in and motility of rat spermatozoa, by W. C. Ford, et al. JOURNAL OF REPRODUCTIVE FERTILITY. 63(1):75-79, September 1981

The effect of some long acting steroid contraceptives on some enzymes in goats and rabbits, by M. M. Kader, et al. EGYPTIAN

JOURNAL OF VETERINARY SCIENCE. 16(1/2):151-158, 1981

Effects in vitro of medroxyprogesterone acete on steroid metabolizing enzymes in the rat: selective inhibition of 3 alpha-
hydroxysteroid oxidoreductase activity, by A. Sunde, et al.
JOURNAL OF STEROID BIOCHEMISTRY. 17(2):197-203, August 1982

Effects of antiandrogens on glycogen metabolism of spermatozoa
from caput epididymidis, by G. T. Panse. INDIAN JOURNAL OF
EXPERIMENTAL BIOLOGY. 19(9):872-873, September 1981

Effects of antifertility drugs on epididymal protein secretion,
acquisition of sperm surface proteins and fertility in male
rats, by A. Y. Tsang, et al. INTERNATIONAL JOURNAL OF ANDROL-
OGY. 4(6):703-712, December 1981

Effects of calmodulin-binding drugs on the guinea pig spermatozoon acrosome reaction and the use of these drugs as vaginal
contraceptive agents in rabbits, by R. W. Lenz, et al. ANNALS
OF THE NEW YORK ACADEMY OF SCIENCES. 383:85-97, 1982

Effects of oral contraceptive steroids on serum lipid and aortic
glycosaminoglycans levels in iron-deficient rats, by Y. Kanke,
et al. INTERNATIONAL JOURNAL FOR VITAMIN AND NUTRITION RE-
SEARCH. 51(4):416-420, 1981

Effects of 17 beta-hydroxy-7 alpha-methylandrost-5-en-3-one on
early pregnancy in the rat, by S. Saksena, et al. ACTA ENDO-
CRINOLOGICA. 98(4):614-618, December 1981

Effects of 6-chloro-6-deoxysugars on glucose oxidation in rat
spermatozoa, by W. C. Ford, et al. JOURNAL OF REPRODUCTIVE
FERTILITY. 63(1):67-73, September 1981

The four-day pill (work of Etienne-Emile Baulieu), by R. Mason.
HEALTH. 14:20, July 1982

Half-life and metabolism of 3H-folic acid in oral contraceptive
treated rats, by N. Lakshmaiah, et al. HORMONE AND METABOLIC
RESEARCH. 13(7):404-407, July 1981

Histology of the rat vas deferens after injection of a non-occlusive chemical contraceptive, by K. Verma, et al. JOURNAL
OF REPRODUCTIVE FERTILITY. 63(2):539-542, November 1981

Immunologic contraception, by O. I. Polevaia, et al. AKUSHERST-
VO I GINEKOLOGIIA. (2):3-5, February 1982

Immunological studies of the vaginal secretion in women using
contraceptive preparations, by B. Nalbanski, et al. AKUSHER-
STVO I GINEKOLOGIIA. 20(4):337-340, 1981

In vivo production of nucleolar channel system in human endocervical secretory cells, by G. Yasuzumi, et al. JOURNAL OF
SUBMICROSCOPIC CYTOLOGY. 13(4):639-647, October 1981

Influence of contraceptive pill and menstrual cycle on serum
lipids and high-density lipoprotein cholesterol concentra-

tions, by P. N. M. Dermacker, et al. BRITISH MEDICAL JOURNAL. 6324:1213-1215, April 24, 1982

Influence of metabolism on the activity of a new anti-fertility agent, 2-(3-ethoxyphenyl)-5,6-dihydro-s-triazolo [5,1-a]isoui-noline (DL 204-IT), in the rat and the hamster, by A. Assandri, et al. ARZNEIMITTEL-FORSCHUNG. 31(12):2104-2111, 1981

The influence of oral contraceptive therapy on the periodontium --duration of drug therapy, by C. L. Pankhurst, et al. JOURNAL OF PERIODONTOLOGY. 52(10):617-620, October 1981

The influence of oral contraceptives on lipoprotein status, by H. Wieland, et al. DEUTSCHE MEDIZINISCHE WOCHENSCHRIFT. 107(17):649-653, April 30, 1982

Influence of sex difference and oral contraceptives on forearm reactive hyperemia, by R. C. Webb, et al. BLOOD VESSELS. 18(4-5):161-170, 1981

Influence of sex, menstrual cycle an oral contraception on the disposition of nitrazepam, by R. Jochemsen, et al. BRITISH JOURNAL OF CLINICAL PHARMACOLOGY. 13(3):319-324, March 1982

Interactions between antibiotics and oral contraceptives [letter], by R. J. True. JAMA: JOURNAL OF THE AMERICAN MEDICAL ASSOCIATION. 247(10):1408, March 12, 1982

An intravasal non-occlusive contraceptive device in rats, by M. M. Misro, et al. JOURNAL OF REPRODUCTIVE FERTILITY. 65(1): 9-13, May 1982

Kinetic studies of the human renin and human substrate reaction, by A. B. Gould, et al. BIOCHEMICAL MEDICINE. 24(3):321-326, December 1980

The law of human reproduction [an overview], by D. G. Warren. JOURNAL OF LEGAL MEDICINE. 3(1):1-57, March 1982

Letting intrauterine devices lie [research review], by M. Pollock. BRITISH MEDICAL JOURNAL. 6339:395-396, August 7, 1982

Liver regeneration after partial hepatectomy in oral contraceptive-treated female rats, by M. A. Mukundan, et al. BIOCHEMICAL MEDICINE. 26(2):222-230, October 1981

The mechanism of action of vacation pills, by Z. Y. Hu. CHUNG HUA FU CHAN KO TSA CHIH. 16(2):73-77, April 1981

Medical intervention in the field of human reproduction, by J. Cruz y Hermida. ANALES DE LA ACADEMIA NACIONAL DE MEDICINA. 98(3):369-394, 1981

Metabolic studies in gestational diabetic women during contraceptive treatment: effects on glucose tolerance and fatty acid composition of serum lipids, by T. Radberg, et al. GYNECOLOGIC AND OBSTETRIC INVESTIGATION. 13(1):17-29, 1982

Minigest--a new Czechoslovak contraceptive and its side-effects, by E. Zizkovska, et al. CESKOSLOVENSKA GYNEKOLOGIE. 45(9): 649-652, November 1980

Mutagenic evaluation of two male contraceptives: 5-thio-d-glucose and gossypol acetic acid, by S. K. Majumdar, et al. JOURNAL OF HEREDITY. 73(1):76-77, January-February 1982

The neurotoxicity and antifertility properties of 6-chloro-6-deoxyglucose in the mouse, by J. M. Jacobs, et al. NEUROTOXI-COLOGY. 2(3):405-417, November 1981

A new delivery system for metals as contraceptives in animals, by S. S. Riar, et al. INDIAN JOURNAL OF EXPERIMENTAL BIOLOGY. 19(12):1124-1126, December 1981

A new look at contraception, by P. M. Brunetti. ECOLOGIST. 11(4):174, 1981

The NORPLANT contraceptive method: a report on three years of use, by I. Sivin, et al. STUDIES IN FAMILY PLANNING. 13:258-261, August-September 1982

Oestrogenic activity of cyproterone acetate in female mice, by N. K. Lohiya, et al. ENDOKRINOLOGIE. 78(1):21-27, October 1981

On the track of a new fertility control?, by J. Grinsted, et al. NORDISK MEDICIN. 96(11):280-281, November 1981

Oral contraception: mechanism of action, by R. A. Bronson. CLINICAL OBSTETRICS AND GYNECOLOGY. 24(3):869-877, September 1981

Oral contraceptive and platelet lipid biosynthesis in female rats: dose-response relationship, by M. Ciavatti, et al. LIPIDS. 17(2):111-114, February 1982

Oral contraceptives: technical and safety aspects. WHO OFFSET PUBLICATIONS. (64):1-45, 1982

Organic changes as affected by oral steroid contraception in female inbred Buffalo rats, by C. Markuszewski. PATOLOGIA POLSKA. 32(4):487-503, October-December 1981

Pharmacokinetic and pharmacodynamic studies with vaginal devices releasing norethisterone at a constant, near zero order, by B. M. Landgren, et al. CONTRACEPTION. 24(1):29-44, July 1981

Pharmacologic control of estrus in bitch and queen, by T. J. Burke. VETERINARY CLINICS OF NORTH AMERICA. SMALL ANIMAL PRACTICE. 12(1):79-84, February 1982

The pill: an evaluation of recent studies, by A. Rosenfield. JOHNS HOPKINS MEDICAL JOURNAL. 150(5):177-180, May 1982

Plasminogen, fibrinogen, alpha 2-antiplasmin and antithrombin-III levels during a single cycle of a combined oral contraceptive regime, by G. Baele, et al. ACTA CLINICA BELGICA. 36(6):280-285, 1981

A preliminary pharmacological trial of the monthly injectable contraceptive CycloProvera, by K. Fotherby, et al. CONTRA-CEPTION. 25(3):261-272, 1982

A randomized, double-blind study of 6 combined oral contraceptives, by S. Koetsawang, et al. CONTRACEPTION. 25(3):231-242, March 1982

Rejecting scientific advice [editorial]. BRITISH MEDICAL JOURNAL. 284(6372):1426, May 15, 1982

The relationship of static muscle function to use of oral contraceptives, by J. C. Wirth, et al. MEDICINE AND SCIENCE IN SPORTS AND EXERCISE. 14(1):16-20, 1982

Research activities in the field of oral contraceptives in the People's Republic of China, by Z. De-Wei. ACTA OBSTETRICIA ET GYNECOLOGICA SCANDINAVICA. SUPPLEMENT. 105:51-60, 1982

Review and prospect of gossypol research, by H. P. Lei. YAO HSUEH HSUEH PAO: ACTA PHARMACEUTICA SINICA. 17(1):1-4, January 1982

Sex hormone binding globulin: effect of synthetic steroids on the assay and effect of oral contraceptives, by S. M. Bowles, et al. ANNALS OF CLINICAL BIOCHEMISTRY. 18(Pt 4):226-231, July 1981

Size distribution, forms and variations of glandular tissue of the breast. Histometric examination on the question of the effect of contraceptives on the lobular parenchyma, by C. Theele, et al. PATHOLOGE. 2(4):208-219, August 1981

Spermatogenesis and SRBC haemolysin formation in various inbred mouse strains treated with cyproterone acetate, by Z. Pokorna, et al. FLORIDA STATE UNIVERSITY LAW REVIEW. 27(5):354-359, 1981

Structure and biological function of 16a,17a-cycloprogesterones (Pregna-D'-pentarans), by V. I. Simonov, et al. BIOORGANI-CHESKAYA KHIMIYA. 7(6):920-926, 1981

Studies of synthetic contraceptives. III. Stereospecific total synthesis of racemic prostaglandin F2 alpha, by G. D. Han, et al. YAO HSUEH HSUEH PAO: ACTA PHARMACEUTICA SINICA. 16(2):114-121, February 1981

Studies on the mechanism of action of me-quingestanol on fertility in the rabbit, by Y. M. Wei. CHUNG HUA FU CHAN KO TSA CHIH. 14(2):73-78, April 1979

A study on toxicity of bakuchiol to mice's kidney, by Y. S. Zhang. CHUNG-KUO YAO LI HSUEH PAO. 6(3):30-32, May 1981

Teratology study of intravaginally administered nonoxynol-9-

containing contraceptive cream in rats, by D. Abrutyn, et al.
FERTILITY AND STERILITY. 37(1):113-117, January 1982

A theoretical framework for studying adolescent contraceptive
use, by K. Urberg. ADOLESCENCE. 17:527-540, Fall 1982

Triquilar/trinordiol. A new pill with 3 sequences, by E. B.
Obel. UGESKRIFT FOR LAEGER. 143(25):1610-1611, June 15, 1981

Unlikely role of tryptophan metabolites in glucose tolerance
and gluconeogenesis in oral contraceptive and pyridoxine
treated rats, by S. Safaya, et al. INDIAN JOURNAL OF MEDICAL
RESEARCH. 74:236-243, August 1981

Use of mepregenol diacetate (Diamol), a gestagen preparation,
for estrus synchronization in caracul sheep during mating
season, by IuD. Klinskii, et al. ARCHIV FUR EXPERIMENTELLE
VETERINARMEDIZIN. 36(1):159-162, January 1982

WHO special programme of research, development and research
training in human reproduction. Task force on long-acting
agents for the regulation of fertility. CONTRACEPTION.
25(1):1-11, January 1982

What value (risks) do today's modern possibilities of contraception have?. MEDIZINISCHE WELT. 32(39):1456-1459, September
25, 1981

Women saying no to pill, by M. Neilson. NATIONAL CATHOLIC RE-
PORTER. 18(1):23, January 15, 1982

CONTRACEPTIVE AGENTS
Antifertility effects of GnRH, by H. M. Fraser. JOURNAL OF RE-
PRODUCTIVE FERTILITY. 64(2):503-515, March 1982

Chronic treatment with a LH-RH-agonist: a new contraceptive
method?, by M. Schmidt-Gollwitzer, et al. ACTA EUROPAEA
FERTILITATIS. 12(3):275-276, September 1981

The clinical use of me-quingestanol contraceptive pill. CHUNG
HUA FU CHAN KO TSA CHIH. 14(2):68-72, April 1979

Contraception with LHRH agonists, a new physiological approach,
by F. Labrie, et al. REPRODUCCION. 5(4):229-241, October-
December 1981

Effect of aflatoxin B1 on hepatic drug-metabolizing enzymes in
female rats. Interaction with a contraceptive agent, by L.
Kamdem, et al. XENOBIOTICA. 11(4):275-279, April 1981

Effect of contraceptive steroids on creatine kinase activity in
serum [letter], by U. Gupta, et al. CLINICAL CHEMISTRY.
28(6):1402-1403, June 1982

A new class of contraceptives? [news], by H. M. Fraser. NATURE.
296(5856):391-392, April 1, 1982

Plants of Haiti used as antifertility agents, by B. Weniger, et

CONTRACEPTIVE AGENTS (continued)

    al. JOURNAL OF ETHNOPHARMACOLOGY. 6(1):67-84, July 1982

CONTRACEPTIVE AGENTS: COMPLICATIONS
Clinical, epidemiological, morphological and etiopathogenetic
aspects of benign tumors of hepatocytic derivation, with description of a case of focal nodular hyperplasia, by L. Bontempini, et al. ARCHIVIO DE VECCHI PER L ANATOMIA PATOLOGICA
E LA MEDICINA CLINICA. 64(3):547-568, December 1981

Contraception and multiple sclerosis, by S. Poser. NERVENARZT.
53(6):323-326, June 1982

Contraceptives go on trial for diabetics. NEW SCIENTIST. 91:
463, August 20, 1981

Failure of contraceptive steroids to modify human chorionic
gonadotrophin secretion by hydatidiform mole tissue and
choriocarcinoma cells in culture, by D. Gal, et al. STEROIDS.
37(6):663-671, June 1981

From contraception to cancer: a review of the therapeutic appli-
cations of LHRH analogues as antitumor agents, by a. Corbin.
YALE JOURNAL OF BIOLOGY AND MEDICINE. 55(1):27-47, January-
February 1982

A review of enzyme changes in serum an urine due to treatment
with drugs (tuberculostatics, contraceptive medication, diagnostics and drugs in real diseases), by R. J. Hashen. FOLIA
MEDICA CRACOVIENSIA. 22(3-4):279-291, 1980

CONTRACEPTIVE AGENTS: FEMALE
Cervical mucus penetration test for in vitro assay of vaginal
contraceptive agents, by N. J. Alexander, et al. FERTILITY
AND STERILITY. 36(4):516-520, October 1981

Clinical and immunological responses with Pr-beta-hCG-TT vaccine
by S. M. Shahani, et al. CONTRACEPTION. 25(4):421-434, April
1982

Contraceptive use, pregnancy intentions and pregnancy outcomes
among U.S. women, by J. G. Dryfoos. FAMILY PLANNING PERSPEC-
TIVES. 14(2):81-94, March-April 1982

CONTRACEPTIVE AGENTS: FEMALE: ORAL: COMPLICATIONS
Actinomyces-like organisms and IUD use linked but clinical im-
portance of the finding is unclear. FAMILY PLANNING PERSPEC-
TIVES. 14:34-35, January-February 1982

Biliary lipids, bile acids, and gallbladder function in the
human female: effects of contraceptive steroids, by F. Kern,
Jr., et al. JOURNAL OF LABORATORY AND CLINICAL MEDICINE.
99(6):798-805, June 1982

Hepatic lesions caused by anabolic and contraceptive steroids,
by K. G. Ishak. SEMINARS IN LIVER DISEASE. 1(2):116-128, May
1981

CONTRACEPTIVE AGENTS: MALE

Clinical study of gossypol as a male contraceptive, by G. Z.
Liu. REPRODUCCION. 5(3):189-193, July-September 1981

Copper as a male contraceptive, by S. S. Riar, et al. INDIAN
JOURNAL OF EXPERIMENTAL BIOLOGY. 19(12):1121-1123, December
1981

Effects of low doses of cyproterone acete on sperm morphology
and some other parameters of reproduction in normal men, by B.
Fredricsson, et al. ANDROLOGIA. 13(4):369-375, July-August
1981

Gossypol: a potential male contraceptive?, by S. V. Lawrence.
AMERICAN PHARMACY. 21(11):57-59, November 1981

Interference with epididymal physiology as possible site of male
contraception, by A. Reyes, et al. ARCHIVES OF ANDROLOGY.
7(2):159-168, September 1981

Novel mode of contraception using polymeric hydrogels, by H.
Singh, et al. JOURNAL OF BIOMEDICAL MATERIALS RESEARCH.
16(1):3-9, January 1982

Synthesis and evaluation of the male antifertility properties
of a series of N-unsubstituted sulfamates, by A. F. Hirsch,
et al. JOURNAL OF MEDICINAL CHEMISTRY. 24(7):901-903, July
1981

Toward a male contraceptive [letter], by J. S. Morrill. NEW
ENGLAND JOURNAL OF MEDICINE. 306(3):177, January 21, 1982

CONTRACEPTIVES: GENERAL
Abortions preventable by contraceptive practice, by C. F. West-
off, et al. FAMILY PLANNING PERSPECTIVES. 13(5):218-223,
September-October 1981

Birth control: contraception, by A. Bicego, et al. PROFESSIONI
INFERMIERISTICHE. 34(3):149-159, July-September 1981

Characteristics of contraceptive acceptors in rural Zaire, by J.
E. Brown, et al. STUDIES IN FAMILY PLANNING. 11(12):378-384,
December 1980

Community available of contraceptives and family limitation, by
A. O. Tsui, et al. DEMOGRAPHY. 18:615-625, November 1981

Contraceptive availability differentials in use and fertility,
by A. O. Tsui, et al. STUDIES IN FAMILY PLANNING. 12(11):
381-393, November 1981

Contraceptive use, pregnancy intentions and pregnancy outcomes
among U.S. women, by J. G. Dryfoos. FAMILY PLANNING PERSPEC-
TIVES. 14(2):81-94, March-April 1982

Contraceptives, by I. R. McFadyen. INFORMATION. (5):95, 1981

--, by B. P. Quinby. MADEMOISELLE. 88:66-67, January 1982

CONTRACEPTIVES: GENERAL (continued)

Education and contraceptive choice: a conditional demand framework, by M. R. Rosenzweig, et al. INTERNATIONAL ECONOMIC REVIEW. 23:171-198, February 1982

Find patients at Oxford clinic have very few contraceptive failures. FAMILY PLANNING PERSPECTIVES. 14:150-151, May-June 1982

Taking liberties with women: abortion, sterilization, and contraception, by W. Savage. INTERNATIONAL JOURNAL OF HEALTH EDUCATION. 12(2):293-308, 1982

Voluntary childlessness and contraception: problems and practices, by F. Baum. JOURNAL OF BIOSOCIAL SCIENCE. 14(1):17-23, January 1982

AFRICA
Characteristics of contraceptive acceptors in rural Zaire, by J. E. Brown, et al. STUDIES IN FAMILY PLANNING. 11(12): 378-384, December 1980

Modern, transitional and traditional demographic and contraceptive patterns among Kenyan women, by T. E. Dow, et al. STUDIES IN FAMILY PLANNING. 13:12-23, January 1982

BANGLADESH
The demographic impact of the contraceptive distribution pro-project in Matlab, Bangladesh, by W. S. Stinson, et al. STUDIES IN FAMILY PLANNING. 13(5):141-148, May 1982

CARIBBEAN
The impact on breastfeeding and pregnancy status of household contraceptive distribution in rural Haiti [research], by A. Bordes, et al. AMERICAN JOURNAL OF PUBLIC HEALTH. 72:835-838, August 1982

CENTRAL AMERICA
Characteristics of successful distributors in the community-base distribution of contraceptives in Guatemala, by J. T. Bertrand, et al. STUDIES IN FAMILIY PLANNING. 11(9-10): 274-285, September-October 1980

Contraceptive use and fertility in the Republic of Panama, by R. S. Monteith, et al. STUDIES IN FAMILY PLANNING. 12(10): 331, October 1981

Family planning communications and contraceptive use in Guatemala, El Salvador, and Panama, by J. T. Bertrand, et al. STUDIES IN FAMILY PLANNING. 13(6-7):190-199, June-July 1982

ENGLAND
Contraception in ethnic minority groups in Bedford [research], by P. Beard. HEALTH VISITOR. 55:417+, August 1982

GREAT BRITAIN
British embrace a gentler postcoital contraceptive. MEDICAL WORLD NEWS. 23:28-29, October 11, 1982

CONTRACEPTIVES: GENERAL (continued)

INDIA
Contraceptive intentions and subsequent behavior in rural
Bangladesh, by S. Bhatia. STUDIES IN FAMILY PLANNING. 13:
24, January 1982

The effect on fecundity of pill acceptance during postpartum
amenorrhea in rural Bangladesh, by S. Bhatia, et al. STUD-
IES IN FAMILY PLANNING. 13:200-207, June-July 1982

Patterns of IUD acceptance and removals in a geographically
defined urban slum area in Ludhiana, Punjab, by P. S.
Zachariah, et al. JOURNAL OF FAMILY WELFARE. 28:70-76,
March 1982

User preferences for contraceptive methods in India, Korea,
the Philippines, and Turkey. STUDIES IN FAMILY PLANNING.
11(9-10):267-273, September-October 1980

ITALY
Contracetpion, pregnancy management and the clinic: opinions
of 1271 puerperas in a large hospital on the northern border
of Milan, by P. Dall'Aglio. ANNALI DI OSTETRICIA GINECOLO-
GIA, MEDICINA PERINATALE. 103(1):48-59, January-February
1982

KOREA
Abortion and contraception in the Korean fertility transition,
by P. J. Donaldson, et al. POPULATION STUDIES. 36:227-235,
July 1982

User preferences for contraceptive methods in India, Korea,
the Philippines, and Turkey. STUDIES IN FAMILY PLANNING.
11(9-10):267-273, September-October 1980

LATIN AMERICA
Contraceptive sterilization in four Latin American countries,
by J. McCarthy. JOURNAL OF BIOLOGICAL SCIENCE. 14(2):189-
201, April 1982

NIGERIA
Contraceptives and the female undergraduates in Ibadan,
Nigeria, by J. A. Adeleye. EAST AFRICAN MEDICAL JOURNAL.
58(8):616-621, August 1981

Response of unmarried adolescents to contraceptive advice and
service in Nigeria, by M. Ezimokhai, et al. INTERNATIONAL
JOURNAL OF GYNAECOLOGY AND OBSTETRICS. 19(6):481-485,
December 1981

THE PHILIPPINES
Effects of Philippine family planning outreached project on
contraceptive prevalence: a multivariate analysis, by J. E.
Laing. STUDIES IN FAMILY PLANNING. 12(11):367, November
1981

User preferences for contraceptive methods in India, Korea,
the Philippines, and Turkey. STUDIES IN FAMILY PLANNING.
11(9-10):267-273, September-October 1980

CONTRACEPTIVES: GENERAL (continued)

THAILAND
Antecedents to contraceptive innovation: evidence from rural
Northern Thailand, by D. P. Hogan, et al. DEMOGRAPHY. 18:
597-614, November 1981

Continuation of injectable contraceptions in Thailand, by T.
Narkavonnakit, et al. STUDIES IN FAMILY PLANNING. 13:99-
105, April 1982

TURKEY
User preferences for contraceptive methods in India, Korea,
the Philippines, and Turkey. STUDIES IN FAMILY PLANNING.
11(9-10):267-273, September-October 1980

UNITED STATES
Contraceptive failure in the United States: the impact of
social econimic and demographic factors [research], by A. L.
Schirm, et al. FAMILY PLANNING PERSPECTIVES. 14:68-74,
March-April 1982

Contraceptive use, pregnancy intentions and pregnancy outcomes
among U.S. women [research], by J. G. Dryfoos. FAMILY PLAN-
NING PERSPECTIVES. 14(2):81-94, March-April 1982

CONTRACEPTIVES: ADVERTISING
Airing contraceptive commercials, by P. Donovan. FAMILY PLAN-
NING PERSPECTIVES. 14:321-323, November-December 1982

High court strikes down ad circular ban. ADVERTISING AGE. 53:
73, May 24, 1982

Should contraceptives be advertised on television?, by R. Horowitz. CHANNELS. 1(3):64-66, October-November 1981

CONTRACEPTIVES: ATTITUDES
Contraception, pregnancy management and the family-planning
clinic (findings on 410 puerperas in a Lombard hospital), by
M. Semeria. ANNALI DI OSTETRICIA GINECOLOGIA, MEDICINA
PERINATALE. 103(1):93-101, January-February 1982

Contraceptive methods and abortion: one question, by L. Bale-
striere. ANNALES MEDICO-PSYCHOLOGIQUES. 139(5):513-528, May
1981

Contraceptive use, pregnancy intentions and pregnancy outcomes
among U.S. women, by J. G. Dryfoos. FAMILY PLANNING PERSPEC-
TIVES. 14(2):81, March-April 1982

The dream of love and the reality of contraception. Current
adolescent sexual behaviour and contraceptive methods, by K.
Thormann, et al. THERAPEUTISCHE UMSCHAU. 39(6):462-468, June
1982

The first abortion--and the last? A study of the personality
factors underlying repeated failure of contraception, by P.
Niemela, et al. INTERNATIONAL JOURNAL OF GYNAECOLOGY AND
OBSTETRICS. 19(3):193-200, June 1981

Kinship dependence and contraceptive use among Navaho women, by S. J. Kunitz, et al. HUMAN BIOLOGY. 53:439-452, September 1981

An organizational and behavioral analysis of the contraceptive compliance process, by D. F. Winokur. DISSERTATION ABSTRACTS INTERNATIONAL. A. p. 4950, 1982

Pregnancy, contraception and the family-planning clinic: from the woman's point of view (studies of 3635 puerperas in 6 Lombard hospital obstetrical departments), by G. Remotti, et al. ANNALI DI OSTETRICIA GINECOLOGIA, MEDICINA PERINATALE. 103(1):7-47, January-February 1982

Psychic attitude of women to irreversible contraception, by R. Sudik, et al. ZENTRALBLATT FUR GYNAEKOLOGIE. 103(2):1242-1254, 1981

Relationship between women's attitudes and choice of birth control, by K. I. Hunter, et al. PSYCHOLOGICAL REPORTS. 49(2):372-374, October 1981

Studies of the attitudes of a group of puerapas of the Brianza region toward contraception and the services offered for such purposes of the public health organizations, by G. Remotti, et al. ANNALI DI OSTETRICIA GINECOLOGIA, MEDICINA PERINATALE. 103(1):68-92, January-February 1982

Women saying no to pill, by M. Nielsen. NATIONAL CATHOLIC RE-PORTER. 18:23, January 15, 1982

CONTRACEPTIVES: COMPLICATIONS
Blood pressure and contraceptive use, by K-T. Khaw, et al. BRITISH MEDICAL JOURNAL. 6339:403-407, August 7, 1982

Cerebral circulation disturbances due to the use of contraceptives, by D. Khadzhiev, et al. ZHURNAL NEVROPATOLOGII I PSIKHIATRII. 81(1):64-67, 1981

Effect of menstrual cycle and method of contraception on recover of neisseria gonorrhoeae, by W. M. McCormack, et al. JAMA: JOURNAL OF THE AMERICAN MEDICAL ASSOCIATION. 247(9):1292-1294, 1982

Psychological aspects of contraception with the multiload Cu250, by U. Rauchfleisch. GYNAEKOLOGISCHE RUNDSCHAU. 21(3):159-165, 1981

The Rov v. Wade and Doe v. Bolton decisions on abortion: an analysis critique, and examination of related issues, by A. P. Smith. DISSERTATION ABSTRACTS INTERNATIONAL. A. p. 4037, 1982

CONTRACEPTIVES: COUNSELING
Contraceptive preferences of adolescents and the role of counseling, by M. Endler, et al. THERAPEUTISCHE UMSCHAU. 39(6): 458-461, June 1982

CONTRACEPTIVES: COUNSELING (continued)

Counseling on contraception following interruption of pregnancy. Responsibility of the hospital gynecologist. Model of contraceptive counseling at the Gynecological Clinic Berlin-Neukolln, by S. Ufer, et al. FORTSCHRITTE DER MEDIZIN. 100(16): 746-748, April 29, 1982

Couple-directed contraceptive counseling, by M. A. Redmond. CANADIAN NURSE. 78:38-39, September 1982

Model for effective contraceptive counseling on campus, by G. A. Bachmann. JOURNAL OF THE AMERICAN COLLEGE HEALTH ASSOCIATION. 30(3):119-121, December 1981

Pregnancy, contraception and the family-planning clinic: from the woman's point of view (studies of 3635 puerperas in 6 Lombard hospital obstetical departments), by G. Remotti, et al. ANNALI DI OSTETRICIA GINECOLOGIA, MEDICINA PERINATALE. 103(1):7-47, January-February 1982

CONTRACEPTIVES: FEMALE

Contraception--a woman's delimma, by S. Wigington. NURSING TIMES. 77:1765-1768, October 1981

Contraceptives and the female undergraduates in Ibadan, Nigeria, by J. A. Adeleye. EAST AFRICAN MEDICAL JOURNAL. 58(8):616-621, August 1981

Disposition of intravenous diazepam in young men and women, by H. G. Giles, et al. EUROPEAN JOURNAL OF CLINICAL PHARMACOLOGY. 20(3):207-213, 1981

The doubtful value of transitory contraception after laparoscopic electrocoagulation of the fallopian tubes, by J. J. Kjer, et al. ACTA OBSTETRICIA ET GYNECOLOGICA SCANDINAVICA. 60(4):403-405, 1981

Injectable contraception (Depo-Provera and Norigest), by P. E. Hall, et al. WORLD HEALTH. pp. 2-4, May 1982

Kinship dependence and contraceptive use among Navajo women, by S. J. Kunitz, et al. HUMAN BIOLOGY. 53(3):439-452, September 1981

Maternal nutrition, breast feeding, and contraception [editorial], by J. Dobbing. BRITISH MEDICAL JOURNAL. 284(6331): 1725-1726, June 12, 1982

Seasonal conception by women in various age groups compared with the season of menarche, by F. Ronnike. DANISH MEDICAL BULLETIN. 28(4):148-153, September 1981

Sex guilt and the use of contraception among unmarried women, by J. F. Keller, et al. CONTRACEPTION. 25(4):387-394, 1982

Taking liberties with women: abortion, sterilization, and contraception, by W. Savage. INTERNATIONAL JOURNAL OF HEALTH SERVICES. 12(2):293-308, 1982

CONTRACEPTIVES: FEMALE (continued)

Transfer of contraceptive steroids in milk of women using long-acting gestagens, by S. Koetsawang, et al. CONTRACEPTION. 25(4):321-331, April 1982

Women's health care: approaches in delivery to physically disabled women, by L. Peters. NURSE PRACTITIONER. 7(1):34-37+, January 1982

CONTRACEPTIVES: FEMALE: BARRIER
Barrier contraception: a trend toward older methods, by R. L. Young. CONSULTANT. 22:297-301, June 1982

Birth control plugs (silicon plug for Fallopian tubes). SCIENCE NEWS. 122:41, July 17, 1982

The cervical cap. An alternate barier contraceptive method, by W. M. Gilbirds, 2nd, et al. MISSOURI MEDICINE. 79(4):216-218+, April 1982

Contraceptives: back to the barriers, by R. Serlin. NEW SCIENTIST. 91(1264):281, July 30, 1981

Diaphragms rediscovered, by S. O'Malley. COSMOPOLITAN. 192(3):171+, March 1982

Doing as the ancient Egyptians did--the sponge by V. Morgan. TIMES (London). p. 9, March 16, 1982

Frontlines: shot felt around the world (FD will decide whether Depo-Provera should be approved for use in U.S.), by K. Brannan. MOTHER JONES. 7:10+, May 1982

In vitro method for evaluation of spermicides by hemolytic potency, by M. M. Dolan. FERTILITY AND STERILITY. 36(2):248-249, 1981

In vitro testing for potency of various spermicidal agents, by H. P. Lee. SEOUL JOURNAL OF MEDICINE. 22(4):525-540, 1981

New sponge contraceptive, by S. Katz. CHATELAINE. 55:26, August 1982

Of menses--pills and IUDs--neisseria--and flings--(with apologies to Lewis Carroll) [editorial], by J. C. Hume. JAMA: JOURNAL OF THE AMERICAN MEDICAL ASSOCIATION. 247(9):1321-1322, March 5, 1982

Pill and IUD use at PPFA clinics decline: diaphragm use rises. FAMILY PLANNING PERSPECTIVES. 14:152-153, May-June 1982

Polyurethane contraceptive vaginal sponge: product modifications resulting from user experience, by R. Aznar, et al. CONTRACEPTION. 24(3):235-244, September 1981

The Prentif contraceptive cervical cap: acceptability aspects and their implications for future cap design, by J. P. Koch. CONTRACEPTION. 25(2):161-174, 1982

CONTRACEPTIVES: FEMALE: BARRIER (continued)

--: a contemporary study of its clinical safety and effectiveness, by J. P. Koch. CONTRACEPTION. 25(2):135-160, 1982

Relationship of weight change to required size of vaginal diaphragm [research], by K. Fiscella. NURSE PRACTITIONER. 7:
21+, July-August 1982

A throw-away diaphragm, by R. Kall. HEALTH. 14:18, March 1982

Vaginal spermicidal activity of gossypol in Macaca arctoides, by
S. M. Cameron, et al. FERTILITY AND STERILITY. 37(2):273-
274, 1982

Vaginal spermicides and outcome of pregancy: findings in a large
cohort study, by G. Huggins, et al. CONTRACEPTION. 25(3):
219-230, 1982

CONTRACEPTIVES: FEMALE: BARRIER: COMPLICATIONS
Are spermicides dangerous?. READERS DIGEST. 120:44, June 1982

Barrier-method contraceptives and pelvic inflammatory disease,
by J. Kelaghan, et al. JAMA: JOURNAL OF THE AMERICAN MEDICAL
ASSOCIATION. 248(2):184-187, July 9, 1982

Birth defects and vaginal spermicides, by S. Shapiro, et al.
JAMA: JOURNAL OF THE AMERICAN MEDICAL ASSOCIATION. 247(17):
2381, May 7, 1982

Condom sales surge, as venereal diseases rise, by R. Raldt.
AMERICAN DRUGGIST. 185:60+, January 1982

Dalkon shield controversy continues. TRIAL. 17(6):13, June
1981

Depo-Provera for better or worse?, by P. MacMillan. NURSING
TIMES. 78(11):467, March 17-23, 1982

Diaphragm failure [letter], by W. R. Atkinson. MEDICAL JOURNAL
OF AUSTRALIA. 2(4):206-207, August 22, 1981

Evaluation of the spring coil and Dalkon shield, by H. A.
Kisnisci. ACTA REPRODUCTION TURCICA. 3(2):67-72, 1981

Just when you thought you were safe ... today's contraceptive
controversy (spermicides and birth defects), by D. Weinberg.
MADEMOISELLE. 88:159-161, March 1982

Monica was reported when she refused to give Depo-Provera
[interview by Susanne Gare], by M. Blomster. VARDFACKET.
6(7):53, April 8, 1982

The Prentif contraceptive cervical cap: acceptability aspects
and their implications for future cap design, by J. P. Koch.
CONTRACEPTION. 25(2):161-173, February 1982

--: a contemporary study of its clinical safety and effectiveness, by J. P. Koch. CONTRACEPTION. 25(2):135-159, February
1982

CONTRACEPTIVES: FEMALE: BARRIER: COMPLICATIONS (continued)

Prolonged use of a diaphragm and toxic shock syndrome, by E. A. Baehler, et al. FERTILITY AND STERILITY. 38(2):248-250, August 1982

Spermicide use and Down's syndrome, by K. J. Rothman. AMERICAN JOURNAL OF PUBLIC HEALTH. 72;399-401, April 1982

Sweden approved of Depo-Provera sales promotion in developing countries [interview by Elisabeth Magnusson], by B. Rubensson. VARDFACKET. 6(7):54, April 8, 1982

Toxic-shock syndrome associated with diaphragm use [letter]. NEW ENGLAND JOURNAL OF MEDICINE. 305(26):1585-1586, December 24, 1981

Toxic-shock syndrome associated with diaphragm use for only nine hours [letter], by D. V. Alcid, et al. LANCET. 1(8285):1363-1364, June 12, 1982

Why the diaphragm doesn't work, by G. Berkowitz. SAN FRANCISCO. 23(4):72-75, December 1981

CONTRACEPTIVES: FEMALE: COMPLICATIONS
Cholesterol ester metabolism in plasma during estrogen and anti-androgen treatment in men with carcinoma of the prostate, by L. Wallentin, et al. JOURNAL OF LABORATORY AND CLINICAL MEDICINE. 98(6):906-916, December 1981

Chorea associated with the use of oral contraceptives: report of a case and review of the literature, by W. B. Wadlington, et al. CLINICAL PEDIATRICS. 20(12):804-806, December 1981

Contraceptive effect of breast feeding, by P. W. Howie, et al. JOURNAL OF TROPICAL PEDIATRICS. 28(1):ii-v, February 1982

Cyproterone acetate in the treatment of acne vulgaris in adult females, by B. Hansted, et al. DERMATOLOGICA. 164(2):117-126, February 1982

The effect of cyproterone acetate on pituitary-ovarian function and clinical symptoms in hirsute women, by N. O. Lunell, et al. ACTA ENDOCRINOLOGICA. 100(1):91-97, May 1982

Gallbladder function in the human female: effect of the ovulator cycle: pregnancy and contraceptive steroids, by G. T. Everson, et al. GASTROENTEROLOGY. 82(4):711-719, 1982

Psychic attitude of women to irreversible contraception, by R. Sudik, et al. ZENTRALBLATT FUR GYNAEKOLOGIE. 103(20):1242-1254, 1981

A test of the Luker theory of contraceptive risk-taking, by P. V. Crosbie, et al. STUDIES IN FAMILY PLANNING. 13:67-78, March 1982

Wrongful birth. What is the damage?, by V. R. Greenfield. JAMA: JOURNAL OF THE AMERICAN MEDICAL ASSOCIATION. 248(8):926-927, August 27, 1982

Cu-7 IUD can be used up to 4 years with low pregnancy rates.
FAMILY PLANNING PERSPECTIVES. 14:35-36, January-February
1982

Changing profile of IUD users in family planning clinics in
rural Bangladesh, by S. Bhatia, et al. JOURNAL OF BIOSOCIAL
SCIENCE. 13(2):169-177, April 1981

Clinical performance of a new levonorgestrel-releasing intrauterine device: a randomized comparison with a nova-T-copper
device, by C. G. Nilsson, et al. CONTRACEPTION. 25(4):345-
356, 1982

Effect of intrauterine drug contraceptives on the endometrium,
by T. A. Shirokova, et al. LABORATORNOE DELO. (11):665-667,
1981

Fertility after discontinuation of levo-norgestrel-releasing
intrauterine devices, by C. G. Nilsson. CONTRACEPTION.
25(3):273-278, 1982

IUD under the aspects of sexual medicine, by J. M. Wenderlein,
et al. GEBURTSHILFE UND FRAUENHEILKUNDE. 42(2):115-117,
February 1982

Intrauterine contraception from the viewpoint of an ambulatorty
gynecologic department, by P. Hagen. ZEITSCHRIFT FUR ARZT-
LICHE FORTBILDUNG. 75(17):800-804, September 1, 1981

Letting intrauterine devices lie [research review], by M.
Pollock. BRITISH MEDICAL JOURNAL. 6339:395-396, August 7,
1982

The mechanism of action of intrauterine contraceptive devices,
by J. Lippes. MIDWIFE, HEALTH VISITOR AND COMMUNITY NURSE.
17:518-521, December 1981

The multiload intra-uterine contraceptiv device: comparison of 4
different models, by W. A. A. Van Os, et al. SOUTH AFRICAN
MEDICAL JOURNAL. 60(24):938-940, 1981

Patentex-Oval: contraceptive intrauterine device, by B.
Horoszko-Husiatynska, et al. WIADOMOSCI LEKARSKIE. 34(12):
985-989, 1982

Pill and IUD use at PPFA clinics decline: diaphragm use rises.
FAMILY PLANNING PERSPECTIVES. 14:152-153, May-June 1982

Study finds lactation has no adverse effect on IUD performance.
FAMILY PLANNING PERSPECTIVES. 14:338-339, November-December
1982

Time of application of intrauterine devices in women with prior
voluntary abortions, by C. Balbi, et al. ARCHIVES OF OBSTE-
TRICS AND GYNECOLOGY. 85(3):195-198, May-June 1980

CONTRACEPTIVES: FEMALE: IUD: COMPLICATIONS
Comparison of the Lippes Loop D and tapered Lippes Loop D intra-

uterine devices, by B. Behlilovic, et al. CONTRACEPTION. 25(3):293-298, 1982

Contact dermatitis from a copper-containing intrauterine contraceptive device, by C. Romaguera, et al. CONTACT DERMATITIS. 7(3):163-164, May 1981

Duration of brest-feeding and development of children after insertion of a levo-norgestrel-releasing intrauterine contraceptive device, by M. heikkila, et al. CONTRACEPTION. 25(3):279-292, 1982

Duration of lactation and return of menstruation in lactating women using hormonal contraception and intrauterine devices, by K. Prema. CONTRACEPTIVE DELIVERY SYSTEMS. 3(1):39-46, 1982

Early pregnancy factor as a monitor for fertilization in women wearing intrauterine devices, by Y. C. Smart, et al. FERTILITY AND STERILITY. 37(2):201-204, 1982

Evaluation of the spring coil and Dalkon shield, by H. A. Kisnisci. ACTA REPRODUCTION TURCICA. 3(2):67-72, 1981

Fincoid: a new copper intrauterine device [a preliminary report], by E. Hirvonen, et al. CONTRACEPTIVE DELIVERY SYSTEMS. 3(2):83-90, 1982

Intrauterine devices: mechanism and management of uterine bleeding, by K. Srivastava. JOURNAL OF FAMILY WELFARE. 28:26-33, March 1982

'Lupus' anticoagulant and inhibition of prostacyclin formation in patients with repeated abortions, intrauterine growth retardation and intrauterine death, by L. O. Carreras, et al. BRITISH JOURNAL OF OBSTETRICS AND GYNAECOLOGY. 88(9):890-894, September 1981

Management of amenorrhea due to contraceptive injectables by temporary intrauterine device insertion, by M. Toppozada, et al. CONTRACEPTIVE DELIVERY SYSTEMS. 3(2):127-132, 1982

Menstrual pattern and blood loss with U-coil inert progesterone-releasing intrauterine devices, by F. Hefnawi, et al. CONTRACEPTIVE DELIVERY SYSTEMS. 3(2):91-98, 1982

Ovarian pregnancy: association with IUD, pelvic pathology and recurrent abortion, by J. Reichman, et al. EUROPEAN JOURNAL OF OBSTETRICS, GYNECOLOGY AND REPRODUCTIVE BIOLOGY. 12(6):333-337, December 1981

Patterns of IUD acceptance and removals in a geographically defined urban slum area in Ludhiana, Punjab, by P. S. Zachariah, et al. JOURNAL OF FAMILY WELFARE. 28:70-76, March 1982

Pregnancy rates during long-term use of copper intrauterine devices, by A. Huber, et al. CONTRACEPTIVE DELIVERY SYSTEMS. 3(2):99-102, 1982

CONTRACEPTIVES: FEMALE: IUD: COMPLICATIONS (continued)

The relationship of intrauterine device dimensions to event
rates, by N. D. Goldstuck. CONTRACEPTIVE DELIVERY SYSTEMS.
3(2):103-106, 1982

The role of copper iron in contraception, by E. Kobylec, et al.
GINEKOLOGIA POLSKA. 52(8):751-754, 1981

Role of retention in avoiding expulsion of intrauterine devices:
measuring devices for basic research, by K. H. Kurz. CONTRA-
CEPTIVE DELIVERY SYSTEMS. 3(2):107-116, 1982

CONTRACEPTIVES: FEMALE: IMPLANTED

An intravasal nonocclusive contraceptive device in rats, by M.
m. Misro, et al. JOURNAL OF REPRODUCTIVE FERTILITY. 65(1):
9-14, 1982

Laparoscopic removal of translocated intrauterine contraceptive
devices, by P. J. McKenna, et al. BRITISH JOURNAL OF OBSTE-
TRICS AND GYNAECOLOGY. 89(2):163-165, 1982

Long-term intracervical contraception with a levonorgestrel device, by S. El Mahgoub. CONTRACEPTION. 25(4):357-374, 1982

Menstrual behaviour with steroid implant, by M. N. Pal, et al.
JOURNAL OF THE INDIAN MEDICAL ASSOCIATION. 77(1):16-17, July
1, 1981

Microbial presence in the uterine cavity as affected by varieties of intrauterine contraceptive devices, by M. Skangalils,
et al. FERTILITY AND STERILITY. 37(2):263-269, 1982

Pituitary and ovarian function during contraception with one
subcutaneous implant releasing a progestin, St-1435, by P.
Lahteenmaki, et al. CONTRACEPTION. 25(3):299-306, March 1982

A preliminary report on the intracervical contraceptive device--
its effect on cervical mucus, by H. A. Pattinson, et al. AD-
VANCES IN EXPERIMENTAL MEDICINE AND BIOLOGY. 144:289-291,
1982

A study of the characteristics of acceptors of the Copper-T
device, by V. B. Jalagar, et al. JOURNAL OF FAMILY WELFARE.
28:54-61, June 1982

CONTRACEPTIVES: FEMALE: INJECTED

A clinical trial of norethisterone oenanthate (Norigest) injected every two months, by G. Howard, et al. CONTRACEPTION.
25(4):333-340, April 1982

Continuation of injectable contraceptives in Thailand, by T.
Narkavonnakit, et al. STUDIES IN FAMILY PLANNING. 13(4):99,
April 1982

Curbing sexual appetite (Depo Provera lowers testosterone levels
work of Fred S. Berlin and John Money), by W. Herbert. SCI-
ENCE NEWS. 122:270, October 23, 1982

Depo-Provera debate revs up at FDA, by M. Sun. SCIENCE. 217:

424-428, July 30, 1982

Depo-provera: an injectable contraceptive, by S. Wigington.
NURSING TIMES. 77:1794-1798, October 1981

Experimental study of the effec of rabbits on the injectable
contraceptive medroxyprogesterone acetate, cholesterol feeding
and drug-atherogenic diet combination, by T. H. Al-Shebib, et
al. LABORATORY ANIMALS. 16(1):78-83, January 1982

Fertility regulation in nursing women. II. Comparative perform-
ance of progesterone implants versus placebo and copper T, by
H. B. Croxatto, et al. AMERICAN JOURNAL OF OBSTETRICS AND
GYNECOLOGY. 144(2):201-208, September 15, 1982

Injectable contraception, by P. E. Hall, et al. WORLD HEALTH.
pp. 2-4, May 1982

--. Depo Provera, by G. Howard. LISTENER. 107:4-5, March 4,
1982

Injectable hormonal contraceptives: technical and safety aspects
WHO OFFSET PUBLICATIONS. (65):1-45, 1982

Long-term intracervical contraception with a levonorgestrel device, by S. El Mahgoub. CONTRACEPTION. 25(4):357-374, April
1982

Management of amenorrhea due to contraceptive injectables by
temporary intrauterine device insertion, by M. Toppozada, et
al. CONTRACEPTIVE DELIVERY SYSTEMS. 3(2):127-132, 1982

New hope for the puppy problem (vaccination). TODAY. p. 6,
February 27, 1982

Nine Thai women had cancer--none of them took Depo-provera;
therefore, Depo-provera is safe, by S. Minkin. MOTHER JONES.
6:34+, November 1981

Plasma levels of medroxyprogesterone acetate, sex-hormone binding globulin, gonadal steroids, gonadotropins and prolactin in
women during long-term use of depo-medroxy-progesterone acetate (Depo-Provera) as a contraceptive agent, by S. Jeppsson,
et al. ACTA ENDOCRINOLOGICA. 99(3):339-343, 1982

A preliminary pharmacological trial of the monthly injectable
contraceptive cycloprovera, by K. Fotherby, et al. CONTRACEP-
TION. 25(3):261-272, March 1982

Reduction of fertility of mice by the intrauterine injection
of prostaglandin antagonists, by J. D. Biggers, et al. JOUR-
NAL OF REPRODUCTIVE FERTILITY. 63(2):365-372, November
1981

Some metabolic effects of long-term use of the injectable contraceptive norethisterone oenanthate, by G. Howard, et al.
LANCET. 1(8269):423-425, February 20, 1982

Age-specific secular changes in oral contraceptive use [letter], by S. Shapiro, et al. AMERICAN JOURNAL OF EPIDEMIOLOGY. 114(4):604, October 1981

Better birth control pill seen. NEW YORK TIMES MAGAZINE. p. 33, January 1, 1982

Birth control: 4-day pill is promising in early test, by R. Eder. NEW YORK TIMES MAGAZINE. p. C1, April 20, 1982

Budd-Chiari syndrome and OCs ... oral contraceptives. NURSES DRUG ALERT. 5:86, September 1981

Clinical trial of an oral contraceptive containing desogestrel and ethynyl estradiol, by M. J. Weijerss. CLINICAL THERAPEUTICS. 4(5):359-366, 1982

Contraception: the pill, by V. A. Serrano. AMERICAN DRUGGIST. 185:45+, March 1982

Depo provera in perspective, by I. A. McGoldrick. PAPAU NEW GUINEA MEDICAL JOURNAL. 24(4):274-279, December 1981

The effect on fecundity of pill acceptance during postpartum amenorrhea in rural Bangladesh, by S. Bhatia, et al. STUDIES IN FAMILY PLANNING. 13:200-207, June-July 1982

The enzyme inducing effect of rifampicin in the rhesus monkey (Macaca mulatta) and its lack of interaction with oral contraceptive steroids, by D. J. Back, et al. CONTRACEPTION. 25(3):307-317, 1982

Four-day birth control pill, by S. Katz. CHATELAINE. 55:16, October 1982

The four-day pill (work of Etienne-Emile Baulieu) by R. Mason. HEALTH. 14:20, July 1982

Frank estrogenic action of 1,2-diethyl-1,3-bis-(p-methoxyphenyl)-1-propene: a new oral contraceptive, by A. O. Prakash, et al. INDIAN JOURNAL OF EXPERIMENTAL BIOLOGY. 20(3):253-254, 1982

Hard pill to swallow?, by B. Brophy. FORBES. 129:99, May 10, 1982

Improvement in cervical dysplasia associated with folic acid therapy in users of oral contraceptives, by C. E. Butterworth, Jr., et al. AMERICAN JOURNAL OF CLINICAL NUTRITION. 35:73-82, January 1982

Influence of contraceptive pill and menstrual cycle on serum lipids and high-density lipoprotein cholesterol concentrations, by P. N. M. Dermacker, et al. BRITISH MEDICAL JOURNAL. 6324:1213-1215, April 24, 1982

Living without the pill, by L. McQuaig. MACLEAN'S. 95:40-42+, March 15, 1982

Low dosage oral contraception in women with previous gestational diabetes, by S. O. Skouby, et al. OBSTETRICS AND GYNECOLOGY. 59(3):324-328, 1982

The noncontraceptive health benefits from oral contraceptive use, by H. W. Ory. FAMILY PLANNING PERSPECTIVES. 14:182-184, July-August 1982

Noncontraceptive uses of the pill, by D. R. Halbert. CLINICAL OBSTETRICS AND GYNECOLOGY. 24(3):987-993, September 1981

Normal sister--chromatid exchanges in oral contraceptive users, by B. Husum, et al. MUTATION RESEARCH. 103(2):161-164, 1982

Of menses--pills and IUDs--neisseria--and flings--(with apologies to Lewis Carroll) [editorial], by J. C. Hume. JAMA: JOURNAL OF THE AMERICAN MEDICAL ASSOCIATION. 247(9):1321-1322, March 5, 1982

Oral contraceptive during lactation: a global survey of physician practice, by L. T. Strauss, et al. INTERNATIONAL JOURNAL OF GYNAECOLOGY AND OBSTETRICS. 19(3):169-175, June 1981

The oral contraceptive: past, present and future use, by J. J. Speidel, et al. JOHNS HOPKINS MEDICAL JOURNAL. 150(5):161, 1982

Oral contraceptives in the 1980s. POPULATION REPORTS. 10(3): , May-June 1982

Pill and IUD use at PPFA clinics decline: diaphragm use rises. FAMILY PLANNING PERSPECTIVES. 14:152-153, May-June 1982

Pill does not increase risk of breast cancer, even after years of use. FAMILY PLANNING PERSPECTIVES. 14:216-219, July-August 1982

Pill users protected against PID if they have used OCs for longer than one year. FAMILY PLANNING PERSPECTIVES. 14:32-33, January-February 1982

Prudence since the pill, by H. Chappell. NEW SOCIETY. pp. 372-374, September 2, 1982

A randomized, double-blind study of 2 combined and 2 progestogen-only oral contraceptives, by A. Sheth, et al. CONTRACEPTION. 25(3):243-252, 1982

The risk of myocardial infarction in former users of oral contraceptives, by P. M. Layde, et al. FAMILY PLANNING PERSPECTIVES. 14:78-80, March-April 1982

Sex of offspring of women using oral contraceptives, rhythm and other methods of birth control around the time of conception, by P. H. Shiono, et al. FERTILITY AND STERILITY. 37(3):367-372, 1982

CONTRACEPTIVES: FEMALE: ORAL (continued)

Testing a better birth-control pill. NEWSWEEK. 99:86, May 3, 1982

Twenty years progress in oral contraception. Based on the symposium arranged by Shering Nordiska AB in Stockholm on March 21, 1981 ACTA OBSTETRICIA ET GYNECOLOGICA SCANDINAVICA. SUPPLEMENT. 105:1-71, 1982

Update on oral contraception. CLINICAL OBSTETRICS AND GYNECOLOGY. 24(30:867-996, September 1981

Women who never used pill are twice as likely as users to develop endometrial or ovarian cancer. FAMILY PLANNING PERSPECTIVES. 14:145-146, May-June 1982

CONTRACEPTIVES: FEMALE: ORAL: COMPLICATIONS
Access to data and the information explosion: oral contraceptives and risk of cancer, by J. M. Weiner, et al. CONTRACEPTION. 24(3):301-313, September 1981

Action of oral contraceptives on circulating immune complexes, by B. Petermann, et al. ZENTRALBLATT FUR GYNAEKOLOGIE. 104(6):349-353, 1982

Adrenal function in hirsutism. II. Effect of an oral contraceptive, by R. A. Wild, et al. JOURNAL OF CLINICAL ENDOCRINOLOGY AND METABOLISM. 54(4):676-681, April 1982

Alteration in blood pressures associated with combined alcohol and oral contraceptive use: the Lipid Research Clinics Prevalence study, by R. B. Wallace, et al. JOURNAL OF CHRONIC DISEASES. 35(4):251-258, 1982

Atherosclerosis and oral contraceptive use. Serum from oral contraceptive users stimulates growth of arterial smooth muscle cells, by J. D. Bagdade, et al. ARTERIOSCLEROSIS. 2(2):170-176, March-April 1982

Atypical reserve cell hyperplasia of cervical glands, simulating adenocarcinoma. An undescribed reversible lesion in a woman taking oral contraceptives, by M. Filotico, et al. TUMORI. 67(5):491-496, October 31, 1981

Benefit of the 'pill' may outweigh the risks [news]. AMERICAN FAMILY PHYSICIAN. 26(3):258-259, September 1982

Benign hepatic tumour and oral contraception, by A. Lavy, et al. HAREFUAH. 102(3):107-108, February 1, 1982

Birth control pills and pancreatitis, by J. W. Liu. MARYLAND STATE MEDICAL JOURNAL. 31(2):66-67, February 1982

Bitter pill: the birth control pill is losing popularity as evidence mounts about its harmful side effects, by G. B. Sinclair. SATURDAY NIGHT. 96:13, December 16, 1981

Blood levels of ethynylestradiol, caffeine, aldosterone and desoxycorticosterone in hypertensive oral contraceptive users, by L. Kaul, et al. CONTRACEPTION. 23(6):643-651, June 1981

Blood pressure and contraceptive use, by C. R. Kay. BRITISH
MEDICAL JOURNAL. 285(6343):737-738, September 11, 1982

--, by K. T. Khaw, et al. BRITISH MEDICAL JOURNAL. 285(6339):
403-407, August 7, 1982

Breast cancer and oral contraception: findings in Oxford-Family
Planning Association contraceptive study, by M. P. Vessey, et
al. BRITISH MEDICAL JOURNAL. 282(6282):2093-2094, 1981

Breast cancer and the pill [editorial], by I. S. Fraser. MEDI-
CAL JOURNAL OF AUSTRALIA. 1(1):6, January 9, 1982

Breast cancer and use of antihypertensive drugs and oral contraceptives: results of a case-control study, by F. Clavel, et
al. BULLETIN DU CANCER. 68(5):449-455, 1981

Breast cancer, pregnancy, and the pill, by J. O. Drife. BRITISH
MEDICAL JOURNAL. 283(6294):778-779, September 19, 1981

Budd-Chiari syndrome and hepatic adenomas associated with oral
contraceptives [a case report], by H. K. Tong, et al. SINGA-
PORE MEDICAL JOURNAL. 22(3):168-172, June 1981

Cardiovascular effects and progestins in oral contraceptives,
by V. Wynn. AMERICAN JOURNAL OF OBSTETRICS AND GYNECOLOGY.
142(6 Pt 2):718, March 15, 1982

A case-control study of cancer of the endometrium, by J. L. Kelsey, et al. AMERICAN JOURNAL OF EPIDEMIOLOGY. 116(2):333-
342, August 1982

A case of hepatoma in pregnancy associated with earlier oral
contraception, by S. E. Christensen, et al. ACTA OBSTETRICIA
ET GYNECOLOGICA SCANDINAVICA. 60(5):519, 1981

Case records of the Massachusetts General Hospital. Weekly
clinicopathological exercises. Case 40-1982. Tender hepatomegaly in a 29-year-old woman. NEW ENGLAND JOURNAL OF MED-
ICINE. 307(15):934-942, October 7, 1982

Cervical adenocarcinoma in users of oral contraceptives [clini-
cal case], by E. Roa, et al. REVISTA CHILENA DE OBSTETRICIA Y
GINECOLOGIA. 45(4):225-228, 1980

Changes in physiological, EEG, and psychological paremeters in
women during the spontaneous menstrual cycle and following
oral contraceptives, by D. Becker, et al. PSYCHONEUROEN-
DOCRINOLOGY. 7(1):75-90, March 1982

The chromosomal effects of the oral contraceptive, by N. P. Bishun. JOURNAL OF SURGICAL ONCOLOGY. 20(2):115-118, June 1982

Chronic intestinal ischemia associated with oral contraceptive
use, by G. L. Arnold, et al. AMERICAN JOURNAL OF GASTROEN-
TEROLOGY. 77(1):32-34, January 1982

Clinical and biochemical results during the treatment with marvelon, a new oral contraceptive, by M. Mall-Haefeli, et al. GEBURTSHILFE UND FRAUENHEILKUNDE. 42(3):215-222, March 1982

Clinical pharmacology and common minor side effects of oral contraceptives, by J. E. DeLia, et al. CLINICAL OBSTETRICS AND GYNECOLOGY. 24(3):879-892, September 1981

Coagulation factors in women using oral contraceptives or intrauterine contraceptive devices immediately after abortion, by P. Lahteenmaki, et al. AMERICAN JOURNAL OF OBSTETRICS AND GYNECOLOGY. 141(2):175-179, September 15, 1981

Complications and contraindications of oral contraception, by W. W. Beck, Jr. CLINICAL OBSTETRICS AND GYNECOLOGY. 24(3):893-901, September 1981

Complications of pregnancy and labor in former oral contraceptive users, by S. Harlap, et al. CONTRACEPTION. 24(1):1-13, July 1981

Contraception and toxic-shock syndrome: a reanalysis, by J. D. Shelton, et al. CONTRACEPTION. 24(6):631-634, December 1981

Contraceptive steroids, age, and the cardiovascular system, by E. R. Plunkett. AMERICAN JOURNAL OF OBSTETRICS AND GYNECOLOGY. 142(6 Pt 2):747-751, March 15, 1982

Contraceptives and the conceptus. II. Sex of the fetus and neonate after oral contraceptive use, by H. P. Klinger, et al. CONTRACEPTION. 23(4):367-374, April 1981

Contraceptives and the liver, by M. Schmid. LEBER, MAGEN, DARM. 11(5):216-226, September 1981

Court finds pill defectively designed. TRIAL. 17(6):13, June 1981

Delay in conception for former pill users, by S. Linn, et al. JAMA: JOURNAL OF THE AMERICAN MEDICAL ASSOCIATION. 247(5): 629-632, February 5, 1982

Dilatation of hepatic sinusoids after use of oral contraceptives by M. Balazs, et al. DEUTSCHE MEDIZINISCHE WOCHENSCHRIFT. 106(41):1345-1349, October 9, 1981

Dilatation of hepatic sinusoids caused by oral contraceptives, by M. Balazs, et al. ORVOSI HETILAP. 122(34):2071-2074, August 23, 1981

Discontinuance of oral contraceptives [letter], by P. T. Hohe. ARCHIVES OF INTERNAL MEDICINE. 142(8):1585, August 1982

Does oral contraception cause deep venous thromboses?, by R. Lambrecht, et al. ZENTRALBLATT FUR CHIRURGIE. 106(6):1074-1080, 1981

Effect of blood pressure or changing from high to low dose

steroid preparations in women with oral contraceptive induced hypertension, by R. J. Weir. SCOTTISH MEDICAL JOURNAL. 27(3):212-215, July 1982

Effect of combined oral contraceptives on glycosylated haemo-globin, by N. Oakley, et al. JOURNAL OF THE ROYAL SOCIETY OF MEDICINE. 75(4):234-236, April 1982

The effect of a contraceptive vaginal ring and oral contracep-tives on the vaginal flora, by S. Roy, et al. CONTRACEPTION. 24(4):481-491, October 1981

Effect of contraceptives on the digestibility of dietary protein and nitrogen balance, by K. Gruhn, et al. NAHRUNG. 25(8): 779-788, 1981

Effect of duration of low-dose oral contraceptive administration on carbohydrate metabolism, by V. Wynn. AMERICAN JOURNAL OF OBSTETRICS AND GYNECOLOGY. 142(6 Pt 2):739-746, March 15, 1982

Effect of low gestagen doses on the kidneys and urodynamics of the upper urinary tract, by A. G. Khomauridze, et al. AKU-SHERSTVO I GINEKOLOGIIA. (4):56-57, April 1982

Effect of menstrual cycle and method of contraception on recover of neisseria gonorrhoeae, by W. M. McCormack, et al. JAMA: JOURNAL OF THE AMERICAN MEDICAL ASSOCIATION. 247(9):1292-1294, March 5, 1982

The effect of oral contraceptive on serum bile acids and liver function routine tests, by R. Ferraris, et al. PANMINERVA MEDICA. 23(2):89-92, April-June 1981

The effect of oral contraceptives on antiaggregatory prostacyc-lin and proaggregatory thromboxane A2 in humans, by O. Ylikor-kala, et al. AMERICAN JOURNAL OF OBSTETRICS AND GYNECOLOGY. 142(5):573-576, March 1, 1982

Effect of oral contraceptives on reproductive function during semichronic exposure to ethanol in the female rat, by C. D. Lox, et al. GENERAL PHARMACOLOGY. 13(1):53-56, 1982

The effects of ampicillin oral contraceptive steroids in women, by D. J. Back, et al. BRITISH JOURNAL OF CLINICAL PHARMA-COLOGY. 14(1):43-48, July 1982

Effects of smoking and the pill on the blood count, by H. Dods-worth, et al. BRITISH JOURNAL OF HAEMATOLOGY. 49(3):484-488, November 1981

"Effort thrombosis" of the subclavian vein associated with oral contraceptives ... [case report], by S. J. Stricker, et al. ANNALS OF EMERGENCY MEDICINE. 10:596-599, November 1981

Endocrinological changes in depression caused by oral contracep-tives, by T. Namba, et al. JOURNAL OF THE MEDICAL SOCIETY OF TOKO UNIVERSITY. 28(4):594-599, 1981

Endometrial cancer, epidemiology, and medical practice [editorial], by K. J. Ryan. JAMA: JOURNAL OF THE AMERICAN MEDICAL ASSOCIATION. 247(4):496, January 22-29, 1982

Endometrial morphology and peripheal steroid levels in women with and without intermenstrual bleeding during contraception with the 300 microgram norethisteone minipill, by E. Johannisson, et al. CONTRACEPTION. 25(1):13-30, 1982

Epistaxis secondary to oral contraceptive, by A. Man, et al. ACTA OTO-LARYNGOLOGICA. 92(3-4):383-384, September-October 1981

Epithelial ovarian cancer and combination oral contraceptives, by L. Rosenberg, et al. JAMA: JOURNAL OF THE AMERICAN MEDICAL ASSOCIATION. 247(23):3210-3212, June 18, 1982

Evidence against oral contraceptives as a cause of neural-tube defects, by H. S. Cuckle, et al. BRITISH JOURNAL OF OBSTETRICS AND GYNAECOLOGY. 89(7):547-549, July 1982

Factors affecting riboflavin requirements of oral contraceptive users and nonusers, by D. A. Roe, et al. AMERICAN JOURNAL OF CLINICAL NUTRITION. 35(3):495-501, March 1982

Failure of p-pills and anticonvulsants, by L. Gram. UGESKRIFT FOR LAEGER. 143(37):2364-2365, September 7, 1981

Failure with the new triphasic oral contraceptive Logynon [letter]. BRITISH MEDICAL JOURNAL. 284(6313):422-423, February 6, 1982

--[letter], by R. A. Fay. BRITISH MEDICAL JOURNAL. 284(6308): 17-18, June 2, 1982

The fallacy of the postpill amenorrhea syndrome, by D. F. Archer, et al. CLINICAL OBSTETRICS AND GYNECOLOGY. 24(3): 943-950, September 1981

Fibrinolytic activity of uterine fluid in oral contraceptive users, by B. Casslen. CONTRACEPTION. 25(5):515-521, May 1982

Flow properties of blood in women on oral contraceptives, by L. Heilmann, et al. ZENTRALBLATT FUR GYNAEKOLOGIE. 103(12):678-686, 1981

Free norethisterone as reflected by saliva concentrations of norethisterone during oral contraceptive use, by V. Odinod, et al. ACTA ENDOCRINOLOGICA. 98(3):470-476, November 1981

Galactorrhea in oral contraceptive users, by G. Holtz. JOURNAL OF REPRODUCTIVE MEDICINE. 27(4):210-212, April 1982

Gallbladder function in the human female: effect of the ovulator cycle, pregnancy, and contraceptive steroids, by G. T. Everson, et al. GASTROENTEROLOGY. 82(4):711-719, April 1982

Headache and oral contraceptives, by W. Farias da Silva, et al.

NEUROBIOLOGIA. 41(1):29-42, January-March 1978

Hepatic adenoma associated with oral contraceptives, by A. B. Woodyer. JOURNAL OF THE ROYAL COLLEGE OF SURGEONS OF EDIN- BURGH. 27(1):59-60, January 1982

Hepatocellular carcinoma in women: probable lack of etiologic association with oral contraceptive steroids, by Z. D. Good- man, et al. HEPATOLOGY. 2(4):440-444, July-August 1982

High density lipoprotein choleteron and apolipoprotein A-I level in 32-33-year-old women on steroid contraceptive-differences between two frequently used low-estrogen pills, by L. Havekes, et al. CLINICA CHIMICA ACTA. 116(2):223-229, October 26, 1981

Hypophyseal reaction state during oral contraception, by E. Gitsch, et al. WIENER KLINISCHE WOCHENSCHRIFT. 93(19):599- 601, October 16, 1981

Ileitis (probable Crohn's disease) and oral contraceptives, by J. Husson. SEMAINES DES HOPITAUX DE PARIS. 57(41-42):1750- 1751, November 8-25, 1981

Immune reactivity and the vascular risk in oral contraceptive users, by J. L. Beaumont, et al. AMERICAN JOURNAL OF REPRO- DUCTIVE IMMUNOLOGY. 1(3):119-125, 1981

Impact of synthetic sexual steroids on blood volume, by G. Klinger, et al. ZENTRALBLATT FUR GYNAEKOLOGIE. 104(6):343- 348, 1982

Improvement in cervical dysplasia associated with folic acid therapy in users of oral contraceptives, by C. E. Butterworth, et al. AMERICAN JOURNAL OF CLINICAL NUTRITION. 35(1):73-82, January 1982

Incidence of ovarian cancer in relation to the use of oral con- traceptives, by N. S. Weiss, et al. INTERNATIONAL JOURNAL OF CANCER. 28(6):669-671, December 1981

Inferior vena cava stenosis and Budd-Chiari syndrome in a woman taking oral contraceptives, by G. Lalonde, et al. GASTROEN- TEROLOGY. 82(6):1452-1456, June 1982

Inflammatory disease associated with oral contraceptive use [letter], by S. H. Swan. LANCET. 2(8250):809, October 10, 1981

Influence of contraceptive pill and menstrual cycle on serum lipids and high-density lipoprotein cholesterol concentra- tions, by P. N. Demacker, et al. BRITISH MEDICAL JOURNAL. 284(6324):1213-1215, April 24, 1982

Influence of estrogen content of oral contraceptives and con- sumption of sucrose on blood parameters, by K. E. M. Behall. DISSERTATION ABSTRACTS INTERNATIONAL. B. p. 1437, 1982

Influence of oral contraceptive therapy on the activity of systemic lupus erythematosus, by P. Jungers, et al. ARTHRITIS
AND RHEUMATISM. 25(6):618-623, June 1982

The influence of oral contraceptives on the composition of bile,
by P. Brockerhoff, et al. KLINISCHE WOCHENSCHRFIT. 60(3):
153-157, February 1, 1982

The influence of pregnancy and contraceptive pills upon oxygen
consumption during phagocytosis by human leukocytes, by B.
Kvarstein, et al. ACTA OBSTETRICIA ET GYNECOLOGICA SCANDINA-
VICA. 60(5):505-506, 1981

Influence of sex and oral contraceptive steroids on antipyrine
metabolite formation, by M. W. Teunissen, et al. CLINICAL
PHARMACOLOGY AND THERAPEUTICS. 32(2):240-246, August 1982

The interaction of cigarette smoking, oral contraceptive use,
and cardiovascular risk factor variables in children: the
Bogalusa Heart Study, by L. S. Webber, et al. AMERICAN JOUR-
NAL OF PUBLIC HEALTH. 72(3):266-274, March 1982

Interactions between contraceptive pills and other drugs, by L.
Nir, et al. HAREFUAH. 100(12):590-591, June 15, 1981

Interactions with the p-pill [letter], by M. B. Kristensen.
UGESKRIFT FOR LAEGER. 143(11):698, March 15, 1981

Is there good news about the pill?, by C. Safran. MADEMOISELLE.
88:150-151+, December 1982

Liver adenoma with granulomas. The appearance of granulomas in
oral contraceptive-related hepatocellular adenoma and in the
surrounding nontumorous liver, by D. A. Malatjalian, et al.
ARCHIVES OF PATHOLOGY AND LABORATORY MEDICINE. 106(5):244-
246, May 1982

The liver and the 'pill'. 1: Disorders of bile secretion and
vessel changes, by J. Eisenburg. FORTSCHRITTE DER MEDIZIN.
99(37):1479-1483, October 1, 1981

--2: Liver tumors, by J. Eisenburg. FORTSCHRITTE DER MEDIZIN.
99(38):1527-1532, October 8, 1981

Liver lesions and oral contraceptives [letter], by A. N. Freedman. CANADIAN MEDICAL ASSOCIATION JOURNAL. 126(10):1149-
1150, May 15, 1982

Living without the pill, by L. McQuaig. MACLEAN'S. 95:40-42+,
March 15, 1982

Low dosage oral contraception in women with previous gestational
diabetes, by S. O. Skouby, et al. OBSTETRICS AND GYNECOLOGY.
59(3):325-328, March 1982

Malignant hypertension and oral contraceptives: four cases, with
two due to the 30 micrograms oestrogen pill, by G. P. Hodsman,
et al. EUROPEAN HEART JOURNAL. 3(3):255-259, June 1982

Malignant mammary tumors in beagle dogs dosed with investigational oral contraceptive steroids, by R. P. Kwapien, et al.
JNCI: JOURNAL OF THE NATIONAL CANCER INSTITUTE. 65(1):137-
144, July 1980

Megadose vitamin C and metabolic effects of the pill [letter],
by M. H. Briggs. BRITISH MEDICAL JOURNAL. 283(6305):1547,
December 5, 1981

Menstrual cycle and oral contraceptive effects on alcohol pharmacokinetics in caucasian females, by A. R. Zeiner, et al.
CURRENTS IN ALCOHOLISM. 8:47-56, 1981

Metabolic effects of the birth control pill, by S. Sondheimer.
CLINICAL OBSTETRICS AND GYNECOLOGY. 24(3):927-941, September
1981

Metabolic studies in gestational diabetic women during contraceptive treatment: effects on glucose tolerance and fatty acid
composition of serum lipids, by T. Radberg, et al. GYNECOL-
OGIC AND OBSTETRIC INVESTIGATION. 13(1):17-29, 1982

Metoprolol pharmacokinetics and the oral contraceptive pill, by
M. J. Kendall, et al. BRITISH JOURNAL OF CLINICAL PHARMA-
COLOGY. 14(1):120-122, July 1982

Microcirculation and oral contraceptives, by J. F. Merlen.
PHLEBOLOGIE. 35(2):631-637, April-June 1982

Multiple pregnancy and fetal abnormalities in association with
oral contraceptive usage, by D. C. Macourt, et al. AUSTRALIAN
AND NEW ZEALAND JOURNAL OF OBSTETRICS AND GYNAECOLOGY. 22(1):
25-28, February 1982

Neurologic and cerebrovascular pathology during treatment with
oral contraceptives, by V. Sbarbaro, et al. RIVISTA DI NEURO-
BIOLOGIA. 26(4):453-462, October-December 1980

New studies of malignant melanoma, gallbladder and heart disease
help further define pill risk. FAMILY PLANNING PERSPECTIVES.
14:95-97, March-April 1982

Noncontraceptive health benefits of oral steroidal contraceptives, by D. R. Mishell, Jr. AMERICAN JOURNAL OF OBSTETRICS
AND GYNECOLOGY. 142(6 Pt 2):809-816, March 15, 1982

Norethisterone, a major ingredient of contraceptive pills, is a
suicide inhibitor of estrogen biosynthesis (inhibitor of estrogen synthetase), by Y. Osawa, et al. SCIENCE. 215(4537):
1249-1251, March 5, 1982

Normal sister-chromatid exchanges in oral contraceptive users,
by B. Husum, et al. MUTATION RESEARCH. 103(2):161-164,
February 1982

OCs do not add to risk of birth defects. NURSES DRUG ALERT.
6:3, January 1982

Occurrence and histological structure of adenocarcinoma of the endocervix after long-term use of oral contraceptives, by G. Dallenbach-Hellweg. GEBURTSHILFE UND FRAUENHEILKUNDE. 42(4): 249-255, April 1982

Optic nerve drusen and pseudopapilledema, by I. F. Gutteridge. AMERICAN JOURNAL OF OPTOMETRY AND PHYSIOLOGICAL OPTICS. 58(8):671-676, August 1981

Oral contraception and breast pathology, by N. Ragni, et al. ACTA EUROPAEA FERTILITATIS. 12(2):141-163, June 1981

Oral contraception and cancer risk, by C. Y. Genton. SCHWEIZERISCHE MEDIZINISCHE WOCHENSCHRIFT. 111(46):1742-1748, November 14, 1981

Oral contraception and cerebrovascular accidents, by J. Nick, et al. BULLETIN DE L'ACADEMIE NATIONALE DE MEDICINE. 165(6): 723-730, June 1981

Oral contraception and myocardial infarction revisited: the effects of new preparations and prescribing patterns, by P. Bye. BRITISH JOURNAL OF OBSTETRICS AND GYNAECOLOGY. 88(11): 1167-1168, November 1981

Oral contraception and some debatable side effects, by B. Astedt. ACTA OBSTETRICIA ET GYNECOLOGICA SCANDINAVICA. SUPPLEMENT. 105:17-23, 1982

Oral contraception as a risk factor for preeclampsia, by M. B. Bracken, et al. AMERICAN JOURNAL OF OBSTETRICS AND GYNECOLOGY. 142(2):191-196, January 15, 1982

Oral contraception, circulating immune complexes, antiethinylestradiol antibodies, and thrombosis, by V. Beaumont, et al. AMERICAN JOURNAL OF REPRODUCTIVE IMMUNOLOGY. 2(1):8-12, February 1982

Oral contraception in diabetic women. Diabetes control, serum and high density lipoprtein lipids during low-dose progestogen, combined oestrogen/progestogen and non-hormonal contraception, by Radberg, et al. ACTA ENDOCRINOLOGICA. 98(2):246-251, October 1981

Oral contraception in patients with hyperprolactinaemia, by P. J. Moult, et al. BRITISH MEDICAL JOURNAL. 284(6319):868, March 20, 1982

Oral contraceptive and cardiovascular disease: some questions and answers, by M. P. Vessey. BRITISH MEDICAL JOURNAL. 6316: 615-616, February 27, 1982

Oral contraceptive exposure of amenorrheic women with and without prolactinomas, by J. R. Jones, et al. INTERNATIONAL JOURNAL OF GYNAECOLOGY AND OBSTETRICS. 19(5):381-387, October 1981

On oral contraceptive safety: cardiovascular problems [editor-

ial], by R. A. Edgren. INTERNATIONAL JOURNAL OF FERTILITY.
26(4):241-244, 1981

Oral contraceptive steroid concentrations in smokers and nonsmokers, by F. E. Crawford, et al. BRITISH MEDICAL JOURNAL.
282(6279):1824, 1981

Oral contraceptive steroids and malignancy, by E. Grant. CLINI-
CAL ONCOLOGY. 8(2):97-102, June 1982

Oral contraceptive use and abortion before first term pregnancy
in relation to breast cancer risk, by M. P. Vessey, et al.
BRITISH JOURNAL OF CANCER. 45(3):327-331, March 1982

Oral contraceptive use and malignant melanoma, by C. Bain, et
al. JNCI: JOURNAL OF THE NATIONAL CANCER INSTITUTE. 68(4):
537-539, April 1982

Oral contraceptives and blood coagulation [a critical review],
by E. F. Mammen. AMERICAN JOURNAL OF OBSTETRICS AND GYNE-
COLOGY. 142(6 Pt 2):781-790, March 15, 1982

Oral contraceptives and cancer of the liver: a review with two
additional cases, by T. S. Helling, et al. AMERICAN JOURNAL
OF GASTROENTEROLOGY. 77(7):504-508, July 1982

Oral contraceptives and cardiovascular disease [letter], by H.
Ratner. NEW ENGLAND JOURNAL OF MEDICINE. 306(17):1052-1053,
April 29, 1982

--: some questions and answers [editorial], by M. P. Vessey.
BRITISH MEDICAL JOURNAL. 284(6316):615-616, February 27, 1982

Oral contraceptives and circulatory disease [letter]. FERTILITY
AND STERILITY. 36(3):412-417, September 1981

Oral contraceptives and depression: impact, prevalence and cause
by G. B. Slap. JOURNAL OF ADOLESCENT HEALTH CARE. 2(1):53-
64, September 1981

Oral contraceptives and diabetes mellitus, by L. M. Pedersen.
UGESKRIFT FOR LAEGER. 144(4):261-263, January 25, 1982

Oral contraceptives and hepatic tumors, by J. H. Wilson. AGRES-
SOLOGIE. 23(A):21-23, January 1982

Oral contraceptives and hepatocellular carcinoma, by S. R. Shar,
et al. CANCER. 49(2):407-410, January 15, 1982

Oral contraceptives and nonfatal vascular disease--recent experience, by J. B. Porter, et al. OBSTETRICS AND GYNECOLOGY.
59(3):299-302, March 1982

Oral contraceptives and postoperative venous thrombosis, by F.
DeStefano, et al. AMERICAN JOURNAL OF OBSTETRICS AND GYNE-
COLOGY. 143(2):227-228, May 15, 1982

Oral contraceptives and prolactinomas [a case-control study], by

R. Maheux, et al. AMERICAN JOURNAL OF OBSTETRICS AND GYNE-
COLOGY. 143(2):134-138, May 15, 1982

Oral contraceptives and the risk of myocardial infarction
[letter]. NEW ENGLAND JOURNAL OF MEDICINE. 305(25):1530-
1531, December 17, 1981

Oral contraceptives and risk of ovarian cancer, by W. C. Willett, et al. CANCER. 48(7):1684-1687, October 1, 1981

Oral contraceptives and venous thromboembolism, by A. Bergqvist,
et al. BRITISH JOURNAL OF OBSTETRICS AND GYNAECOLOGY. 89(5):
381-386, May 1982

Oral contraceptives, clotting factors, and thrombosis, by T. W.
Meade. AMERICAN JOURNAL OF OBSTETRICS AND GYNECOLOGY. 142(6
Pt 2):758-761, March 15, 1982

Oral contraceptives: effect of folate and vitamin B12 metabolism, by A. M. Shojania. CANADIAN MEDICAL ASSOCIATION JOURNAL.
126(3):244-247, February 1, 1982

Oral contraceptives: where are the excess deaths?, by R. P.
Shearman. MEDICAL JOURNAL OF AUSTRALIA. 1(13):698-700, June
27, 1981

--[letter], by M. P. Vessey, et al. MEDICAL JOURNAL OF AUS-
TRALIA. 2(8):390, October 17, 1981

Oral hormonal contraceptives and benign liver tumors, by J.
Giedl, et al. FORTSCHRITTE DER MEDIZIN. 99(6):165-170,
February 12, 1981

The P pill and liver disease, by L. Ranek, et al. UGESKRIFT FOR
LAEGER. 144(3):165-166, January 18, 1982

P-pills [letter]. UGESKRIFT FOR LAEGER. 143(12):768-769, March
16, 1981

P-pills and hypertension, by K. Rasmussen. UGESKRIFT FOR
LAEGER. 144(7):491-492, February 15, 1982

P-pills nad inflammatory intestinal disease, by J. N. Sørensen, et al. UGESKRIFT FOR LAEGER. 143(37):2365-2366, September 7, 1981

Peliosis hepatis, oral contraceptives and hepatic carcinoma: a
case treated surgically, by J. Tocornal, et al. REVISTA MED-
ICA DE CHILE. 109(3):236-238, March 1981

Pelvic inflammatory disease among women using copper intrauterine devices, progestasert, oral contraceptive pills or vaginal
contraceptive pills. A 4-year prospective investigation, by B.
Larsson, et al. CONTRACEPTIVE DELIVERY SYSTEMS. 2(3):237-
242, 1981

Perceived physician humaneness, patient atitude, and satisfaction with the pill as a contraceptive, by D. J. Kallen, et al.

JOURNAL OF HEALTH AND SOCIAL BEHAVIOR. 22(3):256-267, September 1981

Phlegmasia cerulea dolens as a complication of short-course oral contraceptives for dysfunctional bleeding, by C. C. Coddington. SOUTHERN MEDICAL JOURNAL. 75(3):377-378, March 1982

Pill and breast cancer; few answers yet. NEW SCIENTIST. 91:7, July 2, 1981

Pill & diazepam, by S. Katz. CHATELAINE. 55:26, August 1982

The pill and the thoracic outlet and bilatera carpal tunnel syndromes, by J. C. Chisholm. JOURNAL OF THE NATIONAL MEDICAL ASSOCIATION. 73(10):995-996, October 1981

Pill-induced disability (information from interview with Susan Odgers), by A. Fugh-Berman. OFF OUR BACKS. 12:11+, January 1982

Pituitary response to LHRH stimulation in women on oral contraceptives: a followup dose rsponse study, by L. S. Wan, et al. CONTRACEPTION. 24(3):229-234, September 1981

Plasma and erythrocyte membrane fatty acids in oral contraceptive users, by A. M. Fehily, et al. CLINICA CHIMICA ACTA. 120(1):41-47, March 26, 1982

Plasma levels of ethinylestradiol (EE) during cyclic treatment with combined oral contraceptives, by J. M. Kaufman, et al. CONTRACEPTION. 24(5):589-602, November 1981

Platelet aggregation in response to 5-HT in migraine patients taking oral contraceptives [letter], by E. Hanington, et al. LANCET. 1(8278):967-968, April 24, 1982

Portal and superior mesenteric venous thrombosis secondary to oral contraceptive trreatment, by D. Abet, et al. JOURNAL DES MALADIES VASCULAIRES. 7(1):59-63, 1982

Portal vein thrombosis and fatal pulmonary thromboembolism associated with oral contraceptive treatment, by J. P. Capron, et al. JOURNAL OF CLINICAL GASTROENTEROLOGY. 3(3):295-298, September 1981

Possible interactions of antihistamines and antibiotics with oral contraceptive effectiveness, by E. A. DeSano, Jr., et al. FERTILITY AND STERILITY. 37(6):853-854, June 1982

Post-pill amenorrhea [a causal study], by M. G. Hull, et al. FERTILITY AND STERILITY. 36(4):472-476, October 1981

Postpill pregnancies last longer. NURSES DRUG ALERT. 6:10, February 1982

The post-pill secondary amenorrhea: etiology and treatment, by J. Del Olmo, et al. ACTA EUROPAEA FERTILITATIS. 12(2):133-139, June 1981

A preliminary report on the relationship between serum antithrombin III concentration in pre- and post-operative patients
and in women on oral contraceptives, by S. H. Ton, et al.
MEDICAL JOURNAL OF MALAYSIA. 36(4):212-214, December 1981

Premenstrual complaints II. Influence of oral contraceptives, by
B. Andersch, et al. ACTA OBSTETRICIA ET GYNECOLOGICA SCAN-
DINAVICA. 60(6):579-583, 1981

A prospective cohort study of oral contraceptives and breast
cancer, by E. J. Trapido. JNCI: JOURNAL OF THE NATIONAL
CANCER INSTITUTE. 67(5):1011-1015, November 1981

Protection against endometrial carcinoma by combination-product
oral contraceptives, by B. S. Hulka, et al. JAMA: JOURNAL OF
THE AMERICAN MEDICAL ASSOCIATION. 247(4):475-477, January
22-29, 1982

--[letter], by J. R. Evrard. JAMA: JOURNAL OF THE AMERICAN
MEDICAL ASSOCIATION. 248(6):647-648, August 13, 1982

Protection of ovarian function by oral contraceptives in women
receiving chemotherapy for Hodgkin's disease, by R. M. Chapman, et al. BLOOD. 58(4):849-851, October 1981

Quantitative analysis of ethynodiol diacetate and ethynyl
estradiol--mestranol in oral contraceptive tablets by
high-performane liquid chromatography, by G. B. Carignan, et
al. JOURNAL OF PHARMACEUTICAL SCIENCES. 71(2):264-266, 1982

A randomized, double-blind study of 6 combined oral contraceptives, by S. Koetsawang, et al. CONTRACEPTION. 25(3):231-
242, 1982

Randomized prospective studies on metabolic effects of oral
contraceptives, by M. H. Briggs, et al. ACTA OBSTETRICIA ET
GYNECOLOGICA SCANDINAVICA. SUPPLEMENT. 105:25-32, 1982

Recurrent hemolytic uremic syndrome during oral contraception,
by D. Hauglustaine, et al. CLINICAL NEPHROLOGY. 15(3):148-
153, March 1981

Regression of liver cell adenoma. A follow-up study of three
consecutive patients after discontinuation of oral contraceptive use, by H. Buhler, et al. GASTROENTEROLOGY. 82(4):775-
782, April 1982

The relation between oral contraceptive use and subsequent
development of hyperprolactinemia, by S. Z. Badawy, et al.
FERTILITY AND STERILITY. 36(4):464-467, October 1981

The relationship of static muscle function to use of oral contraceptives, by J. C. Wirth, et al. MEDICINE AND SCIENCE IN
SPORTS AND EXERCISE. 14(1):16-20, 1982

Report from an international symposium about advantages and
risks of oral contraceptives, Amsterdam, March 1982, by K.
Andersson. JORDEMODERN. 95(7-8):244-251, July-August 1982

A review of problems of bias and confounding in epidemiologic studies of cervical neoplasia and oral contraceptive use, by S. H. Swan, et al. AMERICAN JOURNAL OF EPIDEMIOLOGY. 115(1): 10-18, January 1982

Review: oral contraceptives and menopausal estrogens in relation to breast neoplasia, by A. Brzezinski, et al. ISRAEL JOURNAL OF MEDICAL SCIENCES. 18(4):433-438, April 1982

Risk factors for benign breast disease [letter], by D. Glebatis. AMERICAN JOURNAL OF EPIDEMIOLOGY. 115(5):795-797, May 1982

Risk factors in breast cancer, by R. Scolozzi, et al. RECENTI PROGRESSI IN MEDICINA. 70(5):463-486, May 1981

The risk of myocardial infarction in former users of oral contraceptives, by P. M. Layde, et al. FAMILY PLANNING PERSPECTIVES. 14(2):78-80, March-April 1982

Risk of myocardial infarction in relation to current and discontinued use of oral contraceptives, by D. Slone, et al. NEW ENGLAND JOURNAL OF MEDICINE. 305:420-424, August 20, 1981

The risks and benefits of oral contraceptives in the developing world. Past experiences and future perspectives, by M. A. Belsey. ACTA OBSTETRICIA ET GYNECOLOGICA SCANDINAVICA. SUPPLEMENT. 105:61-70, 1982

The role of augmented Hageman factor (factor XII) titers in the cold-promoted activation of factor VII and spontaneous shortening of the prothrombin time in women using oral contraceptives, by E. M. Gordon, et al. JOURNAL OF LABORATORY AND CLINICAL MEDICINE. 99(3):363-369, March 1982

Secondary hyperparathyroidism caused by oral contraceptives, by A. M. Moses, et al. ARCHIVES OF INTERNAL MEDICINE. 142(1): 128-129, January 1982

Serum iron concentrations in women applying Angravid (Polfa) preparation as contraceptive means, by R. Mierzwinski, et al. GINEKOLOGIA POLSKA. 52(8):747-750, 1981

Serum 25-hydroxycholecalciferol levels in women using oral contraceptives, by W. H. Schreurs, et al. CONTRACEPTION. 23(4):399-406, April 1981

Sex hormone binding globulin levels in hirsuite patients: the effect of combined oral contraceptives, by O. F. Giwa-Osagie, et al. CONTRACEPTIVE DELIVERY SYSTEMS. 3(2):155-160, 1982

Sex of offspring of women using oral contraceptives, rhythm, and other methods of birth control around the time of conception, by P. H. Shiono, ete al. FERTILITY AND STERILITY. 37(3):367-372, March 1982

Skin changes caused by oral contraceptives. Interview with Dr. H. Zaun, Director of the University Skin Clinic, Homburg/Saar [interview by M. Minker], by H. Zaun. THERAPIE DER GEGENWART.

121(3):146-151, March 1982

Smoking, oral contraceptives, and serum lipid and lipoprotein
levels in youths, by A. W. Voors, et al. PREVENTIVE MEDICINE.
11(1):1-12, January 1982

Smoking, oral contraceptives, and thromboembolic disease, by F.
M. Sturtevant. INTERNATIONAL JOURNAL OF FERTILITY. 27(1):2-
26, 1982

Some long term problems with the pill [editorial]. NEW ZEALAND
MEDICAL JOURNAL. 94(689):92, August 12, 1982

Status of the reproductive system in women taking oral contraceptive for a long time, by A. G. Khomasuridze, et al.
AKUSHERSTVO I GINEKOLOGIIA. (12):17-20, December 1981

Studies continue to explore possible association between pill
and breast cancer; most find none. FAMILY PLANNING PERSPEC-
TIVES. 13:232-235, September-October 1981

Studies on the role of oral contraceptive use in the etiology of
benign and malignant liver tumors, by C. Mettlin, et al.
JOURNAL OF SURGICAL ONCOLOGY. 18(1):73-85, 1981

Subjective assessment and cardiovascular response to ischemic
pain in young, healthy women and users and non-users of oral
contraceptives, by E. J. Stein, et al. JOURNAL OF PSYCHO-
SOMATIC RESEARCH. 25(6):579-586, 1981

Teratogenic hazards of oral contraceptives [letter], by M.
Labbok. AMERICAN JOURNAL OF OBSTETRICS AND GYNECOLOGY.
142(8):1066, April 15, 1982

Thrombosis and oral contraception [letter], by P. Armitage.
BRITISH JOURNAL OF HOSPITAL MEDICINE. 26(2):185-186, August
1981

Thrombotic disorders associated with pregnancy and the pill, by
J. E. Tooke, et al. CLINICS IN HAEMOTOLOGY. 10(2):613-630,
June 1981

Transposition of the great vessels in an infant exposed to massive doses of oral contraceptives, by R. W. Redline, et al.
AMERICAN JOURNAL OF OBSTETRICS AND GYNECOLOGY. 141(4):468-
469, October 15, 1981

Twinning following oral contraceptive discontinuation, by D.
Hemon, et al. INTERNATIONAL JOURNAL OF EPIDEMIOLOGY. 10(4):
319-328, December 1981

Ultrastructure of cervical mucus and sperm penetration during
use of a triphasic oral contraceptive, by M. Ulstein, et al.
ACTA OBSTETRICIA ET GYNECOLOGICA SCANDINAVICA. SUPPLEMENT.
105:45-49, 1982

Urine free dopamine in normal primigravid pregnancy and women
taking oral contraceptives, by C. M. Perkins, et al. CLINICAL

CONTRACEPTIVES: FEMALE: ORAL: COMPLICATIONS (continued)

SCIENCE. 61(4):423-428, October 1981

The use of birth control pills in women with medical disorders, by A. H. Decherney. CLINICAL OBSTETRICS AND GYNECOLOGY. 24(3):965-975, September 1981

Uterine leiomyomas, serum cholesterol, and oral contraceptives. A preliminary study of epidemiologic differences in Los Angeles, California and Albany, New York, by H. Ratech, et al. DIAGNOSTIC GYNECOLOGY AND OBSTETRICS. 4(1):21-24, Spring 1982

Vascular thrombosis related to oral contraceptives and anti- ethinylestradiol antibodies--epidemiology and prevention, by V. Beaumont, et al. THERAPEUTISCHE UMSCHAU. 39(2):109-113, 1982

Ventilatory response of humans to chronic contraceptive pill administration, by C. A. Smith, et al. RESPIRATION. 43(3): 179-185, May-June 1982

Vestibular side effects of contraceptives, by F. Nagymajtenyi, et al. ORVOSI HETILAP. 122(8):455-457, February 22, 1981

Will consumption or oral contraceptives enhance the gastro- intestinal absorption of lead, by E. J. Calabrese. MEDICAL HYPOTHESES. 8(1):11-15, January 1982

Women and the pill: from panacea to catalyst, by S. C. M. Scrim- shaw. FAMILY PLANNING PERSPECTIVES. 13(6):254-256+, Novem- ber-December 1981

CONTRACEPTIVES: FEMALE: ORAL: THERAPEUTIC USE
The noncontraceptive health benefits from oral contraceptive use, by H. W. Ory. FAMILY PLANNING PERSPECTIVES. 14:182-184, July-August 1982

Premenstrual complaints: 2. Influence of oral contraceptives, by B. Andersch, et al. ACTA OBSTETRICIA ET GYNECOLOGICA SCAN- DINAVICA. 60(6):579-583, 1981

Serum bile acids during biphasic contraceptive treatment with ethynyl estradiol and norgestel, by J. Heikkinen, et al. CONTRACEPTION. 25(1):89-96, 1982

CONTRACEPTIVES: FEMALE: POST-COITAL
Alpha-difluoromethylornithine as a postcoitally effective anti- fertility agent in female rats, by P. R. Reddy, et al. CON- TRACEPTION. 24(2):215-221, August 1981

British embrace a gentler postcoital contraceptive. MEDICAL WORLD NEWS. 23:28-29, October 11, 1982

Chromosomal analysis of baboons and their mothers, following ap- plication to mothers of potentially post-ovulation fertility- inhibiting steroids, by Z. A. Jemilev, et al. ZENTRALBLATT FUR GYNAEKOLOGIE. 103(20):1215-1219, 1981

Effects of 17 beta-hydroxy-7 alpha-methylandrost-5-en-3-one on

CONTRACEPTIVES: FEMALE: POST-COITAL (continued)

early pregnancy in the rat, by S. Saksena, et al. ACTA EN-
DOCRINOLOGICA. 98(4):614-618, December 1981

Influence of metabolism on the activity of a new anti-fertility
agent, 2-(3-ethoxyphenyl)-5,6-dihydro-s-triazolo [5,1-a]isoui-
noline (DL 204-IT), in the rat and the hamster, by A. Assandri, et al. ARZNEIMITTEL-FORSCHUNG. 31(12):2104-2111, 1981

Morning-after pills [editorial], by S. Rowlands. BRITISH MEDI-
CAL JOURNAL. 285(6338):322-323, July 31, 1982

A multicenter clinical investigation employing ethinyl estradiol
combined with dl-norgestrel as postcoital contraceptive agent,
by A. A. Yuzpe, et al. FERTILITY AND STERILITY. 37(4):508-
513, April 1982

CONTRACEPTIVES: FEMALE: PSYCHOLOGY
A psychological investigation of contraceptive behavior, by V.
A. Byron. DISSERTATION ABSTRACTS INTERNATIONAL. B. p. 242,
1982

CONTRACEPTIVES: FEMALE: SUPPOSITORY
Use of a contraceptive suppository as chemoprophylaxis against
sexually-transmitted diseases, by G. Marion-Landais. SPM:
SALUD PUBLICA DE MEXICO. 23(4):345-352, July-August 1981

CONTRACEPTIVES: FEMALE: TECHNIQUES
Contraception by diet probed, by P. Lefervere. NATIONAL CATHO-
LIC REPORTER. 18(1):5, February 12, 1982

Cottonseed oil as a vaginal contraceptive. ARCHIVES OF ANDROLO-
GY. 8(1):11-14, 1982

Long-term intranasal luteinizing hormone-releasing hormone
agonist treatment for contraception in women, by C. Bergquist,
et al. FERTILITY AND STTERILITY. 38(2):190-193, August 1982

CONTRACEPTIVES: MALE
Antisperm antibodies in infertility: the role of condom therapy
[letter], by L. B. Greentree. FERTILITY AND STERILITY.
37(3):451-452, March 1982

Breast cancer and the condom [editorial], by G. Tibblin.
CLINICAL AND INVESTIGATIVE MEDICINE. 4(3-4):153-154, 1981

The condom as contraceptive and prophylactic [a reappraisal], by
P. D. Shenefelt. WISCONSIN MEDICAL JOURNAL. 80(9):19-20,
September 1981

Development of a male contraceptive--a beginning [editorial], by
W. J. Crowley, Jr. NEW ENGLAND JOURNAL OF MEDICINE. 305:695-
696, September 17, 1981

Disposition of intravenous diazepam in young men and women, by
H. G. Giles, et al. EUROPEAN JOURNAL OF CLINICAL PHARMACOL-
OGY. 20(3):207-213, 1981

Immunological control of male fertility, by G. P. Talwar, et al.

CONTRACEPTIVES: MALE (continued)

ARCHIVES OF ANDROLOGY. 7(2):177-185, September 1981

Mutagenic evaluation of two male contraceptives: 5-thio-D-glu-
cose and gossypol acetic acid, by S. K. Majumdar, et al.
JOURNAL OF HEREDITY. 73:76-77, January-February 1982

Potential use of male antifertility agents in developed countries, by G. Bialy, et al. CHEMOTHERAPY. 27(Suppl 2):102-
106, 1981

Reversible inhibition of testicular steroidogenesis and spermatogenesis by a potent gonadotropin-releasing hormone agonist
in normal men; an approach toward the development of a male
contraceptive, by R. Linde, et al. NEW ENGLAND JOURNAL OF
MEDICINE. 305(12):663-667, September 17, 1981

The search for male contraception reveals exciting photographs
too, by D. M. Phillips. LABOUR WORLD. 32:48-51, August 1981

Toward a taxonomy of contraceptive behaviors and attitudes of
single college men, by D. B. Stephen. DISSERTATION ABSTRACTS
INTERNATIONAL. A. p. 1431, 1982

CONTRACEPTIVES: MALE: ORAL
Attitudes toward male oral contraceptives: implications for
models of the relationship between beliefs and attitudes, by
J. Jaccard, et al. JOURNAL OF APPLIED SOCIAL PSYCHOLOGY.
11(3):181-191, May-June 1981

Mutagenic evaluation of 2 male contraceptives: 5-thio-D-glucose
and gossypol acetic acid, by S. K. Majudmar, et al. JOURNAL
OF HEREDITY. 73(1):76-77, 1982

Myocardial infarction in a man handling oral contraceptives.
Immunologic study [letter], by B. Ponge, et al. NOUVELLE
PRESSE MEDICALE. 10(37):3076, October 17, 1981

CONTRACEPTIVES: METHODS
Continuation of injectable contraceptions in Thailand, by T.
Narkavonnakit, et al. STUDIES IN FAMILY PLANNING. 13:99-105,
April 1982

Contraception by diet probed, by P. S. Lefevere. NATIONAL
CATHOLIC REPORTER. 18:5, February 12, 1982

Contraception: condoms, rhythm, spermicidal agents, diaphragms,
intrauterine devices, by J. A. Gans. AMERICAN DRUGGIST.
185:35-38+, March 1982

Contraception: which method will you prescribe, and why?, by G.
Weiss. CONSULTANT. 21:285-286+, November 1981

Contraceptive methods. NUEVA ENFERMERIA. (11):12-16, May 1980

--, by M. E. Creus. REVISTA DE ENFERMAGEN. 4(34):36-40, May
1981

Efficacy of different contraceptive methods, by M. Vessey, et

CONTRACEPTIVES: METHODS (continued)

al. LANCET. 1(8276):841-842, April 10, 1982

Feminine hygiene: the news in napkins. PROGRESSIVE GROCER. 61:98-99, March 1982

Human action, natural rhythms, and contraception: a response to Noonan, by j. Boyle. AMERICAN JOURNAL OF JURISPRUDENCE. 26: 32-46, 1981

Immunocontraception: consideration of the zona pellucida as a target antigen, by A. G. Sacco. OBSTETRICS AND GYNECOLOGY ANNUAL. 10:1-26, 1981

Methods of contraception. Educational chart at the University Gynecological Clinic, Mannheim. FORTSCHRITTE DER MEDIZIN. 100(16):743-745, April 29, 1982

Mid-cycle contraception with LHRH i women, by H. Maia, Jr., et al. REPRODUCCION. 5(4):251-260, October-December 1981

Natural family planning: when other contraceptive methods won't do, by J. J. McCarthy. CONSULTANT. 21:109-110+, December 1981

Oral hormonal contraceptives and benign liver tumors, by J. Giedl, et al. FORTSCHRITTE DER MEDIZIN. 99(6):165-170, February 12, 1981

Periodic abstinence: how well do new approaches work?. POPULA-TION REPORTS. (3):133-171, September 1981

Postcoital antifertility effect of mentha arvensis, by D. Kanjanapothi, et al. CONTRACEPTION. 24(5):559-567, November 1981

Postpartum contraception, by D. A. Edelman, et al. INTERNATION-AL JOURNAL OF GYNAECOLOGY AND OBSTETRICS. 19(4):305-312, 1981

CONTRACEPTIVES: PARENTAL CONSENT
Confidentiality and the pill [letter], by R. Taines. AMERICAN FAMILY PHYSICIAN. 25(5):53, May 1982

Informed consent and contraceptive order, by E. T. Wimberley. DISSERTATION ABSTRACTS INTERNATIONAL. A. p. 1683, 1982

Reagan wants parents to be told when teens get contraceptives. CHRISTIANITY TODAY. 26:41, April 23, 1982

Storm over Washington: the parental notification proposal (re-quiring family planning clinics to notify the parents of minors when prescription contraceptives are provided), by A. M. Kenney, et al. FAMILY PLANNING PERSPECTIVES. 14:185+, July-August 1982

Teens and contraception (parental notification proposal), by A. J. Fugh-Berman. OFF OUR BACKS. 12:13, June 1982

Telltale birth control (proposal to require federally funded

CONTRACEPTIVES: PARENTAL CONSENT (continued)

    family-planning clinics to notify parents when their teen-
    agers receive contraceptives), by M. Beck. NEWSWEEK. 99:33,
    April 5, 1982

  Unmarried black adolescent father's attitudes toward abortion,
    contraception, and sexuality [a preliminary report], by L. E.
    Hendricks. JOURNAL OF ADOLESCENT HEALTH CARE. 2(3):199-203,
    March 1982

  When teens want contraceptives, should their parents know? Two
    impassioned advocates face off (views of M. Mecklenburg and F.
    Wattleton), by K. Huff, et al. PEOPLE WEEKLY. 17:44-45, May
    24, 1982

CONTRACEPTIVES: STATISTICS
  Breast cancer and oral contraception: findings in Oxford-Family
    Planning Association contraceptive study, by M. P. Vessey, et
    al. BRITISH MEDICAL JOURNAL. 282(6282):2093-2094, 1981

  Changing contraceptive usage intentions: a test of the Fishbein
    model of intention, by D. McCarty. JOURNAL OF APPLIED SOCIAL
    PSYCHOLOGY. 11(3):192-211, May-June 1981

  Contraception is less risky for teenagers than is pregnancy,
    worldwide study finds. FAMILY PLANNING PERSPECTIVES. 14:274-
    275, September-October 1982

  Contraception, pregnancy management and the family-planning
    clinic (findings on 410 puerperas in a Lombard hospital), by
    M. Semeria. ANNALI DI OSTETRICIA GINECOLOGIA, MEDICINA
    PERINATALE. 103(1):93-101, January-February 1982

  Contraceptive availability differentials in use and fertility,
    by A. O. Tsui, et al. STUDIES IN FAMILY PLANNING. 12:381-
    393, November 1981

  Contraceptive failure in the United States: the impact of social
    economic and demographic factors, by A. I. Schirm, et al.
    FAMILY PLANNING PERSPECTIVES. 14(2):68-75, March-April 1982

  IPPF international medical advisory panel meetings May and
    October 1981 and policy statements on contraceptives. IPPF:
    INTERNATIONAL PLANNED PARENTHOOD FEDERATION MEDICAL BULLETIN.
    15(6):6, December 1981

  Knowledge of contraceptives: an assessment of world fertility
    survey data collection procedures, by M. Vaessen. POPULATION
    STUDIES. 35(3):357, November 1981

  The oral contraceptive: past, present and future use, by J. J.
    Speidel, et al. JOHNS HOPKINS MEDICAL JOURNAL. 150(5):161,
    1982

  Oral contraceptives in the 1980s. POPULATION REPORTS. 10(3): ,
    May-June 1982

  Perception of methods of contraception: a semantic differential
    study, by P. K. Kee, et al. JOURNAL OF BIOSOCIAL SCIENCE.

CONTRACEPTIVES: STATISTICS (continued)

13(2):209-218, April 1981

Sequences of events following adoption of contraception: an
exploratory analysis of 1973 United States fertility history
data, by G. Pickens, et al. SOCIAL BIOLOGY. 28:111-125,
Spring-Summer 1981

Studies of the attitude of a group of puerperas of the Brianza
region toward contraception and the services offered for such
purposes by the public health organizations, by G. Remotti, et
al. ANNALI DI OSTETRICIA GINECOLOGIA, MEDICINA PERINATALE.
103(1):68-92, January-February 1982

A study of the characteristics of acceptors of the Copper-T
device, by V. B. Jalagar, et al. JOURNAL OF FAMILY WELFARE.
28:54-61, June 1982

CONTRACEPTIVES: TECHNIQUES
Contraception during lactation, by I. Aref, et al. CONTRACEP-
TIVE DELIVERY SYSTEMS. 3(1):47-52, 1982

A preliminary pharmacological trial of the monthly injectable
contraceptive CycloProvera, by K. Fotherby, et al. CONTRA-
CEPTION. 25(3):261-272, 1982

Searching for an ideal contraceptive method, by L. B. Tyrer.
USA TODAY. 110:31-33, March 1982

Topical contraceptives, by V. I. Alipov, et al. AKUSHERSTVO I
GINEKOLOGIIA. (2):5-7, February 1982

CONTRACEPTIVES AND COLLEGE STUDENTS
Body image of and contraceptive use by college females, by M.
Young. PERCEPTUAL AND MOTOR SKILLS. 53(2):456-458, October
1981

Contraception choices of female university students [research],
by A. Ayvazian. JOGN NURSING: JOURNAL OF OBSTETRIC GYNECOLO-
GIC AND NEONATAL NURSING. 10(6):426-429, November-December 1981

Contraceptive patterns of college students who experienced early
coitus, by M. L. Vincent, et al. JOURNAL OF SCHOOL HEALTH.
51(10):667-672, December 1981

The effects of microcomputer assisted instruction on the contraceptive knowledge attitudes, and behavior of college students,
by L. G. DeSonier. DISSERTATION ABSTRACTS INTERNATIONAL. A.
p. 399, 1982

Knowledge and attitudes toward Tay-Sachs disease among a college
student population, by C. F. Austein, et al. YALE JOURNAL OF
BIOLOGY AND MEDICINE. 54(5):345-354, September-October 1981

Locus of control of increasing specificity reinforcement value
and contraceptive use among sexually experienced college
females who are knowledgeable about contraception, by S. J.
Albano. DISSERTATION ABSTRACTS INTERNATIONAL. A. p. 5058,
1982

CONTRACEPTIVES AND COLLEGE STUDENTS (continued)

Model for effective contraceptive counseling on campus, by G. A. Bachmann. JOURNAL OF THE AMERICAN COLLEGE HEALTH ASSOCIATION. 30(3):119-121, December 1981

A perilous paradox: the contraceptive behavior of college students, by K. D. Rindskopf. JOURNAL OF THE AMERICAN COLLEGE HEALTH ASSOCIATION. 30(3):113-118, December 1981

Risk-taking and contraceptive behavior among unmarried college students, by J. R. Foreit, et al. POPULATION AND ENVIRONMENT. 4(3):174, Fall 1981

Sexual and contraceptive behavior on a college campus. A five-year follow-up, by R. W. Hale, et al. CONTRACEPTION. 25(2):125-134, February 1982

The sexually liberated college student--fact or fancy, by P. Murphy, et al. JOURNAL OF THE AMERICAN COLLEGE HEALTH ASSO-CIATION. 30(2):87-89, October 1981

The theory of reasoned action and health belief model applied to contraception of college women, by S. McCammon. DISSERTATION ABSTRACTS INTERNATIONAL. B. p. 72, 1982

Toward a taxonomy of contraceptive behaviors and attitudes of single college men, by D. B. Stephen. DISSERTATION ABSTRACTS INTERNATIONAL. A. p. 1431, 1982

CONTRACEPTIVES AND FUNDING

Community availability of contraceptives and family limitation, by A. O. Tsui, et al. DEMOGRAPHY. 18(4):615-625, November 1981

Public funding of contraceptive services, 1980-1982 (United States) [research], by B. Nestor. FAMILY PLANNING PERSPEC-TIVES. 14:198-203, July-August 1982

CONTRACEPTIVES AND HORMONES

Advantages and risks of hormonal contraception, by M. Mall-Haefeli. FORTSCHRITTE DER MEDIZIN. 100(16):723-728, April 29, 1982

Alterations in clinical chemistry measures associated with oral contraceptive and estrogen use: the Lipid Research Clinics Program Prevalence Study, by L. D. Cowan, et al. JOURNAL OF REPRODUCTIVE MEDICINE. 27(5):275-282, May 1982

Antifertility effects of luteinizing hormone-releasing hormone (LHRH) agonists, by F. Labrie, et al. PROGRESS IN CLINICAL AND BIOLOGICAL RESEARCH. 74:273-291, 1981

Antipyrine elimination in saliva after low-dose combined or progestogen-only oral contraceptive steroids, by D. M. Cham-bers, et al. BRITISH JOURNAL OF CLINICAL PHARMACOLOGY. 13(2):229-232, February 1982

Are hormonal contraceptives relevant for family planning?, by J. M. Wenderlein. MMW: MUENCHENER MEDIZINISCHE WOCHENSCHRIFT.

124(20):487-488, May 21, 1982

The beginnings of hormonal contraception and the Munchener
Medizinische Wochenschrift, by H. H. Summer. MMW: MUENCHENER
MEDIZINISCHE WOCHENSCHRIFT. 124(2):499-503, May 21, 1982

Behaviour of ujoviridin exposures test (ICG) in conjunction with
application of hormonal contraceptives, by E. Brugmann, et al.
ZENTRALBLATT FUR GYNAEKOLOGIE. 103(14):823-826, 1981

Biochemical and steroidal indicators in the use of monogest, a
progesterone contraceptive, by J. Kobiikova, et al. ČESKO-
SLOVENSKA GYNEKOLOGIE. 46(7):540-541, August 1981

Carbohydrate metabolism during treatment with estrogen, progestogen, and low-dose oral contraceptives, by W. N. Spellacy.
AMERICAN JOURNAL OF OBSTETRICS AND GYNECOLOGY. 142(6 Pt 2):
732-734, March 15, 1982

Clinical trial of an oral contraceptive containing desogestrel
and ethynyl estradiol, by M. J. Weijerss. CLINICAL THERA-
PEUTICS. 4(5):359-366, 1982

Colposcopic study of the effect of steroid contraceptives on the
uterine cervix, by J. Y. Zhou. CHUNG HUA FU CHAN KO TSA CHIH.
16(1):55-58, January 1981

Comparison of the metabolic effects of two hormonal contraceptive methods: an oral formulation and a vaginal ring. I. Carbohydrate metabolism and liver function, by T. Ahren, et al.
CONTRACEPTION. 24(4):415-427, October 1981

--II. Serum lipoproteins and apolipoproteins by T. Ahren et
al. CONTRACEPTION. 24(4):451-468, October 1981

Contraceptive activity and mechanism of action of 6-methylsub-
stituted D'_6-pentaranes combined with nestranol, by V. V.
Korkhov, et al. FARMAKOLOGYA I TOKSIKOLOGYA. 44(1):95-98,
1981

Dermal changes in response to hormonal contraceptives, by C.
Scholz, et al. ZENTRALBLATT FUR GYNAEKOLOGIE. 103(19):1158-
1164, 1981

Does progestogen reduction in oral contraception parallel re-
duce lipid metabolic effects?, by N. Crona, et al. ACTA
OBSTETRICIA ET GYNECOLOGICA SCANDINAVICA. SUPPLEMENT. 105:
41-44, 1982

Duration of lactation and return of menstruation in lactating
women using hormonal contraception and intrauterine devices,
by K. Prema. CONTRACEPTIVE DELIVERY SYSTEMS. 3(1):39-46,
1982

Effect of hormonal contraceptives containing 0.05 mg ethinyl
estradiol and 0.125 mg desogestrel in normophasic regimen
(Oviol), by M. J. Weijers. FORTSCHRITTE DER MEDIZIN.
100(16):764-767, April 29, 1982

The effect of progestins in combined oral contraceptives on serum lipids with special reference to high-density lipoproteins, by V. Wynn, et al. AMERICAN JOURNAL OF OBSTETRICS AND GYNECOLOGY. 142(6 Pt 2):766-771, March 15, 1982

The effect of prolonged oral contraceptive steroid use on erythrocyte glutathione peroxidase activity, by I. D. Capel, et al. JOURNAL OF STEROID BIOCHEMISTRY. 14(8):729-732, August 1981

The effect on lipids and lipoproteins of a contraceptive vaginal ring containing levonorgestrel and estradiol, by S. Roy, et al. CONTRACEPTION. 24(4):429-449, October 1981

Effects of the estrogenicity of levonorgestrel/ethinylestradiol combinations of the lipoprotein status, by U. Larsson-Cohn, et al. ACTA OBSTETRICIA ET GYNECOLOGICA SCANDINAVICA. SUPPLE-MENT. 105:37-40, 1982

Effects of estrogens and progestogens on lipid metabolism, by P. Oster, et al. AMERICAN JOURNAL OF OBSTETRICS AND GYNECOLOGY. 142(6 Pt 2):773-775, March 15, 1982

Effects of oral contraceptive combinations containing levonor-gestrel or desogestrel on serum proteins and androgen binding, by E. W. Bergink, et al. SCANDINAVIAN JOURNAL OF CLINICAL AND LABORATORY INVESTIGATION. 41(7):663-668, November 1981

Effects of oral contraceptive steroids on serum lipid and aortic glycosaminoglycans levels in iron-deficient rats, by Y. Kanke, et al. INTERNATIONAL JOURNAL FOR VITAMIN AND NUTRITION RE-SEARCH. 51(4):416-420, 1981

Effects of oral contraceptives on lipoprotein triglyceride and cholesterol: relationships to estrogen and progestin potency, by R. H. Knopp, et al. AMERICAN JOURNAL OF OBSTETRICS AND GYNECOLOGY. 142(6 Pt 2):725-731, March 15, 1982

Effects of progestogens on the cardiovascular system, by T. W. Meade. AMERICAN JOURNAL OF OBSTETRICS AND GYNECOLOGY. 142(6 Pt 2):776-780, March 15, 1982

Endometrial morphology and peripheal steroid levels in women with and without intermenstrual bleeding during contraception with the 300 microgram norethisteone minipill, by E. Johannis-son, et al. CONTRACEPTION. 25(1):13-30, 1982

Endometrial patterns in women on chronic luteinizing hormone-releasing hormone agonist treatment for contraception, by C. Bergquist, et al. FERTILITY AND STERILITY. 36(3):339-342, September 1981

Estrogens and hypertension, by M. H. Weinberger. COMPREHENSIVE THERAPY. 8(6):71-75, June 1982

Estrogens in oral contraceptives: historical perspectives, by J. W. Goldzieher. JOHNS HOPKINS MEDICAL JOURNAL. 150(5):165-169, May 1982

Extragenital changes caused by intake of hormonal contraceptives --marginal periodontium. by M. Arnold, et al. ZENTRALBLATT FUR GYNAEKOLOGIE. 103(14):827-834, 1981

Fertility after discontinuation of levo-norgestrel-releasing intrauterine devices, by C. G. Nilsson. CONTRACEPTION. 25(3):273-278, 1982

The formulation of oral contraceptives: does the amount of estrogen make any clinical difference?, by L. Speroff. JOHNS HOPKINS MEDICAL JOURNAL. 150(5):170-176, May 1982

Further studies on pituitary and ovarian function in women receiving hormonal contraception, by B. L. Cohen, et al. CONTRACEPTION. 24(2):159-172, August 1981

Hormonal contraception and hearing disorders, by K. Kvorak. CESKOSLOVENSKA GYNEKOLOGIE. 45(9):653-655, November 1980

Hormonal contraception and hypertension, by K. M. Hamann, et al. ZEITSCHRIFT FUR ARZTLICHE FORTBILDUNG. 76(5):198-201, March 1, 1982

Hormonal contraceptive therapy and thromboembolic disease, by M. J. Narvaiza, et al. REVISTA DE MEDICINA DE LA UNIVERSIDAD DE NAVARRA. 24(4):49-53, December 1980

Hormonal factors in fertility, infertility and contraception. JOURNAL OF STEROID BIOCHEMISTRY. 14(11):i-xxxvii, November 1981

Hormone replacement treatment and benign intracranial hypertension [letter], by K. L. Woods. BRITISH MEDICAL JOURNAL. 285(6336):215, July 1982

Impairment of diazepam metabolism by low-dose estrogen-containing oral-contraceptive steroids, by D. R. Abernethy, et al. NEW ENGLAND JOURNAL OF MEDICINE. 306(13):791-792, April 1, 1982

Influence of oral hormonal contraceptives on multiple pregnancy, by I. Halmos. MEDICINSKI RAZGLEDI. 20(2):131-136, 1981

LH, FSH, estradiol and progesterone levels after discontinuation of hormonal contraception, by A. Balogh, et al. ACTA UNIVERSITATIS PALACKIANAE OLOMUCENSIS FACULTATIS MEDICAE. 101:95-101, 1981

Levonorgestrel and estradiol release from an improved contraceptive vaginal ring, by T. M. Jackanicz. CONTRACEPTION. 24(4):323-339, October 1981

Lipid metabolic effects induced by two estradiol/norgestrel combinations in women around forty, by A. Hagstad, et al. ACTA OBSTETRICIA ET GYNECOLOGICA SCANDINAVICA. SUPPLEMENT. 106:57-62, 1981

Liver diseases when using hormonal contraceptives, by T. S. Lie. MMW: MUENCHENER MEDIZINISCHE WOCHENSCHRIFT. 124(20):489-494, May 21, 1982

Liver tumours in pregnancy, following previous intake of hormonal contraceptives, by P. Pietsch, et al. ZENTRALBLATT FUR GYNAEKOLOGIE. 103(13):772-780, 1981

Massive, painful hepatomegaly, sinusoidal dilation and prolonged use of estroprogestational agents [letter], by D. Fischer, et al. GASTROENTEROLOGIE CLINIQUE ET BIOLOGIQUE. 6(3):302-304, March 1982

Measurement of serum activity in short and long-term application of various hormonal contraceptives, by G. Klinger, et al. ZEITSCHRIFT FUR DIE GESAMTE INNERE MEDIZIN. 36(17):611-620, September 1, 1981

Metabolic clearance rates of luteinizing hormone in women during different phases of the menstrual cycle and while taking an oral contraceptive, by R. E. Wehmann, et al. JOURNAL OF CLINICAL ENDOCRINOLOGY AND METABOLISM. 55(4):654-659, October 1982

Metabolism of (6, 7-3H) norethisterone enanthate in rats, by G. W. Sang, et al. CHUNG-KUO YAO LI HSUEH PAO. 2(1):37-41, March 1981

A multicenter clinical investigation employing ethinyl estradiol combined with dl-norgestrel as postcoital contraceptive agent, by A. A. Yuzpe, et al. FERTILITY AND STERILITY. 37(4):508-513, April 1982

A multicenter study of levonorgestrel-estradiol contraceptive vaginal rings. I. Use effectiveness. An international comparative trial, by I. Sivin, et al. CONTRACEPTION. 24(4):341-358, October 1981

--II. Subjective and objective measures of effects. An international comparative trial, by I. Sivin, et al. CONTRACEPTION. 24(4):359-376 October 1981

--III. Menstrual patterns. An international comparative trial, by I. Sivin, et al. CONTRACEPTION. 24(4):377-392, October 1981

Neonatal malformations and hormone therapy during pregnancy, by L. Pacilli, et al. MINERVA GINECOLOGIA. 33(7-8):659-665, July-August 1981

Neoplasia and hormonal contraception, by G. R. Huggins. CLINICAL OBSTETRICS AND GYNECOLOGY. 24(3):903-925, September 1981

A new key to the use of hormonal contraception, by C. Berger. PRAXIS. 70(51):2312-2315, December 15, 1981

Norethisterone, a major ingredient of contraceptive pills, is a suicide inhibitor of estrogen biosynthesis, by Y. Osawa, et al. SCIENCE. 215(4537):1249-1251, March 5, 1982

Normalization of testosterone levels using a low polycystic ovary syndrome, by S. G. Raj, et al. OBSTETRICS AND GYNE-COLOGY. 60(1):15-19, July 1982

Observations with a combined oral contraceptive (Rigevidon) containing minimum oestrogen dose, by K. Karsay. THERAPIE HUNAGIRCA. 28(1):17-20, 1980

Oestrogens and hypertension, by J. M. Roberts. CLINICAL EN-DOCRINOLOGY. 10(3):489-512, November 1981

Oral and vaginal Candida colonization under the influence of hormonal contraception, by G. Klinger, et al. ZAHN-, MUND-, UND KIEFERHEILKUNDE MIT ZENTRALBLATT. 70(2):120-125, 1982

Oral contraception in diabetic women. Diabetes control, serum and high density lipoprtein lipids during low-dose progesto-gen, combined oestrogen/progestogen and non-hormonal contra-ception, by Radberg, et al. ACTA ENDOCRINOLOGICA. 98(2):246-251, October 1981

Oral contraceptive and postmenopausal estrogen effects on lipo-protein triglyceride and cholesterol in an adult female popu-lation: relationships to estrogen and progestin potency, by R. H. Knopp, et al. JOURNAL OF CLINICAL ENDOCRINOLOGY AND ME-TABOLISM. 53(6):1123-1132, December 1981

An overview of studies on estrogens, ora contraceptives and breast cancer, by V. A. Drill. PROGRESS IN DRUG RESEARCH. 25:159-187, 1981

A perspective on progestogens in oral contraceptives, by W. N. Spellacy. AMERICAN JOURNAL OF OBSTETRICS AND GYNECOLOGY. 142(6 Pt 2):717, March 15, 1982

Pituitary and gonadal function during the use of progesterone-or progesterone-estradiol-releasing vaginal rings, by J. Toivonen. INTERNATIONAL JOURNAL OF FERTILITY. 25(2):106-111, 1980

Pituitary responsiveness to gonadotropin-releasing hormone (GnRH and thyrotropin-releasing hormone (TRH) during different phases of the same cycle of oral contraceptive steroid ther-apy, by F. R. Perez-Lopez, et al. FERTILITY AND STERILITY. 37(6):767-772, June 1982

Plasma levels of medroxyprogesterone acetate (MPA), sex-hormone binding globulin, gonadal steroids, gonadotrophins and prolac-tin in women during long-term use of depo-MPA (Depo-Provera) as a contraceptive agent, by S. Jeppsson, et al. ACTA EN-DOCRINOLOGICA. 99(3):339-343, March 1982

Population-based lipoprotein lipid reference values for pregnant women compared to nonpregnant women classified by sex hormone usage, by R. H. Knopp, et al. AMERICAN JOURNAL OF OBSTETRICS

AND GYNECOLOGY. 143(6):626-637, July 15, 1982

Porphyria cutanea tarda in female patients with speical regard
to hormonal contraception, by H. Fiedler, et al. DERMATOLO-
GISCHE MONATSSCHRIFT. 167(8):481-485, 1981

Possible interference of synthetic estroprogestins with thyroid
hormone production, by A. Paggi, et al. CLINICAL THERA-
PEUTICS. 98(4):349-363, August 31, 1981

Post-bill amenorrhea following hormonal contraceptive therapy in
adolescence, by M. Brandt, et al. ARZTLICHE JUGENDKUNDE.
72(4):241-245, 1981

Progestogen effects and their relationship to lipoprotein
changes. A report from the Oral Contraception Study of the
Royal College of General Practitioners, by S. J. Wingrave.
ACTA OBSTETRICIA ET GYNECOLOGICA SCANDINAVICA. SUPPLEMENT.
105:33-36, 1982

Progestogens and arterial disease--evidence from the Royal Col-
lege of General Practitioners' study, by C. R. Kay. AMERICAN
JOURNAL OF OBSTETRICS AND GYNECOLOGY. 142(6 Pt 2):762-765,
March 15, 1982

Progestogens in cardiovascular diseases: an introduction to
the epidemiologic data, by J. I. Mann. AMERICAN JOURNAL OF
OBSTETRICS AND GYNECOLOGY. 142(6 Pt 2):752-757, March 15,
1982

Psychiatric complications of progesterone and oral contraceptives, by I. D. Glick, et al. JOURNAL OF CLINICAL PSYCHO-
PHARMACOLOGY. 1(6):350-367, November 1981

Quantitative analysis of ethynodiol diacetate and ethinyl estra-
diol/mestranol in oral contraceptive tablets by high-performance liquid chromatography, by G. B. Carignan, et al. JOURNAL
OF PHARMACEUTICAL SCIENCES. 71(2):264-266, February 1982

RIA of insulin in the determination of aberrations in the glycide metabolism in women using steroidal contraceptive preparations, by V. Dvorak, et al. ACTA UNIVERSITATIS PALACKI-
ANAE OLOMUCENSIS FACULTATIS MEDICAE. 101:149-154, 1981

A randomized double-blind study of two combined and two progestogen-only oral contraceptives, by A. Sheth, et al. CONTRA-
CEPTION. 25(3):243-252, March 1982

A randomized study of metabolic effects of four low-estrogen
oral contraceptives: I. Results after 6 cycles, by M. Briggs,
et al. CONTRACEPTION. 23(5):463-471, May 1981

Recurring inflammation of optic nerve after long-time therapy
with hormonal contraceptive anacyclin 28, by H. Huismans.
KLINISCHE MONATSBLAETTER FUR AUGENHEILKUNDE. 180(2):173-175,
February 1982

Reversible inhibition of testicular steroidogenesis and spermatogenesis by a potent gonadotropin-releasing hormone agonist in normal men; an approach toward the development of a male contraceptive, by R. Linde, et al. NEW ENGLAND JOURNAL OF MEDICINE. 305:663-667, September 17, 1981

Risks and perspectives of steroid contraceptives, by J. Presl. CESKOSLOVENSKA GYNEKOLOGIE. 46(1):50-58, February 1981

The role of estrogens as a risk factor for stroke in postmeno-pausal women, by S. H. Rosenberg, et al. WESTERN JOURNAL OF MEDICINE. 133(4):292-296, October 1980

Role of hormones including diethylstibestrol (DES) in the patho-genesis of cervical and vaginal intraepithelial neoplasia, by S. J. Robboy, et al. GYNECOLOGIC ONCOLOGY. 12(2 Pt 2):S98-110, October 1981

Serum bile acids during biphasic contraceptive treatment with ethinyl estradiol and norgestrel, by J. Heikkinen, et al. CONTRACEPTION. 25(1):89-95, January 1982

Sex hormone binding globulin levels in hirsuite patients: the effect of combined oral contraceptives, by O. F. Giwa-Osagie, et al. CONTRACEPTIVE DELIVERY SYSTEMS. 3(2):155-160, 1982

Sex hormones and gynaecological cancer [editorial], by J. S. Scott. BRITISH MEDICAL JOURNAL. 284(6330):1657-1658, June 5, 1982

Sex hormones and liver cancer, by G. M. Williams. LABORATORY INVESTIGATION. 46(3):352-353, March 1982

Side effects of hormonal contraception, by W. Carol, et al. ZEITSCHRIFT FUR DIE GESAMTE INNERE MEDIZIN. 36(8):253-260, April 15, 1981

Steroidal contraceptives and the immune system, by J. Presl. CESKOSLOVENSKA GYNEKOLOGIE. 47(2):143-148, March 1982

Structural variations of cervical cancer and its precursors under the influence of exogenous hormones, by G. Dallenbach-Hellweg. CURRENT TOPICS IN PATHOLOGY. 70:143-170, 1981

Suppression of ovulation in the rat by an orally active antagon-ist of luteinizing hormone-releasing hormone, by M. V. Nekola, et al. SCIENCE. 218:160-162, October 8, 1982

The third S.K. & F. Prize lecture, University o London, December 1981. The clinical pharmacology of oral contraceptive ster-oids, by M. L. Orme. BRITISH JOURNAL OF CLINICAL PHARMACOL-OGY. 14(1):31-42, July 1982

25 years of hormonal contraception, by M. Sas. ORVOSI HETILAP. 123(4):195-200, January 24, 1982

Vascular effects of hormonal contraception, by L. C. Huppert. CLINICAL OBSTETRICS AND GYNECOLOGY. 24(3):951-963, September 1981

CONTRACEPTIVES AND THE MENTALLY RETARDED

Special considerations in pregnancy prevention for the mentally
subnormal adolescent female, by K. Hein, et al. JOURNAL OF
ADOLESCENT HEALTH CARE. 1(1):46-49, September 1980

CONTRACEPTIVES AND PHYSICIANS
Oral contraceptive during lactation: a global survey of physi-
cian practice, by L. T. Strauss, et al. INTERNATIONAL JOURNAL
OF GYNAECOLOGY AND OBSTETRICS. 19(3):169-175, June 1981

Perceived physician humaneness, patient attitude, and satisfaction with the pill as a contraceptive, by D. Kallen, et al.
JOURNAL OF HEALTH AND SOCIAL BEHAVIOR. 22(3):256-267, September 1981

Toledo doctor wages compaign against the pill, by A. Jones.
NATIONAL CATHOLIC REPORTER. 18:1+, October 15, 1982+

CONTRACEPTIVES AND POLITICS
Depo-Provera debate revs up at FDA, by M. Sun. SCIENCE. 217:
424-428, July 30, 1982

Politics of contraception, by A. Charney. CHATELAINE. 55:57+,
April 1982

Reagan: la grande croisade dans les chambres a coucher [adoles-
cents], by L. Wiznitzer. L'ACTUALITE. 7:26, September 1982

Statutes and ordinances--contraceptives and sex aids. CRIMINAL
LAW REPORTER: COURT DECISIONS AND PROCEEDINGS. 30(4):2086,
October 28, 1981

CONTRACEPTIVES AND RELIGION
Church teaching and the immorality of contraception, by W. E.
May. HOMILETIC AND PASTORAL REVIEW. 18:23, January 15, 1982

Contraception: how many will heed the Pope?, by C. Longley.
TIMES (London). p. 10, May 7, 1982

CONTRACEPTIVES AND SEXUAL BEHAVIOR
Can contraception kill romance?, by J. Labreche. CHATELAINE.
55:47+, August 1982

Curbing sexual appetite (Depo Provera lowers testosterone levels
work of Fred S. Berlin and John Money), by W. Herbert. SCI-
ENCE NEWS. 122:270, October 23, 1982

Effects of medroxyprogesterone acete on socio-sexual behavior of
stumptail macaques, by H. D. Steklis, et al. PHYSIOLOGY AND
BEHAVIOR. 28(3):535-544, March 1982

Locus of control of increasing specificity reinforcement value
and contraceptive use among sexually experienced college
females who are knowledgeable about contraception, by S. J.
Albano. DISSERTATION ABSTRACTS INTERNATIONAL. A. p. 5058,
1982

Sex and contraceptive behavior among young single persons, by E.
Garcia Hassey, et al. GINECOLOGIA Y OBSTETRICIA DE MEXICO.

CONTRACEPTIVES AND SEXUAL BEHAVIOR (continued)

49(296):343-357, June 1981

Sex guilt and the use of contraception among unmarried women, by
J. F. Keller, et al. CONTRACEPTION. 25(4):387-393, April
1982

Sex, sex guilt, and contraceptive use, by M. Gerrard. JOURNAL
OF PERSONALITY AND SOCIAL PSYCHOLOGY. 42(1):153-158, January
1982

Sexual practice and the use of contraception, by J. Bell. HIGH
SCHOOL JOURNAL. 65:241-244, April 1982

CONTRACEPTIVES AND YOUTH
Adolescent contraception, by G. C. Bolton. CLINICAL OBSTETRICS
AND GYNECOLOGY. 24(3):977-986, September 1981

Adolescent sex, by W. Girstenbrey. MEDIZINISCHE WELT. 32(44):
3, October 30, 1981

Adolescents' use of a hospital-based contraceptive program
(based on a study of the Adolescent Reproductive Health Care
Program Columbia-Presbyterian Medical Center, New York City,
1977-80), by J. B. Jones, et al. FAMILY PLANNING PERSPEC-
TIVES. 14:224-225+, July-August 1982

Biology--contraception--adolescence (part 2), by P. Lonchambon,
et al. INFIRMIERE FRANCAISE. (237):7-16, July 1982

--. From the physiology of puberty to the possible physiopathology of contraception in the formative years, by P. Lonchambon, et al. INFIRMIERE FRANCAISE. (236):21-30+, June
1982

Constitutional law--fourteenth amendment--right to privacy--con-
traceptives--minors--the United States Court of Appeals for
the Sixth Circuit has held that a state-funded family planning
cen- ter's distribution of contraceptives to minors without
parental notice does not violate the parents' constitutional
rights. DUSQUESNE LAW REVIEW. 20:111-121, Fall 1981

Contraception for adolescent girls, by J. E. DeLia. CONSULTANT.
21:63-64+, March 1981

Contraception for adolescents, by J. Huber. THERAPEUTISCHE
UMSCHAU. 39(6):469-471, June 1982

Contraception for adolescents ... test yourself, AMERICAN JOUR-
NAL OF NURSING. 81:2191+, December 1981

Contraception for the under 16s: better safe than sorry [re-
search], by A. Cook. NURSING MIRROR AND MIDWIVE'S JOURNAL.
153(12):24-26, September 16, 1981

Contraception in adolescence, by S. Vandal. NURSING QUEBEC.
2(2):18-23, January-February 1982

Contraception in adolescents according to recent scientific

understanding, by M. Mall-Haefeli. THERAPEUTISCHE UMSCHAU. 39(6):448-457, June 1982

Contraception is less risky for teenagers than is pregnancy, worldwide study finds. FAMILY PLANNING PERSPECTIVES. 14:274-275, September-October 1982

Contraceptive method switching among American female adolescents 1979, by M. B. Hirsch. DISSERTATION ABSTRACTS INTERNATIONAL. A. p. 1303, 1982

Contraceptive preferences of adolescents and the role of counseling, by M. Endler, et al. THERAPEUTISCHE UMSCHAU. 39(6):458-461, June 1982

Cyclic hepatitis' in a young woman [case presentation], by H. J. Dworken, et al. HOSPITAL PRACTICE. 16(11):48G-H, November 1981

The dream of love and the reality of contraception. Current adolescent sexual behaviour and contraceptive methods, by K. Thormann, et al. THERAPEUTISCHE UMSCHAU. 39(6):462-468, June 1982

The effectiveness of contraceptive programs for teenagers, by P. B. Namerow, et al. JOURNAL OF ADOLESCENT HEALTH CARE. 2(3): 189-198, March 1982

An empirical assessment of a decision making model of contraceptive use and nonuse among adolescent girls, by N. B. Peacock. DISSERTATION ABSTRACTS INTERNATIONAL. A. p. 3774, 1982

Fatal subarachnoid haemorrhage in young women: role of oral contraceptives, by M. Thorogood, et al. BRITISH MEDICAL JOURNAL. 283(6294):762, September 19, 1981

A hard pill to swallow? (proposal to require Federally funded family-planning clinics to notify parents when their adolescents receive contraceptives), by B. Brophy. FORBES. 129:99, May 10, 1982

The influence of oral contraception on the sex life of adolescents, by B. Bourrit, et al. THERAPEUTISCHE UMSCHAU. 38(11): 1098-1102, November 1981

The interaction of cigarette smoking, oral contraceptive use and cardiovascular risk factor variables in children: the Bogalusa Heart Study, by L. S. Webber, et al. AMERICAN JOURNAL OF PUBLIC HEALTH. 72;266-274, March 1982

Measurement issues involved in examining contraceptive use among young single women, by E. S. Herold. POPULATION AND ENVIRONMENT. 4(2):128-144, Summer 1981

Never-pregnant adolescents and family planning programs: contraception, continuation, and pregnancy risk [research], by E. W. Freeman, et al. AMERICAN JOURNAL OF PUBLIC HEALTH. 72(8):

822, August 1982

The nurse listening to the adolescent. Contraception problems in adolescents, by A. Perron. NURSING MONTREAL. 6(3):4, June 1982

Post-bill amenorrhea following hormonal contraceptive therapy in adolescence, by M. Brandt, et al. ARZTLICHE JUGENDKUNDE. 72(4):241-245, 1981

Post-partum development of a mesenteric venous infarct and portal thrombosis in a young woman taking an oral contraceptive, by X. Quancard, et al. JOURNAL DES MALADIES VASCU-LAIRES. 6(4):307-311, 1981

Prescribing the 'pill' for minors [letter], by P. Gerber. MEDI-CAL JOURNAL OF AUSTRALIA. 1(11):483, May 29, 1982

Problems in adolescent contraception, by L. Aresin. ZEITSCHRIFT FUR DIE GESAMTE HYGIENE. 27(7):560-561, July 7, 1981

Problems of contraception in adolescents, by P. O. Hubinont. REVUE MEDICALE DE BRUXELLES. 3(6):425-430, June 1982

Problems of contraception in sexually active female adolescents. Results of an empirical study, by S. Rehpenning. ZEITSCHRIFT FUR DIE GESAMTE HYGIENE. 27(7):556-559, July 7, 1981

Psychosocial maturity and teenage contraceptive use: an investigation of decision-making and communication skills, by G. Cvetkovich, et al. POPULATION AND ENVIRONMENT: BEHAVIORAL AND SOCIAL ISSUES. 4(4):211-226, Winter 1981

Reagan: la grande croisade dans les chambres a coucher [adolescentes], by L. Wiznitzer. L'ACTUALITE. 7:26, September 1982

Reagan wants parents to be told when teens get contraceptives. CHRISTIANITY TODAY. 26:41, April 23, 1982

The relationship of abortion attitudes and contraceptive behavior among young single women [research], by E. S. Herold. CANADIAN JOURNAL OF PUBLIC HEALTH. 73(2):101-104, March-April 1982

Response of unmarried adolescents to contraceptive advice and service in Nigeria, by M. Ezimokhai, et al. INTERNATIONAL JOURNAL OF GYNAECOLOGY AND OBSTETRICS. 19(6):481-485, December 1981

The sensibility of the hypophysis, th gonads and the thyroid of adolescents before and after the administration of oral contraceptives [a resume], by I. Rey-Stocker, et al. PEDIATRIC ANNALS. 10(12):15-20, December 1981

Sex and contraceptive behavior among young single persons, by E. Garcia Hassey, et al. GINECOLOGIA Y OBSTETRICIA DE MEXICO. 49(296):343-357, June 1981

Sex education and contraceptive education in U.S. public high schools, by M. T. Orr. FAMILY PLANNING PERSPECTIVES. 14:304-313, November-December 1982

Sex education and its association with teenage sexual activity, pregnancy and contraceptive use, by M. Zelnik, et al. FAMILY PLANNING PERSPECTIVES. 14:117-125, May-June 1982

Sex education and its association with teenage sexual activity, pregnancy and contraceptive use [research], by M. Zelnik, et al. FAMILY PLANNING PERSPECTIVES. 14:117-119+, May-June 1982

Smoking, oral contraceptives and serum lipid and lipoprotein levels in youths, by A. W. Voors, et al. PREVENTIVE MEDICINE. 11(1):1-12, 1982

Social and affective factors associated with adolescent pregnancy, by P. B. Smith, et al. JOURNAL OF SCHOOL HEALTH. 52(2):90-93, February 1982

Social support for contraceptive utilization in adolescence, by J. A. Shea. DISSERTATION ABSTRACTS INTERNATIONAL. B. p. 4008, 1982

Special considerations in pregnancy prevention for the mentally subnormal adolescent female, by K. Hein, et al. JOURNAL OF ADOLESCENT HEALTH CARE. 1(1):46-49, September 1980

Staffing a contraceptive service for adolescents: the importance of sex, race, and age, by S. G. Philliber, et al. PUBLIC HEALTH REPORTS. 97(2):165-169, March-April 1982

Subjective assessment and cardiovasallar response to ischemic pain in young healthy women users and nonusers of oral contraceptives, by E. J. Stein, et al. JOURNAL OF PSYCHOSOMATIC RESEARCH. 25(6):579-586, 1981

Talking to parents about sex does not affect teens' contraceptive use. FAMILY PLANNING PERSPECTIVES. 14:279-280, September-October 1982

Teenage women and contraceptive behavior: focus on self-efficacy in sexual and contraceptive situations, by R. A. Levinson. DISSERTATION ABSTRACTS INTERNATIONAL. A. p. 151, 1982

Teens and contraception (parental notification proposal), by A. J. Fugh-Berman. OFF OUR BACKS. 12:13, June 1982

Theoretical framework for studying adolescent contraceptive use, by K. A. Urberg. ADOLESCENCE. 17:527-540, Fall, 1982

When teens want contraceptives, should their parents know? Two impassioned advocates face off (views of M. Mecklenburg and F. Wattleton), by K. Huff, et al. PEOPLE WEEKLY. 17:44-45, May 24, 1982

Abortion--referrals--family planning services. FAMILY LAW RE-
PORTER: COURT OPINIONS. 8(1):2009, November 3, 1981

Are hormonal contraceptives relevant for family planning?, by J.
M. Wenderlein. MMW: MUENCHENER MEDIZINISCHE WOCHENSCHRIFT.
124(20):487-488, May 21, 1982

Birth planning in Cuba: a basic human right, by J. M. Swanson.
INTERNATIONAL JOURNAL OF NURSING STUDIES. 18(2):81-88,
1981

Breast-feeding and family planning: a review of the relationships between breast-feeding and family planning, by R. E.
Brown. AMERICAN JOURNAL OF CLINICAL NUTRITION. 35(1):162-
171, January 1982

Breast-feeding, fertility and family planning, by M. F. McCann,
et al. POPULATION REPORTS. (24):J525-575, November-December
1981

The Brook Advisory Centres. HELATH VISITOR. 55:177-178, April
1982

Careers: family planning, fundamental to care, by A. Cowper.
NURSING MIRROR AND MIDWIVE'S JOURNAL. 154(25):58, June 23,
1982

Clinical forum 9. Obstetrics II: Postpartum family planning, by
S. Walker. NURSING MIRROR AND MIDWIVE'S JOURNAL. 153(11
Suppl):xxii-xxiv, September 9, 1981

Consultorio familiare e politica sociale. Un approccio sociologico-giuridico, by M. Corsale. SOCIOLOGIA DEL DIRITTO.
7(2):35-62, 1980

Elaboration and development of a family planning program for
pharmacists in Mexico, by C. Gutierrez Martinez, et al. SPM:
SALUD PUBLICA DE MEXICO. 23(4):405-411, July-August 1981

Evaluation of family planning communications in El Salvador, by
J. T. Bertrand, et al. INTERNATIONAL JOURNAL OF HEALTH
EDUCATION. 24(3):183-194, 1982

An evaluation of the use-effectiveness of fertility awareness
methods of family planning, by J. R. Weeks. JOURNAL OF BIO-
SOCIAL SCIENCE. 14(1):25-32, January 1982

Family planning, by R. Munoz, et al. NUEVA ENFERMERIA. (11):
11-12, May 1980

--, by P. Stoll. LEBENSVERSICHERUNGSMEDIZIN. 34(2):42-45,
February 11, 1982

--, by Z. Wei-sen, et al. AMERICAN JOURNAL OF PUBLIC HEALTH.
72:24-26, September 1982

Family planning and abortion: have they affected fertility in
Tennessee?, by H. K. Atrash, et al. AMERICAN JOURNAL OF PUB-

LIC HEALTH. 72(6):608-610, June 1982

Family planning and contraception, by D. Fock. KATILOLEHTI.
87(3):91-93, March 1982

Family planning and increased fitness of the child to survive,
by J. R. Kumari, et al. JOURNAL OF FAMILY WELFARE. 28:77,
March 1982

The family planning component, by U. Bhandari, et al. NURSING
JOURNAL OF INDIA. 73:141-143, May 1982

Family planning concept, by J. B. Dumindin. NEWSETTE. 21:9-13,
April-June 1981

Family planning. Contraception, sterilization, abortion, by H.
Ludwig. FORTSCHRITTE DER MEDIZIN. 100(16):721-722+, April
29, 1982

Family planning: fundamental to care, by A. Cowper. NURSING
MIRROR AND MIDWIVE'S JOURNAL. 154:58, June 23, 1982

Family planning in primary health care. NUEVA ENFERMERIA.
(17):28, January 1981

Family planning in a suburban development of Mexico City, by J.
H. Gutierrez Avila, et al. SPM: SALUD PUBLICA DE MEXICO.
24(1):39-47, January-February 1982

Family planning--paragraph 218 StGB, by E. Jakob. OEFFENTLICHE
GESUNDHEITSWESEN. 43(9):421-422, September 1981

Health services in Shanghai County; family planning, by W. S.
Zheng, et al. AMERICAN JOURNAL OF PUBLIC HEALTH. 72(9
Suppl):24-25, September 1982

Integrated family planning activities in maternal and child
health centres in Cap Bon, Tunisia. III: Impact on some
maternal and child health indicators, by I. De Schampheleire.
JOURNAL OF TROPICAL PEDIATRICS. 27(6):304-307, December 1981

Iowa Family Planning Program, by C. S. Adams. JOURNAL OF THE
IOWA MEDICAL SOCIETY. 72(4):165-168, April 1982

Maternal and child health and family planning in an island
village locality, by S. R. Mehta. JOURNAL OF FAMILY WELFARE.
28:66-77, June 1982

A note on measuring the independent impact of family planning
programs on fertility declines, by D. J. Hernadez. DEMOGRA-
PHY. 18(4):627-634, November 1981

A people's movement for health and family planning, by I. Gandhi.
INDIAN JOURNAL OF PEDIATRICS. 48(393):389-394, July-August
1981

Peptid contraception--new principles for family planning, by S.
J. Nillius. LAKARTIDNINGEN. 78(34):2845-2848, August 19, 1978

FAMILY PLANNING: GENERAL (continued)

Planificaria familiei in perspectiva sociologica, by V. Trebici. VIITORUL SOCIAL. 8(1):171-176, January-March 1981

Planning the family way, by Z. Pauncefort. NURSING MIRROR AND MIDWIVE'S JOURNAL. 154(Community Forum #2):ii+, February 10, 1982

Population and birth planning in the People's Republic of China, by P. C. Chen, et al. POPULATION REPORTS. (25):J577-618, January-February 1982

Preliminary experience with a family planning risk-scoring system, by W. N. Spellacy, et al. FERTILITY AND STERILITY. 36(4):527-528, October 1981

Prospects for planning in the global family. NEW SCIENTIST. 94:291, April 29, 1982

Reproductive health care: delivery of services and organization- al structure, by J. M. Johnson. FAMILY COMMUNITY HEALTH. 5(1):41-46, May 1982

Should we have children? A decision-making group for couples, by K. K. Kimball, et al. PERSONNEL AND GUIDANCE JOURNAL. 60(3): 153-156, November 1981

Teenagers who use organized family planning services: United States, 1978, by E. Eckard. VITAL HEALTH STATISTICS. 13(57): 1-18, August 1981

The trend toward delayed parenthood, by J. R. Wilkie. JOURNAL OF MARRIAGE AND THE FAMILY. 43(3):583-591, August 1981

Unplanned pregnancies in a midwestern community, by D. Hilliard, et al. JOURNAL OF FAMILY PRACTICE. 15(2):259-263, August 1982

Voluntary childlessness and contraception: problems and prac- tices, by F. Baum. JOURNAL OF BIOSOCIAL SCIENCE. 14:17-24, January 1982

AFRICA
Characteristics and attitudes of family planners in Khartoum, Sudan, by M. A. Khalifa. JOURNAL OF BIOSOCIAL SCIENCE. 14(1):7-16, January 1982

Factors influencing the acceptance of family planning by blacks in Salisbury, Zimbabwe, by D. S. MacDonald. SOUTH AFRICAN MEDICAL JOURNAL. 61(12):437-439, March 20, 1982

Integrated family planning activities in maternal and child health centres in Cap Bon, Tunisia. I. Methodology and re- sults, by I. De Schampheleire, et al. JOURNAL OF TROPICAL PEDIATRICS. 27(4):190-195, August 1981

--II. Use of a family planning technical card in an integrated maternal and child health program, by I. De Schampheleire. JOURNAL OF TROPICAL PEDIATRICS. 27(4):196-198, August 1981

--III. Impact on some maternal and child health indicators, by I. De Schampheleire. JOURNAL OF TROPICAL PEDIATRICS. 27(6):304-307, December 1981

Maternal and child health and family planning in Nigeria, by M. A. Oyediran. PUBLIC HEALTH. 95(6):344-346, November 1981

Polygyny and family planning in Sub-Saharan Africa, by J. E. Brown. STUDIES IN FAMILY PLANNING. 12(8-9):322, August-September 1981

Rwanda: too many people too little land, by J. Hammand. WORLD HEALTH. pp. 12-15, June 1982

U. S. population policies, development, and the rural poor of Africa, by E. Green. JOURNAL OF MODERN AFRICAN STUDIES. 20:45-67, March 1982

ASIA
Incentives, reproductive behavior, and integrated community development in Asia, by H. P. David. STUDIES IN FAMILY PLANNING. 13(5):159-173, May 1982

BANGKOK
Factors associated with family planning acceptance in Bangkok metropolis health clinic areas (MHCs), by T. Chumnijarakij, et al. CONTRACEPTION. 23(5):517-525, May 1981

BRAZIL
Consultori per la pianificazione familiare in Brasile, by C. Souto, et al. SOCIOLOGIA DEL DIRITTO. 7(2):125-137, 1980

CARIBBEAN
Fertility and family planning in Haiti, by J. Allman. STUDIES IN FAMILY PLANNING. 13:237-245, August-September 1982

Post family planning acceptance experience in the Caribbean: St. Kitts-Nevis and St. Vincent, by J. Bailey, et al. STUDIES IN FAMILY PLANNING. 13(2):44-58, February 1982

CENTRAL AMERICA
Family planning communications and contraceptive use in Guatemala, El Salvador, and Panama, by J. T. Bertrand, et al. STUDIES IN FAMILY PLANNING. 13(6-7):190-199, June-July 1982

CHINA
China: planning or persecution? China is using a mix of incentives and deterrents to meet its population reduction target; but the campaign has led to excesses, by D. Lee. SOUTH. pp. 35-37, November 1981

China's one-child drive: another long march, by L. C. Landman. INTERNATIONAL FAMILY PLANNING PERSPECTIVES. 7:102-107, September 1981

FAMILY PLANNING: GENERAL (continued)

China's one-child family: policy and public response, by L. F.
Goodstadt. POPULATION AND DEVELOPMENT REVIEW. 8:37-58,
March 1982

One is enough: the Chinese way of population control, by L. R.
Brown. ACROSS THE BOARD. 19:27-28, March 1982

1000m people, 800m peasants (population policies; China), by
L. Zheng. POPULI. 8(3):36-43, 1981

Population and birth planning in the People's Republic of
China. POPULATION REPORTS. 10(1): , January-February
1982

Population studies and population policy in China, by J. S.
Aird. POPULATION AND DEVELOPMENT REVIEW. 8:267-297, June
1982

COLOMBIA
Child mortality and fertility in Colombia: individual and com-
munity effects, by M. R. Rosenzweig, et al. HEALTH POLICY
AND EDUCATION. 2(3-4):305-348, March 1982

COSTA RICA
A decline of fertility in Costa Rica: literacy, modernization
and family planning, by J. M. Stycos. POPULATION STUDIES.
36(1):15-30, March 1982

DEVELOPING COUNTRIES
Impact of family planning programs on fertility in developing
countries: a critical evaluation, by J. J. Hernandez. SO-
CIAL SCIENCE RESEARCH. 10:63-66, March 1981

EAST GERMANY
Changes in the reproductive behavior in East Germany (1970-
1979) in connection with measures of family policy. I., by
U. Fritsche. ZEITSCHRIFT FUR ARZTLICHE FORTBILDUNG.
75(10):489-492, May 15, 1981

The development and role of the Marriage and Family Section in
the establishment of socialist family policies in East
Germany. ZEITSCHRIFT FUR DIE GESAMTE HYGIENE. 27(7):514-
516, July 7, 1981

EL SALVADOR
Evaluation of family planning communications in El Salvador,
by J. T. Bertrand, et al. INTERNATIONAL JOURNAL OF HEALTH
EDUCATION. 24(3):183-194, 1982

EUROPE
Ideal family size, fertility, and population policy in Western
Europe, by A. Girard, et al. POPULATION AND DEVELOPMENT RE-
VIEW. 8:323-345, June 1982

FRANCE
Le conseil familial et conjugal en France, by J. Rigaux.
SOCIOLOGIA DEL DIRITTO. 7(2):111-124, 1980

FAMILY PLANNING: GENERAL (continued)

GUATEMALA
Nutrition, family planning, and health promotion: the Guate-
malan program of primary health care, by A. Lechtig, et al.
BIRTH. 9:97-104, Summer 1982

INDIA
The demographic impact of the contraceptive distribution pro-
ject in Matlab, Bangladesh, by W. S. Stinson, et al. STUD-
DIES IN FAMILY PLANNING. 13(5):141-148, May 1982

The demographic impact of the family planning--health services
project in Matlab, Bangladesh, by J. F. Phillips, et al.
STUDIES IN FAMILY PLANNING. 13(5):131-140, May 1982

Indira Gandhi calls for revitalization of India's family
planning program. FAMILY PLANNING PERSPECTIVES. 14:149-
150, May-June 1982

Migrant-nonmigrant differentials in socioeconomic status, fertility and family planning in Nepal, by J. M. Tuladhar, et
al. INTERNATIONAL MIGRATION REVIEW. 16:197-205, Spring
1982

INDONESIA
Family planning attitudes in urban Indonesia: findings from
focus group research, by H. Suyono, ete al. STUDIES IN
FAMILY PLANNING. 12(12 Pt 1):433, December 1981

Focus group research (reports on the use of focus group re-
search in evaluating family planning programs in Mexico and
Indonesia). STUDIES IN FAMILY PLANNING. 12(Pt 1):407-456,
December 1981

IRELAND
Fertility and family planning in the Irish Republic 1975, by
K. Wilson-Davis. JOURNAL OF BIOSOCIAL SCIENCE. 14:343-358,
July 1982

Ideal family size in Northern Ireland, by J. Coward. JOURNAL
OF BIOSOCIAL SCIENCE. 13(4):443-454, October 1981

ITALY
Knowledge concerning the family-planning clinic among the
female population of Milan: studies of a group of 959
puerperas, by A. Bouzin, et al. ANNALI DI OSTETRICIA
GINECOLOGIA, MEDICINA PERINATALE. 103(1):60-67, January-
February 1982

KOREA
The transition in Korean family planning behavior, 1935-1976:
a retrospective cohort analysis, by J. R. Foreit. STUDIES
IN FAMILY PLANNING. 13:227-236, August-September 1982

LEBANON
Marital relations and fertility control decisions among
Lebanese couples, by M. Chamie, et al. POPULATION AND
ENVIRONMENT. 4(3):189, Fall 1981

FAMILY PLANNING: GENERAL (continued)

MEXICO
Contraceptive use and family planning services along the
U.S.-Mexico border, by C. W. Warren, et al. INTERNATIONAL
FAMILY PLANNING PERSPECTIVES. 7:52-59, June 1981

Elaboration and development of a family planning program for
pharmacists in Mexico, by C. Gutierrez Martinez, et al.
SPM: SALUD PUBLICA DE MEXICO. 23(4):405-411, July-August
1981

Family planning in a suburban development of Mexico City, by
J. H. Gutierrez Avila, et al. SPM: SALUD PUBLICA DE
MEXICO. 24(1):39-47, January-February 1982

Focus group and survey research on family planning in Mexico,
by E. Folch-Iyon, et al. STUDIES IN FAMILY PLANNING. 12(12
Pt 1):409, December 1981

Focus group research (reports on the use of focus group re-
search in evaluating family planning programs in Mexico and
Indonesia). STUDIES IN FAMILY PLANNING. 12(Pt 1):407-456,
December 1981

NEW GUINEA
Cultural influenes in birth practices in Papua New Guinea, by
E. E. Drakum. AUSTRALASIAN NURSES JOURNAL. 11:14-15+, June
1982

NIGERIA
Maternal and child health and family planning in Nigeria, by
M. A. Oyediran. PUBLIC HEALTH. 95(6):344-346, November
1981

PAKISTAN
The family planning program in Pakistan: what went wrong?, by
W. C. Robinson, et al. INTERNATIONAL FAMILY PLANNING PER-
SPECTIVES. 7:85-92, September 1981

THE PHILIPPINES
Effects of Philippine family planning outreached project on
contraceptive prevalence: a multivariate analysis, by J. E.
Laing. STUDIES IN FAMILY PLANNING. 12(11):367-380, November 1981

SHANGHAI
Health services in Shanghai County: family planning, by W. S.
Zheng, et al. AMERICAN JOURNAL OF PUBLIC HEALTH. 72(9
Suppl):24-25, September 1982

SINGAPORE
Quantiative analysis of some decision rules for famiy planning
in an oriental sociely, by T. N. Goh. INTERFACES. 11:31-
37, April 1981

Stopping rules for family planning in an oriental society, by
V. M. Ng. INTERFACES. 12:82-84, February 1982

SOUTH PACIFIC
Fertility and family planning in the South Pacific, by D.
Lucas, et al. STUDIES IN FAMILY PLANNING. 12(8-9):303-135,
August-September 1981

SOUTHEAST ASIA
Family planning services for Southeast Asian refugess, by J.
Kubota, et al. FAMILY COMMUNITY HEALTH. 5:19-28, May 1982

TAIWAN
Toward a closer integration of population in development
policies in Taiwan [conference paper], by P. K. C. Liu.
INDUSTRY OF FREE CHINA. 56:9-28, August 1981

THAILAND
Thailand's family planning program: a Asian success story, by
A. Rosenfield, et al. INTERNATIONAL FAMILY PLANNING PER-
SPECTIVES. 8:43-51, June 1982

Thailand's reproductive revolution [update], by P. Kamnuansilpa, et al. INTERNATIONAL FAMILY PLANNING PERSPECTIVES. 8:
51-56, June 1982

TUNISIA
Integrated family planning activities in maternal and child
health centres in Cap Bon, Tunisia. I: Methodology and results, by I. De Schampheleire, et al. JOURNAL OF TROPICAL
PEDIATRICS. 27(4):190-195, August 1981

--II: Use of a family planning technical card in an integrated
maternal and child health program, by I. De Schampheleire.
JOURNAL OF TROPICAL PEDIATRICS. 27(4):196-198, August 1981

--III: Impact on some maternal and child health indicators,
by I. De Schampheleire. JOURNAL OF TROPICAL PEDIATRICS.
27(6):304-307, December 1981

TURKEY
Sources of family size attitudes and family planning knowledge
among rural Turkish youth, by C. E. Carpenter-Yaman. STUD-
IES IN FAMILY PLANNING. 13(5):149-158, May 1982

UNITED KINGDOM
GPs and government clinics provide free family planning to
over 70 percent of all UK women. FAMILY PLANNING PERSPEC-
TIVES. 13:272-273, November-December 1981

UNITED STATES
Contraceptive use and family planning services along the U.S.-
Mexico border, by C. W. Warren, et al. INTERNATIONAL FAMILY
PLANNING PERSPECTIVES. 7:52-59, June 1981

Contraceptive use patterns, prior source, and pregnancy history of female family planning patients: United States,
1980, by E. Eckard. ADVANCE DATA. (82):1-12, June 16,
1982

Dynamics of policy politics: the cases of abortion funding and

FAMILY PLANNING: GENERAL (continued)

> family planning in the state of Oregon, by G. L. Keiser.
> DISSERTATION ABSTRACTS INTERNATIONAL. A. p. 4919, 1982

Family planning and abortion: have they affected fertility in
Tennessee, USA?, by H. K. Atrash, et al. AMERICAN JOURNAL
OF PUBLIC HEALTH. 72(6):608-610, June 1982

Family planning practices among Anglo and Hispanic women in
U.S. counties bordering Mexico, by R. W. Rochat, et al.
FAMILY PLANNING PERSPECTIVES. 13(4):176-180, July-August
1981

Family planning visits by teenagers: United States, 1978, by
J. Foster, et al. VITAL HEALTH STATISTICS. 13(58):1-24,
August 1981

Medicaid funding of family planning clinic services, by M. T.
Orr, et al. FAMILY PLANNING PERSPECTIVES. 13:280-287,
November-December 1981

Need for family planning services among Anglo and Hispanic
women in the United States countries bordering Mexico, by S.
E. Holck, et al. FAMILY PLANNING PERSPECTIVES. 14:155-162,
May-June 1982

Use of services for family planning and infertility: United
States, by G. E. Hendershot, et al. VITAL HEALTH SERVICES.
23(8):1-41, December 1981

Women who use organized family planning services: United
States, 1979, by E. Eckard. VITAL HEALTH STATISTICS.
13(62):1-28, January 1982

FAMILY PLANNING: ATTITUDES
Characteristics and attitudes of family planners in Khartoum,
Sudan, by M. A. Khalifa. JOURNAL OF BIOSOCIAL SCIENCE. 14:
7-16, January 1982

Personal and socio-economic variable in relation with attitudes
toward planned family, by M. Bhargava, et al. INDIAN JOURNAL
OF CLINICAL PSYCHOLOGY. 8(1):35-38, March 1981

The planned family is a misconception (Catholic view), by J.
McGowan. US CATHOLIC. 47:31-32, November 1982

Psychological condition of the desire to have children and its
fulfillment (empirical report), by A. Geissler. ZEITSCHRIFT
FUR DIE GESAMTE HYGIENE. 27(7):522-525, July 7, 1981

Sources of family size attitudes and family planning knowledge
among rural Turkish youth, by C. E. Carpenter-Yaman. STUDIES
IN FAMILY PLANNING. 13(5):149, May 1982

The threat of numbers, by R. W. Peterson. AUDUBON. 84:107,
July 1982

FAMILY PLANNING: LAWS AND LEGISLATION
Fertility-related state laws enacted in 1981, by P. Donovan.

FAMILY PLANNING: LAWS AND LEGISLATION (continued)

FAMILY PLANNING PERSPECTIVES. 14(2):63-67, March-April 1982

The 'squeal rule': government and confidentiality, by D. M.
Prout. AMERICAN COLLEGE OF PHYSICIANS. 2(3):3+, April 1982

FAMILY PLANNING: METHODS
An evaluation of the use-effectiveness of fertility awareness
methods of family planning, by J. R. Weeks. JOURNAL OF BIO-
SOCIAL SCIENCE. 14:25-32, January 1982

Family planning: 'Billing's' ovulation method, by M. S. Bhering,
et al. REVISTA ESPANOLA DE LAS ENFERMEDADES DEL APARATO
DIGESTIVO. 14(3):257-263, December 1980

FAMILY PLANNING: NATURAL
An analysis of continuity-descontinuity in natural family
planning: an Australian factor analysis, by J. A. Johnston.
INTERNATIONAL JOURNAL OF FERTILITY. 26(3):231-238, 1981

Effectiveness of the sympto-thermal method of natural family
planning: an international study, by F. J. Rice, et al.
INTERNATIONAL JOURNAL OF FERTILITY. 26(3):222-230, 1981

Natural family planning, by W. Fijalkowski. PIELEGNIARKA I
POLOZNA. (9):1-2, 1981

--[review], by H. Klaus. OBSTETRICAL AND GYNECOLOGICAL SURVEY.
37(2):128-150, February 1982

Natural family planning: an analysis of change in procreative
intention, by H. Klaus, et al. JOURNAL OF THE AMERICAN MEDI-
CAL WOMEN'S ASSOCIATION. 37:231-237+, September 1982

Natural family planning and instructor training, by M. C.
Martin. NURSING AND HEALTH CARE. 2(10):554-556+, December
1981

Natural family planning at the grassroots, by V. L. Enright.
PRIEST. 38:30-32, September 1982

Natural family planning basis for a happy married life, by V. J.
Dunigan. PRIEST. 38:12-17, January 1982

Natural family planning methods [letter], by J. J. Billings.
AMERICAN JOURNAL OF OBSTETRICS AND GYNECOLOGY. 143(1):114-
115, May 1, 1982

Natural family planning: postpartum period, by A. Perez. INTER-
NATIONAL JOURNAL OF FERTILITY. 26(3):219-221, 1981

Natural family planning: when other contraceptive methods won't
do, by J. J. McCarthy. CONSULTANT. 21:109-110+, December
1981

New light on natural family planning, by K. Banet. LIGUORIAN.
70:34-38, August 1982

A one-sided view of natural family planning; reprint from the

FAMILY PLANNING: NATURAL (continued)

　　International Federation for Family Life Promotion Asia-
　　Oceania Region Newsletter, December 1981. LINACRE QUARTERLY.
　　49:2341-239, August 1982

　　A perspective multicentre trial o the ovulation method of na-
　　tural family planning. II. The effectiveness phase. FERTILITY
　　AND STERILITY. 36(5):591-598, November 1981

　　A randomized prospective study of the use-effectiveness of two
　　methods of natural family planning, by M. E. Wade, et al.
　　AMERICAN JOURNAL OF OBSTETRICS AND GYNECOLOGY. 14(4):368-376,
　　October 15, 1981

　　The sympto-thermal methods, by S. Parenteau-Carreau. INTERNA-
　　TIONAL JOURNAL OF FERTILITY. 26(3):170-181, 1981

　　Terminology and core curricula in natural family planning, by J.
　　J. Brennan, et al. FERTILITY AND STERILITY. 38(1):117-118,
　　July 1982

　　A thirty-month clinical experience in natural family planning,
　　by R. Kambic, et al. AMERICAN JOURNAL OF PUBLIC HEALTH.
　　71(11):1255-1258, November 1981

　　The time has come for pastoral work in natura family planning,
　　by A. Zimmerman. PRIEST. 38:12-15, July-August 1982

FAMILY PLANNING: RESEARCH
　　Research on the determinants of fertility: a note on priorites.
　　POPULATION AND DEVELOPMENT REVIEW. 7(2):311, June 1981

　　Terminology and core curriculum in natural family planning, by
　　J. J. Brennan, et al. LINACRE QUARTERLY. 48:313-315, Novem-
　　ber 1981

　　Utilizing research to manage a family planning project, by N. E.
　　Williamson. STUDIES IN FAMILY PLANNING. 11(9-10):301-307,
　　September-October 1980

FAMILY PLANNING: RURAL
　　A review of midwife training programs in Tami Nadu, by S. B.
　　Mani. STUDIES IN FAMILY PLANNING. 11(12):395-400, December
　　1980

　　U. S. population policies, development, and the rural poor of
　　Africa, by E. Green. JOURNAL OF MODERN AFRICAN STUDIES. 20:
　　45-67, March 1982

FAMILY PLANNING: STATISTICS
　　Consent and privacy in the National Survey of Family Growth: a
　　report on the pilot study for cycle III, by K. Tanfer, et al.
　　VITAL HEALTH STATISTICS. 2(91):1-47, March 1982

　　Family planning by tribals, by N. Y. Naidu. THE EASTERN ANTHRO-
　　POLOGIST. 32(3):205-207, July-September 1979

　　Family welfare and child health: a reappraisal of community base
　　postpartum programme, by S. Kumari, et al. INDIAN JOURNAL OF

PEDIATRICS. 18(9):619-623, September 1981

Fertility and family planning in the 1970s: the National Survey of Family Growth, by W. D. Mosher. FAMILY PLANNING PERSPECTIVES. 14:314-340, November-December 1982

The National Inventory of Family Planning Services: 1978 survey results, by E. Graves. VITAL HEALTH STATISTICS. 14(26):1-34, February 1982

Survey of childbearing women in Qi-yi Commune, by E. S. Gao, et al. AMERICAN JOURNAL OF PUBLIC HEALTH. 72(9 Suppl):27-29, September 1982

A time series of instrumental fertility variables, by N. B. Ryder. DEMOGRAPHY. 18(4):487-509, November 1981

Wanted and unwanted fertility: Victoria 1971 to 1975, by K. Betts. AUSTRALIAN JOURNAL OF SOCIAL ISSUES. 15(3):194-208, 1980

FAMILY PLANNING AND INSURANCE
Medicaid funding of family planning clinic services, by M. T. Orr, et al. FAMILY PLANNING PERSPECTIVES. 13(6):280, November-December 1981

FAMILY PLANNING AND MALES
Breast-feeding and family planning: a review of the relationships between breast-feeding and family planning, by R. E. Brown. AMERICAN JOURNAL OF CLINICAL NUTRITION. 35:162-171, January 1982

FAMILY PLANNING AND NURSES
Family planning in the nursing curriculum, by M. B. Agostino. PROFESSIONI INFERMIERISTICHE. 35(1):14-19, January-March 1982

FAMILY PLANNING AND PARENTAL CONSENT
Parental involvement: selling family planning clinics short [research], by F. F. Furstenberg, Jr., et al. FAMILY PLANNING PERSPECTIVES. 14:140-144, May-June 1982

FAMILY PLANNING AND PHYSICIANS
The baby our doctors told us we'd never have (ed. by M. Fuerst), by J. Koblas. GOOD HOUSEKEEPING. 195:122+, October 1982

FAMILY PLANNING AND POLITICS
The politics of fertility. How the population situation affects political institutions. Part 1, by J. A. Loraine. MIDWIFE, HEALTH VISITOR AND COMMUNITY NURSE. 17:498-499+, December 1981

FAMILY PLANNING AND RELIGION
The planned family is a misconception (Catholic view), by J. McGowan. US CATHOLIC. 47:31-32, November 1982

FAMILY PLANNING AND WOMEN
Women's involvement in socioeconomic projects related to family planning, by A. Duza. POPULATION STUDIES. pp. 3-30, July-September 1981

Factors affecting adolescents' use of family planning clinics (United States) [research], by M. Chamie, et al. FAMILY PLANNING PER SPECTIVES. 14:126-127+, May-June 1982

Family planning clinics: cure or cause of teenage pregnancy?, by M. C. Schwartz, et al. LINACRE QUARTERLY. 49:143-164, May 1982

Gynecology in the young, by S. J. Emans. EMERGENCY MEDICINE. 14:92-96+, April 30, 1982

Hospitals, clinics, agencies sponsor adolescent pregnancy projects [interview], by M. E. Mecklenburg. HOSPITAL PROGRESS. 63(9):46-49, September 1982

Never-pregnant adolescents and family planning programs: contraception, continuation, and pregnancy risk, by E. W. Freeman, et al. AMERICAN JOURNAL OF PUBLIC HEALTH. 72(8):815-822, August 1982

Sources of family size attitudes and family planning knowledge among rural Turkish youth, by C. E. Carpenter-Yaman. STUDIES IN FAMILY PLANNING. 13:149-158, May 1982

Teenagers who use organized family planning services: United States, 1978, by E. Eckard. VITAL HEALTH STATISTICS. 13(57): 1-18, August 1981

Why they delay: a study of teenage family planning clinic patients [research], by L. S. Zabin, et al. FAMILY PLANNING PERSPECTIVES. 13(5):205-207, September-October 1981

FAMILY PLANNING CLINICS

Abortion: Planned Parenthood Association of Kansas City, Missouri, Inc. v. Ashcroft (655 F 2d 848): Missouri loses latest round in battle over permissible abortion regulations. UMKC LAW REVIEW. 50:320-339, Spring 1982

Changing profile of IUD users in family planning clinics in rural Bangladesh, by S. Bhatia, et al. JOURNAL OF BIOSOCIAL SCIENCE. 13(2):169-177, April 1981

Clinical forum 9. Obstetrics II: postpartum family planning, by S. Walker. NURSING MIRROR AND MIDWIVE'S JOURNAL. 153(11 Suppl):xxii-xxiv, September 9, 1981

Computerized patient-flow analysis of local family planning clinics, by J. L. Graves, et al. FAMILY PLANNING PERSPEC-TIVES. 13(4):164-170, July-August 1981

Contraception, pregnancy management and the family-planning clinic (findings on 410 puerperas in a Lombard hospital), by M. Semeria. ANNALI DI OSTETRICIA GINECOLOGIA, MEDICINA PERINATALE. 103(1):93-101, January-February 1982

Factors affecting adolescents' use of family planning clinics (United States) [research], by M. Chamie, et al. FAMILY PLANNING PERSPECTIVES. 14:126-127+, May-June 1982

Family planning clinics: cure or cause of teenage pregnancy?, by
M. C. Schwartz, et al. LINACRE QUARTERLY. 49:143-164, May
1982

Family planning visits by teenagers: United States, 1978, by J.
Foster, et al. VITAL HEALTH STATISTICS. 13(58):1-24, August
1981

Five years' experience of a 'prepregnancy' clinic for insulin-
dependent diabetics, by J. M. Steel, et al. BRITISH MEDICAL
JOURNAL. 285(6338):353-356, July 31, 1982

GPs and government clinics provide free family planning to over
70 percent of all UK women. FAMILY PLANNING PERSPECTIVES.
13:272-273, November-December 1981

A hard pill to swallow? (proposal to require Federally funded
family-planning clinics to notify parents when their adolescents receive contraceptives), by B. Brophy. FORBES. 129:99,
May 10, 1982

Hospitals, clinics, agencies sponsor adolescent pregnancy projects [interview], by M. E. Mecklenburg. HOSPITAL PROGRESS.
63(9):46-49, September 1982

Iowa Family Planning Program, by C. S. Adams. JOURNAL OF THE
IOWA MEDICAL SOCIETY. 72(4):165-168, April 1982

Issues in family planning clinic management, by A. A. Hudgins,
et al. FAMILY COMMUNITY HEALTH. 5(1):47-59, May 1982

Medicaid funding of family planning clinic services, by M. T.
Orr, et al. FAMILY PLANNING PERSPECTIVES. 13:280-286, November-December 1981

Never-pregnant adolescents and family planning programs: contraception, continuation, and pregnancy risk, by E. W. Freeman,
et al. AMERICAN JOURNAL OF PUBLIC HEALTH. 72(8):815, August
1982

Parental involvement: selling family planning clinics short
[research], by F. F. Furstenberg, Jr., et al. FAMILY PLANNING
PERSPECTIVES. 14:140-144, May-June 1982

Planned parenthood: ideas for the 1980s, by C. W. Tyler, Jr.
FAMILY PLANNING PERSPECTIVES. 14:221-223, July-August
1982

Planned Parenthood League of Massachusetts v. Bellotti, 40 U S L
W 2532. AMERICAN JOURNAL OF TRIAL ADVOCACY. 5:166-171, Summer 1981

--, 641 F 2d 1006. JOURNAL OF FAMILY LAW. 20:158-161, September 1981

Pregnancy, contraception and the family-planning clinic: from
the woman's point of view (studies of 3635 puerperas in 6
Lombard hospital obstetrical departments), by G. Remotti, et

FAMILY PLANNING CLINICS (continued)

al. ANNALI DI OSTETRICIA GINECOLOGIA, MEDICINA PERINATALE. 103(1):7-47, January-February 1982

Provision of rubella immunization in general practitioner family planning services, by N. A. Black. JOURNAL OF THE ROYAL COLLEGE OF GENERAL PRACTITIONERS. 31(231):593-595, October 1981

Requirements applicable to projects for family planning services Public Health Service. Proposed rule. FEDERAL REGISTER. 47(35):7699-7701, February 22, 1982

Response to rubella immunisation education in health authority family planning clinics: a controlled clinical trial, by N. A. Black. HEALTH EDUCATION JOURNAL. 40(4):111-118, 1981

A review of midwife training program in Tamil Nadu, by S. B. Mani. STUDIES IN FAMILY PLANNING. 11(12):395-400, December 1980

Schienberg v. Smith, 659 F 2d 476. JOURNAL OF FAMILY LAW. 20:551-554, May 1982

Sex education outreach from a family planning agency, by E. Rosen, et al. HEALTH EDUCATION. 13(2):13-15, March-April 1982

Status of family planning among the patients visiting our clinic, by Y. Miyagawa, et al. JOSANPU ZASSHI. 36(6):500-503, June 1982

Telltale birth control (proposal to require federally funded family-planning clinics to notify parents when their teen-agers receive contraceptives), by M. Beck. NEWSWEEK. 99:33, April 5, 1982

Using model projects to introduce change into family planning programs, by M. H. Bernhart. STUDIES IN FAMILY PLANNING. 12(10):346, October 1981

Visits to family planning clinics: United States, 1979, by B. Bloom. ADVANCE DATA. (74):1-7, September 4, 1981

Visits to family planning service sites: United States, 1978, by B. L. Hudson. ADVANCE DATA. (72):1-7, June 29, 1981

Why they delay: a study of teenage family planning clinic pa-tients, by L. S. Zabin, et al. FAMILY PLANNING PERSPECTIVES. 13(5):205-207+, September-October 1981

FAMILY PLANNING COUNSELING
Attitudes of selected secondary students toward family planning education, by J. Mercier, et al. HOME ECONOMICS RESEARCH JOURNAL. 10(2):127-136, December 1981

The family planning 'turntable': the counsellor in the face of a wide range of requests, by N. Meregaglia, et al. THERAPEUTIS-

FAMILY PLANNING COUNSELING (continued)

      CHE UMSCHAU. 38(11):1103-1106, November 1981

    An investigation into the quality of service provided by tele-
      phone hotlines for family planning services [research], by D.
      Baxter, et al. CANADIAN JOURNAL OF PUBLIC HEALTH. 73:194-
      199, May-June 1982

    Marriage and family counseling, by A. P. Kiriushchenkov.
      FEL'DSHER I AKUSHERKA. 47(1):59-60, 1982

    Measuring family planning acceptance by the criterion of excess
      children, by H. M. Rajyaguru. JOURNAL OF FAMILY WELFARE.
      28:34-45, March 1982

    Midwives as counselors, by P. Woo. JORDEMODERN. 95(20:55-59,
      February 1982

    Prenatal diagnosis and genetic counseling in 21 trisomy: its
      impact on family planning, by G. Evers-Keilbooms, et al.
      JOURNAL DE GENETIQUE HUMAINE. 28(5):147-159, February
      1981

FAMILY PLANNING EDUCATION
    Family planning and sex education, by C. Bailey. NURSING.
      2:32-33, June 1982

FAMILY PLANNING FUNDING
    Medicaid funding of family planning clinic services, by M. T.
      Orr, et al. FAMILY PLANNING PERSPECTIVES. 13(6):280-286,
      November-December 1981

    Public funding of contraceptive services, 1980-1982 [research],
      by B. Nestor. FAMILY PLANNING PERSPECTIVES. 14:198-203,
      July-August 1982

FAMILY PLANNING STATISTICS
    Computerized patient-flow analysis of local family planning
      clinics, by J. L. Graves, et al. FAMILY PLANNING PERSPEC-
      TIVES. 13(4):164-170, July-August 1981

FERTILITY AND FERTILITY CONTROL
    Breast-feeding, fertility and family planning, by M. F. McCann,
      et al. POPULATION REPORTS. (24):J525-575, November-December
      1981

    Contraceptive availability differentials in use and fertility,
      by A. O. Tsui, et al. STUDIES IN FAMILY PLANNING. 12(11):
      381-393, November 1981

    Contraceptive use and fertility in the Republic of Panama, by R.
      S. Monteith, et al. STUDIES IN FAMILY PLANNING. 12(10):331,
      October 1981

    Controlling population growth. BEIJING REVIEW. 25:6-7, May 17,
      1982

    The decline of fertility in Costa Rica: literacy, modernization
      and family planning, by J. M. Stycos. POPULATION STUDIES.

36(1):15, March 1982

Drug blocks pregnancy after fertilization, by J. Fox. CHEMICAL AND ENGINEERING NEWS. 60:26, May 17, 1982

An evaluation of the use-effectiveness of fertility awareness methods of family planning, by J. R. Weeks. JOURNAL OF BIO-SOCIAL SCIENCE. 14(1):25-32, January 1982

Family planning and abortion: have they affected fertility in Tennessee, by H. K. Atrash, et al. AMERICAN JOURNAL OF PUBLIC HEALTH. 72;608-609, June 1982

Fertility and family planning in the Irish Republic 1975, by K. Wilson-Davis. JOURNAL OF BIOSOCIAL SCIENCE. 14:343-358, July 1982

Fertility and family planning in the South Pacific, by D. Lucas, et al. STUDIES IN FAMILY PLANNING. 12(8-9):303-315, August-September 1981

Fertility and family planning in the 1970s: the National Survey of Family Growth, by W. D. Mosher. FAMILY PLANNING PERSPEC-TIVES. 14:314-340, November-December 1982

Fertility control and the voluntarily childless: an exploratory study, by E. Carlisle. JOURNAL OF BIOSOCIAL SCIENCE. 14(2): 203-212, April 1982

Fertility-related state laws enacted in 1981, by P. Donovan. FAMILY PLANNING PERSPECTIVES. 14(2):63-67, March-April 1982

Hormonal factors in fertility, infertility and contraception. JOURNAL OF STEROID BIOCHEMISTRY. 14(11):i-xxxvii, November 1981

The impact of legal abortion on marita and nonmarital fertility in upstate New York, by E. J. Tu, et al. FAMILY PLANNING PERSPECTIVES. 14(1):37-46, January-February 1982

Infertility trends among U.S. couples: 1965-1976, by W. D. Mosher. FAMILY PLANNING PERSPECTIVES. 14(1):22, January-February 1982

Intermediate variables and educational differentials in fertil-ity in Korea and the Philippines, by L. Bumpass, et al. DEMOGRAPHY. 14(2):63-67, March-April 1982

Knowledge of contraceptives: an assessment of world fertility survey data collection procedures, by M. Vaessen. POPULATION STUDIES. 35(3):357, November 1981

Legal aspects of research and practice in fertility control, by J. Stepan. CESKOSLOVENSKA GYNEKOLOGIE. 46(3):212-216, April 1981

Luteal phase defects induced by an agonist of luteinizing

hormone-releasing factor: a model for fertility control, by K. L. Sheehan, et al. SCIENCE. 215(4529):170-172, January 1982

Marital relations and fertility control decisions among Lebanese couples, by M. Chamie, et al. POPULATION AND ENVIRONMENT. 4(3):189, Fall 1981

A note on measuring the independent impact of family planning programs on fertility declines, by D. J. Hernadez. DEMOGRA-PHY. 18(4):627-634, November 1981

One child makes sense (fertility trends in 10 Asian countries, 1950-75), by K. Srinivasan. POPULI. 9(1):27-35, 1982

An oral fertility test, by L. Lang. HEALTH. 14:18-19, March 1982

The politics of fertility. How the population situation affects political institutions. Part 1, by J. A. Loraine. MIDWIFE, HEALTH VISITOR AND COMMUNITY NURSE. 17:498-499+, December 1981

The population debate: a survey of opinions of a professional organization's membership, by M. B. Toney, et al. POPULATION AND ENVIRONMENT. 4(3):156, Fall 1981

Relative risks in fertility control and reproduction: individual choice and medical practice, by S. Teper. PROCEEDINGS OF THE ANNUAL SYMPOSIUM OF EUGENICS SOCIETY. 16:59-101, 1981

Research on the determinants of fertility: a note on priorites. POPULATION AND DEVELOPMENT REVIEW. 7(2):311, June 1981

Rwanda: too many people too little land, by J. Hammand. WORLD HEALTH. pp. 12-15, June 1982

Sequences of events following adoption of contraception: an exploratory analysis of 1973 United States fertility history data, by G. Pickens, et al. SOCIAL BIOLOGY. 28:111-125, Spring-Summer 1981

Sexuality, femininity and fertility control, by A. Woodhouse. WOMEN'S STUDIES INTERNATIONAL FORUM. 5(1):1-15, 1982

The subfertile couple, by M. P. McCusker. JOGN NURSING: JOURNAL OF OBSTETRIC GYNECOLOGIC AND NEONATAL NURSING. 11(3):157-162, May-June 1982

A time series of instrumental fertility variables, by N. B. Ryder. DEMOGRAPHY. 18(4):487-509, November 1981

Use of services for family planning and infertility: United States, by G. E. Hendershot, et al. VITAL HEALTH STATISTICS. 23(8):1-41, December 1981

Wanted and unwanted fertility: Victoria 1971 to 1975, by K. Betts. AUSTRALIAN JOURNAL OF SOCIAL ISSUES. 15(3):194-208, 1980

FERTILITY AND FERTILITY CONTROL (continued)

World fertility survey: charting global childbearing, by R. Lightbourne, Jr., et al. POPULATION BULLETIN. 37:2-54, March 1982

HYSTERECTOMY
Hormonal levels following sterilization and hysterectomy, by S. L. Corson, et al. JOURNAL OF REPRODUCTIVE MEDICINE. 26(7): 363-370, July 1981

Hysterectomy after interval laparoscopic sterilisation [letter], by I. C. Chi, et al. LANCET. 1(8276):848-849, April 10, 1982

Hysterectomy and depression [a clinical study], by D. Raglianti. BOLLETINO DI PSICOLOGIA APPLICATA. (155-156):206-211, July-December 1980

Hysterectomy and psychiatric disorder: I. Levels of psychiatric morbidity before and after hysterectomy, by D. Gath, et al. BRITISH JOURNAL OF PSYCHIATRY. 140:335-342, April 1982

--II. Demographic psychiatric and physical factors in relation to psychiatric outcome, by D. Gath, et al. BRITISH JOURNAL OF PSYCHIATRY. 140:343-350, April 1982

Hysterectomy and reliving the castration fantasy, by B. Teitelroit. PSICO. 1(2):11-33, July-December 1980

Post-tubal ligation hysterectomy, by A. S. Gupta, et al. JOURNAL OF THE INDIAN MEDICAL ASSOCIATION. 76(11):208-210, June 1, 1981

Psychological problems of hysterectomy for patients, gynecologists, and psychiatrists: investigations on 75 women, by M. V. Costantini, et al. PSICHIATRIA GENERALE E DELL ETA EVOLUTIVA. 18(3):229-245, 1980

Psychosomatic aspects of gynecological conditions: psychiatric disorder after hysterectomy, by D. Gath, et al. JOURNAL OF PSYCHOSOMATIC RESEARCH. 25(5):347-355, 1981

The risk of death from combined abortion-sterilization procedures: can hysterotomy or hysterectomy be justified?, by H. K. Atrash, et al. AMERICAN JOURNAL OF OBSTETRICS AND GYNECOLOGY. 142(3):269-274, February 1, 1982

Tubal sterilization and hysterectomy, by J. H. Johnson. FAMILY PLANNING PERSPECTIVES. 14(1):28-30, January-February 1982

SEX AND SEXUALITY
Attitudes of Chinese women towards sexuality and birth control, by D. Ellis, et al. CANADIAN NURSE. 78:28-31, March 1982

Birth control-sex preference and sex ratio, by M. A. Toro. HEREDITY. 47(Pt 3):417-423, December 1981

Catholics and sex, by J. Garvey. COMMONWEAL. 109:134-136, March 12, 1982

SEX AND SEXUALITY (continued)

--[discussion]. COMMONWEAL. 109:412-414, July 16, 1982

Changes in sexual desire after voluntary sterilization, by F. D. Bean, et al. SOCIAL BIOLOGY. 27(3):186-193, Fall 1980

Evaluation of sex education outreach, by K. F. Darabi, et al. ADOLESCENCE. 17:57-64, Spring 1982

Extramarital sexual attitudes and norms of an undergraduate student population, by N. P. Medora, et al. ADOLESCENCE. 16:251-262, Summer 1981

The matron and sex education. NUEVA ENFERMERIA. (11):11, May 1980

NRC launches sexuality series, by A. Jones. NATIONAL CATHOLIC REPORTER. 18:1+, October 1, 1982

The Pope and sexuality, by R. Modras. NATIONAL CATHOLIC RE-PORTER. 18:20+, January 15, 1982

Sex: chastity belts next?. ECONOMIST. 281:32, October 3, 1981

Sex conference--planning--sexually transmitted diseases, by M. Barrette, et al. NURSING MONTREAL. 6(3):7-8, June 1982

Sex differences in correlates of abortion attitudes among college students, by B. A. Finlay. JOURNAL OF MARRIAGE AND THE FAMILY. 43(571-582, August 1981

Sex education, by J. Spray. NURSING. 1:1508-1509, March 1982

Sex education and contraceptive education in U.S. public high schools, by M. T. Orr. FAMILY PLANNING PERSPECTIVES. 14: 304-313, November-December 1982

Sex education and its association with teenage sexual activity, pregnancy and contraceptive use [research], by M. Zelnik, et al. FAMILY PLANNING PERSPECTIVES. 14:117-119+, May-June 1982

Sex education of pregnant women and its relationship with their knowledge and attitude to sex, by N. Ishimatsu, et al. JOSAN-PU ZASSHI. 36(6):481-489, June 1982

Sex guilt and the use of contraception among unmarried women, by J. F. Keller, et al. CONTRACEPTION. 25(4):387-394, 1982

Sex, sex guilt, and contraceptive use, by M. Gerrard. JOURNAL OF PERSONALITY AND SOCIAL PSYCHOLOGY. 42(1):153-158, January 1982

Sexual behavior of castrated sex offenders, by N. Heim. ARCHIVES OF SEXUAL BEHAVIOR. 10(1):11-19, February 1981

Sexuality, femininity and fertility control, by A. Woodhouse. WOMEN'S STUDIES INTERNATIONAL FORUM. 5(1):1-15, 1982

SEX AND SEXUALITY (continued)

Student-parent rapport and parent involvement in sex, birth
control, and venereal disease education, by S. M. Bennett, et
al. JOURNAL OF SEX RESEARCH. 16(2):114-130, May 1980

Talking to parents about sex does not affect teens' contraceptive use. FAMILY PLANNING PERSPECTIVES. 14:279-280, September-October 1982

Unmarried black adolescent father's attitudes toward abortion,
contraception, and sexuality [a preliminary report], by L. E.
Hendricks. JOURNAL OF ADOLESCENT HEALTH CARE. 2(3):199-203,
March 1982

STERILIZATION: GENERAL
The band-aid operation (tubal ligation and vasectomy), by M.
Newton. HEALTH. 14:52, March 1982

Family planning. Contraception, sterilization, abortion, by H.
Ludwig. FORTSCHRITTE DER MEDIZIN. 100(16):721-722+, April
29, 1982

Mahgoub'd reversible sterilization, by S. Ballas. HAREFUAH.
100(9):415-416, May 1, 1981

The pattern of sterilisation [editorial]. NEW ZEALAND MEDICAL
JOURNAL. 94(689):92-93, August 12, 1981

Political economy of sexism in industrial health [with dis-
cussion], by M. Felker. SOCIAL SCIENCE AND MEDICINE. 16(1):
3-18, 1982

Postpartum sterilization in cesarean section and non-cesarean
section deliveries: United States, 1970-75 [research], by P.
J. Placek, et al. AMERICAN JOURNAL OF PUBLIC HEALTH. 71:
1258-1261, November 1981

The risk of death from combined abortion-sterilization pro-
cedures: can hysterotomy or hysterectomy be justified?, by H.
K. Atrash, et al. AMERICAN JOURNAL OF OBSTETRICS AND GYNE-
COLOGY. 142(3):269-274, February 1, 1982

Sterilization and the birth rate, by D. L. Nortman. STUDIES IN
FAMILY PLANNING. 11(9-10):286-300, September-October 1980

Taking liberties with women: abortion, sterilization, and contraception, by W. Savage. INTERNATIONAL JOURNAL OF HEALTH
EDUCATION. 12(2):293-308, 1982

ALASKA
Alaska courts have jurisdiction to order sterilization. FAM-
ILY LAW REPORTER: COURT OPINIONS. 7(28):2452-2453, May 19,
1981

BRAZIL
Access to postpartum sterilization in southeast Brazil, by B.
Janowitz, et al. MEDICAL CARE. 20(5):526-534, May 1982

Castracao, esterilizacao, "mudanca" artificial de sexo (con-

ference paper, some emphasis on Brazil), by A. Chaves.
REVISTA DE INFORMACAO LEGISLATIVA. 18:261-272, January-
March 1981

Post-partum sterilization in Sao Paul state, Brazil, by B.
Janowitz, et al. JOURNAL OF BIOLOGICAL SCIENCE. 14(2):179-
187, April 1982

CANADA
Pour ou contre une politique nataliste au Quebec (eight papers
presented at the 49th meeting of the Association canadienne-francaise pour l'avancement des sciences, Sherbrooke,
May 13-15, 1981). CAHIERS QUEBECOIS DE DEMOGRAPHIE. 10(2):
139-303, 1981

CENTRAL AMERICA
Access to sterilization in two hospitals in Honduras, by B.
Janowitz, et al. BULLETIN OF THE PAN AMERICAN HEALTH
ORGANIZATION. 15(3):226-230, 1981

CHILE
Observations on female sterilization in Chile, by D. Menan-
teau-Horta. BULLETIN OF THE PAN AMERICAN HEALTH ORGANIZA-
TION. 16(2):101, 1982

COSTA RICA
Female sterilization in Costa Rica, by M. G. Barrantes, et al.
STUDIES IN FAMILY PLANNING. 13:3-11, January 1982

INDIA
Decision analysis for assessing the impact of female sterili-
zation in Bangladesh, by M. J. Rosenberg, et al. STUDIES IN
FAMILY PLANNING. 13(2):59, February 1982

Sterilization-attributable deaths in Bangladesh, by D. A.
Grimes, et al. INTERNATIONAL JOURNAL OF GYNAECOLOGY AND
OBSTETRICS. 20(2):149-154, April 1982

A two-year follow-up study of women sterilized in India, by R.
V. Ghatt, et al. CONTRACEPTION. 23(6):603-619, June 1981

LATIN AMERICA
Contraceptive sterilization in four Latin American countries,
by J. McCarthy. JOURNAL OF BIOSOCIAL SCIENCE. 14(2):189-
201, April 1982

MALAYSIA
Laparoscopic sterilization with fallope rings--a Malaysian
experience, by A. A. Rahman, et al. MEDICAL JOURNAL OF
MALAYSIA. 36(2):92-99, June 1981

SOUTH AMERICA
Post-partum sterilization in Sao Paul state, Brazil, by B.
Janawitz, et al. JOURNAL OF BIOSOCIAL SCIENCE. 14:179-188,
April 1982

THAILAND
Postpartum sterilization by operating-room nurses in Thailand,

STERILIZATION: GENERAL (continued)

by S. Koetsawang, et al. INTERNATIONAL JOURNAL OF GYNAE-
COLOGY AND OBSTETRICS. 19(3):201-204, June 1981

UNITED STATES
Demographic trends in tubal sterilization: United States,
1970-1978, by F. DeStefano, et al. AMERICAN JOURNAL OF
PUBLIC HEALTH. 72(5):480-484, May 1982

More than 1,000,000 voluntary sterilizations performed in
United States in 1980. FAMILY PLANNING PERSPECTIVES. 14:
99-100, March-April 1982

Mortality risk associated with tubal sterilization in United
States hospitals, by H. B. Peterson, et al. AMERICAN JOUR-
NAL OF OBSTETRICS AND GYNECOLOGY. 143(2):125-129, May 15,
1982

Postpartum sterilization in cesarean section and non-cesarean
section deliveries: United States, 1970-75, by P. J. Placek,
et al. AMERICAN JOURNAL OF PUBLIC HEALTH. 71(11):1258-
1261, November 1981

Sterilization in Pennsylvania, by P. W. Beck, et al. TEMPLE
LAW QUARTERLY. 54:213-236, 1981

STERILIZATION: ATTITUDES
Aspects of reproduction related to human rights. IV. Steriliza-
tion by surgical means, by C. MacGregor. GACETA MEDICA DE
MEXICO. 117(7):272-274, July 1981

Parents' attitudes toward sterilization of their mentally retarded children, by L. Wolf, et al. AMERICAN JOURNAL OF
MENTAL DEFICIENCY. 87:122-129, September 1982

Psychological preparation for surgery: patient recall of information, by A. E. Reading. JOURNAL OF PSYCHOSOMATIC RESEARCH.
25(1):57-62, 1981

Taking liberties with women: abortion, sterilization, and contraception, by W. Savage. INTERNATIONAL JOURNAL OF HEALTH
SERVICES. 12(2):293-308, 1982

STERILIZATION: COMPLICATIONS
Changes in sexual desire after voluntary sterilization, by F. D.
Bean, et al. SOCIAL BIOLOGY. 27:186-193, Fall 1980

Death following puncture of the aorta during laparoscopic sterilization, by H. B. Peterson, et al. OBSTETRICS AND GYNE-
COLOGY. 59(1):133-134, January 1982

The doubtful value of transitory contraception after laparoscopic electrocoagulation of the fallopian tubes, by J. J.
Kjer, et al. ACTA OBSTETRICIA ET GYNECOLOGICA SCANDINAVICA.
60(4):403-405, 1981

Laparoscopic bladder injury, by A. S. Deshmukh. UROLOGY.
19(3):306-307, March 1982

Late complications of sterilization according to method, by H.
H. Riedel, et al. JOURNAL OF REPRODUCTIVE MEDICINE. 26(7):
353-358, July 1981

A prolonged chloroprocaine epidural block in a postpartum patient with abnormal pseudocholinesterase, by B. R. Kuhnert, et
al. ANESTHESIOLOGY. 56(6):477-478, June 1982

Psychological preparation for surgery: patient recall of information, by A. E. Reading. JOURNAL OF PSYCHOSOMATIC RESEARCH.
25(1):57-62, 1981

Psychological sequelae to elective sterilisation: a prospective
study, by P. Cooper, et al. BRITISH MEDICAL JOURNAL.
284(6314):461-464, February 13, 1982

Women and sterilization: the after effects, by S. Katz.
CHATELAINE. 55:16, October 1982

STERILIZATION: FEMALE
Application of laparoscope for female sterilization (analysis of
74 cases), by C. H. He, et al. CHUNG HUA FU CHAN KO TSA CHIH.
3(2):106-109, June 1981

Decision analysis for assessing the impact of female sterilization in Bangladesh, by M. J. Rosenberg, et al. STUDIES IN
FAMILY PLANNING. 13:59, February 1982

Development of pregnancy following sterilization of the woman,
by L. C. van Otterlo, et al. NEDERLANDS TIJDSCHRIFT VOOR
GENEESKUNDE. 126(6):241-244, February 6, 1982

Emotional reaction to female sterilization: a prospective study,
by S. Aribarg, et al. JOURNAL OF THE MEDICAL ASSOCIATION OF
THAILAND. 65(4):167-171, April 1982

Female sterilization: a follow-up report, by M. Ross, et al.
SOUTH AFRICAN MEDICAL JOURNAL. 61(13):476-479, March 27, 1982

--: guideline for the development of services [second edition].
WHO OFFSET PUBLICATIONS. (26):1-47, 1980

Female sterilization in Costa Rica, by M. G. Barrantes, et al.
STUDIES IN FAMILY PLANNING. 13(1):3-11, January 1982

Frequency of unwanted pregnancies among women on waiting lists
for sterilization, by U. Høding, et al. UGESKRIFT FOR
LAEGER. 144(12):875-876, March 22, 1982

How women felt about their sterilization--a follow-up of 368
patients in a general practice, by A. F. Wright. JOURNAL OF
THE ROYAL COLLEGE OF GENERAL PRACTITIONERS. 31(231):598-604,
October 1981

Luteal phase pregnancies in female sterilization patients, bu I.
Chi, et al. CONTRACEPTION. 23(6):579-589, June 1981

Observations on female sterilization in Chile, by D. Menanteau-

STERILIZATION: FEMALE (continued)

Horta. BULLETIN OF THE PAN AMERICAN HEALTH ORGANIZATION. 16(2):101, 1982

Permanent decision making: counselling women for sterilization, by J. R. Goodman, et al. SOCIAL CASEWORK. 63(2):73-81, February 1982

Potential demand for voluntary female sterilization in the 1980s the compelling need for a nonsurgical method, by E. Kessel, et al. FERTILITY AND STERILITY. 37(6):725-733, June 1982

Reversal of female sterilization, by P. A. Gantt, et al. SOUTHERN MEDICAL JOURNAL. 75(2):161-163, February 1982

Sterilization of women, by P. Fylling. SYKEPLEIEN. 68(8):11+, May 5, 1981

Sterilization rate rose most for women 15-24 between 1976 and 1978 (United States). FAMILY PLANNING PERSPECTIVES. 13:236-237, September-October 1981

Sterilization reversal for more women. MEDICAL WORLD NEWS. 23:18, March 29, 1982

Taking liberties with women: abortion, sterilization, and contraception, by W. Savage. INTERNATIONAL JOURNAL OF HEALTH SERVICES. 12(2):293-308, 1982

STERILIZATION: FEMALE: COMPLICATIONS
Complications in women after operative sterilization, by B. Gavric, et al. JUGOSLAVENSKA GINEKOLOGIJA I OPSTETRICIJA. 21(3-4):81-82, May-August 1981

Deaths following female sterilization with unipolar electro-coagulating devices. CONNECTICUT MEDICINE. 46(1):31-32, January 1982

Endometriosis and tuboperitoneal fistulas after tubal ligation [letter], by J. B. Massey. FERTILITY AND STERILITY. 36(3): 417-418, September 1981

The health of sterilized women, by B. W. McGuinness. PRACTI-TIONER. 226(1367):925-928, May 1982

Inadvertent injuries during gynecologic endoscopy [letter], by G. M. Grunert. FERTILITY AND STERILITY. 37(2):284-285, February 1982

Luteal phase pregnancies in female sterilization patients, by I. Chi, et al. CONTRACEPTION. 23(6):579-590, 1981

Menstrual pattern changes following laparoscopic sterilization: comparative study of electrocoagulation and the tubal ring in 1,025 cases, by P. P. Bhiwandiwala, et al. JOURNAL OF REPRO-DUCTIVE MEDICINE. 27(5):249-255, May 1982

STERILIZATION: FEMALE: TECHNIQUES
Evaluation of contemporary female sterilization methods, by W.

E. Brenner. JOURNAL OF REPRODUCTIVE MEDICINE. 26(9):439-453, September 1981

Evaluation of falope ring sterilization by hysterosalpingogram, by C. L. Cook. JOURNAL OF REPRODUCTIVE MEDICINE. 27(5):243-248, May 1982

Female sterilization by falope ring ligation, by A. B. Lalonde. CANADIAN MEDICAL ASSOCIATION JOURNAL. 126(2):140-144, January 15, 1982

Female sterilization. Comparative study of 3 laparoscopic technics, by L. C. Uribe Ramirez, et al. GINECOLOGIA Y OBSTETRICIA DE MEXICO. 49(295):311-324, May 1981

A new technique for female sterilization, by D. Muzsnai, et al. OBSTETRICS AND GYNECOLOGY. 58(4):508-512, October 1981

Sterilization without surgery: the "ovary plug" is simplicity, by L. Lang. HEALTH. 14:19, March 1982

Tubal occlusion with silicone rubber. Update, 1980, by T. P. Reed, et al. JOURNAL OF REPRODUCTIVE MEDICINE. 26(10):534-537, October 1981

STERILIZATION: LAWS AND LEGISLATION
Alaska courts have jurisdiction to order sterilization. FAMILY LAW REPORTER: COURT OPINIONS. 7(28):2452-2453, May 19, 1981

Buck v. Bell: 'felt necessities' v. fundamental values?, by R. J. Cynkar. COLUMBIA LAW REVIEW. 81(7):1418-1461, November 1981

Civil liability of physicians following unsuccessful sterilization, by H. Franzki. FORTSCHRITTE DER MEDIZIN. 99(4):79-80, January 29, 1981

Compensation for incorrect sterilization--remarks on the judgment of the German Supreme Court of 18 March 1980, by K. Handel. BEITRAEGE ZUR GERICHTLICHEN MEDIZIN. 39:233-237, 1981

Equitable jurisdiction to order sterilizations, by C. L. McIvor. WASHINGTON LAW REVIEW. 57(2):373-387, 1982

Grady, In re (NJ) 426 A 2d 467. JOURNAL OF FAMILY LAW. 20:374-377, January 1982

Guidelines issued on court-ordered sterilization of retarded minors. FAMILY LAW REPORTER: COURT OPINIONS. 8(8):2102-2104, December 22, 1981

In re CDM [627 P 2d 607 (Alaska)]: should involuntary sterilization be within the general jurisdiction of a court?. DETROIT COLLEGE OF LAW REVIEW. 1982:719-736, Fall 1982

Inherent parens patriae authority empowers court of general jurisdiction in order sterilization of incompetents. WASHING-

STERILIZATION: LAWS AND LEGISLATION (continued)

TON UNIVERSITY LAW QUARTERLY. 11:77-96, Fall 1982

The international medicolegal status of sterilization for mentally handicapped people, by B. Gonzales. JOURNAL OF REPRODUCTIVE MEDICINE. 27(5):257-258, May 1982

The law and sterilization or permanent contraception, by G. Brenner. GEBURTSHILFE UND FRAUENHEILKUNDE. 42(3):226-230, March 1982

Legal trends and issues in voluntary sterilization. POPULATION REPORTS. (6):E73-102, March-April 1981

National College of French Gynecologists and Obstetricians. Report on legislation on tubal sterilization, by M. F. Lerat, et al. JOURNAL DE GYNECOLOGIE, OBSTETRIQUE ET BIOLOGIE DE LA REPRODUCTION. 11(1):183-188, 1982

Parens patriae: judicial authority to order the sterilization of mental incompetents, by N. J. West. JOURNAL OF LEGAL MEDICINE. 2(4):523-542, December 1981

Probate courts have power to order mental incompetent's sterilization. FAMILY LAW REPORTER: COURT OPINIONS. 8(24):2344-2347, April 20, 1982

Sterilization of incompetents: the quest for legal authority, by A. H. Bernstein. HOSPITALS. 56(3):13-15, February 1, 1982

Sterilization of the mentally retarded: a decision for the courts, by G. J. Annas. HASTINGS CENTER REPORT. 11(4):18-19, August 1981

--: who decides?, by M. S. Lottman. TRIAL. 18:61-64, April 1982

Sterilization of the mentally retarded adult: the Eve case [Eve, In re (1980, 1981) 115 D L R (3d) 283], by B. Starkman. McGILL LAW JOURNAL. 26:931-950, 1981

Sterilizing the retarded: constitutional, statutory and policy alternatives, by R. K. Sherlock, et al. NORTH CAROLINA LAW REVIEW. 60:943-983, June 1982

What's new in the law: courts ... authority to sterilize, by A. Ashman. AMERICAN BAR ASSOCIATION JOURNAL. 67:1044+, August 1981

--: mentally impaired ... sterilization, by A. Ashman. AMERICAN BAR ASSOCIATION JOURNAL. 67:918-919, July 1981

STERILIZATION: MORTALITY AND MORTALITY STATISTICS
Sterilization-attributable deaths in Bangladesh, by D. A. Grimes, et al. INTERNATIONAL JOURNAL OF GYNAECOLOGY AND OBSTETRICS. 20(2):149-154, April 1982

STERILIZATION: RESEARCH
Bladder perforation owing to a unipolar coagulating device, by

STERILIZATION: RESEARCH (continued)

J. Pakter, et al. AMERICAN JOURNAL OF OBSTETRICS AND GYNE-
COLOGY. 141(2):227, September 15, 1981

Failure rates higher for postpartum sterilizations than for
interval procedures. FAMILY PLANNING PERSPECTIVES. 14:100-
101, March-April 1982

Laparoscopy: a retrospective study with two or more years
follow-up of patients in a small community hospital, by J. D.
Chapman. JAOA: JOURNAL OF THE AMERICAN OPTOMETRIC ASSOCIA-
TION. 81(6 Suppl):429-435, 1982

Sterilization of the male dog and cat by laparoscopic occlusion
of the ductus deferens, by D. E. Wildt, et al. AMERICAN
JOURNAL OF VETERINARY RESERACH. 42(11):1888-1897, November
1981

There is no place in gynecological endoscopy for unipolar of
bipolar high frequency current, by H. H. Riedel, et al. ENDO-
SCOPY. 14(2):51-54, March 1982

Training of doctors in conducting M.T.P. and tubectomy--an
experimental approach, by M. Arundhathi, et al. JOURNAL OF
FAMILY WELFARE. 28:62-65, June 1982

STERILIZATION: STATISTICS
Demographic trends in tubal sterilization: United States, 1970-
1978, by F. DeStefano, et al. AMERICAN JOURNAL OF PUBLIC
HEALTH. 72:480-483, May 1982

Failure rates higher for postpartum sterilizations than for
interval procedures. FAMILY PLANNING PERSPECTIVES. 14:100-
101, March-April 1982

1979 AAGL membership survey, by J. M. Philips, et al. JOURNAL
OF REPRODUCTIVE MEDICINE. 26(10):529-533, October 1981

Sterilization failure. An analysis of 27 pregnancies after a
previous sterilization procedure, by V. P. De Villiers. SOUTH
AFRICAN MEDICAL JOURNAL. 61(16):589-590, April 17, 1982

STERILIZATION: TECHNIQUES
Analysis of pathological process in fallopian tubes after injection with mucilago phenol in relation to its sterilization
effectiveness, by M. Y. Chen. CHUNG HUA FU CHAN KO TSA CHIH.
14(2):84-86, April 1979

The choice of sterilization procedure among married couples, by
L. M. Markman, et al. JOURNAL OF FAMILY PRACTICE. 14(1):27-
30, January 1982

Drug blocks pregnancy after sterilization, by J. Fox. CHEMICAL
AND ENGINEERING NEWS. 60:26, May 17, 1982

Endoscopic salpingectomy, by J. C. Tarasconi. JOURNAL OF
REPRODUCTIVE MEDICINE. 26(10):541-545, October 1981

The hysterophore: a new instrument for uterine manipulation

during laparoscopy, by F. B. Lammes. EUROPEAN JOURNAL OF OBSTETRICS, GYNECOLOGY AND REPRODUCTIVE BIOLOGY. 12(4):243-246, October 1981

An initial comparison of coagulation techniques of sterilization, by H. H. Riedel, et al. JOURNAL OF REPRODUCTIVE MEDICINE. 27(5):261-267, May 1982

Laparoscopic sterilization with fallope rings--a Malaysian experience, by A. A. Rahman, et al. MEDICAL JOURNAL OF MALAYSIA. 36(2):92-99, June 1981

Laparoscopic sterilization with the falope-ring technique, by J. B. Hertz. ACTA OBSTETRICIA ET GYNECOLOGICA SCANDINAVICA. 61(1):13-15, 1982

Late complications after application of different sterilization techniques--a comparison between the monopolar HF-sterilization and the endocoagulation method, by H. H. Riedel, et al. GEBURTSHILFE UND FRAUENHEILKUNDE. 42(4):273-279, April 1982

Ligation of the fallopian tubes by means of minilaprotomy (our modification of Pomeroy's method) and using a laparoscope (falope ring), by K. Kuczewski. GINEKOLOGIA POLSKA. 52(1): 57-62, January 1981

Meleney's gangrene following sterilisation by salpingectomy [case report], by D. F. Badenoch. BRITISH JOURNAL OF OBSTETRICS AND GYNAECOLOGY. 88(10):1061-1062, 1981

Minilaparotomy or laparoscopy for sterilization: a multicenter, multinational randomized study. AMERICAN JOURNAL OF OBSTETRICS AND GYNECOLOGY. 143(6):645-652, July 15, 1982

Outpatient laparoscopic sterilization, by H. Arshat, et al. MEDICAL JOURNAL OF MALAYSIA. 36(1):20-23, March 1981

Reversible sterilization with a physiological solution in the rat: preliminary note, by L. Gianaroli, et al. BOLLETTINO DELLA SOCIETA ITALIANA DE BIOLOGIA SPERIMENTALE. 58(3-4):135-141, February 1982

Risk of death from abortion sterilization is three times greater with hysterotomy or hysterectomy. FAMILY PLANNING PERSPECTIVES. 14:147-148, May-June 1982

Sterilization by occlusion of the fallopian tubes with mulcilago phenol (a seven years' clinical observation). CHUNG HUA FU CHAN KO TSA CHIH. 14(2):79-83, April 1979

Sterilization without surgery, by M. Klitsch. FAMILY PLANNING PERSPECTIVES. 14:324-326, November-December 1982

--(silicon plug that blocks the Fallopian tubes), by L. Lang. HEALTH. 14:13, March 1982

Tubal sterilization and hysterectomy, by J. H. Johnson. FAMILY PLANNING PERSPECTIVES. 14:28-30, January-February 1982

STERILIZATION: TECHNIQUES (continued)

Use of fallopian ring with laparoscopy for closure of oviduct, by F. Zabransky. ZENTRALBLATT FUR GYNAEKOLOGIE. 103(20): 1228-1234, 1981

Uterine cornual cauterization as a sterilization method, by M. Ishikawa, et al. JAPANESE JOURNAL OF FERTILITY AND STERILITY. 27(1):122-125, 1982

--REPRODUCCION. 5(3):157-162, July-September 1981

STERILIZATION: TUBAL
Demographic trends in tubal sterilization: United States, 1970-1978, by F. DeStefano, et al. AMERICAN JOURNAL OF PUBLIC HEALTH. 72(5):480-484, May 1982

Ectopic pregnancy after tubal sterilization. Mechanism of re-canalization [case report], by P. Rimdusit. JOURNAL OF THE MEDICAL ASSOCIATION OF THAILAND. 65(2):101-105, February 1982

Embryo transfer, ectopic pregnancy, and preliminary tubal occlu-sion [letter], by I. Craft, et al. LANCET. 2(8260-8261): 1421, December 19-26, 1981

Endocrine profile of patients with post-tubal-ligation syndrome, by J. T. Hargrove, et al. JOURNAL OF REPRODUCTIVE MEDICINE. 26(7):359-362, July 1981

Endometrial pathological changes after fallopian ring tubal li-gation, by D. de Cristofaro, et al. ENDOSCOPY. 14(4):139-140, July 1982

Endosalpingosis ('endosalpingoblastosis') following laparoscopic tubal coagulation as an etiologic factor of ectopic pregnancy, by A. McCausland. AMERICAN JOURNAL OF OBSTETRICS AND GYNE-COLOGY. 143(1):12-24, May 1, 1982

Evaluation of 2236 tubectomies, by M. Raghav, et al. JOURNAL OF THE INDIAN MEDICAL ASSOCIATION. 77(7):115-117, October 1, 1981

Experimental observation and clinical application on the occlu-sion of fallopian tubes by silver clips, by S. L. Ding. CHUNG HUA FU CHAN KO TSA CHIH. 17(2):105-107, April 1982

Failure of yoon ring tubal sterilization, by P. Chenevart. RE-VUE MEDICALE DE LA SUISSE ROMANDE. 101(11):907-912, November 1981

Failures with the tubal ligation with the Bleier-secuclips, by A. R. Schurz, et al. GEBURTSHILFE UND FRAUENHEILKUNDE. 42(5):376-378, May 1982

Hospitalization for tubal sterilization [letter], by H. P. Brown, et al. JAMA: JOURNAL OF THE AMERICAN MEDICAL ASSOCIA-TION. 246(22):2576, December 4, 1981

Laparoscopic sterilisation using Hulka-Clemens clips, with or without termination of pregnancy. A study of 544 cases, by A.

Tadjerouni, et al. JOURNAL DE GYNECOLOGIE, OBSTETRIQUE ET BIOLOGIE DE LA REPRODUCTION. 10(8):851-856, 1981

Laparoscopic sterilization with falope ring (a preliminary report of 200 cases), by X. J. Zhang. CHUNG HUA FU CHAN KO TSA CHIH. 17(1):60-62, January 1982

Laparoscopic sterilization with thermocoagulation, by P. K. Buchhave, et al. UGESKRIFT FOR LAEGER. 144(3):147-149, January 18, 1982

Laparoscopic sterilizations requiring laparotomy, by I. C. Chi, et al. AMERICAN JOURNAL OF OBSTETRICS AND GYNECOLOGY. 142(6 Pt 1):712-713, March 15, 1982

Microsurgical reanastomosos of the fallopian tube: increasingly successful outcome for reversal of previous sterilization procedures, by M. P. Diamond, et al. SOUTHERN MEDICAL JOURNAL. 75(4):443-445, April 1982

Minilaparotomy tubal sterilization: a comparison between normal and high-risk patients, by M. E. Domenzain, et al. OBSTETRICS AND GYNECOLOGY. 59(2):199-201, February 1982

Mortality risk associated with tubal sterilization in United States hospitals, by H. B. Peterson, et al. AMERICAN JOURNAL OF OBSTETRICS AND GYNECOLOGY. 143(2):125-129, May 15, 1982

Operative complications of laparoscopic tubal sterilization with Bleier clips, by E. Schneller, et al. GEBURTSHILFE UND FRAUENHEILKUNDE. 42(5):379-384, May 1982

Pharmacological study on chemically induced tubal occlusion in rabbits. CHUNG HUA FU CHAN KO TSA CHIH. 14(2):87-90, April 1979

Pituitary-ovarian function after tubal ligation, by F. Alvarez-Sanchez, et al. FERTILITY AND STERILITY. 36(5):606-609, November 1981

Postligation tubal pregnancy, by S. K. Chaudhuri, et al. JOURNAL OF THE INDIAN MEDICAL ASSOCIATION. 78(3):50-51, February 1, 1982

Psychological and physical outcome after elective tubal sterilization, by P. Cooper, et al. JOURNAL OF PSYCHOSOMATIC RESEARCH. 25(5):357-360, 1981

Results with laparoscopic tubal sterilization, by R. Burmucic. WIENER KLINISCHE WOCHENSCHRIFT. 94(3):77-80, February 5, 1982

Risk of ectopic pregnancy following tubectomy, by S. Ghatnagar. INDIAN JOURNAL OF MEDICAL RESEARCH. 75:47-49, January 1982

The role of recanalization in tubal pregnancy after sterilization, by S. Badawy, et al. INTERNATIONAL SURGERY. 64(5):49-51, August-October 1979

Severe pelvic inflammatory disease and peritonitis following falope ring tubal ligation. Case report and review of the literature, by C. LoBue. JOURNAL OF REPRODUCTIVE MEDICINE. 26(11):581-584, November 1981

Should your conscience be your guide? ... a nurse-anesthetist refused to participate in a tubal ligation. NURSINGLIFE. 1:15, July-August 1981

Silicone plugs (plugging the fallopian tubes), by C. SerVaas. SATURDAY EVENING POST. 254:108, May-June 1982

Some problems concerning operations for reconstruction of tubal patency, by Q. B. Chen. CHUNG HUA FU CHAN KO TSA CHIH. 14(2):93-96, April 1979

Sterilization: don't count on (tubal ligation) reversal, warns a Calgary doctor, by M. McKinely. ALBERTA REPORT. 9:34-35, March 22, 1982

Study of 500 cases of sterilization by tubal ligation, by R. J. Leke, et al. UNION MEDICALE DU CANADA. 110(9):807-809, September 1981

Study of sociocultural aspect of tubectomy subjects, by R. Ram, et al. JOURNAL OF THE INDIAN MEDICAL ASSOCIATION. 77(8):130-133, October 16, 1981

Tubal anastomosis following unipolar cautery, by J. A. Rock, et al. FERTILITY AND STERILITY. 37(5):613-618, May 1982

Tubal plugs bar pregnancy (tubal occlusion: silicone plugs block fallopian tubes). SCIENCE DIGEST. 90:89, November 1982

Tubal sterilization and hysterectomy, by J. H. Johnson. FAMILY PLANNING PERSPECTIVES. 14(1):28-30, January-February 1982

Tubal sterilization. Characteristics of women most affected by the option of reversibility, by R. N. Shain, et al. SOCIAL SCIENCE AND MEDICINE. 16(10):1067-1077, 1982

Tubal sterilization with silver clips--clinical observation and follow-up of 1,182 cases. CHUNG HUA FU CHAN KO TSA CHIH. 16(1):52-54, January 1981

Utilization of contralateral fallopian tube segments in tubal reanastomosis, by A. F. Haney. FERTILITY AND STERILITY. 37(5):701-703, May 1982

STERILIZATION: VOLUNTARY
Changes in sexual desire after voluntary sterilization, by F. D. Bean, et al. SOCIAL BIOLOGY. 27(3):186-193, Fall 1980

Legal trends and issues in voluntary sterilization. POPULATION REPORTS. (6):E73-102, March-April 1981

More than 1,000,000 voluntary sterilizations performed in United States in 1980. FAMILY PLANNING PERSPECTIVES. 14:99-100,

STERILIZATION: VOLUNTARY (continued)

March-April 1982

Potential demand for voluntary female sterilization in the 1980s the compelling need for a nonsurgical method, by E. Kessel, et al. FERTILITY AND STERILITY. 37(6):725-733, June 1982

Psychological sequelae to elective sterilisation: a prospective study [letter], by M. Thiery, et al. BRITISH MEDICAL JOURNAL. 284(6328):1557, May 22, 1982

Voluntary sterilization of the non-institutionalized mentally incompetent individual: judicial involvement or abstention?. NEW ENGLAND LAW REVIEW. 17:527-547, 1981-1982

STERILIZATION AND CRIMINALS
Alaska courts have jurisdiction to order sterilization. FAMILY LAW REPORTER: COURT OPINIONS. 7(28):2452-2453, May 19, 1981

Parent's attitudes toward sterilization of their mentally re-tarded children, by L. Wolf, et al. AMERICAN JOURNAL OF MEN-TAL DEFICIENCY. 87:122-129, September 1982

What's new in the law: courts ... authority to sterilize, by A. Ashman. AMERICAN BAR ASSOCIATION JOURNAL. 67:1044+, August 1981

STERILIZATION AND HORMONES
Follicular stimulating hormone and estrogen levels before and after female sterilization, by T. Sørensen, et al. ACTA OBSTETRICIA ET GYNECOLOGICA SCANDINAVICA. 60(6):559-561, 1981

STERILIZATION AND HOSPITALS
Access to sterilization to two hospitals in Honduras, by B. Janowitz. BULLETIN OF THE PAN AMERICAN HEALTH ORGANIZATION. 15(3):226, 1981

Hormonal levels following sterilization and hysterectomy, by S. L. Corson, et al. JOURNAL OF REPRODUCTIVE MEDICINE. 26(7): 363-370, July 1981

STERILIZATION AND INSURANCE
Health group cites multiple violations of Medicaid sterilization rules, by M. F. Docksai. TRIAL. 17:10, October 1981

Medicaid sterilization rules violated: group, by M. Magar. AMERICAN BAR ASSOCIATION JOURNAL. 67:1249, October 1981

STERILIZATION AND THE MENTALLY RETARDED
Conflict of choice: California considers statutory authority for involuntary sterilization of the severely mentally retarded. WHITTIER LAW REVIEW. 4:495-516, 1982

Guidelines issued on court-ordered sterilization of retarded minors. FAMILY LAW REPORTER: COURT OPINIONS. 8(8):2102-2104, December 22, 1981

In re Grady [426 A 2d 467 (NJ)]--voluntary sterilization and the retarded. RUTGERS LAW REVIEW. 34:567-590, Spring 1982

--: the mentally retarded individual's right to choose sterilization, by D. Lachance. AMERICAN JOURNAL OF LAW AND MEDICINE.
6(4):559-590, Winter 1981

Inherent parens patriae authority empowers court of general
jurisdiction in order sterilization of incompetents. WASHING-
TON UNIVERSITY LAW QUARTERLY. 11:77-96, Fall 1982

The international medicolegal status of sterilization for mentally handicapped people, by B. Gonzales. JOURNAL OF REPRO-
DUCTIVE MEDICINE. 27(5):257-258, May 1982

The issue of sterilization and the mentally retarded, by P. S.
Appelbaum. HOSPITAL AND COMMUNITY PSYCHIATRY. 33(7):523-524,
July 1982

The mental health professional, the mentally retarded, and sex,
by E. J. Saunders. HOSPITAL AND COMMUNITY PSYCHIATRY.
32(10):717-721, October 1981

Order to sterilize incompetent minor must be based on medical
necessity. FAMILY LAW REPORTER: COURT OPINIONS. 8(40):2598-
2600, August 17, 1982

Parens patriae: judicial authority to order the sterilization of
mental incompetents, by N. J. West. JOURNAL OF LEGAL MEDI-
CINE. 2(4):523-542, December 1981

Parent's attitudes toward sterilization of their mentally retarded children, by L. Wolf, et al. AMERICAN JOURNAL OF MEN-
TAL DEFICIENCY. 87:122-129, September 1982

Probate courts have power to order mental incompetent's sterilization. FAMILY LAW REPORTER: COURT OPINIONS. 8(24):2344-
2347, April 20, 1982

Sterilization of the developmentally disabled: shedding some
myth-conceptions. FLORIDA STATE UNIVERSITY LAW REVIEW. 9:
599-643, Fall 1981

Sterilization of incompetents: the quest for legal authority, by
A. H. Bernstein. HOSPITALS. 56(3):13-15, February 1, 1982

Sterilization of the mentally retarded: a decision for the
courts, by G. J. Annas. HASTINGS CENTER REPORT. 11(4):18-19,
August 1981

--: who decides?, by M. S. Lottman. TRIAL. 18(4):61-64+, April
1982

Sterilization of the mentally retarded adult: the Eve case [Eve,
In re (1980, 1981) 115 D L R (3d) 283], by B. Starkman.
McGILL LAW JOURNAL. 26:931-950, 1981

Sterilization rights of mental retardates. WASHINGTON AND LEE
LAW REVIEW. 39:207-221, Winter 1982

Sterilizing the retarded: constitutional, statutory and policy

STERILIZATION AND THE MENTALLY RETARDED (continued)

alternatives, by R. K. Sherlock, et al. NORTH CAROLINA LAW REVIEW. 60:943-983, June 1982

Voluntary sterilization for persons with mental disabilities: the need for legislation, by B. A. Burnett. SYRACUSE LAW REVIEW. 32:913-955, Fall 1981

Voluntary sterilization of the non-institutionalized mentally incompetent individual: judicial involvement or abstention?. NEW ENGLAND LAW REVIEW. 17:527-547, 1981-1982

What's new in the law: mentally impaired ... sterilization, by A. Ashman. AMERICAN BAR ASSOCIATION JOURNAL. 67:918-919, July 1981

STERILIZATION AND PHYSICIANS
Can 'doctor's orders' include involuntary sterilization?. RN. 45(1):34-35, January 1982

Training of doctors in conducting M.T.P. and tubectomy--an experimental approach, by M. Arundhathi, et al. JOURNAL OF FAMILY WELFARE. 28:62-65, June 1982

STERILIZATION AND SEXUAL BEHAVIOR
Changes in sexual desire after voluntary sterilization, by F. D. Bean, et al. SOCIAL BIOLOGY. 27(3):186-193, Fall 1980

Psychosexual attitudes in the female following sterilization, by H. H. Wynter, et al. INTERNATIONAL SURGERY. 64(5):31-33, August-October 1979

STERILIZATION AND YOUTH
Order to sterilize incompetent minor must be based on medical necessity. FAMILY LAW REPORTER: COURT OPINIONS. 8(40):2598-2600, August 17, 1982

STERILIZATION COUNSELING
Counseling for sterilization, by B. L. Gonzales. JOURNAL OF REPRODUCTIVE MEDICINE. 26(10):538-540, October 1981

Permanent decision making: counseling women for sterilization, by J. R. Goodman, et al. SOCIAL CASEWORK. 63(2):73-81, February 1982

VASECTOMY
Abnormalities of sperm morphology in cases of persistent in-fertility after vasectomy reversal, by R. J. Pelfrey, et al. FERTILITY AND STERILITY. 38(1):112-114, July 1982

The band-aid operation (tubal ligation and vasectomy). HEALTH. 14:52, March 1982

Clinical experience with vasovasostomy utilizing absorbable in-travasal stent, by J. F. Redman. UROLOGY. 20(1):59-61, July 1982

Innervation of the vas deferons and its importance for vasectomy and vasovasostomy, by P. C. Esk, et al. UROLOGIA INTERNA-

VASECTOMY (continued)

TIONALIS. 37(1):26-33, 1982

A low power magnification technique for reanastomosis of the vas, by D. Urquhart-Hay. BRITISH JOURNAL OF UROLOGY. 53(5): 466-469, October 1981

Macroscopic vasovasostomy, by P. Kessler, et al. FERTILITY AND STERILITY. 36(4):531-532, October 1981

No atherosclerosis risk in vasectomized men, preliminary studies find. FAMILY PLANNING PERSPECTIVES. 13:276-277, November-December 1981

Nonmicroscopic vasovasostomy, by B. Fallon, et al. JOURNAL OF UROLOGY. 126(3):361-362, September 1981

Reversal of vasectomy with microsurgery, by M. C. Ferreira. AMB: REVISTA DA ASSOCIACAO MEDICA BRASILEIRA. 27(3):80-82, March 1981

Survey of personal habits, symptoms of illness, and histories of disease in men with and without vasectomies, by D. B. Petitti, et al. AMERICAN JOURNAL OF PUBLIC HEALTH. 72:476-480, May 1982

Vasectomy: it's simple, it works, but it has drawbacks, too. CHANGING TIMES. 35:63-65, February 1981

Vasectomy reversal: technique and results, by S. S. Schmidt. INFECTION CONTROL AND UROLOGICAL CARE. 6(1):13-16, 1981

--: use of microsurgical technique, by F. C. Derrick, Jr., et al. JOURNAL OF THE SOUTH CAROLINA MEDICAL ASSOCIATION. 78(2):90-91, February 1982

Vasovasostomy-microscopy versus macroscopic techniques, by H. Fenster, et al. ARCHIVES OF ANDROLOGY. 7(2):201-204, September 1981

Vasovasostomy with use of intraoperative vasography, by P. R. Hartig, et al. UROLOGY. 19(4):404-406, April 1982

Vasovasotomy. Refertilizatio after vasectomy illustrated by a questionnaire study, by J. Eldrup, et al. UGESKRIFT FOR LAEGER. 144(16):1160-1162, April 19, 1982

Who asks for vasectomy reversal and why?, by G. Howard. BRITISH MEDICAL JOURNAL. 6340:490-492, August 14, 1982

AUTHOR INDEX

Abelson, I., 63
Abernethy, D. R., 59
Abet, D., 92
Abramovici, H., 117
Abrams, M., 127
Abrutyn, D., 117
Adams, C. S., 65
Adeleye, J. A., 32
Agostino, M. B., 48
Ahren, T., 26
Aird, J. S., 91
Al-Shebib, T. H., 46
Albano, S. J., 69
Alcid, D. V., 120
Alexander, N. J., 21
Algeo, D., 7
Alimova, K. R., 123
Alipov, V. I., 119
Allman, J., 50
Allocca, G., 114
Altrash, H. K., 48
Altukhov, I P., 52
Alvardo Duran, A., 106
Alvarez-Sanchez, F., 89
Alvo, M., 10
Amarin, Z. O., 74
Amaro, H., 67
Andersch, B., 94
Andersson, K., 102
Andrews, M. C., 59
Andrews, T., 23
Angelov, A., 12
Annas, G. J., 113
Anokute, C. C., 44
Antsaklis, A., 61
Appelbaum, P. S., 65
Appleton, S. F., 16
Archer, D. F., 47
Aref, I., 29
Aresin, L., 95
Aribarg, S., 43
Aries, N. R., 6
Armitage, P., 119
Arnold, G. L., 24
Arnold, M., 46
Arshat, H., 86
Arundhathi, M., 120
Asch, R. H., 70
Ashman, A., 126

Ashton, J. R., 11
Assandri, A., 62
Astedt, B., 83
Atanasov, A., 27
Atkinson, W. R., 36
Atrash, H. K., 105
Austein, C. F., 66
Axelsson, G., 93
Ayers, J. W., 38
Ayvazian, A., 29
Aznar, R., 91

Bachmann, G. A., 75
Back, D. J., 41, 44
Badawy, S., 105
Badawy, S. Z., 101
Badenoch, D. F., 73
Baehler, E. A., 97
Baele, G., 90
Bagdade, J. D., 14
Bailey, C., 48
Bailey, J., 92
Bain, C., 84
Baker, R. K., 72
Baker, R., 70
Balazs, M., 36
Balbi, C., 60, 119, 120
Balestriere, L., 31
Ball, G. H., 126
Ballard, C. A., 51, 124
Ballas, S., 71
Balogh, A., 66
Banet, K., 79
Barkley, R. R., 15
Barnartt, S. N., 101
Barrantes, M. G., 50
Barrett, J. M., 61
Barrette, M., 108
Barth , . D., 61
Bassen, P., 95
Baum, F., 125
Bauminger, S., 55
Baxter, D., 65
Beale, C. L., 1
Bean, F. D., 21
Beard, P., 30
Beaumont, J. L., 58
Beaumont, V., 83, 124

310

Gudakova, N. T., 118
Guidotti, R. J., 49
Gupta, A. S., 93
Gupta, U., 39
Gutierrez Avila, J. H., 48
Gutierrez Martinez, C., 43
Gutteridge, I. F., 82
Guttman, A., 76
Guyer, M. J., 22
Guzman, Serani, R., 44

Hackett, G. H., 12
Hagen, P., 64
Hagenfeldt, K., 73
Hagstad, A., 69
Hague, D., 7
Halbert, D. R., 80
Hale, R. W., 109
Hall, P. E., 63
Haller, G., 65
Halmos, I., 62
Hamann, K. M., 55
Hamilton, L., 95
Hammand, J, 106
Han, G. D., 114
Handel, K., 26
Handy, J. A., 98
Haney, A. F., 124
Hanington, E., 91
Hansen, S. B., 116
Hansted, B., 34
Hardin, G., 110
Hardy, D. T., 54
Hare, M. J., 33
Hargrove, J. T., 43
Harlap, S., 27
Harrison, B., 53
Harrison, N., 128
Hartfield, V. J., 4
Hartig, P. R., 125
Harvey, J., 14
Hashen, R. J., 104
Haspels, A. A., 33
Hassold, T., 34
Hatch, M., 1
Hauglustaine, D., 101
Havekes, L., 55
Hay, D. L., 45
He, C. H., 14
He, Z. F., 115
Hecht, F., 122
Hefnawi, F., 73
Heikkila, M., 37
Heikkinen, J, 107
Heilmann, L., 51
Heim, N., 109
Hein, K., 111
Helling, T. S., 84
Helvacioglu, A., 13

Hemminke, K., 111
Hemon, D., 121
Hendershot, G. E., 1
Hendershot, G. E., 123
Hendricks, L. E., 122
Hendricks, N., 29
Henning, G., 88
Henry, A., 6
Henry, N. F., 101, 110
Henshaw, S. H., 5,
Henshaw, S. K., 8, 52
Hepburn, K., 68
Herbert, W., 33
Hern, W. M., 74
Hernandez, D. J., 80
Hernandez, J. J., 58
Herold, E. S., 72, 87, 102
Herrera, M., 46
Herring, R., 111
Hillard, P. A., 92
Hilliard, D., 122
Hirsch, A. F., 116
Hirsch, M. B., 31
Hirvonen, E., 51
Hlinak, Z., 45
Hodicke, H. D., 103
Høding, U., 52
Hodsman, G. P., 71
Hoflehner, G., 53
Hogan, D. P., 12
Hogberg, U., 61
Hohe, P. T., 36
Holahan, M., 13
Holck, S. E., 78
Holland, M., 15, 65, 126
Holman, K., 118
Holton, R. R., 65
Holtz, G., 52
Hook, E. B., 9
Horan, D. J., 33, 56, 115
Horgan, G., 65
Horoszko-Husiatynska, B., 87
Horowitz, R., 109
Howard, G., 25, 63, 111, 126
Hristamian, S., 36
Hu, Z. Y., 72
Huber, A., 94
Huber, J., 29
Hubinont, P. O., 95
Hudgins, A. A., 65
Hudson, B. L., 125
Huff, K., 126
Huggins, G., 124
Huggins, G. R., 79
Huismans, H., 101
Hulka, B. S., 97
Hull, E. M., 42
Hull, M. G., 93
Hume, J. C., 81
Humphries, J., 110

316

MacGregor, C., 14
McGuinnes, B. W., 54
McIvor, C. L., 45
McKenna, C., 55
McKenna, P. J., 66
MacKenzie, I. Z., 97
McKinely, M., 113
McLaughlin, J., 6
MacMillan, P., 35
McMunn, R., 17
McQuaig, L., 69
Macourt, D. C., 77
Made, T. W., 42
Magar, M., 72
Mahajan, R. C., 58
Maheux, R., 84
Mahowald, M. B., 27, 50
Maia, H., Jr., 74
Maine, D., 2
Majumdar, S. K., 77
Malatjalian, D. A., 69
Mall-Haefeli, M., 11, 24, 30
Mallovy, N., 11
Malmstrom, H., 103
Mamlouk, M., 2
Mammen, E. F., 84
Man, A., 44
Manabe, Y., 5, 6, 63, 78, 90
Mandlekar, A. V., 21
Mani, S. B., 104
Mann, J. I., 96
Mannion, M. T., 5
Mantoni, M., 50
Manuilova, I. A., 75
Mapa, M. K., 75
Marean, A. R., 25
Marion-Landais, G., 122
Markman, L. M., 23
Markuszewski, C., 85
Marrs, R. P., 117
Marshall, J. H., 86
Martella, E., 85
Martin, M. C., 78
Martinez-Manautou, J., 14
Marx, P., 97
Mason, R., 52
Mason, R. W., 20
Massey, J. B., 44
Matsumoto, K., 42
Matsuzawa, T., 36
May, W. E., 24
Meade, T. W., 85
Mecklenburg, M. E., 56
Medora, N. P., 46
Meehan, M., 8, 11, 24, 51, 54,
    65, 66, 73, 96, 100, 107,
    112, 116
Mehta, R. R., 13
Mehta, S. R., 71
Meijernik, A., 25

Meirik, O., 124
Mejsnarova, B., 60
Melis, G. B., 123
Menaldo, G., 66
Menanteau-Horta, D., 81
Mensik, J., 76
Mercier, J., 15
Meregaglia, N., 49
Merlen, J. F., 74
Merton, A. H., 2
Merz, M., 98
Messiha, F. S., 38
Mettlin, C., 114
Meuwissen, J. H., 14
Michel, A. E., 5
Michels, V. V., 23
Mierzwinski, R., 107
Mikrut, W., 79
Miller, T., 121
Milunsky, A., 7
Minkin, S., 79
Mirsky, J., 22
Mishell, D., 2
Mishell, D. R., 83
Mishell, D. R., Jr, 80
Mishenin, A. V., 123
Misinger, I., 9
Misro, M. M., 64
Mitchell, N., 77
Mithers, C. L., 17
Miyagawa, Y., 112
Miyake, A., 103
Mizejewski, G. J., 59
Modras, R., 91
Moldando, S. A., 120
Molin, J., 97, 106
Møller, B. R., 87
Monopoli, W., 66
Monteith, R. S., 31
Montgomery, J. W., 2
Montmarquet, J. A., 74
Morano, S., 64
Morgan, S., 2
Morgan, V., 37
Morganthau, T., 104
Morikawa, S., 111
Morrill, J. S., 119
Morrison, B., 30
Moses, A. M., 106
Mosher, S. W., 17
Mosher, W. D., 50, 62, 120
Moskop, J. C., 93
Moult, P. J., 83
Mueller-Heubach, E., 96
Mukundan, M. A., 69
Mulcahy, M. T., 34
Muldoon, M., 2
Muller, H. G., 46
Mumford, S. D., 7
Munoz, R., 47